Editor
Polly Hoffman

Managing Editor
Karen J. Goldfluss, M.S. Ed.

Editor-in-Chief
Sharon Coan, M.S. Ed.

Illustrator
Bruce Hedges
Sue Fullam

Cover Artist
Lesley Palmer

Art Coordinator
Denice Adorno

Imaging
James Edward Grace
Rosa C. See

Product Manager
Phil Garcia

Publishers
Rachelle Cracchiolo, M.S. Ed.
Mary Dupuy Smith, M.S. Ed.

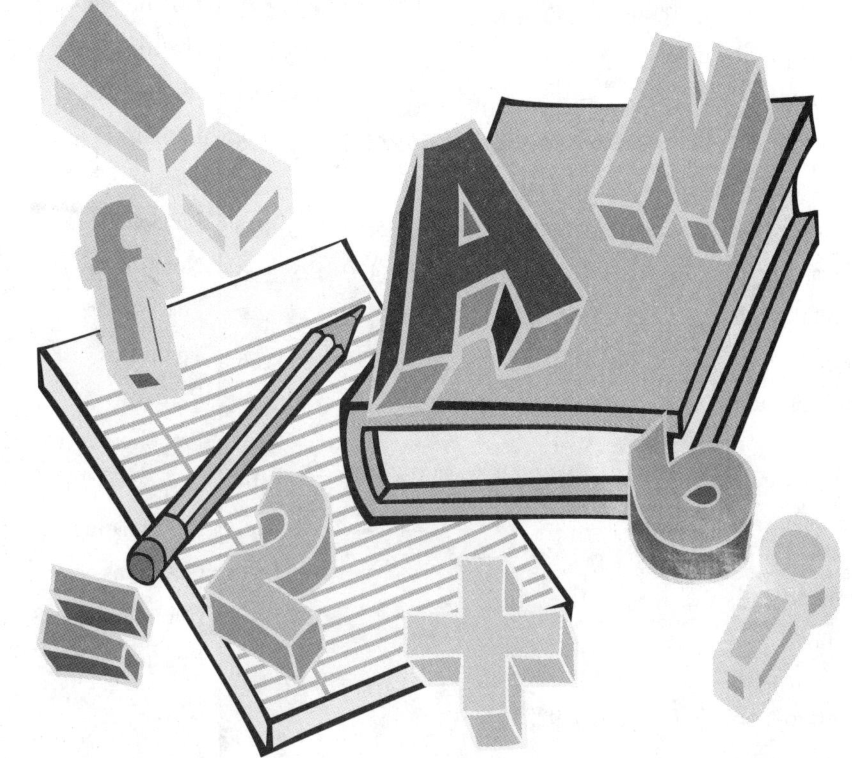

Author
Mary Rosenberg

Teacher Created Materials, Inc.
6421 Industry Way
Westminster, CA 92683
www.teachercreated.com

Reprinted, 2003
Made in U.S.A.
ISBN-0-7439-3305-2

Table of Contents

Introduction

Daily Skills Practice: Grades 3–4 was designed to cover a wide range of skills and concepts typically introduced or reviewed during a school year. The practice pages provide a quick assessment of how a child is performing on a particular skill or with a specific concept. In addition, the activities in this book provide teachers, children, and parents with consistent, daily feedback on a child's academic progress.

How to Use the Practice Pages

In the Classroom

The daily skills pages are easily implemented in the classroom during whole-class instruction. Here are some suggestions for introducing and assigning the pages:

- Give each child a photocopy of the daily practice sheet you wish to use, or prepare a small packet consisting of six to ten practice sheets for each child. (**Note:** A blank skills practice form has been provided on page 4. To add your own lessons to this book, write activities on the form before reproducing the page.) Send the packets home every one to two weeks. Decide how you will review and assess the children's completed work and communicate this to both the children and the parents.
- If you wish to use some or all of the practice sheets for whole-class or group instruction, simply photocopy them onto overhead transparency sheets and use them throughout the year. The transparencies can be organized and stored for use the coming year.

At Home

The practice pages in this book make excellent reinforcement exercises at home. With over 200 daily practice pages from which to chose, a child is given the opportunity to review concepts and skills he or she already knows. For newly acquired skills, the pages provide reinforcement through practice. As pages are completed, parents and children can correct the exercises using the answer key on pages 207–240.

Practice Page Sections

Each practice page is divided into the following two sections:

- **Math Practice**

  Math Practice consists of five math problems. This section covers basic addition, subtraction, multiplication, and division skills. There are also activities related to money, geometry, multiplication, division, measuring, fact families, place value, and time.

- **Language Practice**

  Each day, one specific skill or concept is presented. This section is an effective way to quickly preview or review a skill or to introduce a new concept to the child. Among the skills covered in this section are color words, number words, months of the year, days of the week, abbreviations, compound words, plurals, alphabetical order, nouns, verbs, adjectives, labeling, reading and analyzing charts and graphs, and phonics (vowels, beginning and ending sounds, blends, digraphs). For more specific skills and a listing of pages on which they are found, see the Table of Contents.

Name ______________________ Practice

Math Practice: ______________________

Language Practice: ______________________

Name ______________________________ Practice 1

Math Practice: Adding to 15

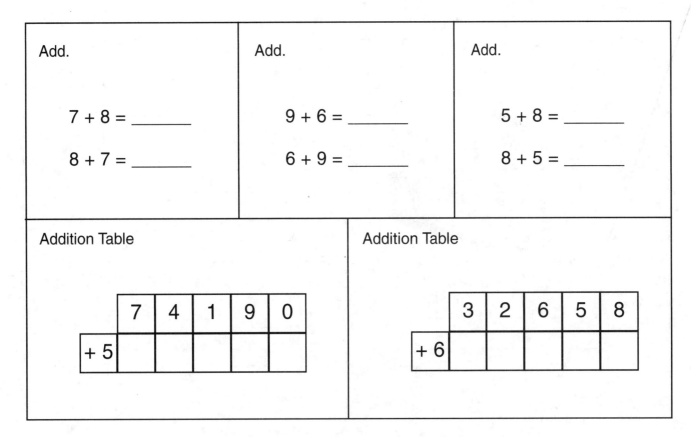

Add.	Add.	Add.
7 + 8 = ______	9 + 6 = ______	5 + 8 = ______
8 + 7 = ______	6 + 9 = ______	8 + 5 = ______

Addition Table

	7	4	1	9	0
+ 5					

Addition Table

	3	2	6	5	8
+ 6					

Language Practice: Common Nouns

Common nouns name people, places, and things. Read each noun. Write person, place, or thing on the line.

uncle	______	mail carrier	______
television	______	skunk	______
car	______	earth	______
the park	______	moon	______
carpet	______	grandma	______
neighbor	______	school	______
pilot	______	mountain	______
mirror	______	surfer	______
magazine	______	piano	______

Name ______________________ Practice 2

Math Practice: Adding to 15

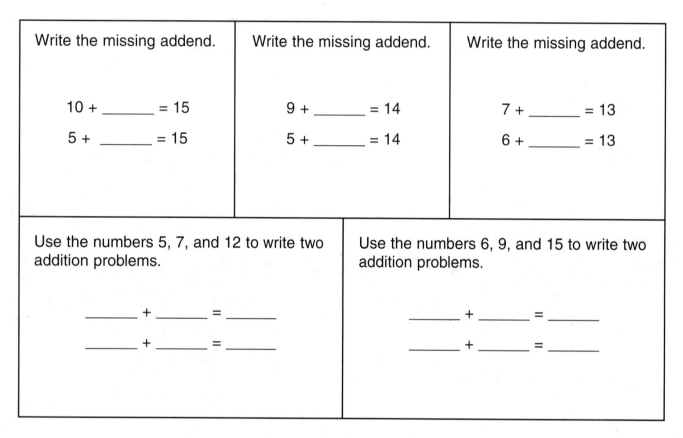

Write the missing addend.	Write the missing addend.	Write the missing addend.
10 + ______ = 15 5 + ______ = 15	9 + ______ = 14 5 + ______ = 14	7 + ______ = 13 6 + ______ = 13

Use the numbers 5, 7, and 12 to write two addition problems.	Use the numbers 6, 9, and 15 to write two addition problems.
______ + ______ = ______ ______ + ______ = ______	______ + ______ = ______ ______ + ______ = ______

Language Practice: Common Nouns

Common nouns name people, places, and things. Write the nouns used in each sentence.

1. The baseball game was exciting! ______________________
2. During the game, people ate hot dogs. ______________________
3. Some people wore hats and carried gloves. ______________________
4. A boy caught a fly ball. ______________________
5. Three girls bought pennants and t-shirts. ______________________
6. The batter caught many foul balls. ______________________
7. The pitcher fell down on the mound. ______________________
8. The center fielder hit the fence. ______________________
9. The umpire stood behind the third baseman. ______________________
10. The visiting team won the game. ______________________

Name ______________________________ Practice 3

Math Practice: Adding to 18

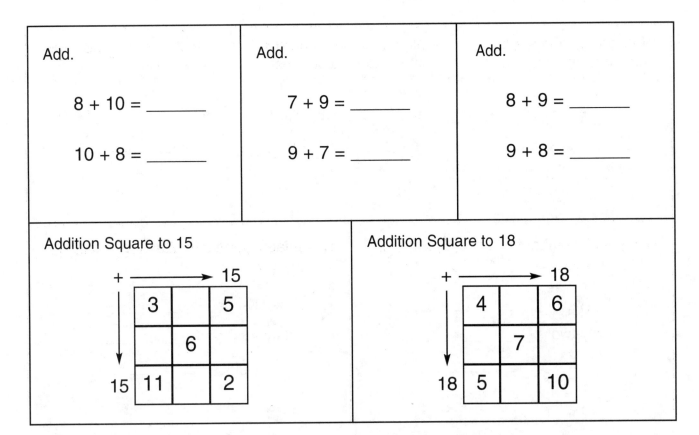

Add.	Add.	Add.
8 + 10 = ______	7 + 9 = ______	8 + 9 = ______
10 + 8 = ______	9 + 7 = ______	9 + 8 = ______

Addition Square to 15

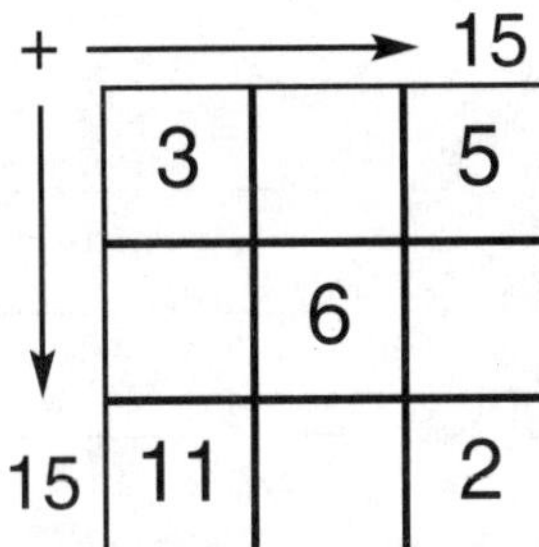

Addition Square to 18

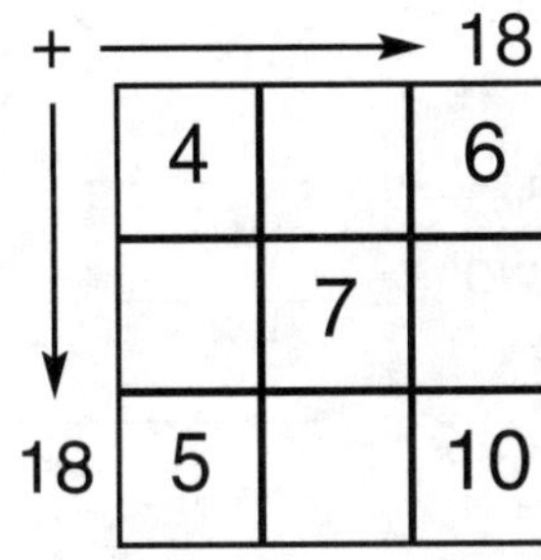

Language Practice: Proper Nouns

Proper nouns name a specific person, place, or thing. Proper nouns begin with a capital letter. Write a proper noun next to the common noun.

month of the year: ______	day of the week: ______
a president: ______	country: ______
city: ______	state: ______
boy: ______	girl: ______
movie theater: ______	game: ______
teacher: ______	holiday: ______
street: ______	restaurant: ______
store: ______	language: ______
car: ______	computer: ______

Name ______________________ Practice 4

Math Practice: Number Sense

Write the numbers in order from smallest to greatest.	Write the numbers in order from smallest to greatest.	Write the numbers in order from smallest to greatest.
86 15 27 4	0 92 18 30	90 15 6 73
____, ____, ____, ____	____, ____, ____, ____	____, ____, ____, ____

Write each number in standard form.	Write each number in standard form.
thirty-eight ____________	ninety-one ____________
sixty-two ____________	fifty-six ____________
forty-five ____________	fifty-eight ____________

Language Practice: Proper Nouns

Proper nouns name a specific person, place or thing. Proper nouns begin with a capital letter. Read each sentence and circle the proper noun. Write the proper noun correctly on the line.

1. The dog is an alaskan husky. ____________________
2. Their friends lives on sierra avenue. ____________________
3. Have you ever been to denver, colorado? ____________________
4. The boys attend redwood high school. ____________________
5. Let's go to aunt betty's pie shop. ____________________
6. They went bowling at bowl-o-rama. ____________________
7. The rose is called a busy lizzie. ____________________
8. dr. nielsen works at the hospital. ____________________
9. The dog's name is dudley. ____________________
10. There are many holidays in december. ____________________

Name ______________________

Math Practice: Number Sense

Write the numbers in order from smallest to greatest.	Write the numbers in order from smallest to greatest.	Write the numbers in order from smallest to greatest.
35 2 14 4	20 62 18 3	95 25 16 7
______________	______________	______________

Write each number in standard form.	Write each number in standard form.
twenty-three ________	eighty-one ________
forty-two ________	fifty-four ________
fifty-three ________	forty-five ________

Language Practice: Proper Nouns

Proper nouns name a specific person, place, or thing. *Proper nouns* begin with a capital letter. Read each sentence. Underline the proper nouns.

August 25

Dear Mom and Dad,

I am having a lot of fun at Camp Bears in the Forest! Yesterday, we had a canoe race against the campers from Camp Tree in the Forest. We won the race!

Thanks for sending the care package. The chocolate chip cookies were delicious. I shared them with my bunk mates, Pat and Chris.

Love,

Alex

Name ______________________________ Practice 6

Math Practice: Subtracting to 15

Subtract.	Subtract.	Subtract.
15 – ______ = 7 15 – ______ = 8	13 – ______ = 6 13 – ______ = 7	14 – ______ = 5 14 – ______ = 9

Solve.	Solve.
Ollie had 14¢. He spent 7¢ at the pet store. How much money does Ollie have left? Ollie has _____¢ left.	Molly had 15¢. She spent 12¢ at the toy store. How much money does Molly have left? Molly has _____¢ left.

Language Practice: Adjectives

Adjectives are used to describe nouns. Adjectives tell *which one*, *what kind*, or *how many*. Read each sentence. Underline the adjectives.

Theodore Roosevelt: Cowboy and President

1. In 1884, Theodore Roosevelt became an adventurous cowboy.
2. He rode with the Rough Riders Calvary.
3. Later, Theodore Roosevelt became the youngest president.
4. He was the 26th president of the United States.
5. He belonged to the Republican Party.
6. Theodore Roosevelt had six children.
7. He was known for having a good sense of humor.
8. His sons were known as the White House Gang.
9. While out hunting, he refused to shoot a black bear cub.
10. Theodore Roosevelt established five national parks.

Name ________________ Practice 7

Math Practice: Subtracting to 18

Subtract.	Subtract.	Subtract.
17 – 10 = ______ 17 – 7 = ______	18 – 6 = ______ 18 – 12 = ______	16 – 9 = ______ 16 – 7 = ______

Use the numbers, 7, 8, and 15 to write two subtraction problems.	Use the numbers 8, 10, and 18 to write two subtraction problems.
______ – ______ = ______ ______ – ______ = ______	______ – ______ = ______ ______ – ______ = ______

Language Practice: Adjectives

Adjectives are used to describe nouns. Adjectives tell *which one, what kind*, and *how many*. Read each sentence and underline the adjective. Write *which one, what kind*, or *how many* on the line.

About Tigers

Example: The tiger is the strongest of all the wild cats. **which one** (Wild describes the kind of cats.)

1. There are about 7,000 tigers in the world. ____________
2. Tigers hunt large mammals. ____________
3. Tigers travel 12 miles in search of food. ____________
4. The Siberian tiger is the largest. ____________
5. A tiger's striped coat is a kind of camouflage. ____________
6. Only a few tigers have become man-eaters. ____________
7. At one time, there were many tigers. ____________

Name ______________________________ Practice 8

Math Practice: Addition and Subtraction to 18

Add and subtract.	Add and subtract.	Add and subtract.
$9 + 9 =$ ____ $17 - 8 =$ ____	$3 + 5$ $12 - 6$	$12 + 5 =$ ____ $14 - 9 =$ ____

Solve.	Solve.
$(17 + 1) - 3 =$ ____ $(4 + 9) - 6 =$ ____	$(18 - 5) + 2 =$ ____ $(16 - 8) + 9 =$ ____

Language Practice: Adjectives

Adjectives are used to describe nouns. Adjectives tell *which one*, *what kind*, and *how many*. Read each word below. Circle the words that are adjectives.

Robert	picture	toasty
accident	bright	horrible
cold	candy	excitement
candle	marshmallow	hearth
green	enormous	shining
tree	shady	two
hospital	wheel	beautiful
tall	refrigerator	red
friendly	lamp	happy
sad	muscle	snowy

Write three adjectives that describe the qualities of a good friend.

______________________, ______________________, ______________________

Name ______________________________ Practice 9

Math Practice: Addition and Subtraction

Write the problem.

______ + ______ = ______

Write the problem.

______ − ______ = ______

Write the problem.

______ + ______ = ______

Circle the operation.

Beth had 15 turtles. She sold 9 to the pet store. How many turtles does Beth have left?

add subtract

Circle the operation.

Niles had 13 peanuts. He fed 7 to the elephant. How many peanuts does Niles have left?

add subtract

Language Practice: Adjectives

Adjectives are used to describe nouns. Adjectives tell *which one*, *what kind*, and *how many*. Read each story. Add the missing adjectives.

475	hard	many	slow-moving

good	strong	long	tree-living

The Turtle

The ____________________ turtle has a ____________ shell. The turtle can live for ____________ years. A turtle can weigh ____________ pounds.

The Chameleon

A chameleon is a ____________________ lizard. It has a ____________ tail and ____________ eyesight. The chameleon also has a ____________ tongue.

Name ______________________________ Practice 10

Math Practice: Number Sense

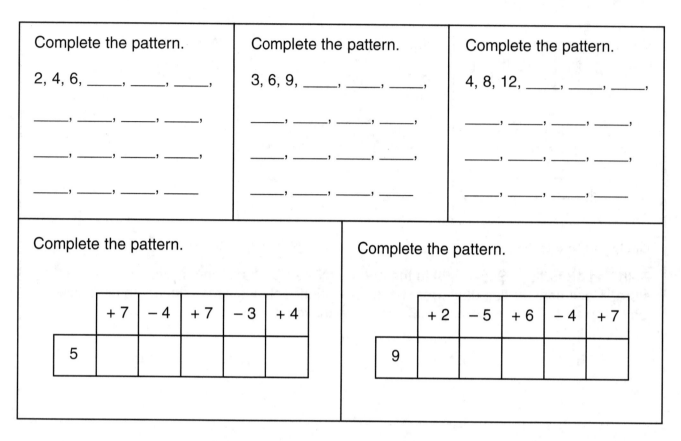

Complete the pattern.	Complete the pattern.	Complete the pattern.
2, 4, 6, ____, ____, ____, ____, ____, ____, ____, ____, ____, ____, ____, ____, ____, ____, ____, ____	3, 6, 9, ____, ____, ____, ____, ____, ____, ____, ____, ____, ____, ____, ____, ____, ____, ____, ____	4, 8, 12, ____, ____, ____, ____, ____, ____, ____, ____, ____, ____, ____, ____, ____, ____, ____, ____

Complete the pattern.

	+ 7	− 4	+ 7	− 3	+ 4
5					

Complete the pattern.

	+ 2	− 5	+ 6	− 4	+ 7
9					

Language Practice: Adjectives

Adjectives are used to describe nouns. Adjectives tell *which one*, *what kind*, and *how many*. Write two descriptive sentences and circle the adjectives used in each sentence.

1. ______________________________

____

____

2. ______________________________

____

____

Name ______________________ Practice 11

Math Practice: Adding and Subtracting to 18

Write the missing "+" or "–" sign.	Write the missing "+" or "–" sign.	Write the missing "+" or "–" sign.
5 ◯ 1 = 4	8 ◯ 3 = 11	9 ◯ 6 = 3
5 ◯ 1 = 6	8 ◯ 3 = 5	9 ◯ 6 = 15

Cross out the addend that does not belong.		Cross out the addend that does not belong.	
9 8 + 7 16	7 3 + 4 7	8 10 + 3 18	0 9 + 6 9

Language Practice: Action Verbs

A verb that tells what the subject is doing is called an *action verb. Action verbs* can be in the present tense (what is happening) or in the past tense (what did happen). Underline the action verb in each sentence. Write *present* or *past* on the line.

Pete's Trip	present or past
1. Pete visits his grandmother every year.	____________
2. His grandmother, Rose, lives in New York.	____________
3. Last week, Pete drove out to see her.	____________
4. She lives near Central Park.	____________
5. Mrs. Moreno lived in Florida at one time.	____________
6. She designed buildings.	____________
7. She retired a few years ago.	____________
8. They saw a baseball game.	____________
9. Grandmother Rose baked Peter a chocolate cake.	____________
10. Peter ate the cake on the drive home.	____________

Name ______

Practice 12

Math Practice: Comparing Numbers

Solve.

9  6 + ____

Solve.

12  3 + ____

Solve.

11  4 + ____

Solve.

Jenna has 9 ducks. Linnea has 12 ducks. Who has more ducks?

____

Solve.

Simon has 10 birds. Lionel has 5 birds. Who has more birds?

____

Language Practice: Compound Words

Read each set of words. Write the one word that can be added before or after each word to make a compound word.

______ cover	______ land	______ card
______ ground	______ pecker	______ woman
______ stand	fire ______	______ office

______ beam	______ mill	home ______
______ flower	______ shield	hand ______
______ set	cross ______	man ______

Name ______ Practice 13

Math Practice: Adding Three Numbers

Add.	Add.	Add.
6 + 8 + 4 = ___ ; 2 + 7 + 9 = ___	3 + 5 + 6 = ___ ; 4 + 0 + 9 = ___	10 + 1 + 4 = ___ ; 8 + 6 + 2 = ___

Solve.
Each vowel is worth 3¢. Each consonant is worth 5¢. How much is the word "mad" worth?

"Mad" is worth ____________ .

Solve.
Each vowel is worth 5¢. Each consonant is worth 3¢. How much is the word "mad" worth?

"Mad" is worth ____________ .

Language Practice: Verb Tenses

Verbs can show whether an action happened (past tense), is happening (present tense), or will happen (future tense). Read each verb below and write whether it represents the *present* or the *past* on the line provided.

1. climbs ____________
2. comes ____________
3. sat ____________
4. say ____________
5. flew ____________
6. grow ____________
7. ate ____________
8. eat ____________
9. win ____________
10. went ____________
11. said ____________
12. see ____________
13. go ____________
14. grew ____________
15. hear ____________
16. sit ____________
17. heard ____________
18. won ____________
19. came ____________
20. saw ____________

Name ______________________________ Practice 14

Math Practice: Number Sense

Write even or odd.	Write even or odd.	Write even or odd.
54 ________ 47 ________	75 ________ 23 ________	18 ________ 92 ________

Using the numbers 0–9, write the even numbers.	Using the numbers 0–9, write the odd numbers.
_____, _____, _____, _____, _____	_____, _____, _____, _____, _____

Language Practice: Word Play

Begin with the complete word. Make a new, smaller word using the same letters. Continue making a smaller word until the final two-letter word is made.

Example: stare (5 letters) ⟶ star (4 letters) ⟶ rat (3 letters) ⟶ at (2 letters)

heart	hover	wreath	please
___ ___ ___ ___	___ ___ ___ ___	___ ___ ___ ___ ___	___ ___ ___ ___ ___
___ ___ ___	___ ___ ___	___ ___ ___ ___	___ ___ ___ ___
___ ___	___ ___	___ ___ ___	___ ___ ___
		___ ___	___ ___

Name ____________________

Math Practice: Tally Marks

Use tally marks to show 10.	Use tally marks to show 12.	Use tally marks to show 9.

Write the number.	Write the number.
卌 卌 卌	卌 卌 卌 卌 ||
______________	______________

Language Practice: Adverbs

Adverbs describe verbs. Adverbs tell *where*, *when*, *how often*, or *how much*. Many adverbs end in *ly*. Read each sentence below. Write the missing adverb correctly on the line.

- Add *ly* to the end of the word to make it an adverb.
- If the word ends in *y*, drop the *y* and add *ily*.

Example: sass**y** sass**ily**

1. The stallion jumped ______________________ over the fence. (easy)
2. The goat chomped ______________________ on the sweet grass. (noisy)
3. The hens clucked ______________________ in the hen house. (loud)
4. The pigs rolled ______________________ in the fresh mud. (happy)
5. The sheep's wool curled ______________________ on its back. (soft)
6. The dog ______________________ chased the farm hand. (playful)
7. The farmer ______________________ gathered the fresh eggs. (careful)
8. The cat ______________________ caught the little mouse. (quick)
9. The cows mooed ______________________ in the pasture. (quiet)

Name ________________________________ Practice 16

Math Practice: Comparing Numbers

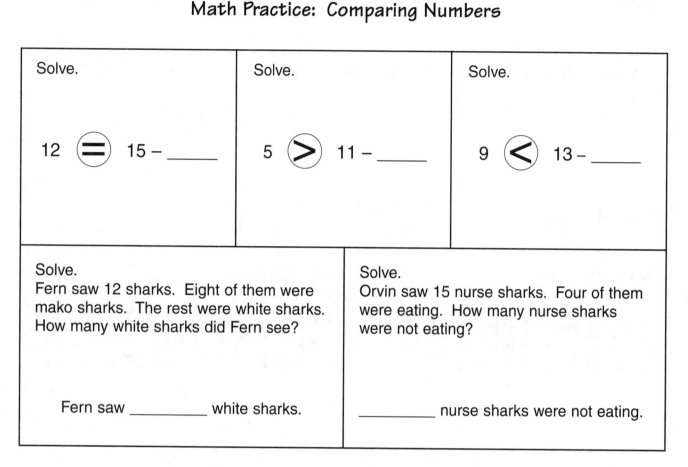

Solve.	Solve.	Solve.
12  15 – ______	5 > 11 – ______	9  13 – ______

Solve.	Solve.
Fern saw 12 sharks. Eight of them were mako sharks. The rest were white sharks. How many white sharks did Fern see? Fern saw __________ white sharks.	Orvin saw 15 nurse sharks. Four of them were eating. How many nurse sharks were not eating? __________ nurse sharks were not eating.

Language Practice: Adjectives and Adverbs

Adjectives describe nouns. *Adverbs* describe verbs. Look at the underlined word in each sentence. Write whether it is an *adjective* or *adverb* on the line.

Sharks

1. The <u>powerful</u> mako shark has a pointed head. ____________________
2. The mako shark <u>usually</u> eats tuna and mackerel. ____________________
3. The whale shark is not a <u>fierce</u> hunter. ____________________
4. The whale shark eats <u>tiny</u> plankton. ____________________
5. The white shark hunts <u>aggressively</u>. ____________________
6. The sea lamprey <u>firmly</u> attaches its mouth to its prey. ____________________
7. The nurse shark moves <u>slowly</u> on the ocean floor. ____________________
8. Sharks are <u>cartilaginous</u> fish. ____________________

Name ______________________________ Practice 17

Math Practice: Ordinals

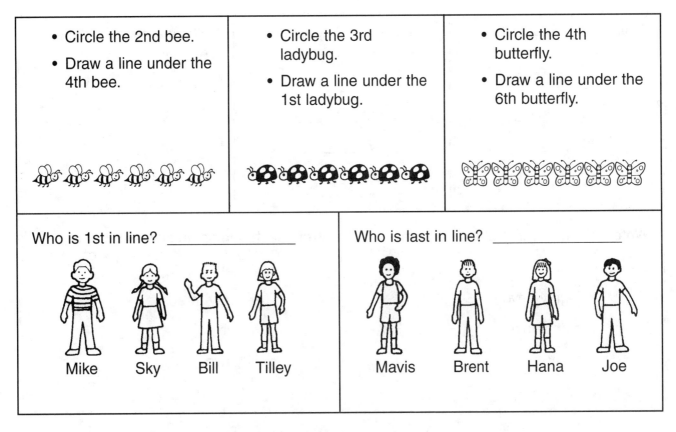

- Circle the 2nd bee.
- Draw a line under the 4th bee.

- Circle the 3rd ladybug.
- Draw a line under the 1st ladybug.

- Circle the 4th butterfly.
- Draw a line under the 6th butterfly.

Who is 1st in line? ____________

Mike Sky Bill Tilley

Who is last in line? ____________

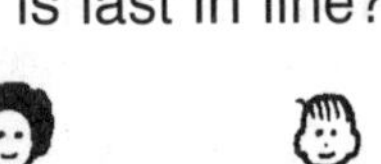

Mavis Brent Hana Joe

Language Practice: Reading and Using Ordinals

Woodland Creatures

Finish writing the ordinal numbers. Answer the questions.

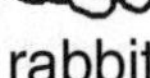

rabbit	possum	mouse	moose	bear	owl	raccoon	fox	rabbit	mouse
1st	____	____	____	5th	____	____	8th	____	____

1. Write the ordinal positions. possum: ________ owl: ________ moose: ________
2. Which animal is last? ______________________________
3. Which animal is first? ______________________________
4. Which animal is after the owl? ______________________________
5. Which animal is after the 2nd rabbit? ______________________________
6. Which animal is before the 1st mouse? ______________________________
7. How many animals are in between the possum and the last mouse? ____________

Name ______________________________ Practice 18

Math Practice: Number Sense

Write the number that is 2 more.	Write the number that is 5 more.	Write the number that is 10 more.
26 _______	39 _______	86 _______
78 _______	95 _______	13 _______
50 _______	47 _______	0 _______
63 _______	55 _______	43 _______

Write each number in standard form.	Write each number in standard form.
eighty-seven _______	seventy-three _______
ninety-five _______	fifteen _______
thirty-six _______	fifty-two _______

Language Practice: Reading and Using Ordinals

Read each sentence and underline the ordinal number. Write the ordinal number on the line.

Example: Margot lives on thirty-third street. 33rd

1. Gilbert is seventeenth in line. ______________________
2. Levi climbed to the fortieth step. ______________________
3. Who's office is on the twenty-ninth floor? ______________________
4. Kay is on her eighty-fifth tour of Egypt. ______________________
5. Mona's song is ninety-first on the music hit list. ______________________
6. Jerome bought his fifty-sixth baseball card. ______________________
7. We have watched our seventy-second TV commercial. ______________________
8. Our home is the fourth brown house on the street. ______________________

Name ______________________ Practice 19

Math Practice: Round Numbers to the Nearest Ten

Round.	Round.	Round.
87 = ______ 31 = ______	59 = ______ 5 = ______	42 = ______ 64 = ______

Round each number to the nearest ten. Add.	Round each number to the nearest ten. Add.
87 + 51 = ______	49 + 3 = ______

Language Practice: Reading and Using a Graph

Use the information in the graph to answer the questions.

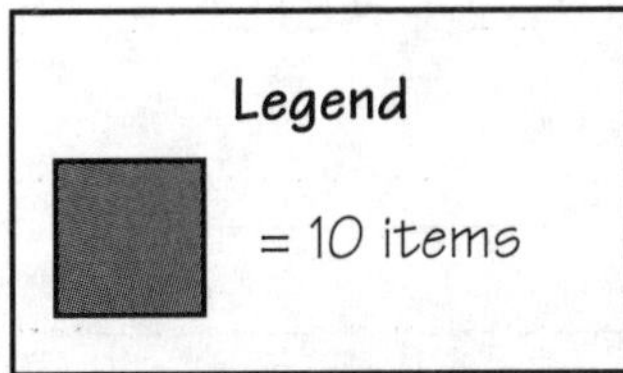

Dessert Sales

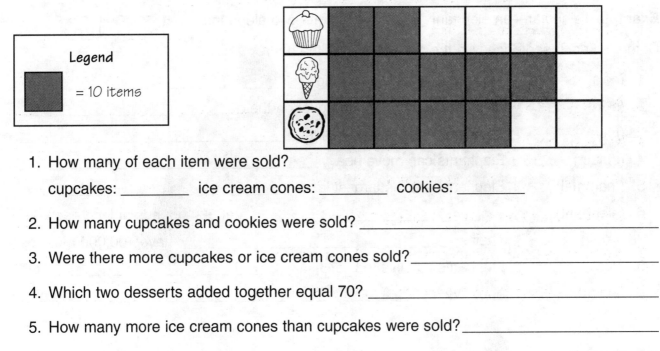

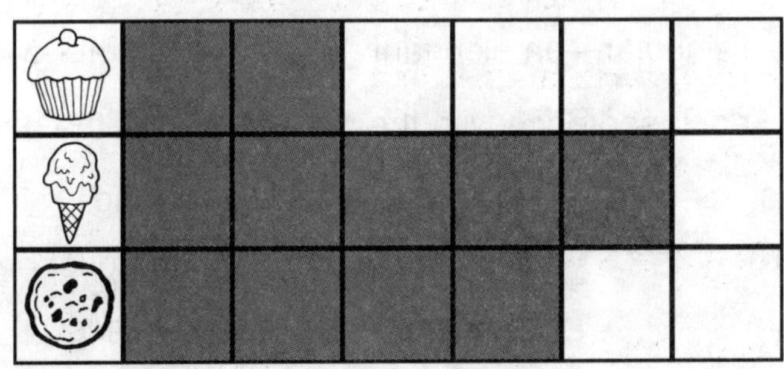

1. How many of each item were sold?
   cupcakes: ________ ice cream cones: ________ cookies: ________
2. How many cupcakes and cookies were sold? ______________________
3. Were there more cupcakes or ice cream cones sold? ______________________
4. Which two desserts added together equal 70? ______________________
5. How many more ice cream cones than cupcakes were sold? ______________________

Name ______________________ Practice 20

Math Practice: Time

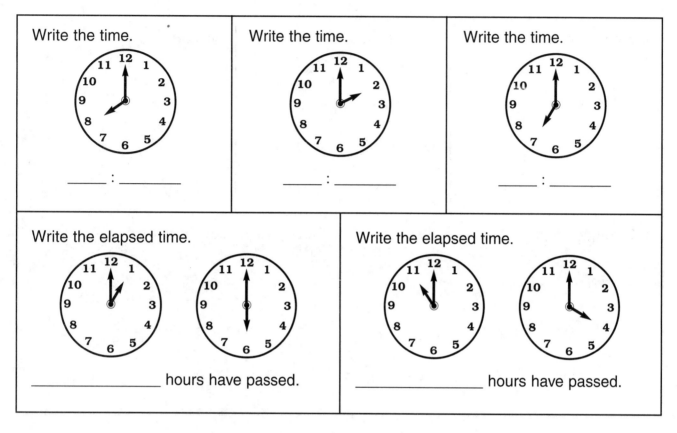

Write the time.	Write the time.	Write the time.
 ____ : ______	 ____ : ______	 ____ : ______

Write the elapsed time.	Write the elapsed time.
  ______________ hours have passed.	  ______________ hours have passed.

Language Practice: Plural Nouns

Nouns (people, places or things) can be either *singular* (meaning one) or *plural* (more than one). To make most words plural, add an "*s*" to the end of the noun.

Example: singular—an elephant  plural—two elephants 

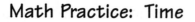

Complete each sentence with the correct form of the noun.

1. (ear) An African elephant has big ______________________.
2. (skin) Elephants spray mud and dust on their ______________________.
3. (tusk) The male Asian elephant has ______________________.
4. (object) Elephants can move heavy ______________________.
5. (mammal) Elephants are the largest land ______________________.
6. (elephant) ______________________ eat 330 pounds of food each day.
7. (trunk) Their ______________________ have 100,000 muscles!
8. (year) Elephants can live to be 78 ______________________ old.
9. (jungle) They live in ______________________ and swamps.

Name ______________________________ Practice 21

Math Practice: Time

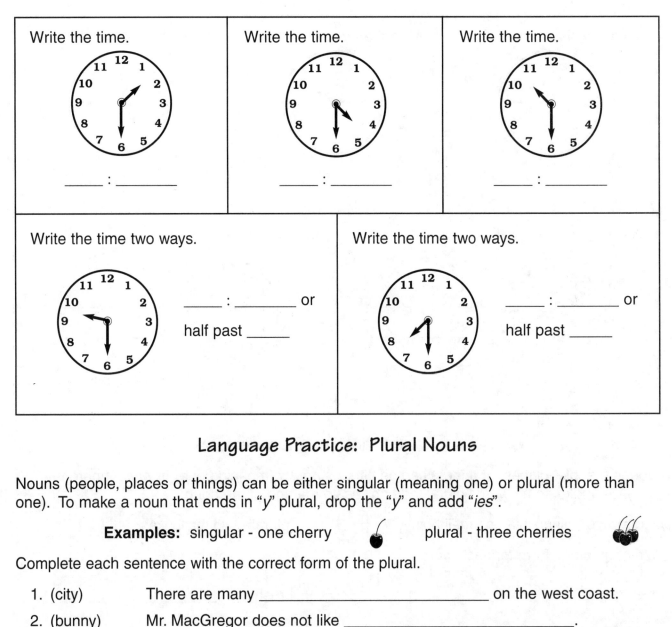

Write the time.	Write the time.	Write the time.
 ____ : ______	 ____ : ______	 ____ : ______

Write the time two ways.	Write the time two ways.
 ____ : ______ or half past ____	 ____ : ______ or half past ____

Language Practice: Plural Nouns

Nouns (people, places or things) can be either singular (meaning one) or plural (more than one). To make a noun that ends in "*y*" plural, drop the "*y*" and add "*ies*".

Examples: singular - one cherry  plural - three cherries 

Complete each sentence with the correct form of the plural.

1. (city) There are many ______________________ on the west coast.
2. (bunny) Mr. MacGregor does not like ______________________.
3. (country) People from many other ______________________ visit Disneyland.
4. (family) Many ______________________ came to the winter program.
5. (hobby) Do you have any ______________________?
6. (penny) How many ______________________ are in the jar?

Write the plural form for each word.

1. baby ____________ 3. copy ____________ 5. story ____________

2. fly ____________ 4. berry ____________ 6. puppy ____________

Name

Math Practice: Time

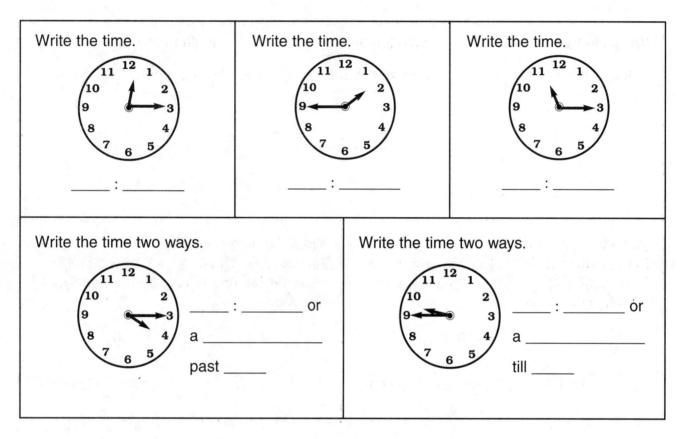

Write the time.	Write the time.	Write the time.
 ____ : ______	 ____ : ______	 ____ : ______

Write the time two ways.	Write the time two ways.
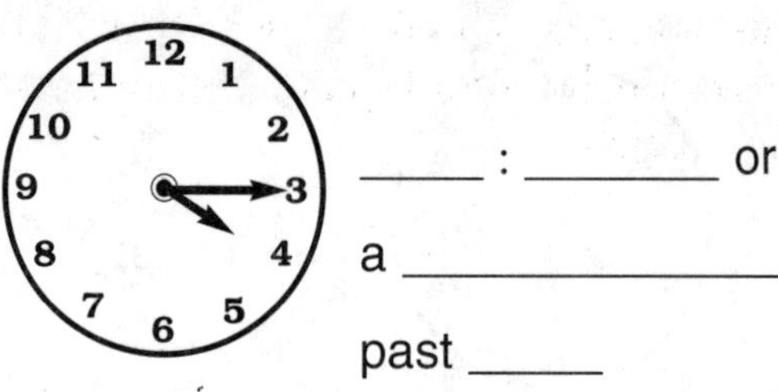 ____ : ______ or a ____________ past ____	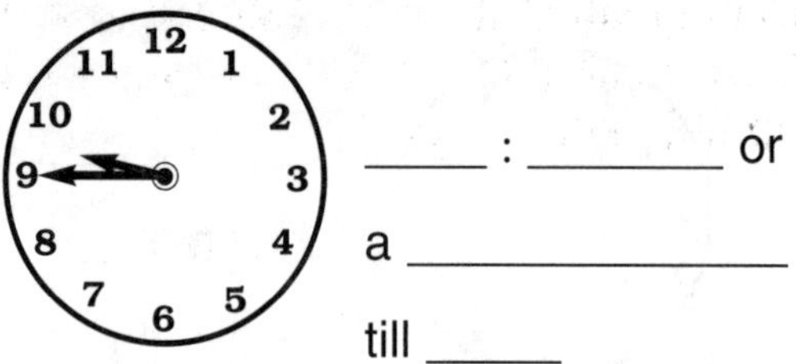 ____ : ______ or a ____________ till ____

Language Practice: Plural Nouns

Nouns (people, places, or things) can be either *singular* (meaning one) or *plural* (more than one). To make some words plural, add an "*es*" to the end of the noun.

Examples: singular - one mail box  plural - two mailboxes 

Write the plural form for each word.

1. guess ______________
2. fox ______________
3. bench ______________
4. bunch ______________
5. class ______________
6. dress ______________
7. sandwich ______________
8. branch ______________
9. brush ______________
10. lunch ______________
11. grass ______________
12. wish ______________
13. flash ______________
14. crash ______________
15. church ______________
16. dish ______________

Name ______________________________ Practice 23

Math Practice: Time

Write the time.	Write the time.	Write the time.
1 hour before 12:00 P.M.	4 hours before 5:00 A.M.	8 hours before 7:00 A.M.
______________	______________	______________

Solve.	Solve.
School starts at 8:00. Recess is at 10:15. How much time elapses between school starting and recess?	Recess is at 10:15. Lunch is at 12:00. How much time elapses between recess and lunch?
______ hours ______ minutes elapses.	______ hour ______ minutes elapses.

Language Practice: Irregular Plurals

Some nouns change form when they are plural.

Examples: singular – child plural - children 

Match the singular form of each word to its plural form. Find and color the plural forms in the word search.

man	feet
woman	geese
mouse	knives
tooth	leaves
foot	lives
goose	men
knife	mice
leaf	teeth
life	women

A	W	W	M	M	E	N	E	G	G
L	N	O	A	V	H	F	F	S	G
L	Z	B	M	N	T	E	E	T	H
K	E	I	G	E	E	S	E	L	R
M	F	A	M	U	N	T	T	I	E
K	C	T	V	I	M	C	D	V	Q
Y	K	J	M	E	C	P	D	E	I
K	N	I	V	E	S	E	J	S	H

Name ______________________________ Practice 24

Math Practice: Time

Write the time. 3 hours after 9:00 A.M. ________	Write the time. 2 hours after 4:00 P.M. ________	Write the time. 6 hours after 4:00 A.M. ________
Solve. The movie lasted 2 hours. It ended at 4:15. What time did the movie start? The movie started at ______.	Solve. Anna took 45 minutes to wash the dishes. She finished at 7:30. What time did she start washing the dishes? Anna started washing the dishes at ______.	

Language Practice: Palindromes

Palindromes are words or numbers that read the same going forwards as backwards.

Example: Hannah hannaH

Read each clue. Unscramble the letters to make the palindrome.

1. a man's name bBo ____________
2. the sound a chick makes ppee ____________
3. a type of boat kkaay ____________
4. to see with yee ____________
5. the sound of a horn otot ____________
6. a musical engagement igg ____________
7. to send elsewhere eefrr ____________
8. a female parent's name Mmo ____________
9. a male parent's name Dda ____________

Name ______________________ Practice 25

Math Practice: Time

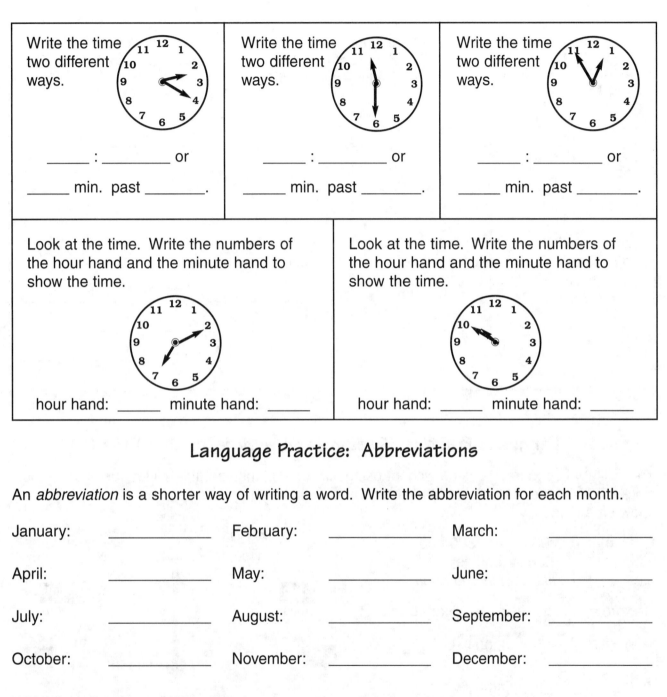

Write the time two different ways.

_____ : ________ or

_____ min. past _______.

Write the time two different ways.

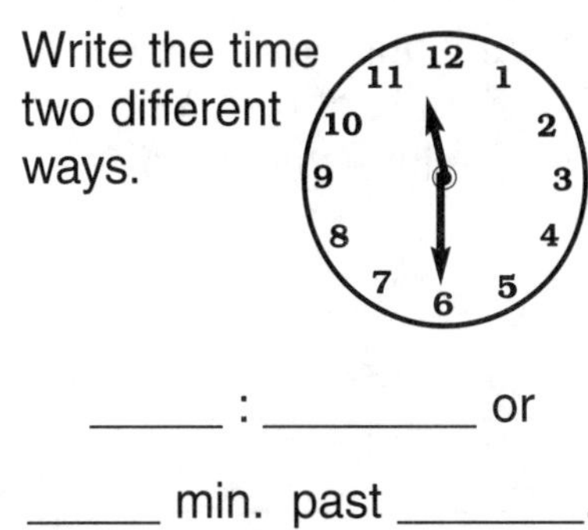

_____ : ________ or

_____ min. past _______.

Write the time two different ways.

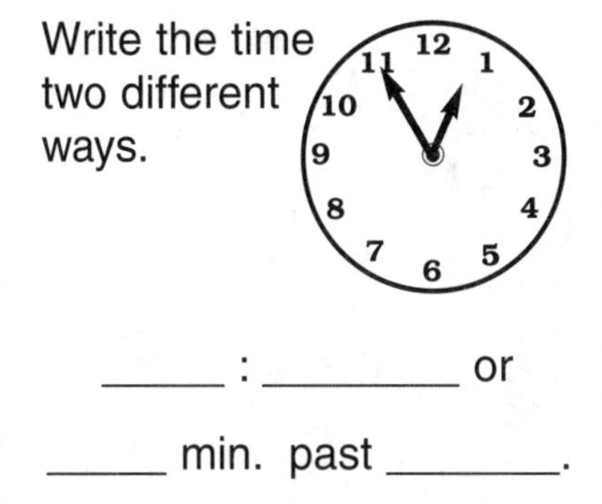

_____ : ________ or

_____ min. past _______.

Look at the time. Write the numbers of the hour hand and the minute hand to show the time.

hour hand: _____ minute hand: _____

Look at the time. Write the numbers of the hour hand and the minute hand to show the time.

hour hand: _____ minute hand: _____

Language Practice: Abbreviations

An *abbreviation* is a shorter way of writing a word. Write the abbreviation for each month.

January:	________	February:	________	March:	________
April:	________	May:	________	June:	________
July:	________	August:	________	September:	________
October:	________	November:	________	December:	________

Which months are not abbreviated: ______________________________

Read the story below. Circle the words that can be abbreviated.

Many schools begin the new year in August or September. Most schools close for a winter break in December and reopen in January after New Year's Day. In the spring, usually in April or May, the students take many academic tests.

Name ______________________ Practice 26

Math Practice: Time

What would you use to tell time?	What would you use to keep track of how long something is cooking?	What would you use to time a fast running race?
______________	______________	______________

What would you use to make sure you get up in time for school each morning?	Make a list of the different items we use to keep track of time.
______________	______________ ______________ ______________ ______________

Language Practice: Reading and Understanding Time

The military keeps track of time without using A.M. or P.M. Instead, the military uses a 24-hour clock. The number 12 is added to each hour to show time in the P.M.

Example: 3:00 P.M. is 1500 hours
1500 is read as
"fifteen hundred hours"

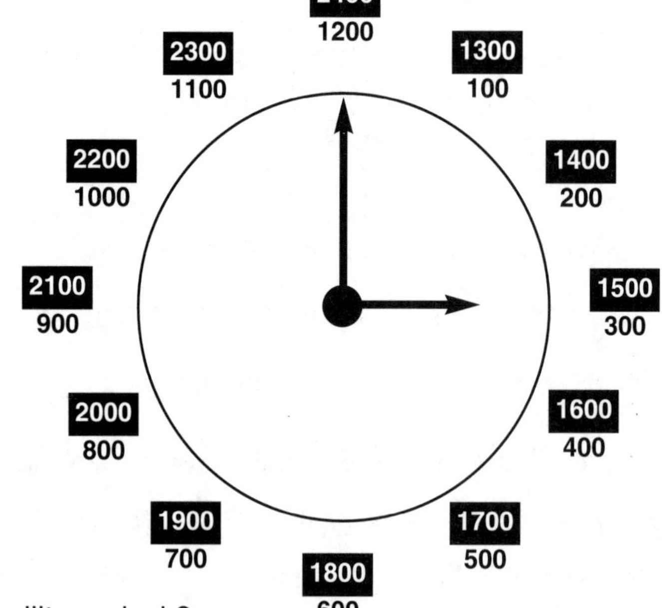

Rewrite each time using a military clock.

1:00 P.M. ______ 9:00 P.M. ______

7:00 A.M. ______ 4:00 P.M. ______

10:00 A.M. ______ 6:00 P.M. ______

8:00 A.M. ______ 2:00 A.M. ______

Why is A.M. or P.M. not needed when using a military clock?

____

Name ______________________________ **Practice 27**

Math Practice: Time

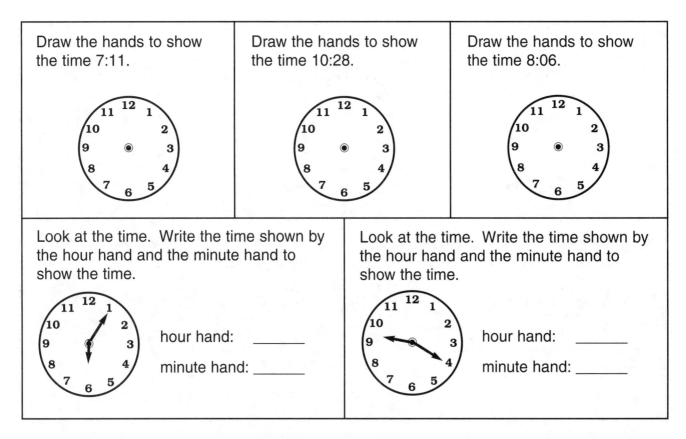

Draw the hands to show the time 7:11. 	Draw the hands to show the time 10:28. 	Draw the hands to show the time 8:06. 

Look at the time. Write the time shown by the hour hand and the minute hand to show the time.  hour hand: ______ minute hand: ______	Look at the time. Write the time shown by the hour hand and the minute hand to show the time.  hour hand: ______ minute hand: ______

Language Practice: Titles

When writing the title of a book, movie, television program, or play, the title is underlined and the important words begin with a capital letter. Read each sentence below.

- If the title is written correctly, write "yes" on the line.
- If the title is written incorrectly, write it correctly on the line.

1. Did you see <u>The Three Stooges</u> movie? ______________________
2. I watch <u>Arthur</u> every afternoon. ______________________
3. Elisabeth had a part in <u>the magic flute</u>. ______________________
4. Andy watches <u>60 Minutes</u> every week. ______________________
5. Ed has read <u>The Secret Garden</u> many times. ______________________
6. The class enjoyed watching <u>the snowman</u>. ______________________
7. Who sang <u>Amazing Grace</u>? ______________________
8. <u>Charlotte's Web</u> is about a pig. ______________________

Name ______________________ Practice 28

Math Practice: Time

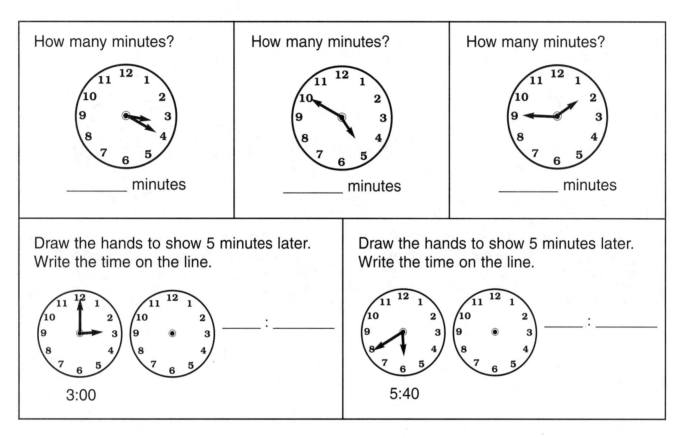

How many minutes?	How many minutes?	How many minutes?
 ________ minutes	 ________ minutes	 ________ minutes

Draw the hands to show 5 minutes later. Write the time on the line.	Draw the hands to show 5 minutes later. Write the time on the line.
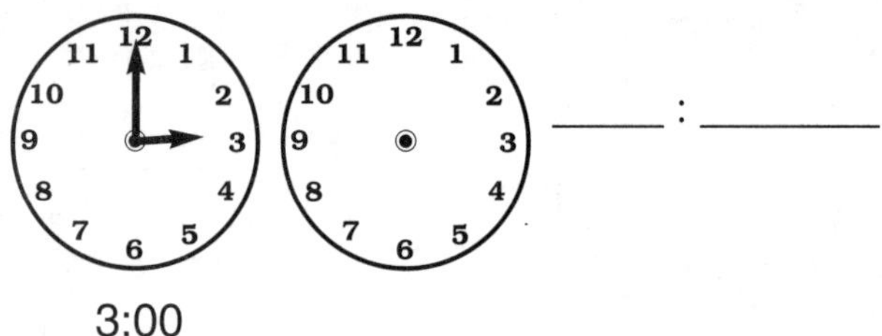 _____ : _______ 3:00	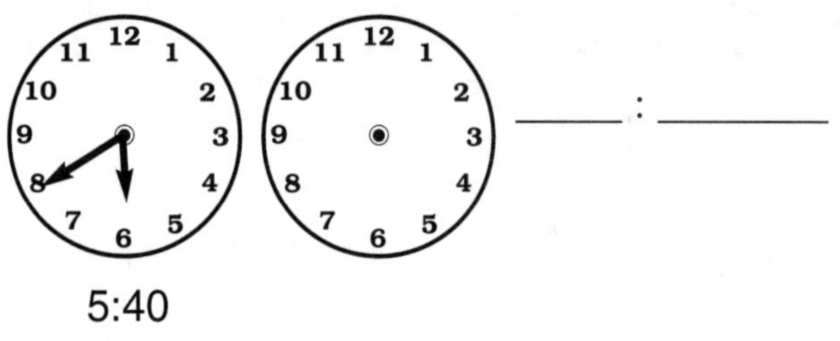 _____ : _______ 5:40

Language Practice: Alphabetical Order

Write the following words in alphabetical order. Find and color the words in the word find.

feet	point	example	country	try
kind	group	sentence	since	light

1. ____________________
2. ____________________
3. ____________________
4. ____________________
5. ____________________
6. ____________________
7. ____________________
8. ____________________
9. ____________________
10. ____________________

E	E	L	I	G	H	T	T	F	L	E	F
G	X	C	O	U	N	T	R	Y	E	C	E
K	R	A	N	T	Y	S	I	N	C	E	N
I	M	O	M	P	K	G	R	I	G	H	T
N	P	C	U	P	O	I	N	T	T	T	I
D	L	O	U	P	L	I	N	O	R	U	S
R	E	S	E	N	T	E	N	C	E	Y	P

Name

Practice 29

Math Practice: Number Lines

Complete the number line.

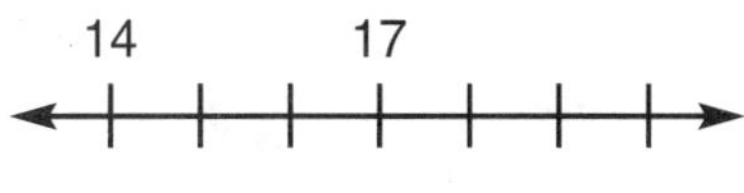

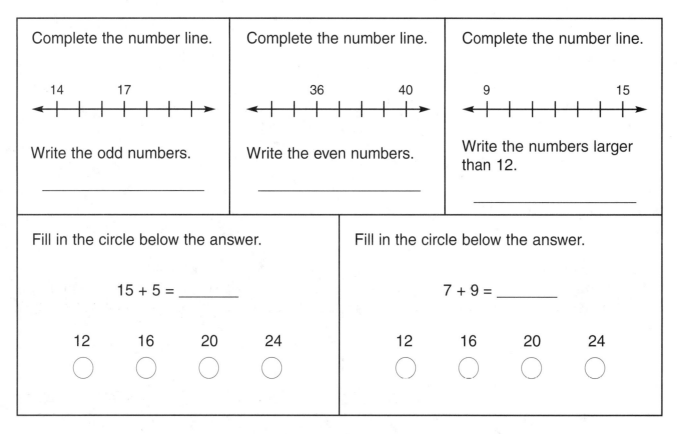

Write the odd numbers.

____

Complete the number line.

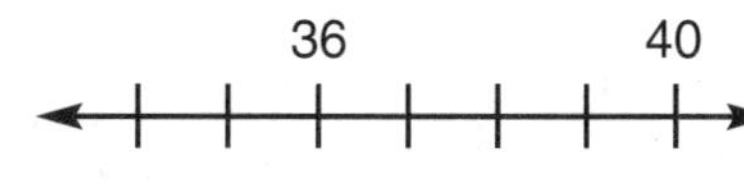

Write the even numbers.

____

Complete the number line.

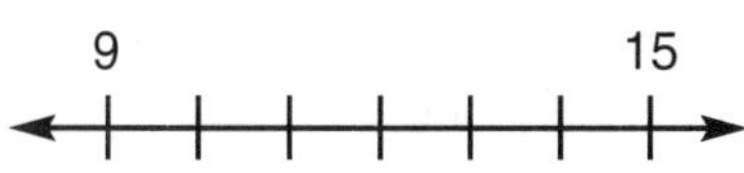

Write the numbers larger than 12.

____

Fill in the circle below the answer.

15 + 5 = _______

12	16	20	24
○	○	○	○

Fill in the circle below the answer.

7 + 9 = _______

12	16	20	24
○	○	○	○

Language Practice: Reading and Using a Graph

Recycling

The graph shows the results of Room 21's recycling efforts. Use the graph to answer the questions.

Legend

each picture square = 10 pounds

1. How many pounds of each item were recycled?

   Bottles: ______________ Cans: ______________ Newspapers: ______________

2. Were more bottles or cans recycled? ____________________
3. Were more newspapers or cans recycled? ____________________
4. Which item had more than 60 pounds recycled? ____________________
5. Which item had fewer than 60 pounds recycled? ____________________

Name ______________________________ Practice 30

Math Practice: Number Sense

Write the missing numbers.	Write the missing numbers.	Write the missing numbers.
24, 28, _______	42, _______, 62	10, _______, 20
32, 36, _______	96, _______, 116	8, _______, 12

Mystery Number	Mystery Number
I am larger than 50 and smaller than 60. When you count by 5s you say my name. What number am I?	I am an odd number. I am larger than 20 and smaller than 25. When you count by 3s you say my name. What number am I?
_______________	_______________

Language Practice: Abbreviations

An *abbreviation* is a shorter way of writing a word. Write the abbreviation for each day of the week.

Sunday: ____________ Monday: ____________ Friday: ____________

Wednesday: ____________ Thursday: ____________

Saturday: ____________ Tuesday: ____________

Read the story. Circle the words that can be abbreviated.

Every Monday, Julian takes piano lessons from Mrs. Hall. On Thursday, Julian has karate lessons. On Tuesday and Friday, Julian has soccer practice with a soccer game on Saturday. On Sunday and Wednesday, Julian can take it easy!

Name ______________________________ Practice 31

Math Practice: Mental Math

Solve.	Solve.	Solve.
12 + 3 – 4 = ________	10 – 8 + 7 = ________	17 – 6 + 2 = ________

Subtraction Square

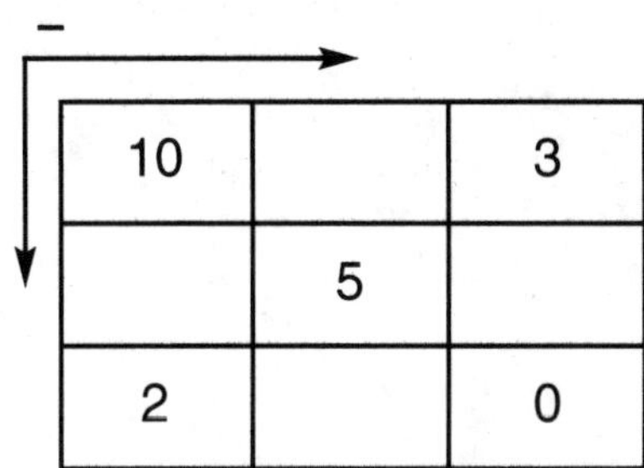

Subtraction Square

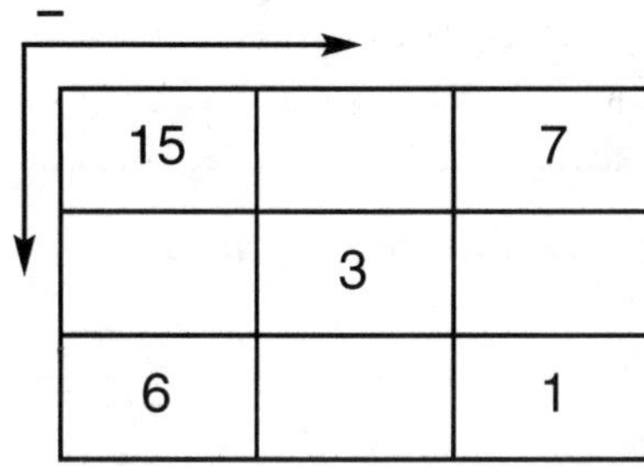

Language Practice: Abbreviations

An *abbreviation* is a shorter way of writing a word. Write the abbreviation for each title.

Governor: ____________ Senator: ____________ Senior: ____________

Representative: ____________ Doctor: ____________ Mister: ____________

Junior: ____________ Honorable: ____________ Professor: ____________

Write the word and its abbreviation next to the definition.

1. ______________________ : congressional representative
2. ______________________ : head of a state
3. ______________________ : someone in the medical profession
4. ______________________ : a teacher at a college or university
5. ______________________ : a man
6. ______________________ : two come from each state
7. ______________________ : a judge
8. ______________________ : a father
9. ______________________ : named after his father

Name ______________________________ Practice 32

Math Practice: Names

Write your first name. Count the letters. There are ______ letters.	Write your middle name. Count the letters. There are ______ letters.	Write your last name. Count the letters. There are ______ letters.

Write the problems. first name + middle name ________ + ________ = ________ first name + last name ________ + ________ = ________	Write a math problem that uses all of the numbers from your fist, middle, and last names.

Language Practice: Abbreviations

An *abbreviation* is a shorter way of writing a word. Write the abbreviation for each kind of street and direction.

Avenue: ______________ Street: ______________ Road: ______________

Boulevard: ______________ Route: ______________ North: ______________

South: ______________ East: ______________ West: ______________

Rewrite each address using the appropriate abbreviation.

1. 2625 West Mooney Boulevard: ______________________________
2. 391 East Lane Avenue: ______________________________
3. 102 South 54th Street: ______________________________
4. 35691 Road 11: ______________________________

Name ______________________________ Practice 33

Math Practice: Number Sense

Circle the correct number sentence.

$4 = 7$

$4 < 7$

$4 > 7$

Circle the correct number sentence.

$88 = 13$

$88 < 13$

$88 > 13$

Circle the correct number sentence.

$24 = 39$

$24 < 39$

$24 > 39$

Circle the correct number sentence.
Queenie had 94 bees. 36 of them flew away.

$94 + 36$ $94 - 36$

Circle the correct number sentence.
Prince had 24 horses. The king gave him 48 more.

$24 + 48$ $24 - 48$

Language Practice: Contractions

A *contraction* is a way of combining two words to make one shorter word. The apostrophe (') takes the place of the missing letters. Rewrite each contraction into its separate words.

Example: needn't ⟶ need not

1. can't ____________	8. I'll ____________
2. don't ____________	9. you'll ____________
3. isn't ____________	10. she'll ____________
4. aren't ____________	11. let's ____________
5. hasn't ____________	12. they've ____________
6. didn't ____________	13. we've ____________
7. who'll ____________	14. we're ____________

Name

Practice 34

Five-a-Day: Subtracting to 18

Subtract. Add to check.	Subtract. Add to check.	Subtract. Add to check.
16 − 4 = ____ ; ____ + 4 = 16	13 − 8 = ____ ; ____ + 8 = 13	18 − 9 = ____ ; ____ + 9 = 18

Solve.	Solve.
Cooper collects flags. He has 17 sea flags and 14 heraldic flags. How many more sea flags does Cooper have?	Diana has collected flags from 12 countries and 15 states. How many more state flags does Diana have?
Cooper has ___________ more sea flags.	Diana has ___________ more state flags.

Language Practice: Proofreading

Proofreading is rereading a sentence and finding the mistakes.

Example: We is saluting the flag. <u>are</u>

"Is" is not the correct verb form. It should be *"are."*

Read each sentence and circle the mistakes. Write the circled word correctly on the line.

1. flags are usually made of fabric. ____________
2. Thay come in different sizes and colors. ____________
3. Military flags is square. ____________
4. Flags used at see are rectangular in shape. ____________
5. Flags was first used to send signals. ____________
6. Heraldic flags are decorated with a cote of arms. ____________
7. Heraldic flags are used by one person? ____________
8. the best known flag is the checkered flag used in racing. ____________

Name

Math Practice: Place Value

Circle sets of ten.	Circle sets of ten.	Circle sets of ten.
_____ tens _____ ones	_____ tens _____ ones	_____ tens _____ ones

Solve.	Solve.
Carlos has 31 pencils. How many sets of ten can he make? How many pencils will be left?	Lara has 40 crayons. How many sets of ten can she make? How many crayons will be left?
_____ sets of ten _____ ones left	_____ sets of ten _____ ones left

Language Practice: Word Play

How many words can you make using the letters in encyclopedia? Write each word in the correct column.

2 Letters	3 Letters	4 Letters	5+ Letters

Name ________________________________ Practice 36

Math Practice: Place Value

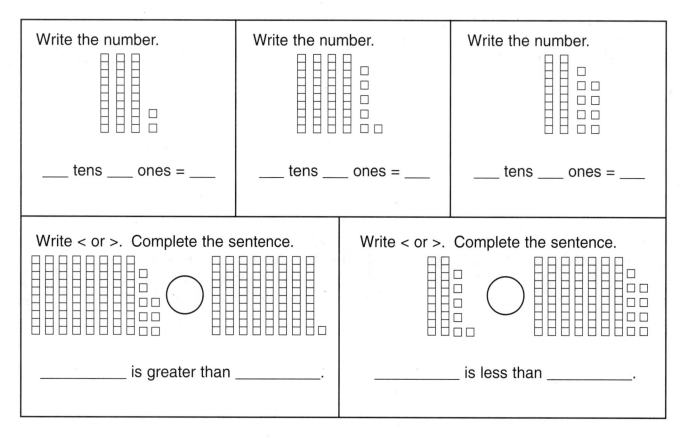

Write the number.	Write the number.	Write the number.
___ tens ___ ones = ___	___ tens ___ ones = ___	___ tens ___ ones = ___

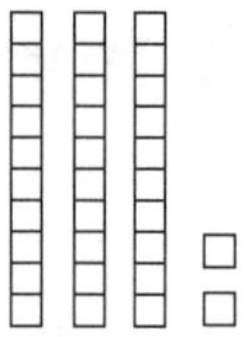

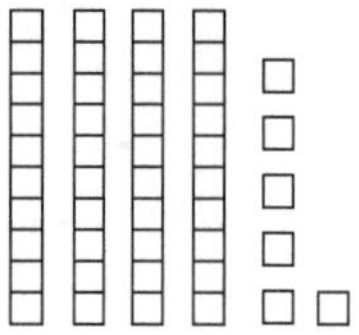

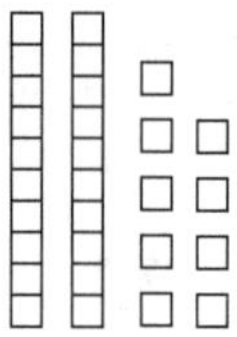

Write < or >. Complete the sentence.	Write < or >. Complete the sentence.
__________ is greater than __________.	__________ is less than __________.

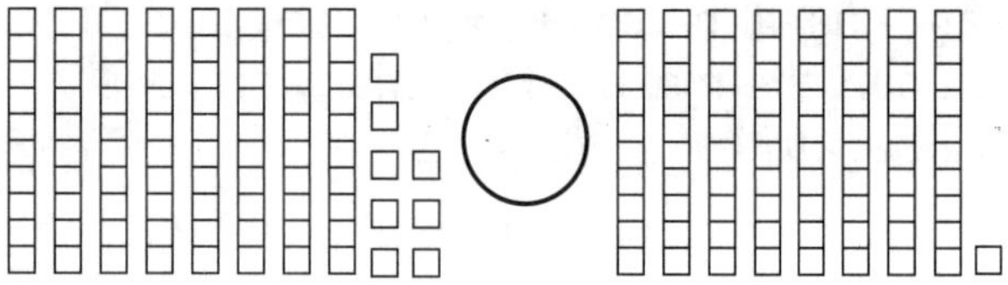

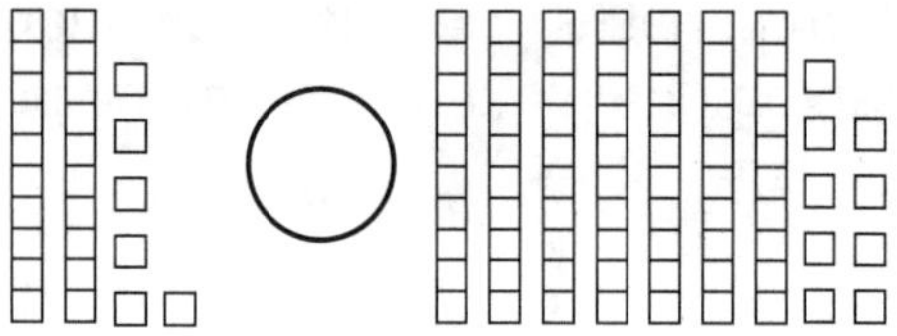

Language Practice: Contractions

A *contraction* is a way of combining two words into one shorter word. The *apostrophe* takes the place of the missing letters. Complete each sentence with the correct word or contraction.

1. wed we'd They were ________________________ on Sunday morning.
2. Wed We'd ________________________ gone to the beautiful ceremony.
3. ill I'll Mrs. Crenshaw is very ________________________.
4. Ill I'll ________________________ take her some chicken soup.
5. well we'll The ________________________ is full of water.
6. Well We'll ________________________ go fill the pail.
7. shell she'll Benita found a conch ________________________.
8. Shell She'll ________________________ fill it with candy.
9. shed she'd Mom was working in the ________________________.
10. Shed She'd ________________________ been out there all day.

Name ______ **Practice 37**

Math Practice: Place Value

Draw the place value blocks to show 9.	Draw the place value blocks to show 52.	Draw the place value blocks to show 60.

Write the number of tens and ones. Write the number.	Write the number of tens and ones. Write the number.
____ tens ____ ones ______	____ tens ____ ones ______

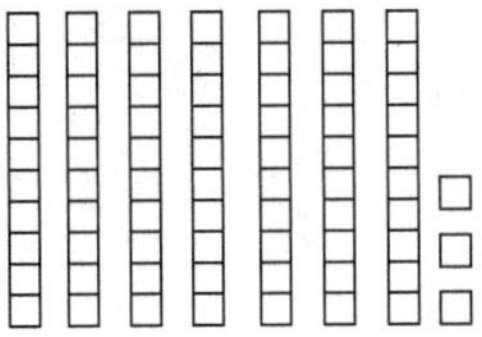

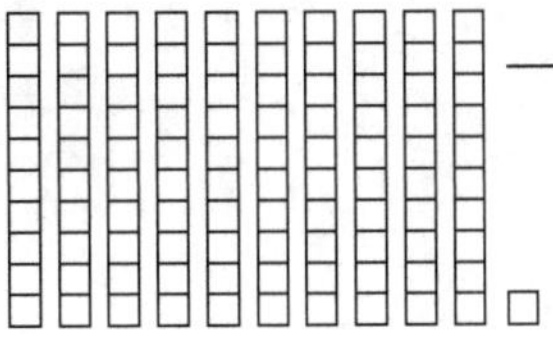

Language Practice: Contractions

A *contraction* is a way of combining two words into one shorter word. The *apostrophe* takes the place of the missing letters. Read each sentence and underline the two words that can be written as a contraction. Write the contraction on the line.

About Squirrels

Example: Some squirrels do not climb trees. don't

1. You will find holes in the ground around the squirrels' home. ______
2. They will bury every nut they collect in a separate hole. ______
3. Kaibab squirrels are not very noisy. ______
4. Kaibab squirrels will not come down from their nests. ______
5. The Douglas' squirrel is not very big. ______
6. It does not weigh more than half a pound. ______
7. Flying squirrels cannot really fly. ______

Name ______________________________________ Practice 38

Math Practice: Place Value

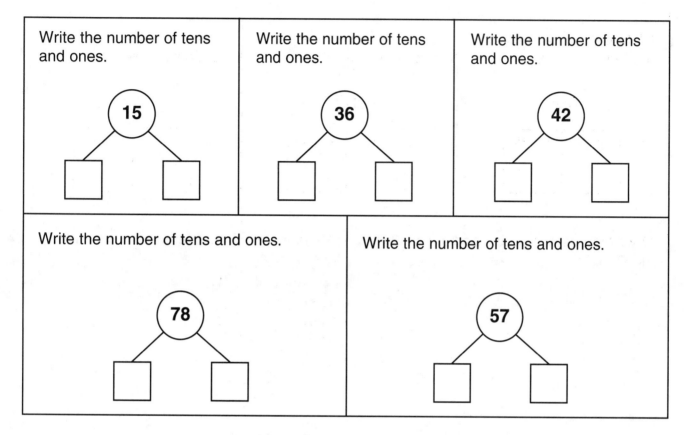

Write the number of tens and ones. 15	Write the number of tens and ones. 36	Write the number of tens and ones. 42
☐ ☐	☐ ☐	☐ ☐

Write the number of tens and ones. 78	Write the number of tens and ones. 57
☐ ☐	☐ ☐

Language Practice: Contractions

A *contraction* is a way of combining two words into one shorter word. The *apostrophe* takes the place of the missing letters. Complete each sentence with the correct word or contraction.

1. your you're ________________ cat caught three mice.
2. your you're ________________ a good friend to have.
3. were we're ________________ you going home for the holidays?
4. were we're ________________ looking forward to seeing you.
5. there they're ________________ are nine girls in our class.
6. there they're ________________ all good students.
7. its it's My dog enjoys chasing ________________ tail.
8. its it's ________________ funny to watch!
9. ones one's How many ________________ do you have?
10. ones one's ________________ plenty to buy the candy bar.

Name

Practice 39

Math Practice: Place Value

Write the number of tens and ones. 39	Write the number of tens and ones. 26	Write the number of tens and ones. 17
Tens | Ones	Tens | Ones	Tens | Ones

Draw the place value blocks to show 86.

Draw the place value blocks to show 45.

Language Practice: Titles

When writing the title of a CD, book, movie, television program, or play, remember to:

- Underline each word in the title.
- Write the important words in the title with a capital letter.

Example: Time for a Story *not* Time For A Story

Underline the titles.

1. The Three Little Pigs
2. I need a binder.
3. Titanic
4. Godzilla
5. television news
6. 'Twas the Night Before Christmas
7. If You Give a Mouse a Cookie
8. The phone is ringing!

Name

Practice 40

Math Practice: Place Value

Circle the larger number.	Circle the larger number.	Circle the larger number.
28 52	61 37	85 19

Write each number in expanded form.

Example: 74 = 70 + 4

95 = _______ + _______

48 = _______ + _______

73 = _______ + _______

Write each number in expanded form.

41 = _______ + _______

19 = _______ + _______

22 = _______ + _______

85 = _______ + _______

Language Practice: Titles

When writing the title of a CD, book, movie, television program, or play, remember to underline each word in the title. Read each sentence and underline the title.

1. The class watched Toy Story 2.
2. The Redfields enjoyed the movie Star Wars.
3. Have you ever seen a performance of The Nutcracker?
4. My favorite movie is Batman.
5. Do you have the video of Cinderella?
6. Superman is a great movie!
7. Vicente played the Sesame Street CD for the young children.
8. Dana had a small part in Romeo and Juliet.
9. I checked out a copy of The Jolly Postman from the local library.
10. Patricia can't wait to read Green Eggs and Ham to her sister.

Name ____________________ Practice 41

Math Practice: Number Sense

Write a number smaller than 20. ______	Write a number between 25 and 50. ______	Write a number larger than 75. ______
Write an odd number between 15 and 35. ______	Write an even number between 80 and 100. ______	

Language Practice: Word Play

Without changing the order of the letters, add a letter to each word to make the name of an animal.

Example: at ⟶ cat

1. money ______
2. got ______
3. do ______
4. muse ______
5. bid ______
6. fog ______
7. ear ______
8. hale ______
9. hark ______
10. be ______
11. he ______
12. ox ______
13. we ______
14. sake ______
15. sunk ______
16. an ______
17. cab ______
18. nail ______

Name

Practice 42

Math Practice: Number Sense

Circle the even numbers.	Circle the odd numbers.	Circle the numbers larger than 50.
8 7 6 4 3 1 0 2	12 79 36 83 57 17 10 41	71 24 85 46 59 62 12 49 5

Write the largest number that can be made using 4, 8, 1 and 5.	Write the smallest number that can be made using 4, 8, 1 and 5.
Write the number that is in the *thousands* place. ________	Write the number that is in the *thousands* place. ________

Language Practice: Titles

When writing the title of a CD, book, movie, television program or play, remember the following:

- Underline each word in the title.
- Write the important words in the title with a capital letter.

Example: Old MacDonald Had a Farm *not* Old MacDonald Had A Farm

Write the titles of your favorite CD, book, movie, television program, or play.

Favorite movie: ______________________________

Favorite CD: ______________________________

Favorite book: ______________________________

Favorite play: ______________________________

Name ______________________ Practice 43

Math Practice: Place Value

Add.	Add.	Add.
10 + 10	10 + 20	20 + 40

Write the problem and then solve it.	Write the problem and then solve it.
Weldon has 20¢. He found 30¢ in his pocket. How much money does Weldon have? Weldon has ______________.	Gayle had 40¢. She found 30¢ in her purse. How much money does Gayle have? Gayle has ______________.

Language Practice: Subjects

The *subject* tells what the sentence is about. The subject can be either singular (about one person, item, or group) or plural (about more than one item, person, or group).

- If the subject is *singular*, the verb ends in *s*.
- If the subject is *plural*, the verb does not end in *s*.

Write the correct form of the verb on the line.

1. Wasp grubs ________________ caterpillars and aphids. (eat)
2. Only the new queen ________________ the winter. (survive)
3. A giant hornet ________________ its nest in a tree. (build)
4. A paper wasp ________________ chewed wood to make her home. (use)
5. Blue-black spider wasps ________________ spiders. (capture)
6. Mud daubers ________________ alone. (live)

Name

Practice 44

Math Practice: Place Value

Write the missing addend.

30
+ □
70

Write the missing addend.

90
+ 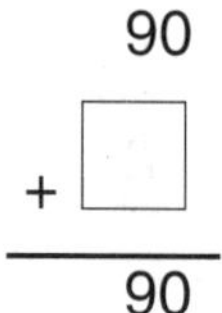
90

Write the missing addend.

20
+ 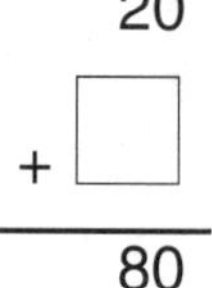
80

Complete the table.

+	1	2	3	4	5	6
10						

Complete the table.

+	10	20	30	40	50	60
5						

Language Practice: Anagrams

Anagrams are words that can be made by rearranging the letters in a word to create a new word.

Example: Noel ——→ Leon

Rearrange the letters in each word to create a new word.

1. three ____________
2. how ____________
3. eon ____________
4. spark ____________
5. earth ____________
6. lips ____________
7. send ____________
8. nose ____________
9. soar ____________
10. bat ____________
11. but ____________
12. stove ____________
13. and ____________
14. Rome ____________
15. lids ____________
16. plea ____________

Name ______________________________ Practice 45

Math Practice: Place Value

Subtract.	Subtract.	Subtract.
80 – 30	70 – 60	50 – 50

Write the problem and then solve it.	Write the problem and then solve it.
Gordon had 20¢ . He spend 10¢ buying a pack of gum. How much money does Gordon have left? Gordon has ______________.	Gertrude had 30¢. She spent 30¢ buying a candy bar. How much money does Gertrude have left? Gordon has ______________.

Language Practice: Subjects

The *subject* tells what the sentence is about. The subject can be either singular (about one person, item, or group) or plural (about more than one item, person, or group). Underline the subject in each sentence.

Flies

1. Flies carry disease.
2. Malaria and yellow fever are spread by flies.
3. They can contaminate food.
4. A fly has two wings instead of four wings.
5. The robber fly can grow to be 3” long.
6. House flies are stronger and faster than gnats.
7. Some flies drink blood.
8. The tsetse fly drinks three times its weight in blood.
9. All flies are able to walk upside down.
10. The fourth largest group of insects is the flies.

Name

Practice 46

Math Practice: Place Value

Round each number to the nearest ten. Solve.	Round each number to the nearest ten. Solve.	Round each number to the nearest ten. Solve.
$39 \longrightarrow 40$ $\underline{-11} \longrightarrow \underline{-10}$	$27 \longrightarrow$ $\underline{+8} \longrightarrow$ _____	$51 \longrightarrow$ $\underline{-27} \longrightarrow$ _____

Circle the estimate.	Circle the estimate.
Jerome had 47 spider eggs. If 12 of the eggs hatched, how many spider eggs are left? < 40 $\quad$ > 40	Adeline had 8 honey combs. Her grandfather gave her 10 more. How many honeycombs does Adeline have? < 10 $\quad$ > 10

Language Practice: Subjects

The *subject* tells what the sentence is about. The subject can be either singular (about one person, item, or group) or plural (about more than one item, person, or group). Underline the subject in each sentence. Write singular or plural on the line provided.

Bees

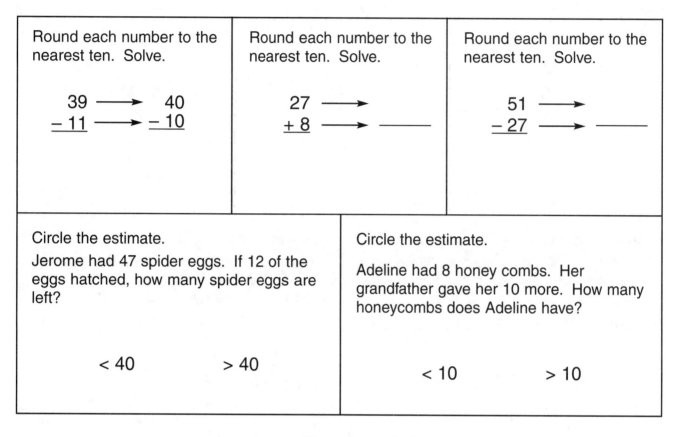

1. Most orchid bees live in tropical areas. ____________
2. The leaf cutter bee is 1/4" long. ____________
3. It uses its jaw to eat pieces of leaves and flowers. ____________
4. Honey bees make honey and wax. ____________
5. Nests are made by the insects. ____________
6. A bee has tiny hairs on its body. ____________
7. A bee colony can have thousands of bees. ____________
8. Bumblebees are large, black insects. ____________

Name _______________ Practice 47

Math Practice: Adding 3 Numbers

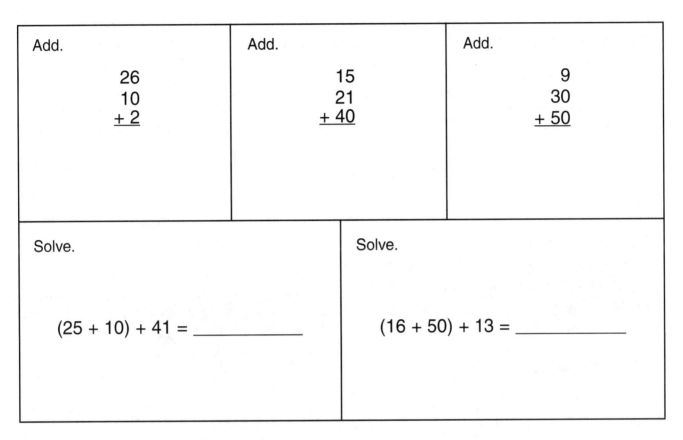

Add.	Add.	Add.
26 10 + 2	15 21 + 40	9 30 + 50

Solve.	Solve.
(25 + 10) + 41 = _______	(16 + 50) + 13 = _______

Language Practice: Alphabetical Order

Write each set of words in alphabetical order.

family	1. _______	tuck	1. _______
face	2. _______	turned	2. _______
far	3. _______	tub	3. _______
paper	1. _______	lift	1. _______
part	2. _______	living	2. _______
pace	3. _______	lick	3. _______
began	1. _______	mother	1. _______
bee	2. _______	money	2. _______
became	3. _______	more	3. _______

Name

Practice 48

Math Practice: Money

Add.	Add.	Add.
26¢ + 3¢	58¢ + 40¢	8¢ + 90¢

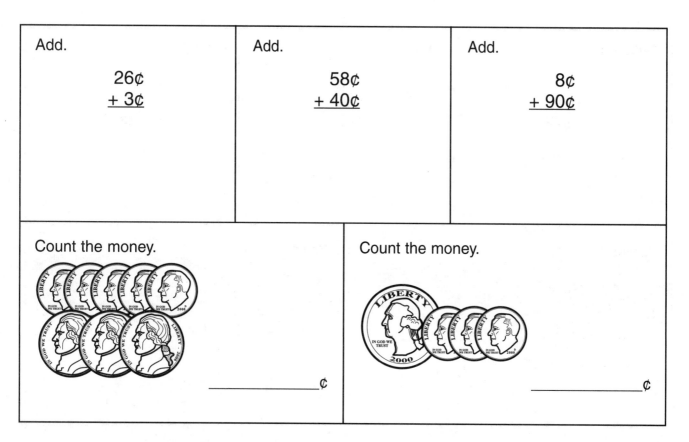

Count the money.

_______________¢

Count the money.

_______________¢

Language Practice: Reading and Using a Chart

Alex's Cleaning Service	
Windows Washed	50¢
Car Washed	35¢
Leaves Raked	25¢
Pets Walked	10¢
Plants Watered	40¢
Carpet Vacuumed	45¢
Floors Mopped	15¢

Use the chart to answer the questions.

1. Which cleaning service is the most expensive?

   ____

2. Which cleaning service is the least expensive?

   ____

3. What is the cost of having the leaves raked combined with walking a pet? _______________________

4. What is the cost of watering the plants combined with vacuuming the carpets? _______________________

5. Mrs. Pettigrew has 60¢ to spend. What two services can Mrs. Pettigrew have done? _______________________

   ____

   ____

Name ______________________________ Practice 49

Math Practice: Subtracting Money

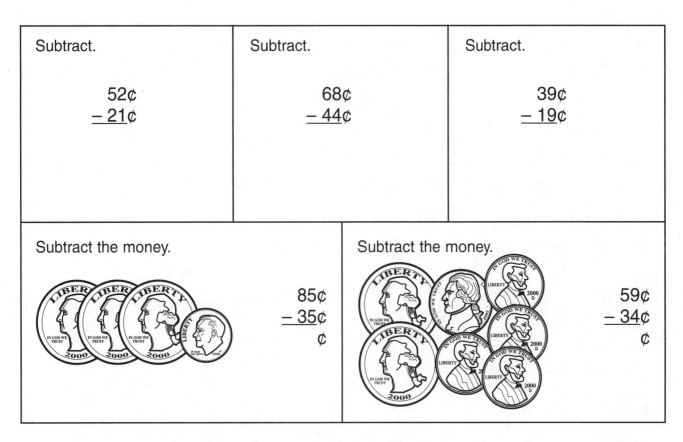

Subtract.	Subtract.	Subtract.
52¢ – 21¢	68¢ – 44¢	39¢ – 19¢

Subtract the money.	Subtract the money.
85¢ – 35¢ ¢	59¢ – 34¢ ¢

Language Practice: Conjunctions

Conjunctions are words that join words, phrases, and sentences. Some conjunctions: *and*, *or*, *but*, *for*, *nor*, *so*, and *yet*.

Example: Kate made the dessert and went to the party.

Complete each sentence with a conjunction.

1. Hadassah and Halima went to the movies ______________ went to lunch.
2. Ogden does not like chocolate cake ______________ chocolate pie.
3. This gift was for Eartha, ______________ I gave it to Bree.
4. Rafi was the last one eating at the dinner table ______________ he had to do the dishes.
5. Would you like to go to the ballet ______________ to the theater?
6. Amos is usually on time, ______________ today he arrived late.

Name ______________________________ Practice 50

Math Practice: Place Value

Write the hundreds, tens, and ones.	Write the hundreds, tens, and ones.	Write the hundreds, tens, and ones.
456	275	981
______ hundreds	______ hundreds	______ hundreds
______ tens	______ tens	______ tens
______ ones	______ ones	______ ones

Write the hundreds, tens, and ones.	Write the hundreds, tens, and ones.
733	659
______ hundreds	______ hundreds
______ tens	______ tens
______ ones	______ ones

Language Practice: Predicates

A *predicate* is the part of a sentence that tells something about the subject. Read each sentence and circle the predicate.

Example: My friend Allen works at an amusement park.
The words *works at an amusement park* explain what Allen does.

Amphibians

1. Salamanders have long bodies, long tails, and four legs.
2. Frogs and toads use their back legs for jumping.
3. Most newts stay near the water.
4. Frogs and toads can swim and hop.
5. Some frogs and toads can even climb trees.
6. Tadpoles breathe through gills.
7. Caecilians are amphibians.
8. They live in underground burrows.

Name ______________________ Practice 51

Math Practice: Place Value

Add.	Add.	Add.
100 + 100	300 + 400	200 + 500

Write the problem. Solve.	Write the problem. Solve.
Rocco had 100 pennies. His dad gave him 200 more. How many pennies does Rocco now have? Rocco has ____________ pennies.	Lourdes planted 400 white roses and 300 yellow roses. How many roses did Lourdes plant? Lourdes planted ____________ roses.

Language Practice: Predicates

A *predicate* is the part of a sentence that tells something about the subject. Read each sentence and circle the predicate.

Example: King Tutankahmun is one of history's most famous pharaohs.
In this sentence, *is one of history's most famous pharaohs* explains who he is.

More About Amphibians

1. Amphibians are vertebrate animals.
2. They evolved from fish millions of years ago.
3. Amphibians spend part of their lives in the water.
4. There are more than 4,550 amphibian species.
5. Salamanders, newts, frogs, and toads are amphibians.
6. Amphibians are cold blooded.
7. They bask in the sun.
8. Amphibians breathe oxygen through their skin.

Name

Practice 52

Math Practice: Place Value

Subtract.	Subtract.	Subtract.
900 – 800	300 – 100	400 – 200

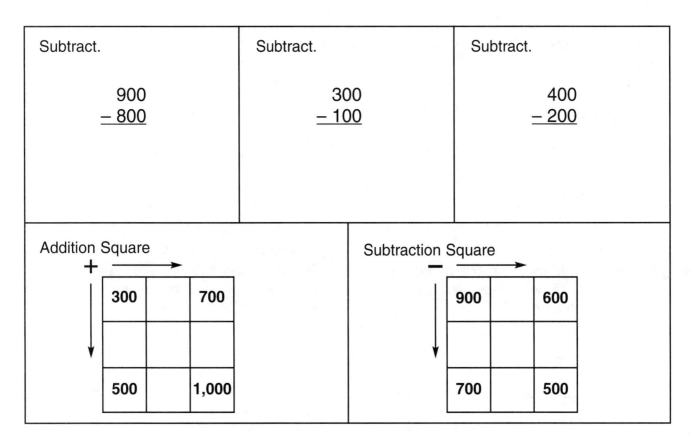

Addition Square

+ →

↓

300		700
500		1,000

Subtraction Square

– →

↓

900		600
700		500

Language Practice: Predicates

Predicates provide information about the subject. Write a predicate to complete each subject.

1. Ladybugs ______________________________
2. Hamburgers ______________________________
3. Grapes ______________________________
4. Recess ______________________________
5. Libraries ______________________________
6. The country fair ______________________________
7. Music ______________________________
8. Rollerblades ______________________________

Name

Math Practice: Place Value

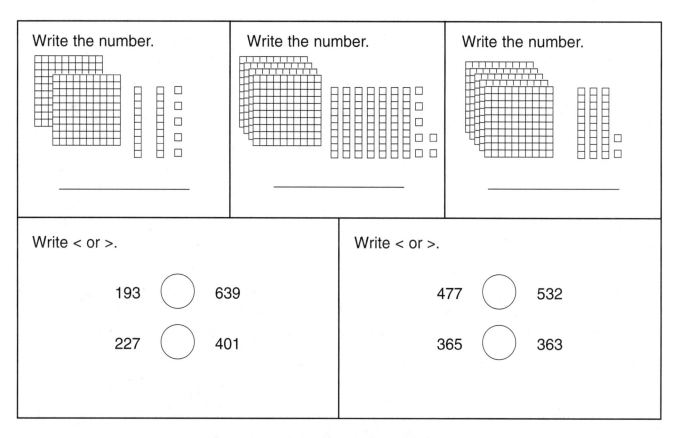

Write the number.	Write the number.	Write the number.
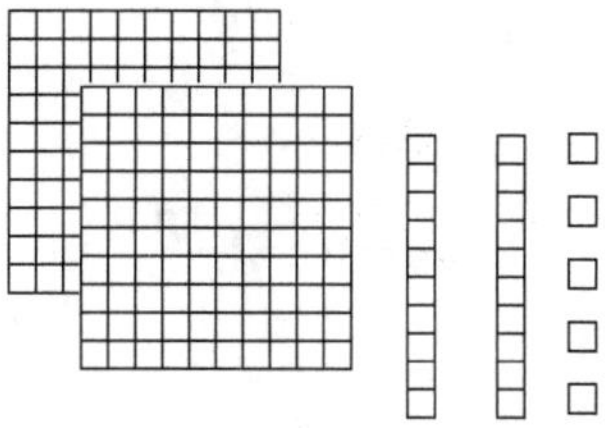 ________	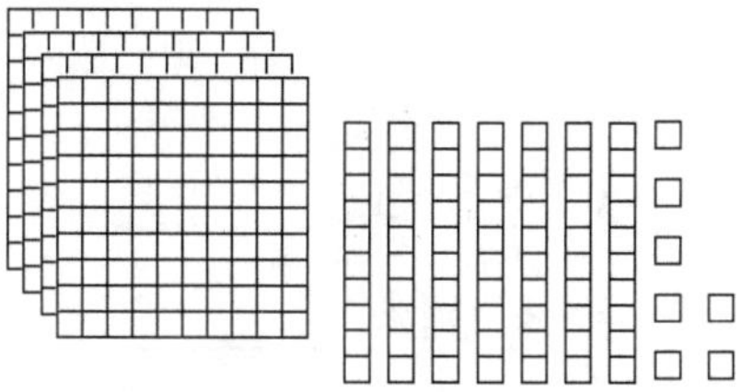 ________	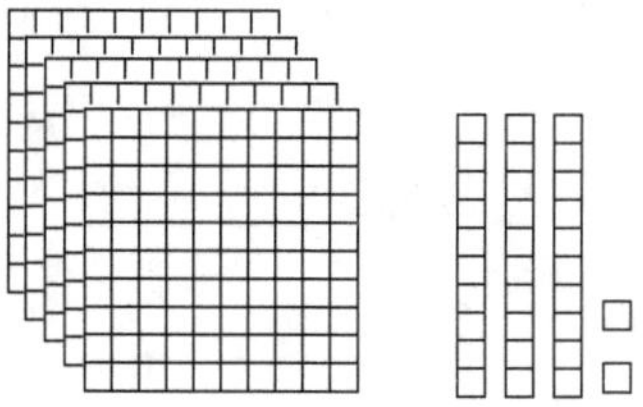 ________

Write < or >.

193 ◯ 639

227 ◯ 401

Write < or >.

477 ◯ 532

365 ◯ 363

Language Practice: Comprehension

Cowboys

Cowboys can be found living and working throughout the world. In Italy, cowboys are called "butteros." In Argentina, they are known as "gouchos." In Spain, they are called "vaqueros."

A cowboy's hat is his trademark. The hats reflect regional differences but are used in much the same way. The hat is used to shade the cowboy's eyes and to protect him from the sun. When it rains, the hat is used like an umbrella. The hat can also be used to carry water and to fan the flames of the campfire. The hat also protects the cowboy's head from low-hanging tree branches and thorny shrubs.

1. What are cowboys called in other parts of the world? ________________________________

____

2. Write at least two other uses for the cowboy's hat. ________________________________

____

____

Name ______________________________ Practice 54

Math Practice: Number Sense

Write the missing numbers.	Write the missing numbers.	Write the missing numbers.
870, 875, ______ 988, 989, ______	362, 363, ______ 913, 914, ______	400, ______, 600 215, ______, 225

Complete the pattern.	Complete the pattern.
150, 200, 250, ______, ______, ______, ______, ______, ______, ______	310, 360, 410, ______, ______, ______, ______, ______, ______, ______

Language Practice: Complete Sentences

A sentence has two parts—the subject and the predicate. The *subject* is a noun. It tells who or what the sentence is about. The *predicate* provides information about the subject. Read each sentence and circle the complete sentences.

1. The telephone.
2. Grew rapidly.
3. The old car drove slowly down the street.
4. Mr. Pletze is having a yard sale.
5. Have you?
6. Who drank all the milk?
7. Made the bed.
8. The lawn.
9. Mrs. Burnett trimmed the hedges.
10. The sky.

Name ______ Practice 55

Math Practice: Place Value

Use the numbers 4, 3, and 6 to make numbers. largest: ______ smallest: ______	Use the numbers 1, 8 and 2 to make an . . . odd number: ______ even number: ______	Use the numbers 5, 9 and 7 to make a number . . . larger than 600: ______ smaller than 600: ______

Mystery Number • The number has the digits 2, 6 and 5. • The number is an even number. • The number has a 2 in the hundreds place. What is the mystery number? ______	Mystery Number • The number has the digits 8, 0 and 3. • The number is an odd number. • The 0 is in the tens place. What is the mystery number? ______

Language Practice: Complete Sentences

A sentence has two parts— the subject and the predicate. The *subject* is a noun. It tells who or what the sentence is about. The *predicate* provides information about the subject. On the lines below, write the correct letter from the box to represent complete sentences, subject only, or predicate only.

> C—for complete sentence
>
> S—for subject only (no predicates)
>
> P—for predicate only (no subject)

Rabbits

1. Rabbits are wild animals. ______
2. Have excellent hearing. ______
3. Their noses. ______
4. Rabbits use their hind legs to thump a warning. ______
5. Hares are bigger, skinnier, and faster than rabbits. ______
6. Rabbits. ______
7. Is a good swimmer. ______

Name ______________________________ Practice 56

Math Practice: Place Value

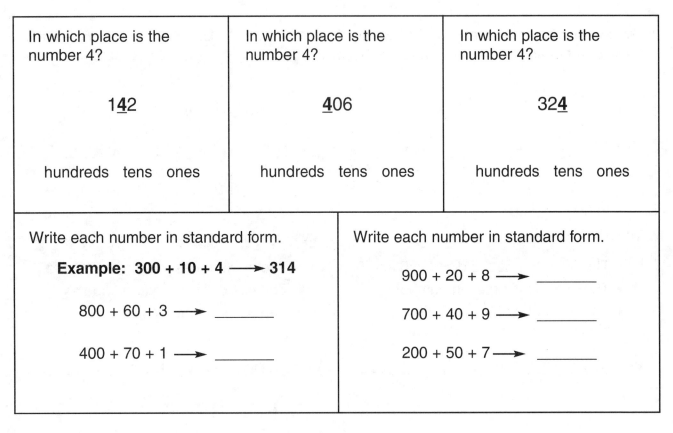

In which place is the number 4?	In which place is the number 4?	In which place is the number 4?
1<u>4</u>2	<u>4</u>06	32<u>4</u>
hundreds tens ones	hundreds tens ones	hundreds tens ones

Write each number in standard form.	Write each number in standard form.
Example: 300 + 10 + 4 ⟶ 314	900 + 20 + 8 ⟶ ______
800 + 60 + 3 ⟶ ______	700 + 40 + 9 ⟶ ______
400 + 70 + 1 ⟶ ______	200 + 50 + 7 ⟶ ______

Language Practice: Research Report

When writing a research report, it is important to use your own words.

Example:

Using my own words: *In 1877, Henry Flipper graduated from West Point.*

Rewrite each sentence using your own words.

Important African Americans

1. Lena Horne received a Tony Award for her one-woman Broadway show.

____

2. In 1844, James Beckwourth discovered a passage through the Sierra Nevada mountain range.

____

3. Ralph Waldo Emerson wrote the novel, *The Invisible Man,* in 1952.

____

Name ______ **Practice 57**

Math Practice: Rounding Numbers

Round each number to the nearest hundred.	Round each number to the nearest hundred.	Round each number to the nearest hundred.
613 ______	879 ______	554 ______
772 ______	921 ______	472 ______
463 ______	548 ______	299 ______

Write the number using words.	Write the number using words.
684	332
______________________	______________________
______________________	______________________

Language Practice: Number Words

Write each number next to its number word. Complete the crossword puzzle.

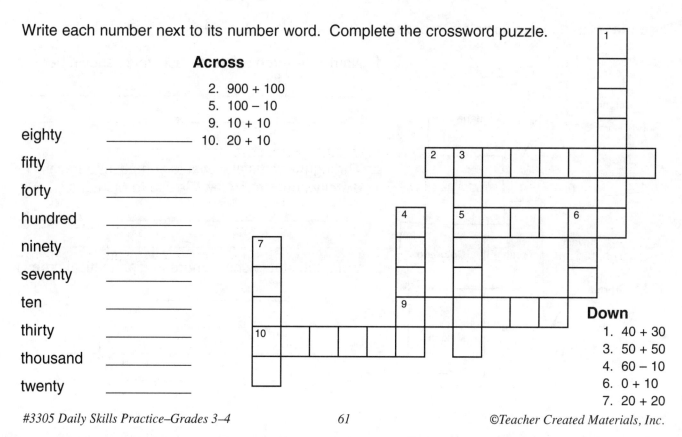

eighty ______
fifty ______
forty ______
hundred ______
ninety ______
seventy ______
ten ______
thirty ______
thousand ______
twenty ______

Across

2. 900 + 100
5. 100 – 10
9. 10 + 10
10. 20 + 10

Down

1. 40 + 30
3. 50 + 50
4. 60 – 10
6. 0 + 10
7. 20 + 20

Name ______________________________ Practice 58

Math Practice: Place Value

Write the numbers in order from smallest to greatest.	Write the numbers in order from smallest to greatest.	Write the numbers in order from smallest to greatest.
434 827 566 139	919 159 127 482	265 773 838 456
____, ____, ____, ____	____, ____, ____, ____	____, ____, ____, ____

Solve. Jade's favorite number is 142. Sade's favorite number is 10 higher than Jade's. What is Sade's favorite number?	Solve. Grant's favorite number is 249. Julian's favorite number is 10 lower than Grant's. What is Julian's favorite number?
Sade's favorite number is ______.	Julian's favorite number is ______.

Language Practice: Reading and Using Maps

Use the map below to complete exercises 1–3.

1. Name the three westernmost states shown here.

   ____

   ____

   ____

2. Through which states would you pass to travel directly north from New Mexico to Montana?

   ____

   ____

3. Write the states shown here in alphabetical order.

   ____

   ____

   ____

   ____

Name ______________________________ Practice 59

Math Practice: 3-Digit Addition Without Regrouping

Add.	Add.	Add.
279 + 300	883 + 112	413 + 274

Solve.	Solve.
Rosa has 200 black ants and 357 red ants in her ant farm. How many ants are there in all? Rosa has ______ ants in all.	Ronny asked people if they liked ants. There were 103 people who said "yes" and 325 who said "no." How many people did Ronny ask? Ronny asked ______ people.

Language Practice: Statements

Statements can either report a fact or an opinion. Read each sentence below. Write *fact* or *opinion* on the line provided.

Ants

1. There are 10 billion ants in the world. ______________
2. Ants are stinky bugs. ______________
3. Ants eat insects, fruit, and crumbs. ______________
4. Ants are smaller than a grain of rice. ______________
5. I don't like ants. ______________
6. Ants use scent signals to communicate with each other. ______________
7. Most ants are female. ______________
8. People should step on all ants. ______________

Name ______________________________ Practice 60

Math Practice: 3-Digit Subtraction Without Regrouping

Subtract.	Subtract.	Subtract.
865 – 341	995 – 364	276 – 213

Solve.	Solve.
Maddie saw 487 whales and 382 star fish. How many more whales than star fish did Maddie see? Maddie saw ______ more whales.	Eric caught 965 bees. Of the bees, 805 buzzed away. How many bees does Eric have left? Eric has ______ bees left.

Language Practice: Questions

A *statement* tells a fact or opinion. A statement has a period at the end. A *question* asks for information and has a question mark at the end. Read each sentence below. Add the missing punctuation mark (. or ?) at the end of each sentence. Write *statement* or *question* on the line.

Unusual Animals

1. A sperm whale's brain can weigh 20 pounds ____ ____________________
2. Some millipedes have only eight legs ____ ____________________
3. Why do slugs have four noses ____ ____________________
4. How many flowers does a hummingbird visit each day ____ ____________________
5. Which deer is nine inches tall ____ ____________________
6. Where do jellyfish live ____ ____________________
7. Who has seen a starfish with 50 arms ____ ____________________
8. When does a seahores lay its egg ____ ____________________
9. One beehive can have 80,000 bees living in it ____ ____________________

Name ______________________ Practice 61

Math Practice: 3-Digit Subtraction Without Regrouping

Write the missing sign.	Write the missing sign.	Write the missing sign.
700 ◯ 600 = 100	700 ◯ 400 = 300	400 ◯ 300 = 700

Solve.

Centerville is 200 miles away and Goshen is another 159 more miles away. How far away is Goshen?

Goshen is ______ miles away.

Solve.

Hanford is 381 miles away. Pixley is 170 miles closer than Hanford. How far away is Pixley?

Pixley is ______ miles away.

Language Practice: Questions

A *statement* tells a fact or opinion. A *question* asks for information. Write a statement and a question for each picture below.

Martin Luther King Jr.

Abraham Lincoln

Rosa Parks

Name ____________________ Practice 62

Math Practice: Place Value

Write the number in standard form. 1,000 + 300 + 80 + 2 ________	Write the number in standard form. 8,000 + 800 + 60 + 1 ________	Write the number in standard form. 2,000 + 400 + 70 + 3 ________

Write the number using words. 8,567 ____________________ ____________________	Write the number using words. 9,325 ____________________ ____________________

Language Practice: Alphabetical Order

Write the presidents' names below in alphabetical order.

Hoover	Carter	Washington	Polk	Johnson	Madison
Lincoln	Ford	Roosevelt	Taft	Kennedy	Van Buren

1. ____________ 5. ____________ 9. ____________
2. ____________ 6. ____________ 10. ____________
3. ____________ 7. ____________ 11. ____________
4. ____________ 8. ____________ 12. ____________

A *syllable* is a part of a word. All words have at least one syllable. Write the number of syllables in each name.

1. Hoover: ______ 5. Washington: ______ 9. Polk: ______
2. Lincoln: ______ 6. Roosevelt: ______ 10. Taft: ______
3. Carter: ______ 7. Johnson: ______ 11. Madison: ______
4. Ford: ______ 8. Kennedy: ______ 12. Van Buren: ______

Name ______________________

Math Practice: Place Value

Write the number in the tens place. 4,681 ________	Write the number in the hundreds place. 4,519 ________	Write the number in the ones place. 3,697 ________

Write the missing numbers. 2,368; 2,369; ________ ; ________ ; ________ ; ________ ; ________ ; ________ ; ________ ; ________	Write the missing numbers. 6,559; 6,560 ________ ; ________ ; ________ ; ________ ; ________ ; ________ ; ________ ; ________

Language Practice: Dictionary Skills

A *dictionary* is a kind of reference book. A dictionary gives the meaning for thousands of words. All of the words are in alphabetical order. Label the parts of word entry.

A. definitions B. entry C. guide words D. part of speech E. pronunciation guide

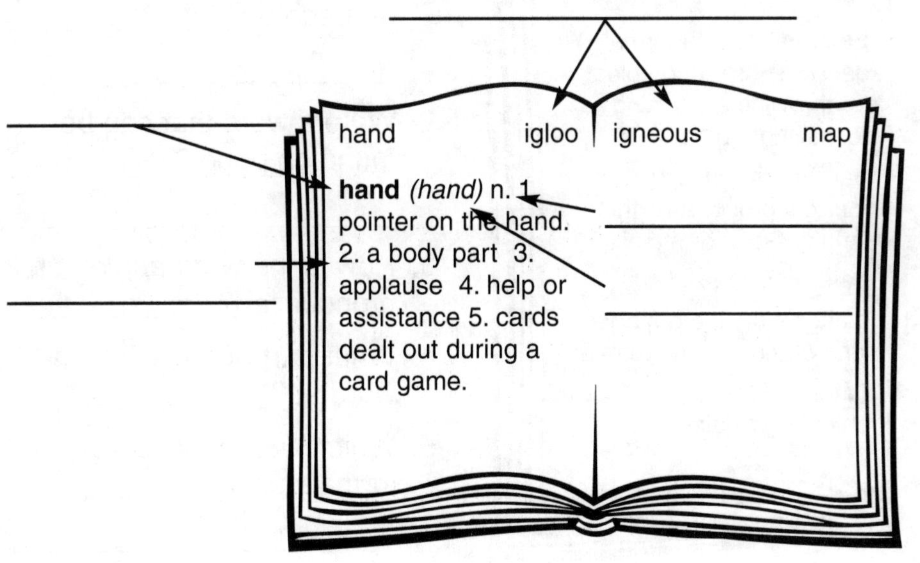

hand
igloo
igneous
map
hand *(hand)* n. 1. pointer on the hand. 2. a body part 3. applause 4. help or assistance 5. cards dealt out during a card game.

Circle the words that could be found on the two dictionary pages.

marry	iguana
help	may
I	milk
next	handy
heart	hae
in	has

Name ______________________________ Practice 64

Math Practice: Comparing Numbers

Write <, >, or = sign.	Write <, >, or = sign.	Write <, >, or = sign.
1,743 ◯ 9,550	8,514 ◯ 6,638	2,128 ◯ 9,773
6,538 ◯ 7,318	6,469 ◯ 2,429	4,865 ◯ 1,465

Write each number using words.	Write each number using words.
6,384	8,651
______________________	______________________
______________________	______________________

Language Practice: Dictionary Skills

A *dictionary* is a kind of reference book. A dictionary tells the meaning for thousands of words. All of the words are in alphabetical order. Use the dictionary pages below to answer the questions.

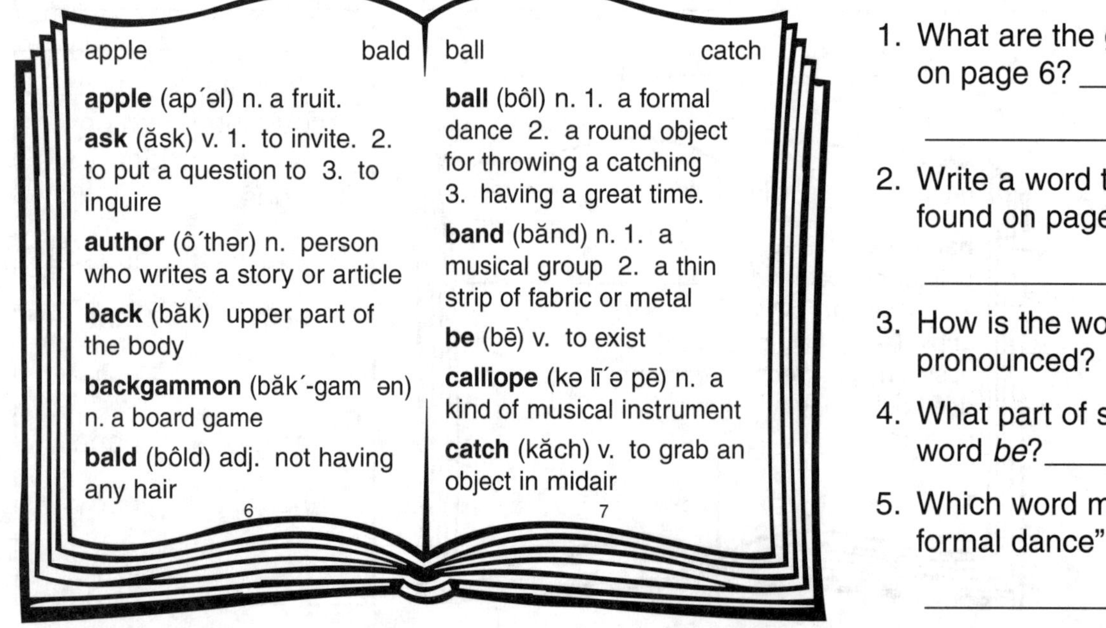

apple bald

apple (ap´əl) n. a fruit.

ask (ăsk) v. 1. to invite. 2. to put a question to 3. to inquire

author (ô´thər) n. person who writes a story or article

back (băk) upper part of the body

backgammon (băk´-gam ən) n. a board game

bald (bôld) adj. not having any hair

6

ball catch

ball (bôl) n. 1. a formal dance 2. a round object for throwing a catching 3. having a great time.

band (bănd) n. 1. a musical group 2. a thin strip of fabric or metal

be (bē) v. to exist

calliope (kə lī´ə pē) n. a kind of musical instrument

catch (kăch) v. to grab an object in midair

7

1. What are the guide words on page 6? ______________ ______________
2. Write a word that can be found on page 7. ______________
3. How is the word *apple* pronounced? ______________
4. What part of speech is the word *be*? ______________
5. Which word means, "a formal dance"? ______________

Name ______________________________ Practice 65

Math Practice: Place Value

Circle the largest number. In which place is the number?	Circle the largest number. In which place is the number?	Circle the largest number. In which place is the number?
4,827	3,385	6,619
________	________	________

Write the numbers in expanded form.	Write the numbers in expanded form.
Example: 1,456 → 1,000 + 400 + 50 + 6	5,391 ____________________
3,927 ____________________	6,594 ____________________
4,145 ____________________	1,382 ____________________

Language Practice: Reading a Chart

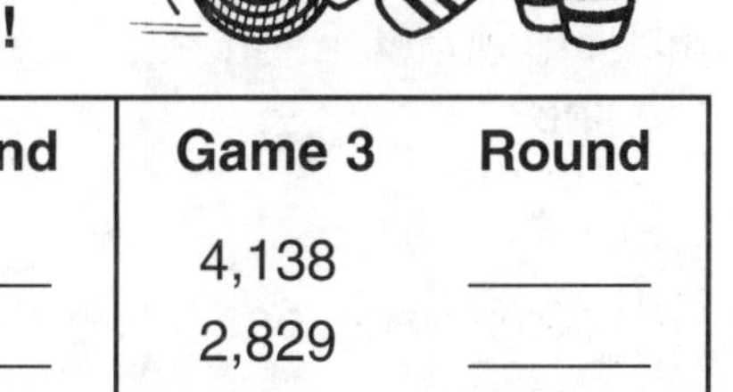

Use the chart to answer the questions.

The Great Bowl-O-Mania Marathon!

Teams	Game 1	Round	Game 2	Round	Game 3	Round
Green Team	799	______	8,566	______	4,138	______
Red Team	1,383	______	1,177	______	2,829	______
Blue Team	927	______	345	______	4,111	______
Purple Team	4,265	______	6,459	______	773	______

1. Circle the highest scores in each column. Write the scores in order from smallest to largest. ______________, ______________, ______________
2. Underline the lowest scores in each column. Write the scores in order from largest to smallest. ______________, ______________, ______________
3. Who won Game 1? ______________ Game 2? ______________ Game 3? ______________

Name

Practice 66

Math Practice: Addition and Subtraction Without Regrouping

Add.	Subtract.	Add.
2,000 + 3,000	8,500 − 6,200	4,700 + 4,100

Solve.	Solve.
The first steam locomotive was invented in 1829. The first jet plane was invented in 1939. How many years separated these two inventions?	The first mini-van was invented in 1983. The first elevator was invented 131 years earlier. In what year was the elevator invented?
They were separated by ______ years.	The elevator was invented in ______ .

Language Practice: Statements and Questions

A *statement* tells a fact or opinion. A statement has a period at the end. A *question* asks for information. A question has a question mark at the end. Read each sentence. Add the missing punctuation mark (. or ?) to the end of each sentence. Write *statement* or *question* on the line.

Weird Animal Facts

1. Do mosquitoes bite _____ ____________________
2. Dolphins sleep at night ______ ____________________
3. Do albatross sleep while flying ______ ____________________
4. Is the Komodo dragon a reptile ______ ____________________
5. What does a leech eat ______ ____________________
6. Amazon ants are fighting ants ______ ____________________
7. How long can a headless cockroach live ______ ____________________

Name ______________________________ Practice 67

Math Practice: Number Sense

Write the missing numbers.	Write the missing numbers.	Write the missing numbers.
5,491; _____ ;5,493 8,190; _____ ; 8,192	_____ ; 9,287; 9,290 _____ ; 9,430; 9,440	4,672; _____ ; 4,676 6,565; _____ ; 6,575

Complete the pattern.	Complete the pattern.
7,623; 7,723; 7,823; _______; _______; _______; _______; _______; _______; _______	4,183; 4,193; 4,203; _______; _______; _______; _______; _______; _______; _______

Language Practice: Statements and Questions

A *statement* tells a fact or opinion. A *question* asks for information. Rewrite each statement as a question.

Just the Facts

Example: George Washington Carver discovered 300 ways to use the peanut.

How many ways did George Washington Carter discover to use the peanut?

1. Arizona has the most telescopes in the world.

____

2. In 1912, Juliette Gordon Law founded the Girl Scouts.

____

3. The typewriter was invented more than 100 years ago.

____

Name

Practice 68

Math Practice: 2 Digit Addition and Subtraction Without Regrouping

Add.	Subtract.	Add.
6,945 + 2,004	9,127 − 8,104	7,161 + 1,525

Estimate.	Estimate.
About how many M&M's® could fit into a shoe box? ten hundred thousand	About how many golf balls could fit in a shoe box? ten hundred thousand

Language Practice: Statements and Questions

A *statement* tells a fact or opinion. A *question* asks for information. Rewrite each question as a statement.

More Facts

Example: Was Elvis Presley's home known as Graceland?

Elvis Presley's home was known as Graceland.

1. Are diamonds mined in Arkansas?

____

2. Was helium discovered in 1905?

____

3. Did Maryland have the first umbrella factory in the United States?

____

Name ________________________________ **Practice 69**

Math Practice: Place Value

Circle the number that is in the ten thousands place.	Circle the number that is in the thousands place.	Circle the number that is in the ten thousands place.
83,347	10,885	29,107

Write the number in standard form.	Write the number in standard form.
Thirty-three thousand, four hundred twenty-one	Ninety-eight thousand, two hundred fifty-four
____________	____________

Language Practice: Reading a Graph

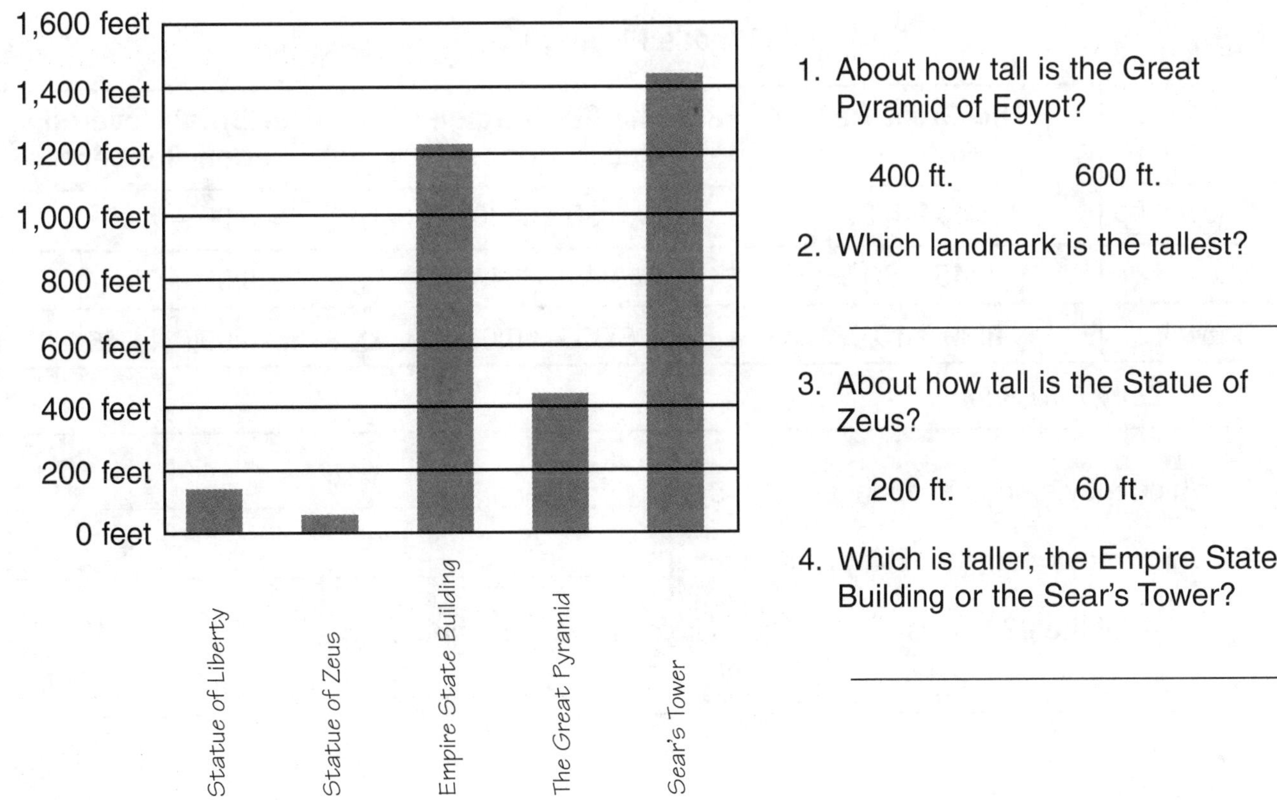

1. About how tall is the Great Pyramid of Egypt?

   400 ft.   600 ft.

2. Which landmark is the tallest?

   ____

3. About how tall is the Statue of Zeus?

   200 ft.   60 ft.

4. Which is taller, the Empire State Building or the Sear's Tower?

   ____

Name

Practice 70

Math Practice: Addition Without Regrouping

Add.

10,200
+ 23,500

Add.

26,900
+ 41,000

Add.

54,000
+ 31,990

Solve.
Alabama covered 52,237 sq. mi. Rhode Island covers 1,231 sq. mi. What is the total area covered by these 2 states?

They cover a total of ___________ sq. mi.

Solve.
Washington covers 70,637 sq. mi. Massachusetts covers 9,241 sq. mi. What is the total area covered by these 2 states?

They cover a total of ___________ sq. mi.

Language Practice: Reading and Using a Chart

What's Playing?

	The Great Train Robbery	**The Great Stage Coach Robbery**	**The Great Covered Wagon Robbery**
Show #1	* 5:00 – 6:30	5:30 – 7:30	6:00 – 7:45
Show #2	6:45 – 8:15	7:45 – 9:45	8:00 – 9:45
Show #3	8:30 – 10:00	8:30 – 10:00	10:00 – 11:45
* = *Early Bird Specal*			

1. Which movie ends at midnight (11:45)? ___________________________

2. Which movie has the "Early Bird Special"? ___________________________

3. Which of the #2 shows can you go to if you have to be home by 9:30?

____

Name

Practice 71

Math Practice: Subtraction Without Regrouping

Subtract.	Subtract.	Subtract.
98,741 – 62,530	54,894 – 53,892	86,543 – 65,440

Estimate.	Estimate.
How much would a new house cost? $5 $500 $150,000	How much would lunch at a fast food restaurant cost? $5 $500 $50,000

Language Practice: Research Report

When writing a research report, it is important to use your own words.

Example: Ayers Rock is located in the Australian desert.

Using My Own Words: *Located in the Australian desert is Ayers Rock.*

Rewrite each sentence using your own words.

Facts from Around the World

1. The Great Wall in China is 2,150 miles long.

   ____

2. The Kruger National Park is a huge nature reserve.

   ____

3. The Leaning Tower of Pisa sinks 1/20th of an inch each year.

   ____

Name ________________ Practice 72

Math Practice: Subtraction Without Regrouping

Subtract.	Subtract.	Subtract.
36,182 − 14,031	42,892 − 31,642	45,577 − 35,157

Write the number using numbers and words.	Write the number using numbers and words.
82,657	23,496
________ thousands, ________ hundreds, ________ tens, ________ ones	________ thousands, ________ hundreds, ________ tens, ________ ones

Language Practice: Alphabetical Order

Make a list of games and toys.

1. ________
2. ________
3. ________
4. ________
5. ________
6. ________
7. ________
8. ________
9. ________
10. ________

Rewrite the list in alphabetical order.

1. ________
2. ________
3. ________
4. ________
5. ________
6. ________
7. ________
8. ________
9. ________
10. ________

Name ______________________________ Practice 73

Math Practice: Rounding Numbers

Round each number to the nearest ten thousand.	Round each number to the nearest ten thousand.	Round each number to the nearest ten thousand.
71,568 ____________	76,526 ____________	35,336 ____________
79,398 ____________	92,892 ____________	84,424 ____________

Write each number in expanded form.	Write each number in expanded form.
Example: 54,913 → 50,000 + 4,000 + 900 + 10 + 3	
27,851 ______________________	44,704 ______________________
30,926 ______________________	86,530 ______________________

Language Practice: Research Report

When writing a research report, it is important to use your own words.

Example: There are more than 80 pyramids in Egypt.

Using My Own Words: *In Egypt, there are more than 80 pyramids.*

Rewrite each sentence using your own words.

The Great Pyramids

1. The Great Pyramid in Giza is the largest and most famous of the Egyptian pyramids.

____

____

2. This pyramid was built for King Khufu around 2550 B.C.

____

____

Name ______________________________ Practice 74

Math Practice: Place Value

In which place is the 8? 836,914 ______________	In which place is the 2? 602,880 ______________	In which place is the 0? 980,733 ______________

Write the number in standard form. One hundred ninety-two thousand, three hundred forty-six ______________	Write the number in standard form. Eight hundred thousand, six hundred one ______________

Language Practice: Reading and Using a Chart

What's the Population?

State Populations

State	Population
Alaska	619,500
Delaware	753,538
Montana	882,779
North Dakota	633,666
Rhode Island	980,819
South Dakota	733,133
Vermont	593,740
Wyoming	479,602

1. Which state has the largest population?

____

2. Which state has the smallest population?

____

3. Which state's population is larger than Vermont's and smaller than North Dakota's?

____

4. Round each state's population to the nearest hundred thousand.

Vermont: ____________ Alaska: ____________

Delaware: ____________ Wyoming: ____________

Name ______________________ Practice 75

Math Practice: Rounding Numbers

Round to the nearest hundred thousand.	Round to the nearest hundred thousand.	Round to the nearest hundred thousand.
198,431 ____________	486,775 ____________	482,165 ____________
312,549 ____________	769,235 ____________	673,289 ____________

Write < or >.	Write < or >.
633,752 ◯ 564,239	871,887 ◯ 519,427
419,918 ◯ 566,243	256,496 ◯ 423,771

Language Practice: Alphabetical Order

Write each set of words in alphabetical order.

land	1. ____________	done	1. ____________
life	2. ____________	didn't	2. ____________
lead	3. ____________	desk	3. ____________
against	1. ____________	earth	1. ____________
animals	2. ____________	egg	2. ____________
almost	3. ____________	English	3. ____________
half	1. ____________	white	1. ____________
himself	2. ____________	without	2. ____________
head	3. ____________	went	3. ____________

Name

Math Practice: Addition Without Regrouping

Add.	Add.	Add.
564,423 +125,276	886,157 +113,342	314,756 +655,140

Write the number in expanded form.	Write the number in expanded form.
842,552 __________ __________ __________	472,975 __________ __________ __________

Language Practice: Comprehension

Louis Doberman

Over 120 years ago in Germany, there lived a tax collector named Louis Doberman. People were not very happy to see Louis Doberman when he knocked on their doors to collect money. To protect himself, Louis Doberman bred a special kind of dog. This dog was bred from German shepherds, rottweilers, terriers, and German pinschers. This dog was very strong, brave, and obedient. This dog was named after Louis Doberman. It is called a Doberman pinscher.

1. What is the main idea of this paragraph?

____

____

2. From what dogs was the Doberman pinscher bred? ______________________________

____

3. Why do you think people were not very happy to see Louis Doberman? ______________

____

Name ______________________ Practice 77

Math Practice: Subtraction Without Regrouping

Subtract.	Subtract.	Subtract.
734,973 – 631,961	294,388 – 160,186	582,791 – 362,740

Solve.	Solve.
In the United States, 843,000 people speak Tagalog and 242,000 people speak Russian. How many more people speak Tagalog than Russian? __________ more people speak Talalog.	In the United States 188,000 people speak French Creole and [illegible] speak Greek. How many more people speak Greek than French Creole? __________ more people speak Greek.

Language Practice: Reading and Solving Logic Problems

Favorite Kind of Dog

Read each clue. If the answer is "yes" make an "O" in the box, if the answer is "no" make an "X" in the box.

	Bulldog	Chihuahua	Poodle	Sheepdog
Diego				
Suraya				
Vincenzo				
Graciela				

Clues

1. Diego and Vincenzo do not like poodles.
2. Suraya names her Chihuahua "Tinkerbelle."
3. Diego has a Sheepdog.

Write the type of dog next to its owner's name.

Diego ______________________

Vincenzo ______________________

Suraya ______________________

Graciela ______________________

Name ____________________ Practice 78

Math Practice: Time

How many minutes in one hour? _______ minutes	How many minutes in half an hour? _______ minutes	How many minutes in a quarter of an hour? _______ minutes

How many minutes in 2 hours? _______ minutes	How many minutes in $1\frac{1}{2}$ hours? _______ minutes

Language Practice: Articles

Articles are used with nouns. Articles tell how the noun is being used. There are three articles. They are: **a**, **an**, and **the**.

- Use *a* before nouns that begin with a consonant.
- Use *an* before nouns that begin with a vowel (a, e, i, o, u).

Write the article for each sentence.

1. (an, the) Reba sat under ___________ apple tree.
2. (a, an) Her dog is ___________ Akita.
3. (a, an) She had ___________ picnic basket with her.
4. (an, the) In ___________ basket were sandwiches.
5. (an, the) Reba and her dog ate ___________ sandwiches.
6. (a, the) Reba drank ___________ juice.
7. (a, an) Before leaving, Reba picked ___________ apple.

Name ______________________________ Practice 79

Math Practice: Time

Use the <, >, or = sign.

1 hour ◯ 32 min.

90 min. ◯ 1 hour

Use the <, >, or = sign.

2 hours ◯ 120 min.

58 min. ◯ $\frac{1}{2}$ hour

Use the <, >, or = sign.

$\frac{1}{4}$ hour ◯ 40 min.

$1\frac{1}{2}$ hours ◯ 35 min.

Solve.
Jeff went to the barbershop at 2:25. It took 22 minutes to have his hair cut. What time did Jeff leave the barbershop?

Jeff left the barbershop at __________.

Solve.
Celeste went to the beauty salon. It took 37 minutes to get a perm and 15 minutes to dry her hair. How long was Celeste at the beauty shop?

Celeste was there for __________ minutes.

Language Practice: Capitalization

Nouns that name a specific person, place or thing are called *proper nouns*. Proper nouns always begin with a capital letter. Read each sentence and underline the proper noun. Write the sentence correctly on the line.

1. farmer macgregor raises cows. ______________________________
2. His farm is in lancaster, california. ______________________________
3. Every day he milks matilda, his favorite cow. ______________________________
4. He sells the milk to the milltown chocolate factory. ______________________________

Name ________________________________ Practice 80

Math Practice: Time

Write the time in standard form.	Write the time in standard form.	Write the time in standard form.
97 minutes	61 minutes	89 minutes
_____ hour(s)_____ minutes	_____ hour(s)_____ minutes	_____ hour(s)_____ minutes

Solve. Red spent 45 minutes waxing the car, 20 minutes vacuuming the car, and 15 minutes washing the car. How much time did Red spend on cleaning the car?	Solve. Sapphire spent 30 minutes raking leaves, 25 minutes panting flowers, and 35 minutes pruning the shrubs. How much time did Sapphire spend doing the yard work?
Red spent ___________ cleaning the car.	Sapphire spent ___________ on the yard.

Language Practice: Capitalization

Nouns that name a specific person, place, or thing are called *proper nouns*. Proper nouns always begin with a capital letter. Read each set of words and circle the word that needs to be capitalized. Write the word correctly on the line provided.

1. city	town	mapleville	____________
2. state	alaska	province	____________
3. canada	country	region	____________
4. pet	barney	animal	____________
5. fast food	sam's	restaurant	____________
6. students	friend	sally	____________
7. eiffel tower	view	monument	____________
8. park	forest	yosemite	____________
9. officer	nurse	ms. hengst	____________
10. osos park	playground	tent	____________

Name ______________________________ **Practice 81**

Math Practice: Money

Write the name and the value of the coin.	Write the name and the value of the coin.	Write the name and the value of the coin.
 ________ ________¢	 ________ ________¢	 ________ ________¢

Write the name and the value of each coin.	Write the name and the value of the coin.
 ____________________ ________¢	 ____________________ ________¢

Language Practice: Collective Nouns

Some groups of nouns (people, places, or things) have special names.

Example: A *band* of musicians

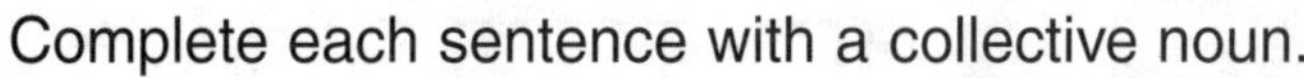

Complete each sentence with a collective noun.

batch	**chest**	**line**	**posse**	**set**	**stack**	**swarm**	**union**

1. Look at the ______________________ of people!
2. My grandma is a member of a ______________________.
3. I put my clean clothes in the ______________________ of drawers.
4. Look out! Here comes a ______________________ of bees!
5. Aunt Celeste bought a new ______________________ of dishes.
6. The ______________________ of deputies will be in the parade.
7. Who made the fresh ______________________ of cookies?
8. I can't believe I ate that huge ______________________ of pancakes!

Name

Practice 82

Math Practice: Money

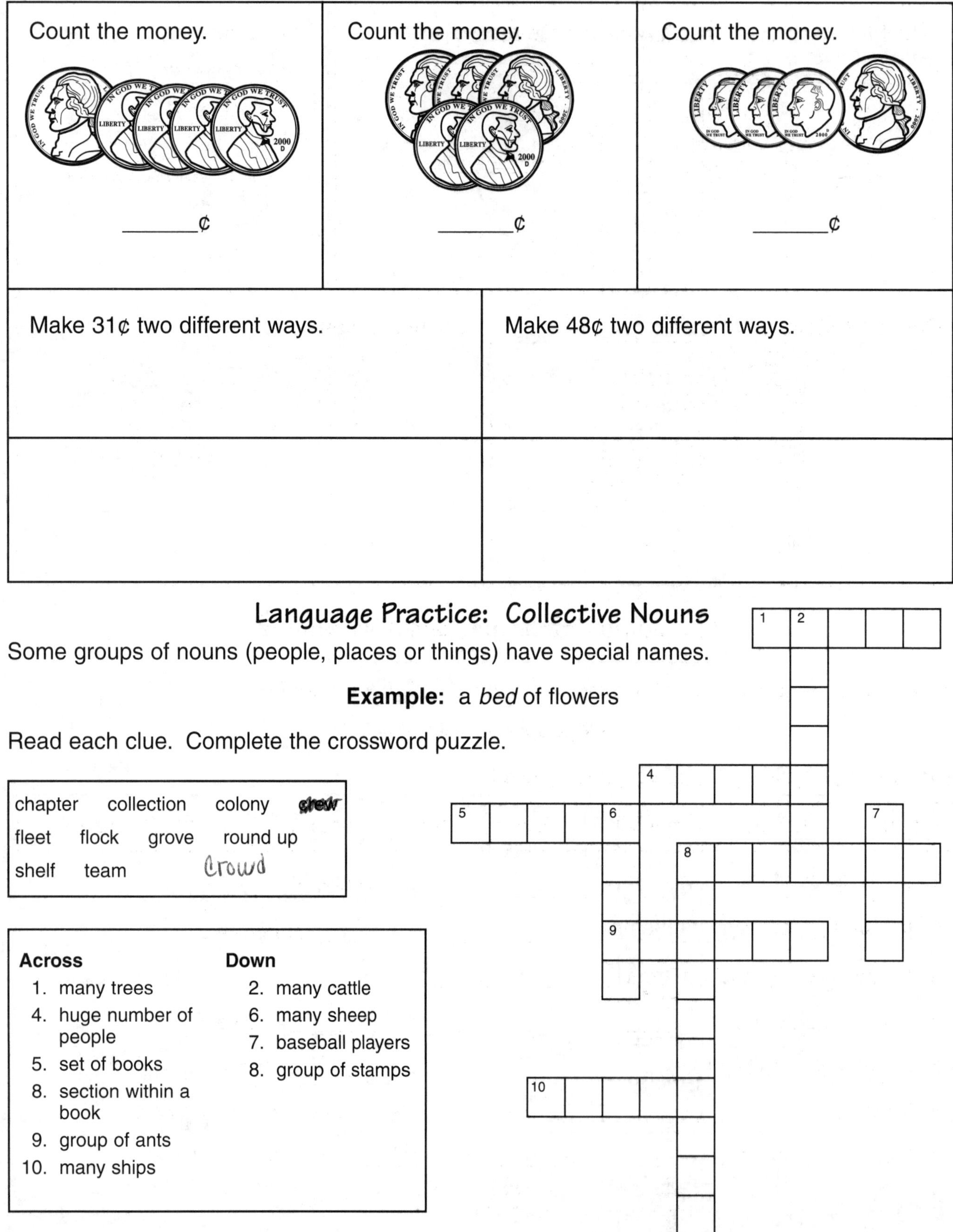

Count the money.	Count the money.	Count the money.
______¢	______¢	______¢

Make 31¢ two different ways.	Make 48¢ two different ways.

Language Practice: *Collective Nouns*

Some groups of nouns (people, places or things) have special names.

Example: a *bed* of flowers

Read each clue. Complete the crossword puzzle.

chapter	collection	colony	crew
fleet	flock	grove	round up
shelf	team	crowd	

Across

1. many trees
4. huge number of people
5. set of books
8. section within a book
9. group of ants
10. many ships

Down

2. many cattle
6. many sheep
7. baseball players
8. group of stamps

Name ______________________________ Practice 83

Math Practice: Money

Count the money.
$ ____________
Count the money.
$ ____________
Count the money.
$ ____________
Count the money.
$ ____________
Count the money.
$ ____________

Language Practice: Collective Nouns

Some groups of nouns (people, places or things) have special names.

Example: A *bed* of flowers

Complete each sentence with a collective noun.

block	clumps	deck	gang	herd	party	pile	troop

1. I put the ______________________________ of cards back in the box.
2. Evelyn lives on that ______________________________ of houses.
3. Dennis belongs to Girl Scout ______________________________ 225.
4. The waiter seated the ______________________________ of diners.
5. Mom is buried under a ______________________________ of papers.
6. There is a ______________________________ of criminals robbing banks.
7. Have you ever seen a ______________________________ of buffaloes?
8. Quit pulling out ______________________________ of grass!

Name

Practice 84

Math Practice: Money

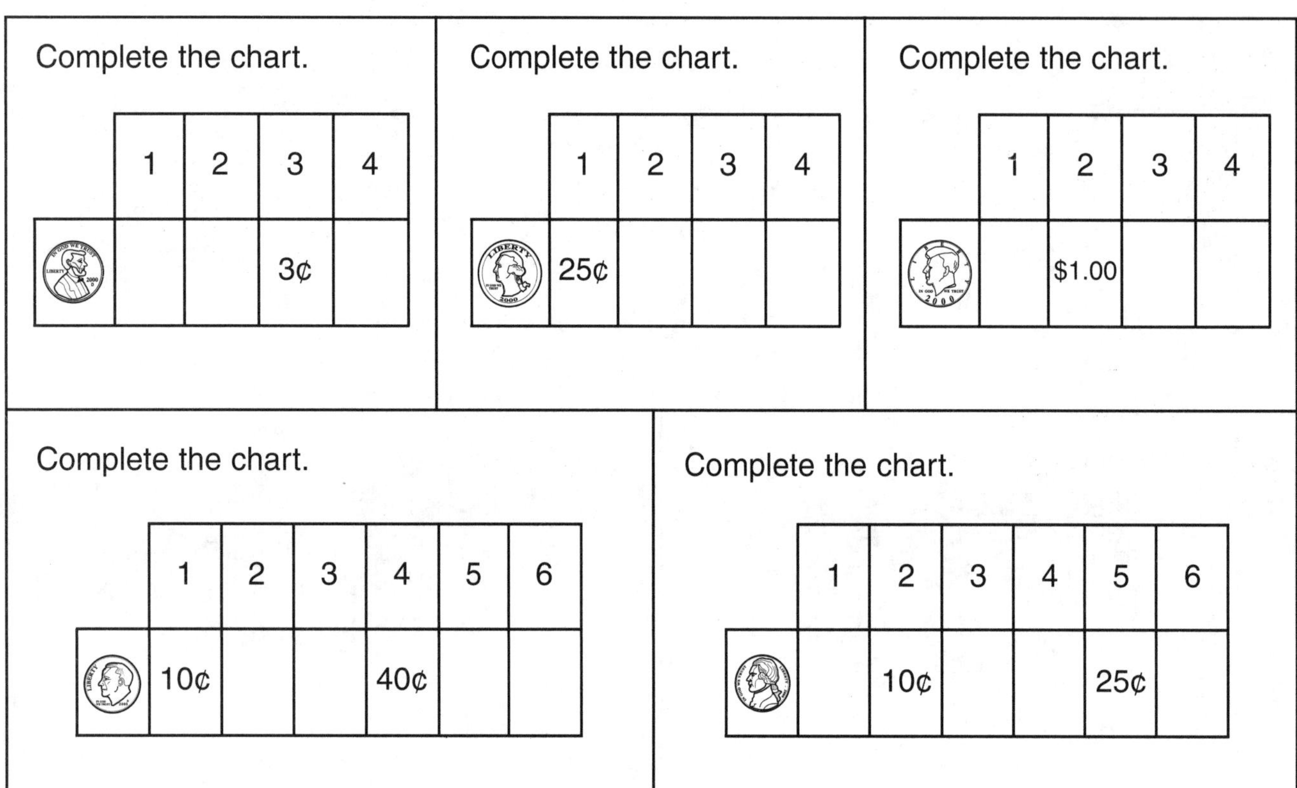

Complete the chart.

	1	2	3	4
			3¢	

Complete the chart.

	1	2	3	4
	25¢			

Complete the chart.

	1	2	3	4
		$1.00		

Complete the chart.

	1	2	3	4	5	6
	10¢			40¢		

Complete the chart.

	1	2	3	4	5	6
		10¢			25¢	

Language Practice: Reading and Using a Chart

Write the cost for each vending-machine item.

Item	Cost
can of soda	
candy	
gum	
soup	
chips	

1. soda: ______________
2. candy: ______________
3. gum: ______________
4. soup: ______________
5. chips: ______________
6. Which items could be purchased with these coins?

   ____

   ____

7. Do you have enough money to buy the soda? ______
8. If you had $1.00, what would you buy? __________

   ____

   ____

Name

Math Practice: Money

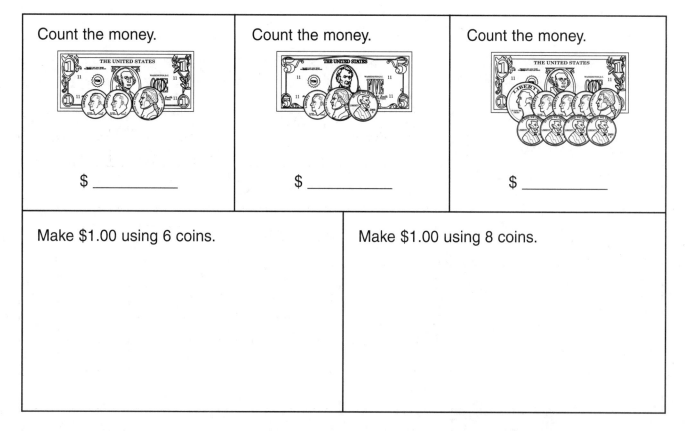

Count the money.	Count the money.	Count the money.
 $ __________	 $ __________	 $ __________

Make $1.00 using 6 coins.	Make $1.00 using 8 coins.

Language Practice: Reading to Solve Math Problems

Use the chart to answer each question below.

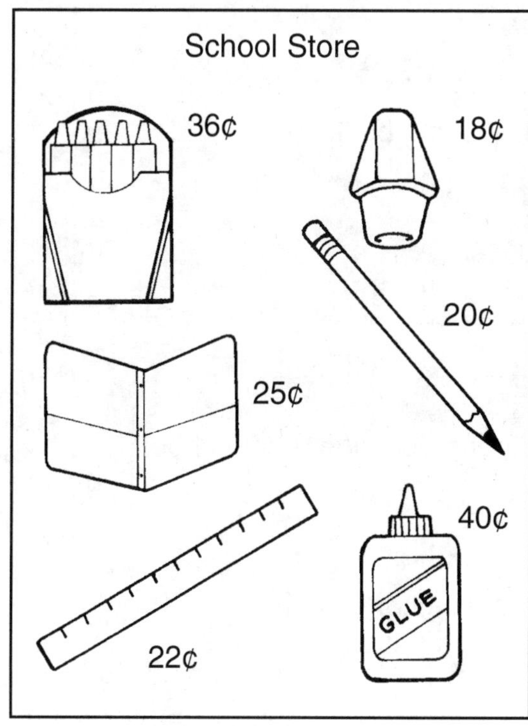

1. Jane has 85¢. She buys a pencil. Jane will have ________ left over.
2. Ryan has 75¢. He buys a ruler. Ryan will have ________ left over.
3. Danielle has 59¢. She buys an eraser. Danielle will have ________ left over.
4. Gregory has 35¢. He buys a folder. Gregory will have ________ left over.
5. Lorenzo has 97¢. He buys glue and a pencil. Lorenzo will have ________ left over.

Name

Math Practice: Money

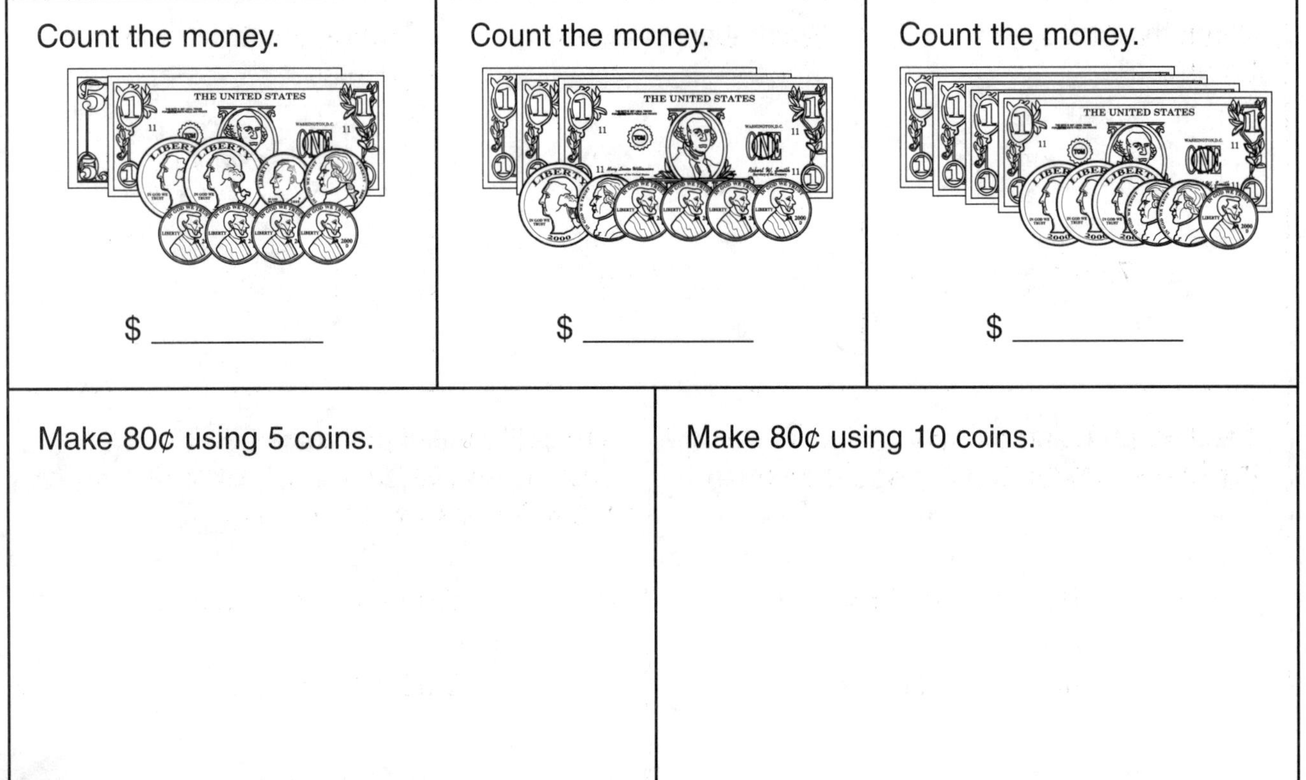

Count the money. $ ______	Count the money. $ ______	Count the money. $ ______

Make 80¢ using 5 coins.	Make 80¢ using 10 coins.

Language Practice: Conjunctions

Correlative conjunctions are used in pairs. If one of the words is used, its partner word must also be used.

Correlative conjunctions are *either-or*, *neither-nor*, *not only-but also*.

Example: *Neither* Duffy *nor* Muffy likes playing basketball.

Underline the correlative conjunctions used in each sentence.

1. Not only Sly but also Carl went to the movies.
2. You can have either cake or pie.
3. Lily can neither sing nor dance.
4. Soledad not only won a blue ribbon at the county fair but also won a blue ribbon at the city fair.
5. I have seen neither hide nor hair of Stephanie.
6. Either Jeffrey or Godfrey needs to take the folder to the office.
7. Neither Dana nor Lana went to the school carnival.

Name ______________________________

Math Practice: Time

When would you eat breakfast?	When would you eat dinner?	When would you go to the matinee?
7:00 A.M.	5:00 A.M.	3:00 A.M.
7:00 P.M.	5:00 P.M.	3:00 P.M.

The bakery is open 7 days a week. Circle the hours that the bakery would be open.	The roller rink has an all night skating session on Saturdays. Circle the hours the roller rink would be open.
7:00 A.M. – 7:00 P.M.	6:00 A.M. – 6:00 P.M.
7:00 P.M. – 7:00 A.M.	6:00 P.M. – 6:00 A.M.

Language Practice: Using a Calendar

Look at the calendar below and answer the following questions.

January

Sun.	Mon.	Tues.	Wed.	Thur.	Fri.	Sat.
	1	2	3 baseball	4 hockey	5 soccer	6 baseball
7 soccer	8 baseball	9 hockey	10 baseball	11 hockey	12 soccer	13 baseball
14 soccer	15 baseball	16 hockey	17 baseball	18 hockey	19 soccer	20 baseball
21 soccer	22 baseball	23 hockey	24 baseball	25 hockey	26 soccer	27 baseball
28 soccer	29 baseball	30 hockey	31 baseball			

1. What is the name of this month? ____________________
2. How many days are in this month? ____________________
3. How many days are in one week? ____________________
4. How many full weeks are in this month? ____________________
5. On what day of the week does this month begin? ____________________
6. On what day of the week does this month end? ____________________

Name ______________________ Practice 88

Math Practice: Place Value

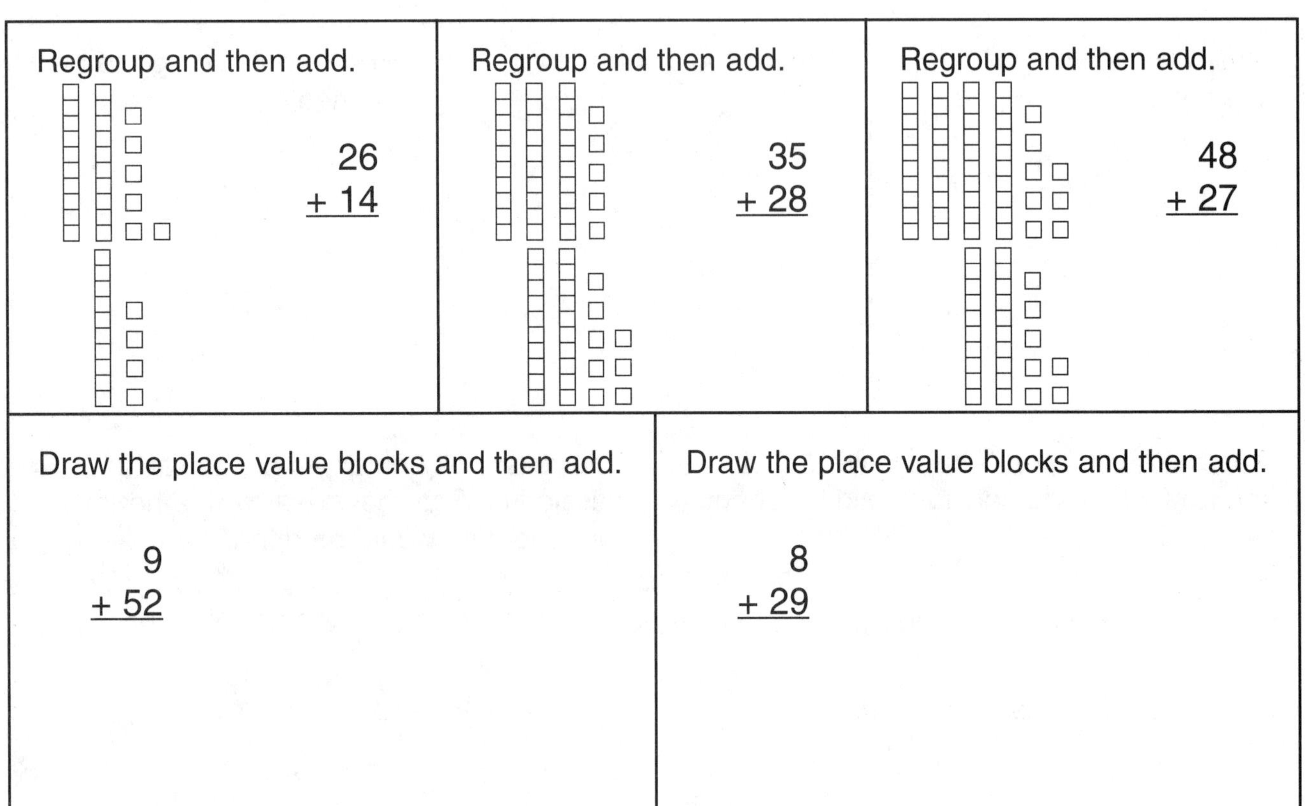

Regroup and then add.
26
+ 14
Regroup and then add.
35
+ 28
Regroup and then add.
48
+ 27
Draw the place value blocks and then add.
9
+ 52
Draw the place value blocks and then add.
8
+ 29

Language Practice: Comprehension

King Tutankahmun

King Tutankahmun is one of the most famous pharaohs. He was born in 1343 B.C. and became king at the age of 9. At the age of 18 he was killed.

Howard Carter was a British archaeologist. Lord Carnarvon was a very rich man who owned the rights to dig in the Valley of the Kings in Egypt. He hired Howard Carter to dig for King Tut's tomb.

It took 5 years of digging, but finally in 1922, Howard Carter unearthed King Tut's mummy and tomb. His tomb was in almost perfect condition as were the fabulous treasures he had been buried with.

1. What year did Howard Carter begin digging for King Tutankhamun's tomb?____________
2. How many years was Tutankhamun king?____________
3. Why do you think they found King Tut's tomb intact?____________

____

Name

Math Practice: Addition with Regrouping

Add.		Add.		Add.	
44 + 27	72 + 19	2 + 89	36 + 56	12 + 48	15 + 75

Rewrite the problem vertically and then solve.	Rewrite the problem vertically and then solve.
36 + 46	52 + 39

Language Practice: Hieroglyphics

	Ă Ĕ		H		P
	Ā		I Y		Q K
	B		J		R
	C K		L		S Z
	D		M		SH
	Ē Y		N		T
	F		UA		U W
	G		O		WR

Hieroglyphics is a pictorial writing system that uses pictures to represent words, objects, or certain sounds. Write your name using hieroglyphics. (If a hieroglyphic letter you need for your name is not there, just write the next letter in your name.)

My name written in English is:

____

My name written in Hieroglyphics is:

Name ______________________ Practice 90

Math Practice: Addition with Regrouping

Add.	Add.	Add.
27¢ + 27¢	36¢ + 9¢	75 + 8

Solve.	Solve.
Marigold has 19¢ . Her sister gives her 26¢ . How much money does Marigold have? Marigold has __________.	Marvin has 37¢. His brother gives him 37¢. How much money does Marvin have? Marvin has __________.

Language Practice: Comparatives

When comparing 2 items, add "*er*" to the end of the descriptive adjective or adverb. If the descriptive word ends in "*y*", drop the "*y*" and add *"ier."*

Example: Justine is *tall.* ("*Tall*" refers to one person.)

Justine is *taller* than Muffy. ("*Taller*" is comparing the size of one person to another.)

Read each sentence and write the correct form of the descriptive word on the line.

1. The Empire State Building is _____________ than my house. (tall)
2. A tiger can run _____________ than a turtle. (fast)
3. It is _____________ today. (cold)
4. A ladybug is _____________ than a butterfly. (tiny)
5. The doorbell rings _____________ than the telephone. (loud)
6. Ernie's room is always _____________ than Norman's room. (messy)
7. The campfire is _____________ than the flashlight. (warm)

Name

Practice 91

Math Practice: Addition with Regrouping

Add.	Add.	Add.
88 + 5 37 + 36	58 + 16 42 + 49	17 + 44 59 + 29

Solve.	Solve.
Brenda delivered 48 papers in the morning and 25 papers in the afternoon. How many papers did Brenda deliver in all?	Neil delivered 34 pieces of mail in the morning and 39 pieces of mail in the afternoon. How many pieces of mail did Neil deliver in all?
Brenda delivered _______ papers in all.	Neil delivered ______ pieces of mail in all.

Language Practice: Comparatives

When comparing more than two items, add "*est*" to the end of the descriptive adjective or adverb. If the descriptive word ends in "*y*", drop the "*y*" and add "*iest*."

Example: Biff is the *friendliest* dog at the pound.

("*Friendliest*" compares more than two dogs.)

Complete each sentence with the correct form of the descriptive word.

1. Oranges are the ________________________ fruit in the produce section. (juicy)
2. Mr. Sims has the ________________________ windows on the block. (clean)
3. Jethro can run very ________________________ . (fast)
4. Saturday was a ________________________ day. (windy)
5. The Arctic has the ________________________ temperature on Earth! (cold)
6. Dominic has the ________________________ pencil in the class. (sharp)
7. Jennifer colored the ________________________ picture in art class. (nice)

Name ______________________ Practice 92

Math Practice: Addition with Regrouping

Use <, >, or = sign.	Use <, >, or = sign.	Use <, >, or = sign.
27 + 15 ◯ 17 + 25	19 + 35 ◯ 9 + 42	15 + 15 ◯ 28 + 2

Circle the estimate.	Circle the estimate.
Angelica invited 45 boys and 19 girls to a party. How many children did Angelica invite?	Maxi made 26 chocolate cupcakes and 37 vanilla cupcakes. How many cupcakes did Maxi make?
< 30 > 30	< 50 > 50

Language Practice: Comparatives

- When comparing two items, add "*er*" to the end of the descriptive word.
  Example: Godzilla is *bigger* than the Swamp Monster.
- When comparing more than two items, add "*est*" to the end of the word.
  Example: King Kong is the *biggest* one of all.
- For words that end in "*y*", drop the "y" and add "*ier*" or "*iest*".

Complete each sentence with the correct form of the descriptive word.

(*clean*) The rug is ______________________.

The carpet is ______________________ than the rug.

The floor is the ______________________ of all.

(*soft*) Puffy's fur is ______________________.

Buffy's fur is ______________________ than Puffy's.

Fluffy's fur is the ______________________ of all.

(*short*) Shanna is ______________________.

Hannah is ______________________ than Shanna.

Vanna is the ______________________ of them all.

Name ______________________________ Practice 93

Math Practice: Addition with Regrouping

Add. 37 36 + 5	Add. 8 28 + 61	Add. 42 9 + 41

Solve. Rogelio saw 13 flies, 57 wasps, and 7 mosquitoes. How many insects did Rogelio see in all? Rogelio saw ______ insects in all.	Solve. Marisa saw 4 orchid bees, 57 leafcutter bees, and 7 bumble bees. How many bees did Marisa see in all? Marisa saw ______ bees in all.

Language Practice: Irregular Comparatives

Irregular comparatives use different words instead of adding "*er*" or "*est*" to the end of the descriptive word.

Example: Mom's pancakes are *good*.

Dad's pancakes are *better*. (Comparing two people's pancakes.)

Grandpa's pancakes are the *best* of all! (Comparing more than two.)

Read the comparative sentence and underline the comparative word.

1. Danny was good at school today.
2. Lance was better than Danny.
3. Guy was the best of all.
4. The sun was brighter today than yesterday.
5. The candy bar costs less than the gum.
6. The chips cost the least of them all.

Name ______________________________ Practice 94

Math Practice: Addition with Regrouping

Add.	Add.	Add.
206 + 185	668 + 127	86 + 106

Solve.	Solve.
Use < or > sign. 400 ◯ 176 + 104	Use < or > sign. 501 + 159 ◯ 600

Language Practice: Irregular Comparatives

For descriptive adjectives or adverbs with two or more syllables, use the words more or most.

Examples: John has *more* marbles than Ted.

Carrie has the *most* marbles.

Complete each sentence with the word *more* or *most.*

1. Heather has ________________ money than Sammy.
2. Is the Rose Bowl the ________________ important football game.
3. Abigail has ________________ coins in her collection than Ali.
4. For Knox is the ________________ secure place to store gold.
5. He ate ________________ of the pizza.
6. Which of the three sweaters cost the ________________?
7. Which animal drinks ________________ water than a camel?
8. Tina has ________________ baseball cards than football cards.

Name ____________________ Practice 95

Math Practice: Addition with Regrouping

Add.	Add.	Add.
3,529 + 1,416	3,915 + 1,045	2,842 + 3,048

Write the numbers in standard form.	Write each number in expanded form.
8,000 + 400 + 60 + 7 ________	7,425 ________
4,000 + 900 + 30 + 2 ________	6,554 ________

Language Practice: Alphabetical Order

Trixie Bell
Ben Stevens
Faye Sweet
Robert Rider
Harry Jacobs
Lyle Mendez
Rafaela Moreno
Buster Robinson
Blair Bates
Cameron Smith

Write each name (first and last) in alphabetical order by first name.

1. ________ 6. ________
2. ________ 7. ________
3. ________ 8. ________
4. ________ 9. ________
5. ________ 10. ________

Write each name (first and last) in alphabetical order by last name.

1. ________ 6. ________
2. ________ 7. ________
3. ________ 8. ________
4. ________ 9. ________
5. ________ 10. ________

Name ______________________________ Practice 96

Math Practice: Addition with Regrouping

Add.	Add.	Add.
2,738 1,045 + 2,112	5,103 2,164 + 1,629	3,219 2,347 + 4,231

Write each number.	Write each number.
One thousand twelve: ________________	Nine hundred fifty-four: _______________
Eight thousand six hundred: ___________	Seven thousand, four hundred eighty-nine: ____________________

Language Practice: the Verb "Lie"

The verb "*lie*" is a *still verb*. This means to *rest or recline in a flat or horizontal position.*

Example: The dog will lie down and take a nap.

The word lie *refers to a resting position.*

The different tenses of lie are: *lay*, *(have, has) lain, lying*

Read each sentence and underline the verb. Write *past* or *present* on the line.

1. The baby lies on the quilt. _______________________
2. Dad is lying on the couch. _______________________
3. Greg has lain in bed all week. _______________________
4. The cat is lying in the tree, fast asleep. _______________________
5. Yesterday, Simone lay on the sand. _______________________

Name ______________________________ Practice 97

Math Practice: Addition with Regrouping

Add.	Add.	Add.
46,552 + 10,319	33,977 + 22,013	29,142 + 60,348

Solve.	Solve.
Hope gathered 56,329 pounds of walnuts and 10,428 pounds of pecans. How many pounds of nuts did Hope gather in all?	Godfrey picked 34,159 pounds of corn and 11,724 pounds of peas. How many pounds of vegetables did Godfrey gather in all?
Hope gathered ________ pounds of nuts.	Godfrey gathered ________ pounds.

Language Practice: the Verb "Lay"

The verb "*lay*" means to place or put something somewhere.

Example: I *laid* the book on the nightstand.
Laid tells what happened to the book.

The different tenses of lay are: *lay*, *laid,* and *laying.*
Complete each sentence with the correct form of the verb.

1. The hen ________________ one egg each morning.
2. I was ________________ the book down when the phone rang.
3. The goose ________________ a golden egg yesterday.
4. Carole ________________ the newspaper on the counter.
5. Who has been ________________ all of the garbage on the ground?
6. The dog ________________ its head in my lap.
7. Grandma ________________ her glasses on the table.

Name ______ Practice 98

Math Practice: Addition with Regrouping

Add.	Add.	Add.
819,734 + 150,217	853,628 + 116,263	317,346 + 572,349

Solve.	Solve.
Mom earned 573,319 frequent flier miles. Dad earned 421,569 frequent flier miles. How many frequent flier miles did they earn in all? They earned _______ frequent flier miles.	Grandma has traveled 765,863 miles. Grandpa has traveled 134,018 miles. How many miles have they traveled in all? They have traveled __________ miles.

Language Practice: The Noun and Verb Forms of "Lie"

The word *lie* means to not tell the truth. Depending on how it is used, this word can be a noun or a verb!

Examples: I would never tell a lie! (*Lie* is a noun.)

He is lying! (*Lie* is a verb.)

Underline the word *lie*. Write whether the word is being used as a noun or a verb in each sentence.

______________________ 1. Do not tell a lie!

______________________ 2. Chris is always lying to the teacher!

______________________ 3. Alberta does not lie to her parents.

______________________ 4. Martin got caught in a lie.

______________________ 5. Who thinks lying is okay?

______________________ 6. Have you ever told a lie?

Name ______________________________ Practice 99

Math Practice: Place Value

Regroup a ten into ones. Write the answer.	Regroup a ten into ones. Write the answer.	Regroup a ten into ones. Write the answer.
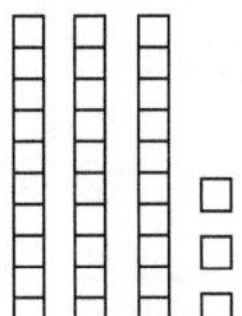	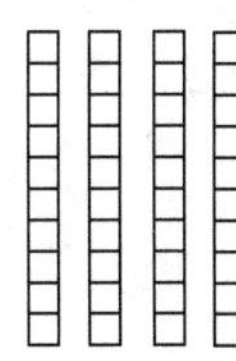	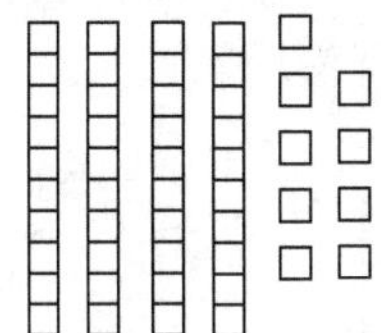
_____ tens = _____ ones	______ tens ______ ones	______ tens ______ ones

Draw the tens and ones. Solve the problem.	Draw the tens and ones. Solve the problem.
41 – 23	54 – 18

Language Practice: Synonyms

Synonyms are two or more words that have similar meanings.

Example: *boy*, *lad*, and *youth*

Circle the two synonyms in each set of words.

1. children	girls	youngsters
2. angry	astonish	amaze
3. never	frequent	often
4. happy	joyful	hurt
5. little	giant	petite
6. thaw	chilled	cold
7. thin	chubby	slender
8. marvelous	okay	extraordinary
9. stop	leave	depart
10. like	dislike	enjoy

Name

Math Practice: Place Value

Regroup and then subtract.	Regroup and then subtract.	Regroup and then subtract.
51 – 9	60 – 22	35 – 17

Draw the place value blocks and then subtract.	Draw the place value blocks and then subtract.
43 – 34	72 – 59

Language Practice: Synonyms

Synonyms are two or more words that have similar meanings.

Example: *big*, *huge,* and *large*

Draw a line matching the synonyms in column A, B, and C.

Column A	Column B	Column C
able	capable	ask
alarm	error	blunder
danger	frighten	competent
divide	globe	earth
hurt	injure	hazard
interrogate	peril	split
mistake	question	terrify
world	separate	wound

Name ______ Practice 101

Math Practice: Number Sense

Write the number that is 100 more and 100 less.	Write the number that is 100 more and 100 less.	Write the number that is 100 more and 100 less.
______ 2,193 ______	______ 4,805 ______	______ 7,628 ______

Solve.	Solve.
Mount Vesuvius erupted in 1979. Kelut erupted in 1586. How many years separate these two eruptions?	Mt. Pinatubo erupted in 1991. Mount Unzen erupted in 1792. How many years separate these two eruptions?
They are ______ years apart.	They are ______ years apart.

Language Practice: Synonyms

Write a sentence for each of these synonym pairs.

1. freedom ______

   liberty ______

2. rough ______

   coarse ______

3. loud ______

   noisy ______

Name

Practice 102

Math Practice: Subtraction with Regrouping

Subtract.	Subtract.	Subtract.
94 − 58 92 − 76	37 − 8 25 − 19	43 − 26 71 − 34

Solve.	Solve.
Lola had 82¢ . She spent 45¢ at the bookstore. How much money does Lola have left?	Mayer had 63¢. He spent 44¢ at the comic book store. How much money does Mayer have left?
Lola has ______ left.	Mayer has ______ left.

Language Practice: Synonyms

Synonyms are two or more words that have similar meanings.

Example: *end*, *finish*, and *complete*

Read each sentence. Write a synonym on the line for the word in italics.

Example: We will have to *depart* soon. go

1. Weddings are a *happy* occasion. ______
2. Abby made a *hasty* departure from the party. ______
3. Herman will *close* the door quietly. ______
4. Veva bought a new *vehicle*. ______
5. Gabriel is a very *helpful* person. ______
6. Mary and her dad go to the library *frequently*. ______
7. Jamie and Heather are quite a *duo*! ______
8. Don't be so *reckless*! ______

Name ______________________________ Practice 103

Math Practice: Subtraction with Regrouping

Subtract.	Subtract.	Subtract.
465 − 48 383 − 34	290 − 81 985 − 76	897 − 88 856 − 47

Complete the pattern.	Complete the pattern.
464, 474, 484, ______, ______, ______, ______, ______, ______, ______, ______	901, 891, 881, ______, ______, ______, ______, ______, ______, ______, ______

Language Practice: Synonyms

Synonyms are two or more words that have similar meanings.

Example: *anger*, *rage*, and *fury*

Read each clue, look at the list on the right, and complete the crossword puzzle.

Across	Down
2. difficult	1. large
5. rear	3. old
7. all	6. sudden
8. help	9. yell
9. end	10. chubby
11. work	

abrupt	enormous	plump
ancient	every	shout
assist	hard	stop
back	job	

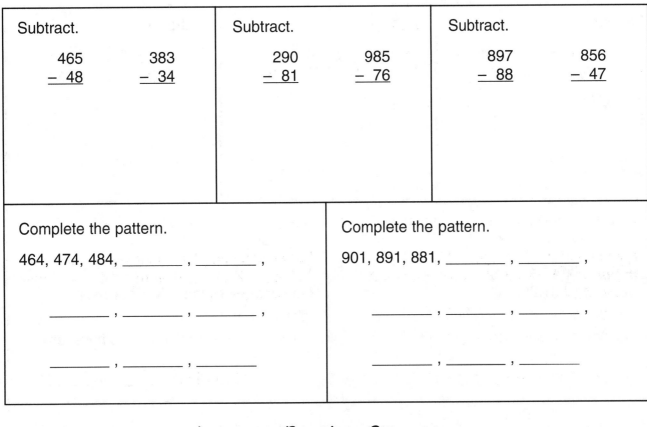

Name

Practice 104

Math Practice: Subtraction with Regrouping

Subtract. $8.14 − 1.83	Subtract. $7.31 − 4.28	Subtract. $3.67 − .00

Cross out the unnecessary piece of information.

Jenny spent 69¢.
Jenny had $1.25.
Jenny likes pennies the best.
How much money does Jenny have left?

______

Cross out the unnecessary piece of information.

Wells had 75¢.
He does not collect silver dollars.
Wells spent 37¢.
How much money does Wells have left?

______

Language Practice: Antonyms

Antonyms are two words that have opposite meanings.

Example: *soft* and *hard*

Draw a line matching each pair of antonyms.

achieve	awake	answer	bad
asleep	back	beautiful	break
come	bent	chilly	copy
down	fail	clean	dirty
fat	freeze	fix	hero
front	go	good	noisy
melt	thin	original	question
play	up	quiet	ugly
straight	work	villain	warm

Name

Math Practice: Subtraction with Regrouping

Subtract.	Subtract.	Subtract.
2,682 – 1,376	6,875 – 5,228	4,531 – 3,104

Solve.	Solve.
Albert had $5,680. He spent $2,226 buying a tree house. How much money does Albert have left?	Ronniese had 9,131 pennies in her piggy bank. She rolled 9,050 of the pennies. How many pennies does Ronniese have left?
Albert has __________ left.	Ronniese has __________ pennies left.

Language Practice: Antonyms

Antonyms are two words that have opposite meanings.

Example: *hot* and *cold*

Draw a line matching each pair of synonyms. Find and color the antonyms in the word search.

hard	tiny
heavy	yes
huge	easy
inside	forget
no	married
poor	light
remember	rich
single	odd
even	she
he	outside

H	A	B	C	M	D	L	I	G	H	T	E	P	I
A	F	O	H	E	A	V	Y	F	G	H	N	O	N
R	C	O	U	D	E	R	P	O	H	I	F	O	S
D	S	B	R	T	R	Q	R	N	U	J	G	R	I
X	I	Y	S	G	S	I	M	I	G	K	Y	H	D
W	N	A	Z	H	E	I	C	L	E	V	E	N	E
V	G	S	R	Q	E	T	D	H	A	D	S	I	J
U	L	T	H	P	O	N	M	E	S	T	I	N	Y
R	E	M	E	M	B	E	R	L	Y	K	O	D	D

Name

Practice 106

Math Practice: Subtraction with Regrouping

Subtract.	Subtract.	Subtract.
7,963 – 4,344	6,584 – 5,409	5,224 – 3,107

Solve.	Solve.
Matthew Henson was born in 1866 and died in 1955. How old was Matthew Henson when he died?	Frederick Douglass was born in 1817 and died in 1895. How old was Frederick Douglass when he died?
Matthew Henson was ________ years old.	Frederick Douglass was _____ years old.

Language Practice: Antonyms

Antonyms are two words that have opposite meanings. Write the antonyms for each clue in the correct space in the crossword puzzle.

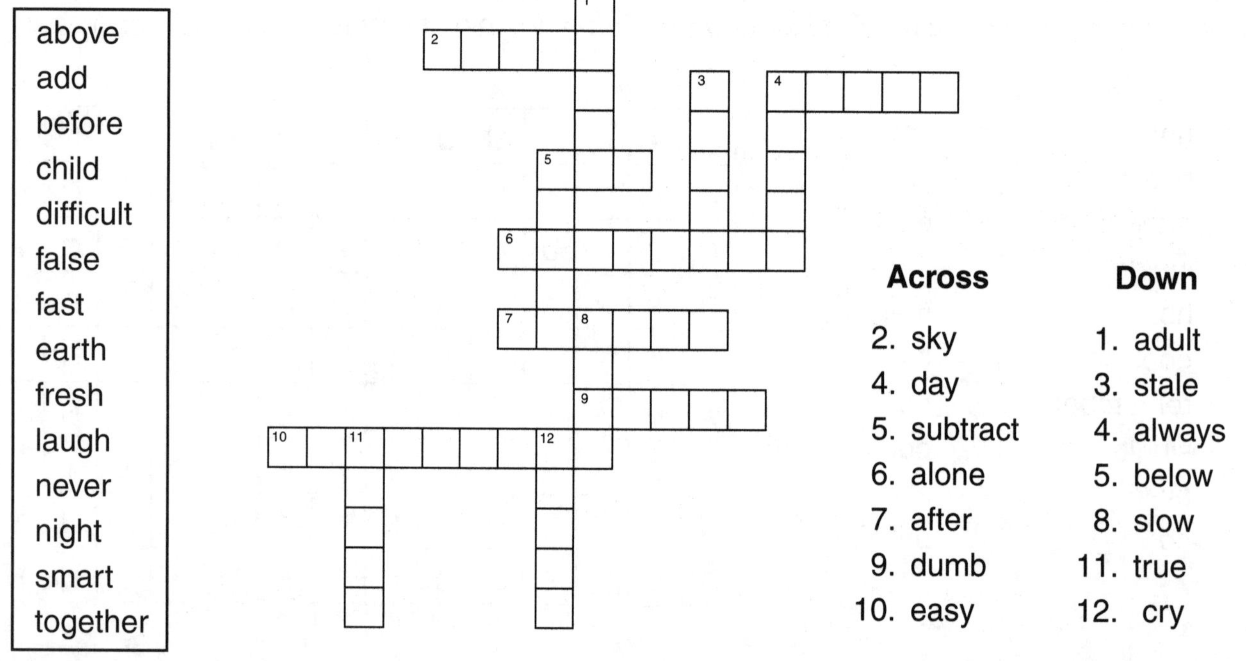

Across

2. sky
4. day
5. subtract
6. alone
7. after
9. dumb
10. easy

Down

1. adult
3. stale
4. always
5. below
8. slow
11. true
12. cry

Name ______________________________ **Practice 107**

Math Practice: Subtraction with Regrouping

Subtract.	Subtract.	Subtract.
$68.26 – 11.38	$83.45 – 70.99	$41.75 – 30.78

Solve.	Solve.
Melanie had $20.00. She spent $11.83 buying a board game. How much change was Melanie given? Melanie was given ________ in change.	Ted had $20.00. He spent $10.25 buying an out door game. How much change was Ted given? Ted was given ________ in change.

Language Practice: Idioms

Idioms are phrases that have special meanings.

Example: The new movie is *not your cup of tea.*

This doesn't mean the movie has anything to do with tea. Instead, it means it isn't something that you would like to see.

Draw a line matching the idiom used in each sentence to its meaning.

1. Justin is always *on the ball.* — not doing anything
2. Dom needs to get to class *on the double.* — acting or looking the same
3. Gordon is skating *on thin ice.* — needs to hurry
4. Quit sitting there *like a bump on a log!* — ready to go
5. Abigail and Ali are *like two peas in a pod!* — in good shape
6. Grandma likes to keep herself *as fit as a fiddle.* — getting into trouble

Name ______________________________ Practice 108

Math Practice: Money

Subtract.	Subtract.	Subtract.
$35.64 – $23.89	$59.61 – $42.95	$47.74 – $30.76

Solve.	Solve.
Sharnelle's house number is 3197. Vance's house number is 364 lower than Sharnelle's. What is Vance's house number? Vance's house number is __________.	Bert needs to drive his truck to its next destination 5,145 miles away. He has already driven 3,728 miles. How many miles does Bert have left to drive? Bert has __________ miles left to drive.

Language Practice: Run-On Sentences

Run-on sentences are two sentences written as one sentence without punctuation. Read each sentence. Rewrite it correctly on the lines.

Reptile Facts

Example: Reptiles are vertebrate animals waterproof scales cover their bodies.

Reptiles are vertebrate animals. Waterproof scales cover their bodies.

1. Crocodiles and alligators are the largest reptiles they hunt other animals for their food.

____

____

2. Most reptiles hatch from eggs the baby reptile looks like its parents.

____

____

Name ______________________________ Practice 109

Math Practice: Subtraction with Regrouping

Subtract.	Subtract.	Subtract.
46,798 – 38,523	78,847 – 45,561	97,453 – 29,210

Solve.	Solve.
Jim Brown rushed for 12,312 yards. Franco Harris rushed for 12,120 yards. How many more yards did Jim Brown rush?	A doctor earns $59,300 a year while a secretary earns $20,600 a year. How much more does a doctor earn?
Jim Brown rushed _______ more yards.	A doctor earns _______ more.

Language Practice: Run-On Sentences

Run-on sentences are two sentences written as one sentence without punctuation. Read each run-on sentence and rewrite it correctly on the lines.

People in the News

Example: Abraham Lincoln was born in 1809 he was our 16th president.

Abraham Lincoln was born in 1809. He was our 16th president.

1. Tiger Woods attended Stanford University in 1997 he won the U.S. Masters.

____

____

2. Michael Jordan played basketball for the Chicago Bulls he played on the 1984 U.S. Olympic basketball team.

____

____

Name

Math Practice: Multiplication

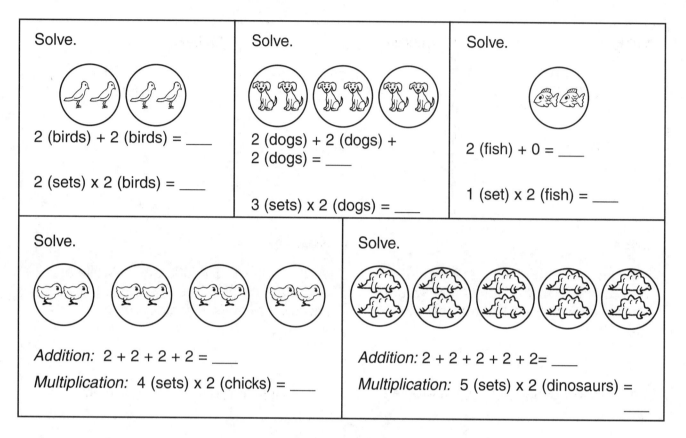

Solve.

2 (birds) + 2 (birds) = ___

2 (sets) x 2 (birds) = ___

Solve.

2 (dogs) + 2 (dogs) + 2 (dogs) = ___

3 (sets) x 2 (dogs) = ___

Solve.

2 (fish) + 0 = ___

1 (set) x 2 (fish) = ___

Solve.

Addition: 2 + 2 + 2 + 2 = ___

Multiplication: 4 (sets) x 2 (chicks) = ___

Solve.

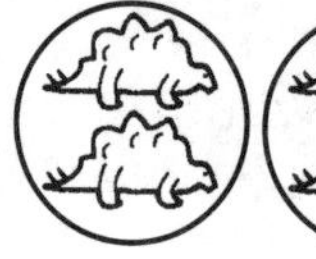
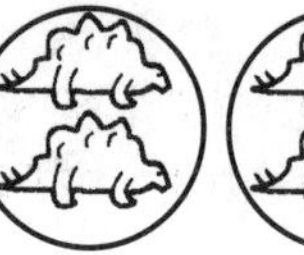
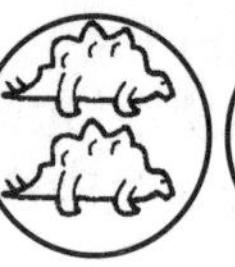

Addition: 2 + 2 + 2 + 2 + 2= ___

Multiplication: 5 (sets) x 2 (dinosaurs) = ___

Language Practice: Alphabetical Order

Make a list of animals. Rewrite the list in alphabetical order.

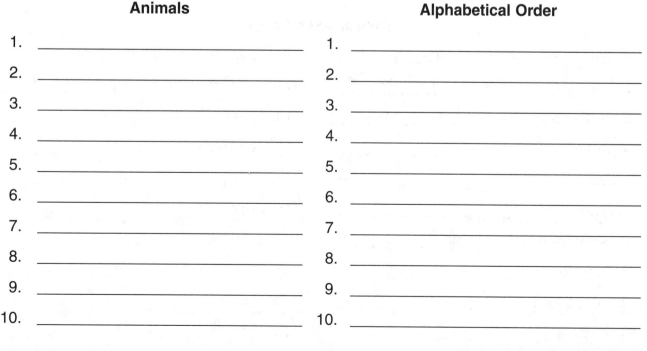

Animals	Alphabetical Order
1. ______	1. ______
2. ______	2. ______
3. ______	3. ______
4. ______	4. ______
5. ______	5. ______
6. ______	6. ______
7. ______	7. ______
8. ______	8. ______
9. ______	9. ______
10. ______	10. ______

Name ______________________________ Practice 111

Math Practice: Multiplying by 2

Multiply.	Multiply.	Multiply.
2 x 1 = ______ 1 x 2 = ______	2 x 3 = ______ 3 x 2 = ______	2 x 4 = ______ 4 x 2 = ______

Solve.	Solve.
There are 4 baskets with 2 apples in each basket. How many apples are there in all? There are ______ apples in all.	There are 2 dogs. Each dog has 2 bones. How many bones are there in all? There are ______ bones in all.

Language Practice: Syllables

Syllables are small segments of a whole word. All words have at least one syllable. Read each word. Write the number of syllables on the line.

Musical Instruments

1. piano ______________
2. clarinet ______________
3. saxophone ______________
4. drums ______________
5. guitar ______________
6. flute ______________
7. piccolo ______________
8. triangle ______________
9. tambourine ______________
10. trumpet ______________
11. oboe ______________
12. violin ______________
13. bass ______________
14. accordion ______________
15. bells ______________
16. xylophone ______________
17. tuba ______________
18. organ ______________
19. cymbal ______________
20. horn ______________

Name ____

Math Practice: Multiplying by 3

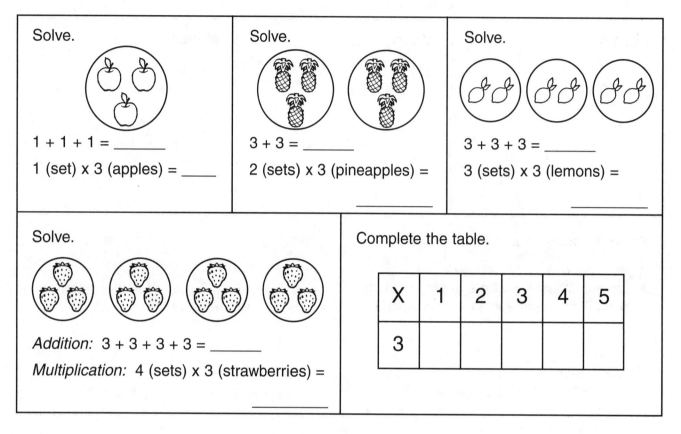

Solve.

1 + 1 + 1 = ______

1 (set) x 3 (apples) = _____

Solve.

3 + 3 = ______

2 (sets) x 3 (pineapples) = ________

Solve.

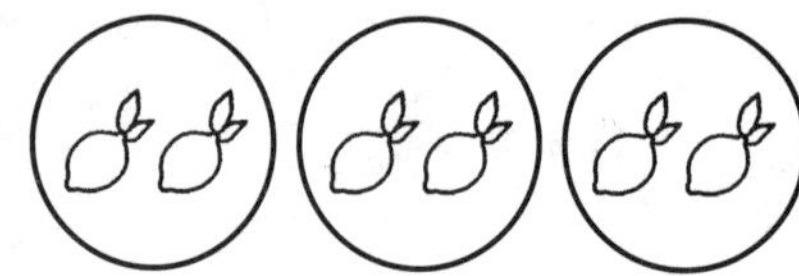

3 + 3 + 3 = ______

3 (sets) x 3 (lemons) = ________

Solve.

Addition: 3 + 3 + 3 + 3 = ______

Multiplication: 4 (sets) x 3 (strawberries) = ________

Complete the table.

X	1	2	3	4	5
3					

Language Practice: Syllables

Syllables are small segments of a whole word. All words have at least one syllable. Arrange the syllables in the word bank to spell each fruit and vegetable's name. Cross off each syllable as it is used.

ip	let	ma	mel	mush	on	po	room
ta	ter	to	to	to	tuce	turn	wa

___ ___ + ___ ___ + ___ ___

___ ___ ___ ___ + ___ ___

___ ___ + ___ ___ ___ + ___ ___ ___ + ___ ___

___ ___ ___ + ___ ___ ___ ___

___ ___ ___ ___ + ___ ___ ___ ___

___ ___ + ___ ___ + ___ ___

Name ______________________________________ Practice 113

Math Practice: Multiplying by 3

Multiply.	Multiply.	Multiply.
3 x 1 = ______	3 x 2 = ______	3 x 4 = ______
1 x 3 = ______	2 x 3 = ______	4 x 3 = ______

Write the problem and then solve it.	Write the problem and then solve it.
A triple cone cost 10¢. How much would 3 triple cones cost?	Pat has 2 bowls. She put 3 scoops of ice cream into each bowl. How many scoops of ice cream are there?
3 triple cones would cost ______.	There are ______ scoops of ice cream.

Language Practice: Idioms

Idioms are phrases that have special meaning.

Example: *R.J. has ants in his pants.*
R.J. doesn't really have *ants in his pants.*
Instead, he is unable to sit still.

Draw a line matching each idiom to its meaning.

1. Carmella is *all ears.*	getting angry
2. Phil is *catching forty winks* before going to work.	listening carefully
3. *"Hold your horses!"* said the police officer.	remind you of something
4. Ava is getting *hot under the collar.*	slow down
5. "Quit *pulling my leg!"* said Mr. Zen.	taking a nap
6. "Doesn't this story *ring a bell*?" asked Ken.	teasing

Name ______________________________ Practice 114

Math Practice: Multiplying by 4

Multiply.	Multiply.	Multiply.
4 x 1 1 x 4	4 x 2 2 x 4	4 x 3 3 x 4

Rewrite as a multiplication problem.	Write the problem and then solve it.
Solve both problems. 4 + 4 + 4 + 4 + 4 = ______ ___ x ___ = ___	Nadine saw 4 cars. Each car had 4 passengers. How many people did Nadine see in all? Nadine saw ______ people in all.

Language Practice: Proofreading

Proofreading is rereading a sentence and finding the mistakes.

Example: *The porcupine poke its enemies with its quills.*

The word "poke" is not the correct verb form. It should be "pokes."

Read each sentence and circle the mistake. Write the circled work correctly on the line.

Animal Self-Defense

1. Plants uses thorns and spines to protect themselves. ________________
2. Many animals run away to a safe plase. ________________
3. some fish live in large schools. ________________
4. Many snakes an opossums "play dead." ________________
5. If a lizard is caught by its tail, the tale breaks off. ________________
6. Armadillos is covered with armor. ________________
7. Sea cucumbers squirt out them insides. ________________
8. Hedgehogs and porcupines is difficult for their enemies to eat. ________________

Name ______________________ Practice 115

Math Practice: Multiplying by 5

Multiply.	Multiply.	Multiply.
5 x 2 = ______	5 x 3 = ______	5 x 5 = ______
2 x 5 = ______	3 x 5 = ______	5 x 1 = ______

Write the multiplication problem.

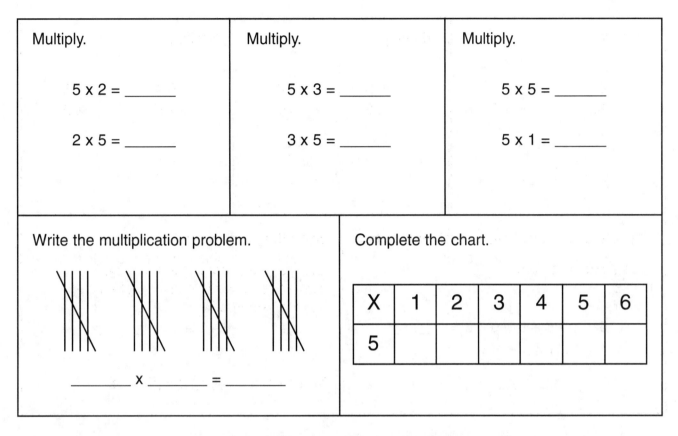

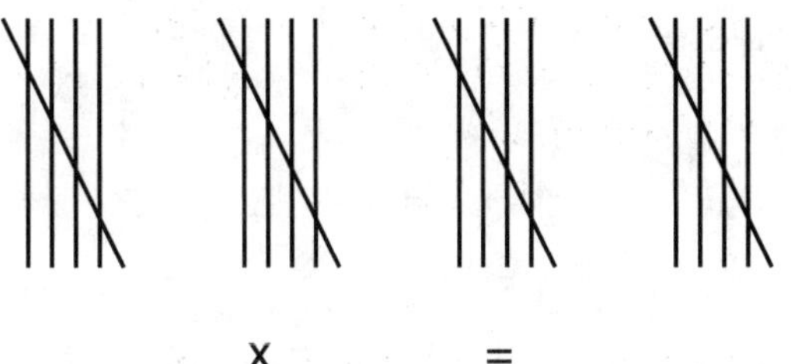

_______ x _______ = _______

Complete the chart.

X	1	2	3	4	5	6
5						

Language Practice: Syllables

Syllables are small segments of a whole word. All words have at least one syllable. Arrange the syllables in the word bank to spell each fruit and vegetable's name. Cross off each syllable as it is used.

ange	ap	ber	cher	cu	cum	kin
le	or	pick	ple	pump	ry	

___ ___ + ___ ___ ___ ___ ___ ___ ___ ___ + ___ ___

___ ___ + ___ ___ ___ ___ ___ ___ ___ + ___ ___

___ ___ ___ ___ + ___ ___ ___ ___ ___ + ___ ___ ___ + ___ ___ ___

Name ______________________________ Practice 116

Math Practice: Multiplying by 6

Multiply.	Multiply.	Multiply.
6 x 3 = ______ 4 x 6 = ______	6 x 2 = ______ 1 x 6 = ______	6 x 6 = ______ 6 x 5 = ______

Solve the addition problem. Then rewrite the addition problem into a multiplication problem.	Solve the addition problem. Then rewrite the addition problem into a multiplication problem.
6 + 6 + 6 + 6 + 6 + 6 = ______ _____ x _____ = _____	6 + 6 + 6 + 6 = ______ _____ x _____ = _____

Language Practice: Syllables

Syllables are small segments of a whole word. All words have at least one syllable. Divide each word into its syllables. If necessary, use a dictionary to help you.

Governmental Words

Word	Number of Syllables	Divided into Syllables
1. president	__________	______________________________
2. executive	__________	______________________________
3. representative	__________	______________________________
4. government	__________	______________________________
5. constitution	__________	______________________________
6. congress	__________	______________________________
7. supreme	__________	______________________________

Name ____________________ Practice 117

Math Practice: Multiplying by 0

Multiply.	Multiply.	Multiply.
0 x 0 = ______ 0 x 10 = ______	4 x 0 = ______ 0 x 7 = ______	9 x 0 = ______ 0 x 6 = ______

What's the rule when multiplying any number by 0?	Solve.
______________________________ ______________________________ ______________________________	There are 6 plates. Each plate has 0 donuts on it. How many donuts are there in all? There are ______ donuts in all.

Language Practice: Syllables

Syllables are small segments of a whole word. All words have at least one syllable. Divide each word into its syllables. If a word has a consonant double, divide the word between the two consonants (example: but/ter).

dinner	______________	berry	______________
supper	______________	summer	______________
jelly	______________	starry	______________
Molly	______________	penny	______________
sitter	______________	babble	______________
collar	______________	collect	______________
runner	______________	digging	______________
pretty	______________	terror	______________

Name ______________________________________ Practice 118

Math Practice: Multiplying by 7

<table>
<tr>
<td>Multiply.

2 x 7 = ______

1 x 7 = ______</td>
<td>Multiply.

7 x 3 = ______

7 x 0 = ______</td>
<td>Multiply.

4 x 7 = ______

7 x 5 = ______</td>
</tr>
<tr>
<td colspan="1">Write the factors for 7.</td>
<td colspan="2">Match the factors to their product.
7 x 6   0
5 x 7   7
0 x 7   42
7 x 1   35</td>
</tr>
</table>

Language Practice: the Verb "Be"

The verb "be" is an *irregular verb.*

- **Present tenses:** am, is, are
- **Past tenses:** was, were

Read each sentence and underline the verb. Write *past* or *present* on the line.

1. Harold was taking a nap. ______________
2. Maude is painting the bathroom. ______________
3. We are going to the baseball game. ______________
4. Jane is running for president. ______________
5. We were rollerblading at the park. ______________
6. Is Jeremiah home? ______________
7. Casper was wearing his batting helmet. ______________
8. They were decorating the house for the holiday. ______________

Name ____________________ Practice 119

Math Practice: Multiplying by 8

Multiply.	Multiply.	Multiply.
8 x 1 2 x 8	3 x 8 8 x 4	8 x 5 6 x 8

Write the multiplication problem.	Write the problem.
There are 8 spiders. Each spider has 8 legs. How many legs in all?	There are 5 octopuses. Each octopus has 8 arms. How many arms in all?
There are ______ legs in all.	There are ______ arms in all.

Language Practice: The Verb "Be"

The verb "*be*" is an irregular verb.

- **Present tense:** am, is, are
- **Past tense:** was, were

Complete each sentence with the correct form of the verb "*be*".

1. Bill, Al, and Ronny __________________ on the team.
2. Sheila __________________ one of the cheerleaders.
3. Steve __________________ ringing the cowbell.
4. I __________________ selling popcorn and hot dogs.
5. Our team __________________ winning the game!
6. Last year, out team __________________ the best!
7. We __________________ at the championship game, but we lost.
8. We __________________ playing better this year!

are am is was were

Name ______________________________ Practice 120

Math Practice: Multiplying by 9

Multiply.	Multiply.	Multiply.
9 x 9 9 x 0	9 x 3 4 x 9	9 x 9 5 x 9

Multiply. Add the digits in each product.	What do you notice about all of the products in the previous problem?
Example: 9 x 5 = 45 4 + 5 = 9 6 x 9 = ____ ____ + ____ = ____ 3 x 9 = ____ ____ + ____ = ____ 9 x 1 = ____ ____ + ____ = ____	

Language Practice: the Verb "Be"

The verb "*be*" is an *irregular verb.*

- **Present tenses:** am, is, are
- **Past tenses:** was, were

Read each sentence and circle the verb. Write the correct form of the verb on the line.

1. Right now, we was playing the game. ____________________
2. Tonight, they is going to the movies. ____________________
3. George are a friendly person. ____________________
4. I is in 6th grade. ____________________
5. She be carving the pumpkin. ____________________
6. We is going to the haunted house tonight. ____________________
7. Last night, Grandpa am barbecuing hamburgers. ____________________
8. Last week, they was planting the seeds in the garden. ____________________

Name ______________________ Practice 121

Math Practice: Division

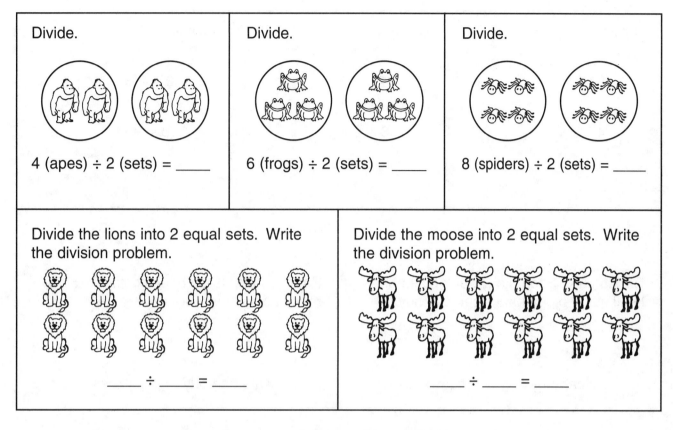

Divide.	Divide.	Divide.
 4 (apes) ÷ 2 (sets) = ____	 6 (frogs) ÷ 2 (sets) = ____	 8 (spiders) ÷ 2 (sets) = ____

Divide the lions into 2 equal sets. Write the division problem.

____ ÷ ____ = ____

Divide the moose into 2 equal sets. Write the division problem.

____ ÷ ____ = ____

Language Practice: Homophones

Homophones are groups of words that sound the same but have different meanings and spellings. Circle the homophone that goes with each picture.

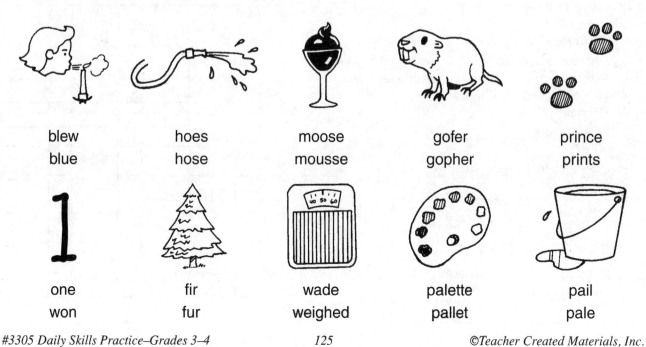

blew
blue

hoes
hose

moose
mousse

gofer
gopher

prince
prints

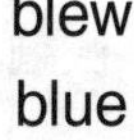

one
won

fir
fur

wade
weighed

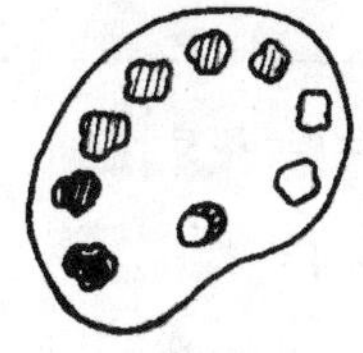

palette
pallet

pail
pale

Name

Math Practice: Dividing by 2

Divide.	Divide.	Divide.
8 ÷ 2 = ______	12 ÷ 2 = ______	2 ÷ 2 = ______
4 ÷ 2 = ______	6 ÷ 2 = ______	10 ÷ 2 = ______

Solve.	Solve.
Cal has $6. Each piggy bank costs $2. How many piggy banks can Cal buy?	Kate has $8. Each book costs $2. How many books can Kate buy?
Cal can buy ______ piggy banks.	Kate can buy ______ books.

Language Practice: Compound Words

A *compound word* is made by combining two separate words into one new word. Write the answer to each clue in the crossword puzzle.

Across

2. placed over a chair or sofa
4. type of painting
6. no shoes
8. an architect's drawing
9. to tighten footwear

Down

1. used to open a door
5. used to tell time
7. kind of pants

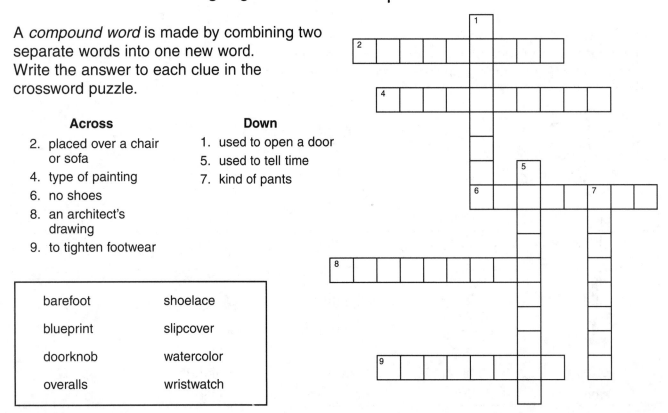

barefoot	shoelace
blueprint	slipcover
doorknob	watercolor
overalls	wristwatch

Name ______________________________

Math Practice: Dividing by 3

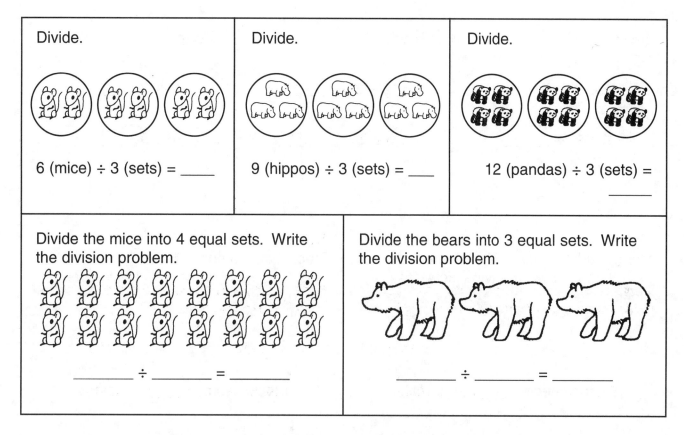

<table>
<tr>
<td>Divide.

6 (mice) ÷ 3 (sets) = ____</td>
<td>Divide.

9 (hippos) ÷ 3 (sets) = ____</td>
<td>Divide.

12 (pandas) ÷ 3 (sets) = ____</td>
</tr>
</table>

<table>
<tr>
<td>Divide the mice into 4 equal sets. Write the division problem.

_______ ÷ _______ = _______</td>
<td>Divide the bears into 3 equal sets. Write the division problem.

_______ ÷ _______ = _______</td>
</tr>
</table>

Language Practice: Reading to Solve Problems

Draw the picture for the problem. Write the division problem.

Grandma baked 12 cookies and divided them equally among the 3 grandchildren.	Sylvester gathered 18 pebbles. He divided them equally among 3 jars.
Josette picked 9 flowers. She divided them equally among 3 vases.	Thomas caught 3 butterflies. He divided them equally among 3 nets.

Name ______________________ Practice 124

Math Practice: Dividing by 3

Divide.	Divide.	Divide.
3 ÷ 3 = ______	12 ÷ 3 = ______	21 ÷ 3 = ______
9 ÷ 3 = ______	15 ÷ 3 = ______	18 ÷ 3 = ______

Solve.
Henny laid 12 eggs. Each basket can hold 3 eggs. How many baskets does Henny need?

Henny needs ______ baskets.

Solve.
Froggy laid 18 eggs. Each lily pad can hold 3 eggs. How many lily pads does Froggy need?

Froggy needs ______ lily pads.

Language Practice: Compound Words

A *compound word* is made by combining two separate words into one new word. Make the compound words using the words in the word bank. Find and color each compound word in the word search.

apple	berry	blue	bread	butter	cake	cheese	corn
meal	melon	milk	nut	oat	pea	pine	water

1. ____________
2. ____________
3. ____________
4. ____________
5. ____________
6. ____________
7. ____________
8. ____________

P	W	A	T	E	R	M	E	L	O	N	A	P	P	L	H
G	E	E	L	O	P	P	I	N	E	A	P	P	L	E	O
R	A	A	I	C	E	C	R	E	A	M	T	G	A	E	T
C	O	R	N	B	R	E	A	D	H	T	O	M	L	S	D
N	D	B	L	U	E	B	E	R	R	Y	R	B	E	A	O
M	O	T	H	E	T	R	S	I	S	T	R	E	F	A	G
O	A	R	C	H	E	E	S	E	C	A	K	E	D	U	L
B	U	T	T	E	R	M	I	L	K	B	P	U	C	C	E

Name ______________________________ Practice 125

Math Practice: Dividing by 4

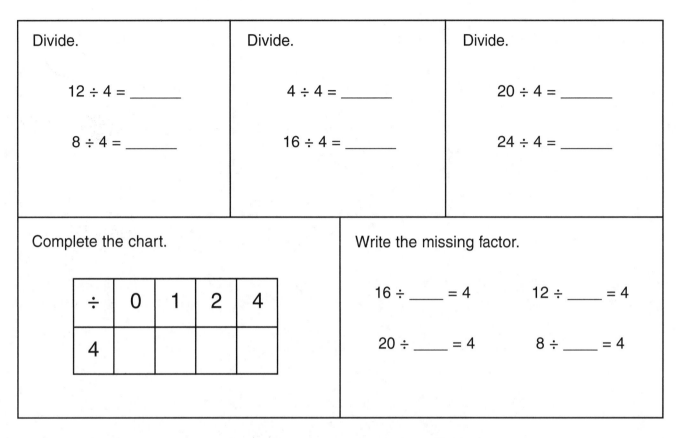

Divide.	Divide.	Divide.
12 ÷ 4 = ______	4 ÷ 4 = ______	20 ÷ 4 = ______
8 ÷ 4 = ______	16 ÷ 4 = ______	24 ÷ 4 = ______

Complete the chart.

÷	0	1	2	4
4				

Write the missing factor.

16 ÷ ____ = 4   12 ÷ ____ = 4

20 ÷ ____ = 4   8 ÷ ____ = 4

Language Practice: Compound Words

A *compound word* is made by combining two separate words into one new word. Write the missing word to complete each set of compound words.

______ board	frog ______	______ bug
______ side	gentle ______	______ room
______ field	weather ______	______ spread

______ pick	______ line	paper ______
______ ache	______ mail	bare ______
______ brush	______ port	______ bone

Name ____________________

Math Practice: Dividing by 5

Divide.	Divide.	Divide.
15 ÷ 5 = ______ 20 ÷ 5 = ______	5 ÷ 5 = ______ 10 ÷ 5 = ______	25 ÷ 5 = ______ 30 ÷ 5 = ______

Count by 5s to 50. Write the numbers.	Rewrite the division problem and then solve.
______, ______, ______, ______ ______, ______, ______, ______ ______, ______	$5\overline{)15}$ $5\overline{)10}$

Language Practice: Compound Words

A *compound word* is made by combining two separate words into one new word. Write eight compound word using the words provided in the box.

anchor	hair	ball	hay	bridge	leap	cracker	nut
crow	pin	cut	scare	draw	stack	frog	woman

______________________ ______________________

______________________ ______________________

______________________ ______________________

______________________ ______________________

Name ______________________________ Practice 127

Math Practice: Dividing by 6

Divide.	Divide.	Divide.
12 ÷ 6 = ______ 6 ÷ 6 = ______	24 ÷ 6 = ______ 18 ÷ 6 = ______	42 ÷ 6 = ______ 36 ÷ 6 = ______

Solve.	Solve.
Nicki has 18 marbles. She puts the marbles into 3 bags. How many marbles are in each bag? There are ______ marbles in each bag.	Nicholas has 12 pieces of bread. For each sandwich, he uses 2 pieces of bread. How many sandwiches did Nicholas make? Nicholas made ______ sandwiches.

Language Practice: Compound Words

A *compound word* is made by combining two separate words into one new word. Write the compound word next to its definition.

another	bareback	eyeball	hardware	outfield
pigtail	skyscraper	stateside	tiptoe	tugboat

1. ______________________________ : a hair style
2. ______________________________ : used to see
3. ______________________________ : used to fix things
4. ______________________________ : of or in the U.S.
5. ______________________________ : a tall building
6. ______________________________ : used to guide big ships into port
7. ______________________________ : to walk quietly
8. ______________________________ : baseball position
9. ______________________________ : to have a second serving
10. ______________________________ : to ride without a saddle

Name ______ Practice 128

Math Practice: Dividing by 10

Divide.	Divide.	Divide.
10 ÷ 10 = ______	30 ÷ 10 = ______	50 ÷ 10 = ______
20 ÷ 10 = ______	40 ÷ 10 = ______	60 ÷ 10 = ______

Solve.

Lazlo had 80 pencils. There were 10 pencils in each box. How many boxes does Lazlo have?

Lazlo has ______ boxes.

Solve.

There are 70 students in fourth grade at Fox Elementary School. They must be arranged in groups of 10 to complete a special project. How many students should be placed in each group?

Each group has ______ students.

Language Practice: Commas

A *comma* is used when writing the date.

- The comma separates the date from the year.
  Example: *February 3, 1999*
- The comma also separates the day of the week from the date.
  Example: *Friday, December 1, 2000*

Read each sentence and write the missing comma or commas.

1. Tuesday March 6 1998
2. February 3 1999
3. Wednesday August 4 1999
4. July 1 1998
5. Sunday October 4 1998
6. October 31 2000
7. Saturday June 3 2000
8. Monday March 22 1999

Name ______________________ Practice 129

Math Practice: Dividing by 1

Divide.	Divide.	Divide.
10 ÷ 1 = ______	6 ÷ 1 = ______	1 ÷ 1 = ______
8 ÷ 1 = ______	7 ÷ 1 = ______	9 ÷ 1 = ______

Solve.	What is the rule when dividing by 1?
Owl had 5 owlets. She put 1 owlet in each nest. How many nests does Owl have? Owl has ______ nests.	______________________ ______________________ ______________________

Language Practice: Commas

Commas are used in a series of words.

Example: I like apples and pears and oranges and plums.
I like apples, pears, oranges, and plums.

Rewrite each sentence using commas.

1. Mrs. Frank went to the bakery and the library and the post office and the beauty salon.

____

____

2. Mr. Brown planted zinnias and chrysanthemums and salvia and ferns and roses.

____

____

Name ____________________ Practice 130

Math Practice: Dividing by 7

Divide.	Divide.	Divide.
7 ÷ 7 = ______	42 ÷ 7 = ______	21 ÷ 7 = ______
49 ÷ 7 = ______	14 ÷ 7 = ______	28 ÷ 7 = ______

Circle the products for 7.

7	14	22	35	41	49
0	21	56	43	27	9

Write the missing factor.

14 ÷ ____ = 7 28 ÷ ____ = 7

21 ÷ ____ = 7 35 ÷ ____ = 7

Language Practice: Commas

Commas are used in a series of words.

Example: *Paul and Dot and Al and Olga are members of the family.*

Paul, Dot, Al, and Olga are members of the family.

Rewrite each sentence using commas.

1. Elizabeth Ann has been to England France Italy and Germany.

   ____

   ____

2. Dad likes cheese lettuce tomatoes and pickles on his hamburger.

   ____

   ____

3. Mom made a skirt a shirt a jacket and a pair of pants.

   ____

   ____

Name ______________________________ Practice 131

Math Practice: Dividing by 8

Divide.	Divide.	Divide.
16 ÷ 8 = ______ 48 ÷ 8 = ______	40 ÷ 8 = ______ 24 ÷ 8 = ______	8 ÷ 8 = ______ 32 ÷ 8 = ______

Solve.	Solve.
Linda put 16 cookies into 8 bags. How many cookies are in each bag? There are ______ cookies in each bag.	John planted 24 flowers in 8 rows. How many flowers did John plant in each row? John planted ______ flowers in each row.

Language Practice: Commas

Commas are used when writing numbers larger than 1,000.

Examples: *12987 ⟶ 12,987 This number is larger than 1,000. It needs a comma.*

39 ⟶ This number is smaller than 1,000. It does not need a comma.

Rewrite each number that needs to have a comma.

17	______	4345	______	7	______
181354	______	211	______	6911	______
738	______	482	______	8790	______
61932	______	862	______	31470	______
265	______	41	______	24587	______

Name ______________________________ Practice 132

Math Practice: Dividing by 9

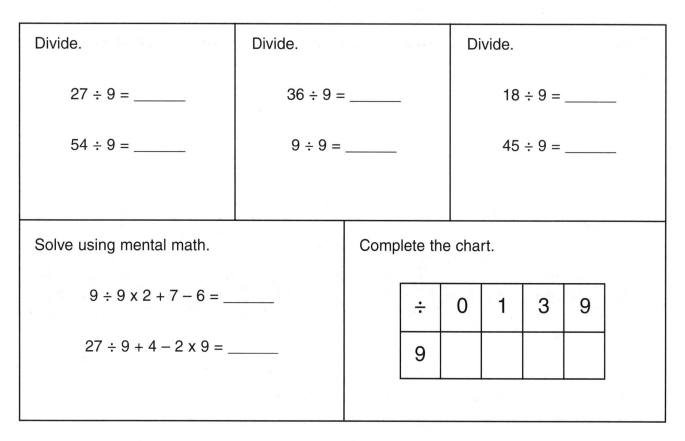

Divide.	Divide.	Divide.
27 ÷ 9 = ______	36 ÷ 9 = ______	18 ÷ 9 = ______
54 ÷ 9 = ______	9 ÷ 9 = ______	45 ÷ 9 = ______

Solve using mental math.

9 ÷ 9 x 2 + 7 – 6 = ______

27 ÷ 9 + 4 – 2 x 9 = ______

Complete the chart.

÷	0	1	3	9
9				

Language Practice: Commas

Commas are used to separate the name of a city from its state or country.

Example: *White Plains, New York*

Write the missing comma in each sentence.

1. Benny visited Little Rock Arkansas.
2. My uncle lives in Fort Lauderdale Florida.
3. Bridget flew to London England for a vacation.
4. Have you ever been to Portland Oregon?
5. My grandparents built a house in Salt Lake City Utah.
6. Barbara's parent retired to Albuquerque New Mexico.
7. Jeremy went to school in Boston Massachusetts.

Write your city and state. Remember to use a comma.

____

Name ______________________ Practice 133

Math Practice: Choosing the Operation

Write +, –, x, or ÷.	Write +, –, x, or ÷.	Write +, –, x, or ÷.
36 ◯ 6 = 6	9 ◯ 3 = 27	5 ◯ 5 = 10

Solve.	Solve.
Tim had 9 baseball caps and 3 hooks. Tim put the same number of caps on each hook. How many caps are on each hook?	Maribel had 4 pastures. There are 6 cows in each pasture. How many cows does Maribel have in all?
Which operation did you use to solve this problem? ______________	Which operation did you use to solve this problem? ______________

Language Practice: Portmanteau Words

Portmanteau words are words that have been blended together to make one unique word.
Example: *brunch (breakfast + lunch)*

Complete the crossword puzzle.

Across

5. of the clock
6. motor + hotel
7. automobile + bus

Down

1. twist + whirl
2. parachute + troops
3. fourteen + nights
4. flame + glare
6. motor + pedal
8. by + cause
9. sky + laboratory

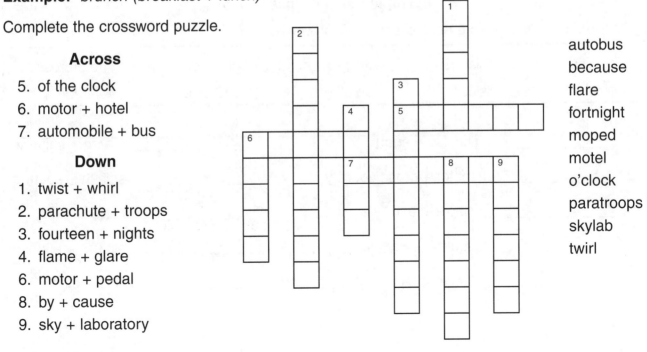

autobus
because
flare
fortnight
moped
motel
o'clock
paratroops
skylab
twirl

Name ______________________________

Math Practice: Mental Math

Solve.	Solve.	Solve.
(3 x 5) x 4 – 10 = ______	(25 ÷ 5) x 5 – 0 = ______	(8 + 2) x 5 ÷ 10 = ______

Write two multiplication problems using the numbers 4, 8, and 32.	Write two division problems using the numbers 4, 8, and 32.
x ______ x ______	$\overline{)\quad}$ $\overline{)\quad}$

Language Practice: Portmanteau Words

Portmanteau words are words that have been blended together to make one unique word.

Example: *smog* (*smoke + fog*)

Write the portmanteau word next to each pair of words.

chortle	clash	flurry	glimmer	motorcross
pixel	slosh	splatter	squiggle	telethon

1. ________________: chuckle + snort
2. ________________: motor + cross country
3. ________________: clap + crash
4. ________________: squirm + wriggle
5. ________________: television + marathon
6. ________________: gleam + shimmer
7. ________________: splash + spatter
8. ________________: flutter + hurry
9. ________________: picture + element
10. ________________: slop + slush

Name

Math Practice: Fractions

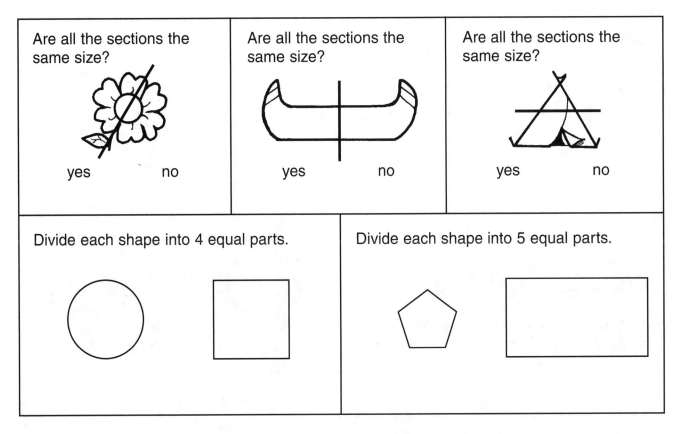

Are all the sections the same size? yes no	Are all the sections the same size? yes no	Are all the sections the same size? yes no

Divide each shape into 4 equal parts.	Divide each shape into 5 equal parts.

Language Practice: Run-On Sentences

Run-on sentences are two sentences written as one sentence without punctuation.

Read each sentence. Rewrite it correctly on the lines.

Example: Lions hunt as a team they chase zebras into a trap.
Lions hunt as a team. They chase zebras into a trap.

1. Lions live in large groups the groups are called "prides."

____

____

2. The male lions protect the prides the lionesses do the hunting.

____

____

Name

Math Practice: Fractions

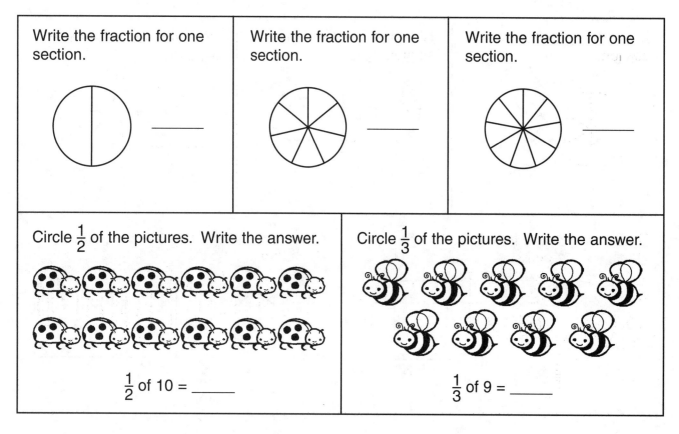

Write the fraction for one section.	Write the fraction for one section.	Write the fraction for one section.
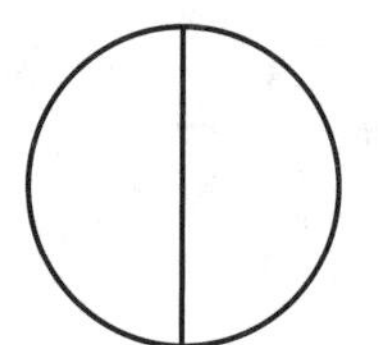 ______	 ______	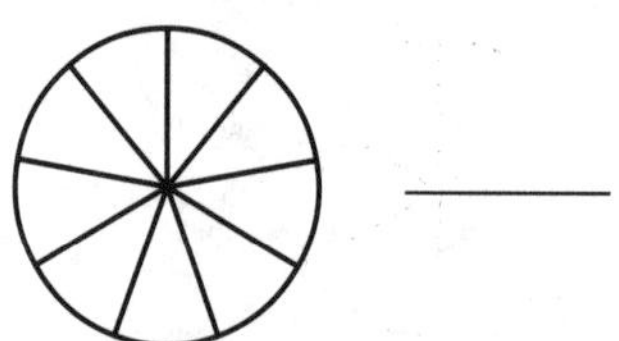 ______

Circle $\frac{1}{2}$ of the pictures. Write the answer.

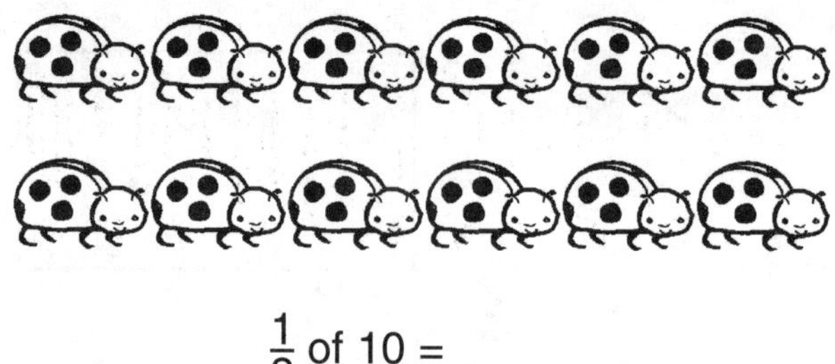

$\frac{1}{2}$ of 10 = ______

Circle $\frac{1}{3}$ of the pictures. Write the answer.

$\frac{1}{3}$ of 9 = ______

Language Practice: Cause and Effect

Cause is an event that happened or did not happen. *Effect* is the result of the event.

Example: "*Barnaby won't stop barking.*" (**cause**)
"*The neighbors are complaining.*" (**effect**)

Draw a line matching each cause to its effect.

1. The phone is ringing.	He got a cold.
2. The windows are dirty.	Her score isn't very good.
3. Andrew is hungry.	She doesn't get her allowance.
4. Kendra didn't study for the test.	The cat is not very happy.
5. Cedric didn't set his alarm.	He will make a snack.
6. Zelda forgets to feed the cat.	Anita will answer it.
7. Zelda didn't do her chores.	Jacob will clean them.
8. Spencer went outside without a coat.	He is late for class.

Name ______________________ Practice 137

Math Practice: Fractions

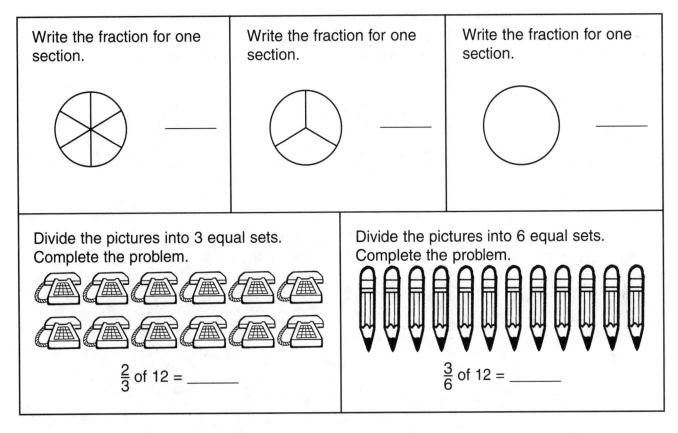

Write the fraction for one section.	Write the fraction for one section.	Write the fraction for one section.
 ______	 ______	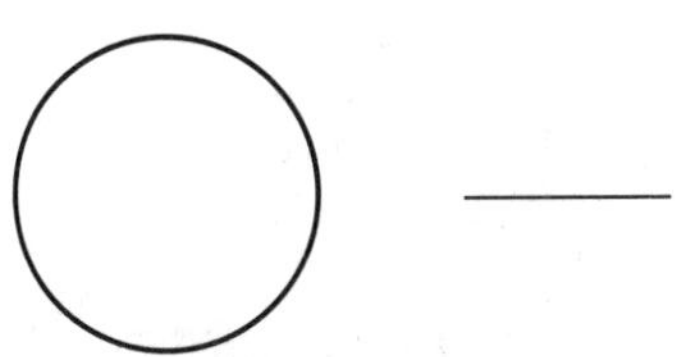

Divide the pictures into 3 equal sets. Complete the problem.	Divide the pictures into 6 equal sets. Complete the problem.
 $\frac{2}{3}$ of 12 = ______	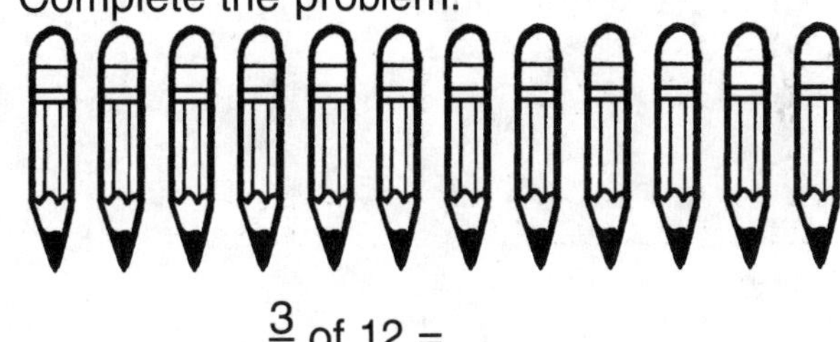 $\frac{3}{6}$ of 12 = ______

Language Practice: Homophones

Homophones are groups of words that sound the same but have different meanings and spellings.

Write the homophones next to its definition.

cheep	creak	freeze	gnu	have
cheap	creek	frees	new	halve

1. ______________: to make a squeaking sound
2. ______________: a bird's call
3. ______________: very cold
4. ______________: a small stream
5. ______________: to obtain or own
6. ______________: releases
7. ______________: fresh, never been used or worn
8. ______________: an antelope
9. ______________: to cut into two parts
10. ______________: inexpensive

Name

Practice 138

Math Practice: Fractions

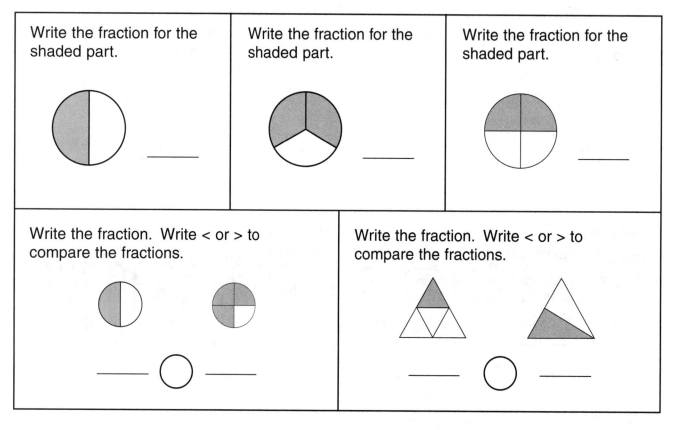

Write the fraction for the shaded part.

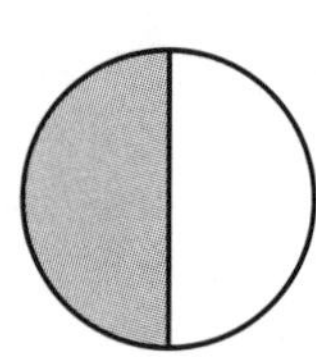 ______

Write the fraction for the shaded part.

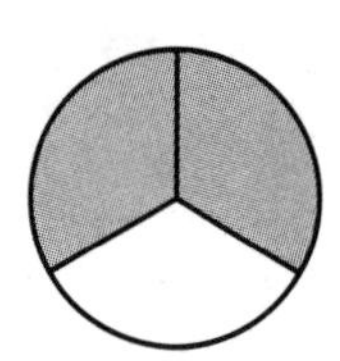 ______

Write the fraction for the shaded part.

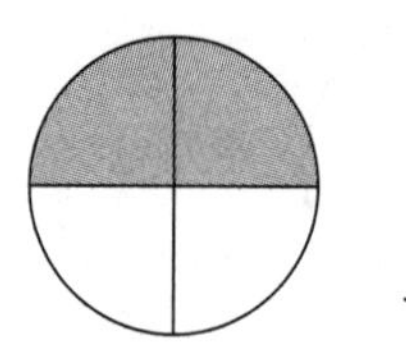 ______

Write the fraction. Write < or > to compare the fractions.

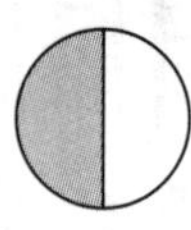 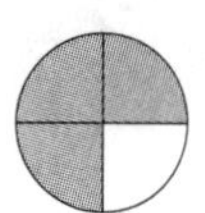

______ ◯ ______

Write the fraction. Write < or > to compare the fractions.

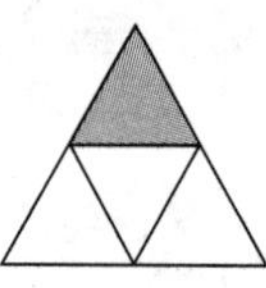 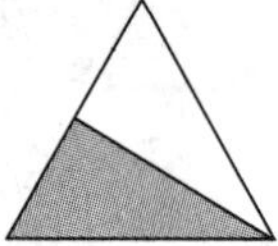

Language Practice: Interjections

Interjections show strong feelings and emotions.

Example: "Owie Mowie! I hurt my finger!"

Owie Mowie is the interjection.

Underline the interjection used in each sentence.

1. Yeah! We won the game!
2. "Hurray!" cheered the crowd.
3. "No way!" said Dwayne.
4. "Eeeeek! I see a mouse!" screamed Hank.
5. Joanie yelled, "Wow!" as she surfed the waves.

Complete each sentence with an interjection.

1. "______________________________! I can't believe I ate the whole thing!"
2. "______________________________! You're running the wrong way!"
3. "______________________________! The ball is going to hit you!"

Name

Practice 139

Math Practice: Fractions

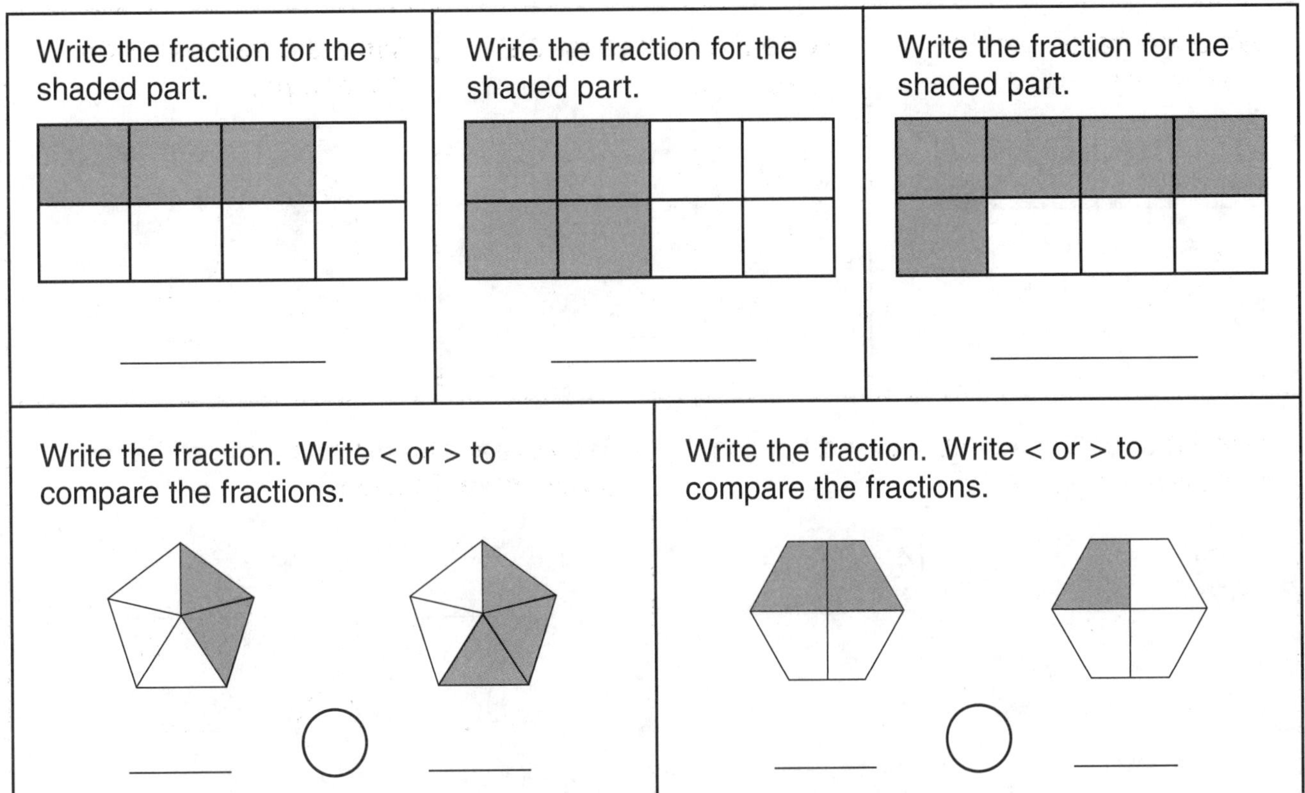

Language Practice: Pronouns

Pronouns can be used in place of nouns. Underline the proper noun in each sentence that can be replaced with a pronoun. Write the pronoun on the line.

he	her	him	it	she

1. Amelia Earhart is a famous pilot. __________
2. Many books have been written about Cleopatra. __________
3. Walt Disney created many cartoon characters. __________
4. Shirley Temple is one of the best known child stars. __________
5. Mickey Mouse is a cartoon character. __________

Name

Math Practice: Fractions

Write the mixed fraction.	Write the mixed fraction.	Write the mixed fraction.
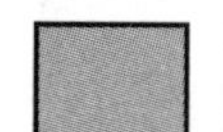  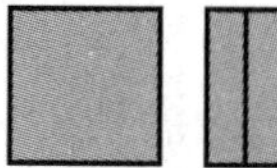  ______	 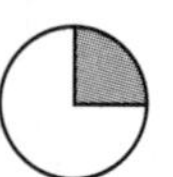 ______	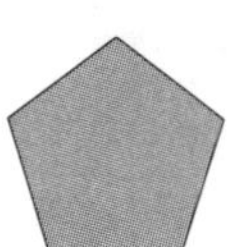 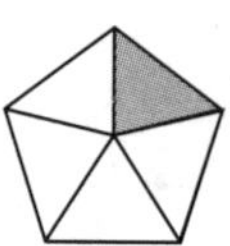 ______

Rewrite each fraction as a mixed fraction.	Rewrite each fraction as a mixed fraction.
$\frac{9}{7}$ = ______ $\frac{14}{3}$ = ______	$\frac{7}{2}$ = ______ $\frac{6}{5}$ = ______

Language Practice: Pronouns

Pronouns can be used in place of nouns. Underline the noun in each sentence that can be replaced with a plural pronoun. Write the pronoun on the line.

them	they	us	we	you

Example: All of the *departing passengers* need to board at Gate 3. *them*

1. My family and I went to England. ______________

2. Our relatives showed us the sights. ______________

3. They took my family and I to see Big Ben. ______________

4. Before we left, we gave our English relatives a gift. ______________

Name ______________________________ Practice 141

Math Practice: Fractions

Add.	Add.	Add.
$\frac{1}{3} + \frac{1}{3} =$ ___	$\frac{4}{8} + \frac{3}{8} =$ ___	$\frac{1}{6} + \frac{1}{6} =$ ___

Write the problem and then solve it.	Write the problem and then solve it.
Clarice ate $\frac{1}{4}$ of a pumpkin pie, and Clarence ate $\frac{2}{4}$ of a pumpkin pie. How much pie did they eat in all?	Pamela and Harrison each ate $\frac{2}{5}$ of a candy bar. How much of the candy bar did they eat in all?
They ate in all ______ of a pie.	They ate ______ of a candy bar.

Language Practice: Possessive Pronouns

Pronouns can be used in place of nouns. A *possessive pronoun* shows ownership. Underline the noun in each sentence that can be replaced with a possessive pronoun. Rewrite the sentence on the line.

her	his	its	our

1. Parker's mom is in the Air Force.

____

2. Minerva's uncle has traveled the world.

____

3. My family's house is near the beach.

____

4. The dog's barking kept us up all night.

____

Name ______________________________ Practice 142

Math Practice: Fractions

Add. $\frac{1}{8} - \frac{5}{8} =$	Add. $\frac{2}{6} - \frac{3}{6} =$	Add. $\frac{4}{7} - \frac{1}{7} =$

Rewrite the answer as a mixed fraction. $\frac{2}{3} + \frac{2}{3} =$	Rewrite the answer as a mixed fraction. $\frac{2}{4} + \frac{3}{4} =$

Language Practice: Clipped Words

Clipped words are words that have been shortened by everyday use.

Example: *lab* is short for laboratory

Write the shortened form for each word.

1. advertisement ______________
2. necktie ______________
3. tuxedo ______________
4. caravan ______________
5. veterinarian ______________
6. photograph ______________
7. cabriolet ______________
8. bicycle ______________
9. examination ______________
10. decaffeinated ______________

Name

Practice 143

Math Practice: Fractions

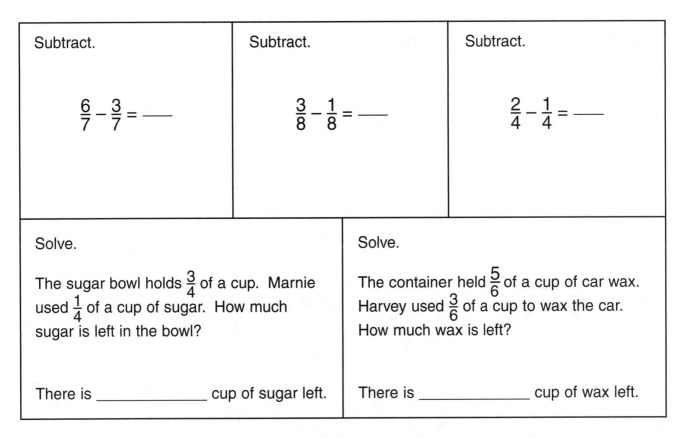

Subtract.	Subtract.	Subtract.
$\frac{6}{7} - \frac{3}{7} =$ ___	$\frac{3}{8} - \frac{1}{8} =$ ___	$\frac{2}{4} - \frac{1}{4} =$ ___

Solve.	Solve.
The sugar bowl holds $\frac{3}{4}$ of a cup. Marnie used $\frac{1}{4}$ of a cup of sugar. How much sugar is left in the bowl?	The container held $\frac{5}{6}$ of a cup of car wax. Harvey used $\frac{3}{6}$ of a cup to wax the car. How much wax is left?
There is ____________ cup of sugar left.	There is ____________ cup of wax left.

Language Practice: Homophones

Homophones are a group of words that sound the same but have different meaning and spellings. Complete each sentence with the correct homophone.

1. Rodney eats ______________________________ for breakfast. (cereal/serial)
2. Lauren ______________________________ her food carefully. (chews/choose)
3. The ______________________________ live in the forest. (dear/deer)
4. Do you like to ______________________________ Easter eggs? (die/dye)
5. The gift is for ______________________________! (ewe/you)
6. The bride will walk down the ______________________________. (aisle/isle)
7. Smoking in not ______________________________. (allowed/aloud)
8. The grass is covered in ______________________________. (dew/do)
9. My muscles are ______________________________. (soar/sore)
10. Would you like cake ______________________________ pie? (oar/or)

Name

Practice 144

Math Practice: Fractions

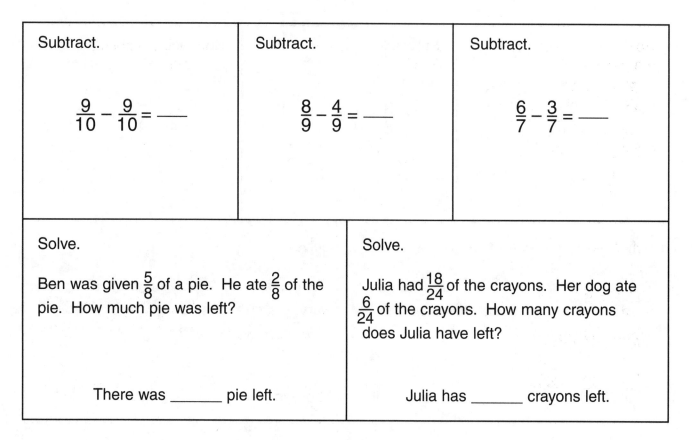

Subtract.	Subtract.	Subtract.
$\frac{9}{10} - \frac{9}{10} = $ ___	$\frac{8}{9} - \frac{4}{9} = $ ___	$\frac{6}{7} - \frac{3}{7} = $ ___

Solve.	Solve.
Ben was given $\frac{5}{8}$ of a pie. He ate $\frac{2}{8}$ of the pie. How much pie was left?	Julia had $\frac{18}{24}$ of the crayons. Her dog ate $\frac{6}{24}$ of the crayons. How many crayons does Julia have left?
There was ______ pie left.	Julia has ______ crayons left.

Language Practice: Prepositions

Prepositions connect nouns or pronouns to the other words in the sentence. Prepositions tell where, when, or why something was done.

Example: *The dog is lying next to me.*

Next to me is the preposition.

It tells where the dog is lying.

Underline the preposition in each sentence. Write *where, when,* or *why* on the line.

1. My sister parked the car in the garage. ______________
2. The birthday party was at 3:00. ______________
3. We were late because our alarm clock broke. ______________
4. They had fun at the picnic. ______________
5. We went to the museum to see the art exhibit. ______________
6. They will bring the new TV on Wednesday. ______________

Name ____________________ Practice 145

Math Practice: Fractions

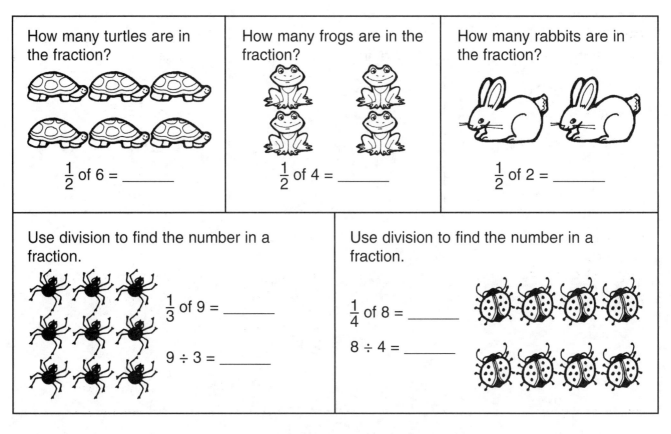

How many turtles are in the fraction?	How many frogs are in the fraction?	How many rabbits are in the fraction?
 $\frac{1}{2}$ of 6 = ______	 $\frac{1}{2}$ of 4 = ______	 $\frac{1}{2}$ of 2 = ______

Use division to find the number in a fraction.	Use division to find the number in a fraction.
 $\frac{1}{3}$ of 9 = ______ $9 \div 3$ = ______	$\frac{1}{4}$ of 8 = ______ $8 \div 4$ = ______ 

Language Practice: Prepositions

Prepositions connect nouns or pronouns to the other words in the sentence. Prepositions tell where, when or why something was done.

Example: The rooster is standing *on the fence.*

On the fence is the prepositional phrase.

Complete each sentence with a prepositional phrase.

1. The train chugged slowly ______________________________.
2. We hurried ______________________________.
3. The television glowed brightly ______________________________.
4. A mouse is a small rodent ______________________________.
5. The heavy book is ______________________________.
6. The soccer ball was kicked ______________________________.
7. Luke is on the swings ______________________________.
8. Have you ever been to the Grand Canyon ______________________________?

Name ______________________ Practice 146

Math Practice: Fractions

Use division to find the number in a fraction.	Use division to find the number in a fraction.	Use division to find the number in a fraction.
$\frac{1}{2}$ of 10 ______	$\frac{1}{3}$ of 12 ______	$\frac{1}{4}$ of 16 ______

Use division to find the number in a fraction.	Use division to find the number in a fraction.
$\frac{1}{5}$ of 10 $\frac{1}{4}$ of 20	$\frac{1}{3}$ of 15 $\frac{1}{2}$ of 24

Language Practice: Comprehension

The Rosetta Stone

A basalt rock was discovered in 1799 by Napoleonic soldiers. It was found in Rosetta, a town in lower Egypt.

The message was inscribed in 196 B.C. The message was written in Egyptian hieroglyphics, Egyptian Demotic, and in Greek. When the stone was deciphered, it told about life in Ancient Egypt. Once the message was deciphered, people were then able to decipher the Egyptian hieroglyphics.

When the British defeated the French, they claimed the Rosetta Stone. The stone is now in a British museum.

1. Who found the Rosetta Stone? ______________________
2. In how many languages was the message written? ______________________
3. Why do you think the writer wrote the message in different languages?

____

____

Name ______________________________ **Practice 147**

Math Practice: Fractions

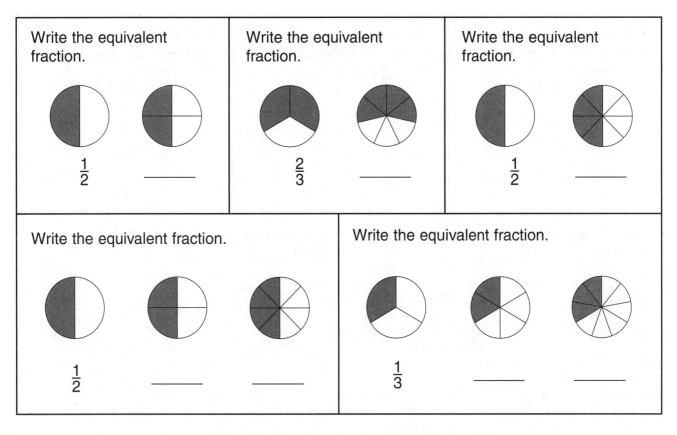

Write the equivalent fraction.

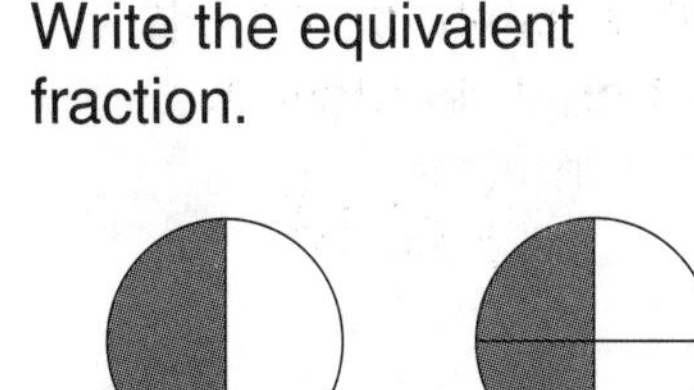

$\frac{1}{2}$ ______

Write the equivalent fraction.

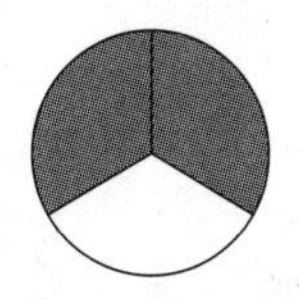

$\frac{2}{3}$ ______

Write the equivalent fraction.

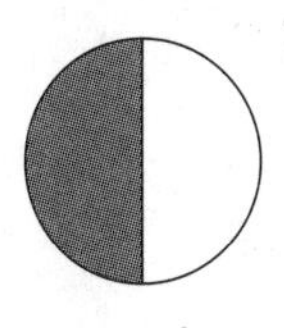 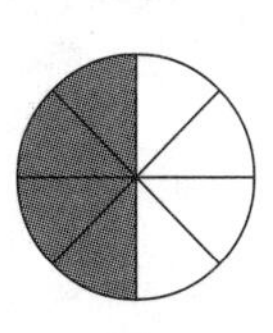

$\frac{1}{2}$ ______

Write the equivalent fraction.

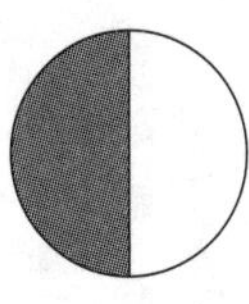 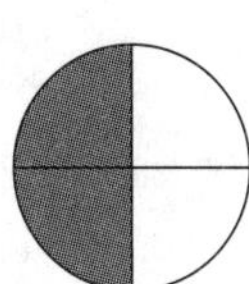

$\frac{1}{2}$ ______ ______

Write the equivalent fraction.

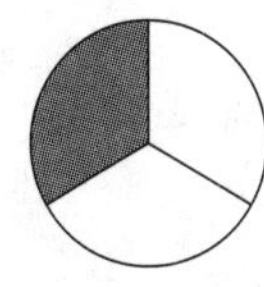 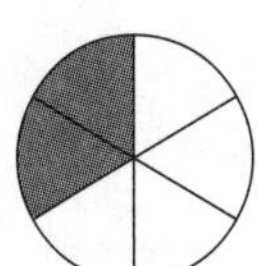 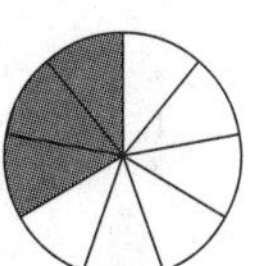

$\frac{1}{3}$ ______ ______

Language Practice: Root Words

Root words are also known as base words. Prefixes are added to the root word to change the meaning.

Prefixes		Root Words	
uni = one	*sub* = below, under	*dict* = speak	*cycle* = circle, wheel
bi or *di* = two	*tri* = three	*tract* = draw	*ped* = foot
	pre = before in time		

Write the meaning for each of the words.

1. unicycle: ______________________
2. predict: ______________________
3. tricycle: ______________________
4. subtract: ______________________
5. bicycle: ______________________
6. biped: ______________________

Name ____________________ **Practice 148**

Math Practice: Fractions

<table>
<tr>
<td>Shade the shape to show the equivalent fraction. Write the fraction.
$\frac{1}{2}$ 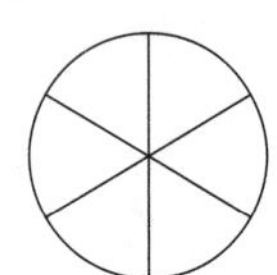
______</td>
<td>Shade the shape to show the equivalent fraction. Write the fraction.
$\frac{2}{3}$ 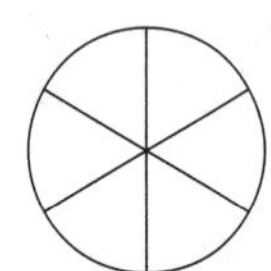
______</td>
<td>Shade the shape to show the equivalent fraction. Write the fraction.
$\frac{3}{4}$ 
______</td>
</tr>
<tr>
<td>Shade the shape to show the equivalent fraction. Write the fraction.
$\frac{1}{3}$ 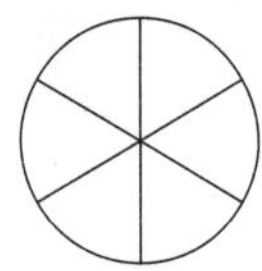 
______ ______</td>
<td colspan="2">Shade the shape to show the equivalent fraction. Write the fraction.
$\frac{1}{2}$  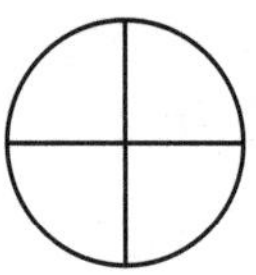
______ ______</td>
</tr>
</table>

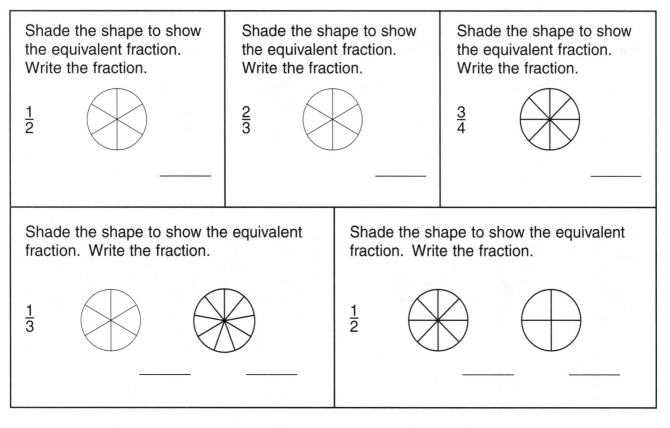

Language Practice: Root Words

Root words are also known as base words. *Suffixes* are added to the root word to change the meaning.

Root Words	**Suffixes**
con = together, with *ex* = out *trans* = across, beyond, through	*port* = carry *tract* = draw, pull

Write the definition for each word.

1. export: ______________________________
2. extract: ______________________________
3. transport: ______________________________
4. contract: ______________________________

Name ______________________________ **Practice 149**

Math Practice: Fractions

Write the fractions in order from smallest to largest.

$\frac{2}{4}$ $\frac{1}{4}$ $\frac{3}{4}$ 1

___, ___, ___, ___

Write the fractions in order from smallest to largest.

1 $\frac{2}{3}$ $\frac{1}{3}$

___, ___, ___

Write the fractions in order from smallest to largest.

1 $\frac{3}{5}$ $\frac{1}{5}$ $\frac{2}{5}$ $\frac{4}{5}$

___, ___, ___, ___, ___

Circle the largest fraction. Draw a line under the smallest fraction.

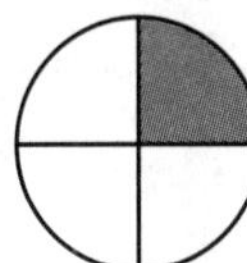
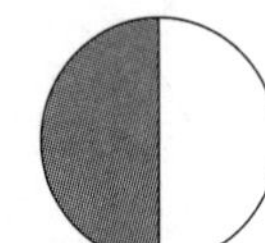
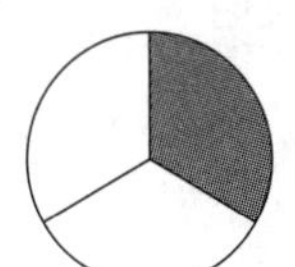

Circle the largest fraction. Draw a line under the smallest fraction.

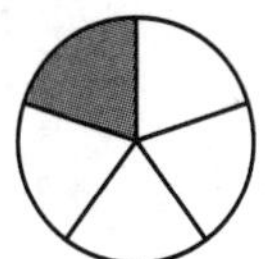
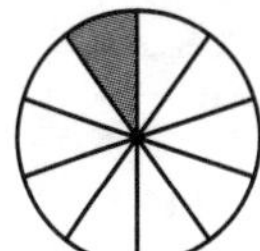
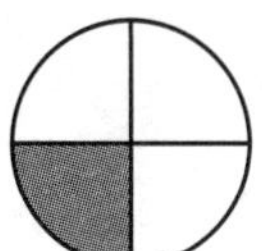

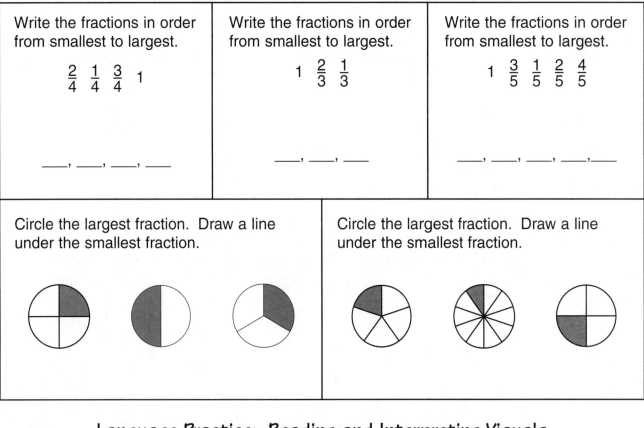

Language Practice: Reading and Interpreting Visuals

Probability tells the chances that a certain letter, number, or color will be chosen.

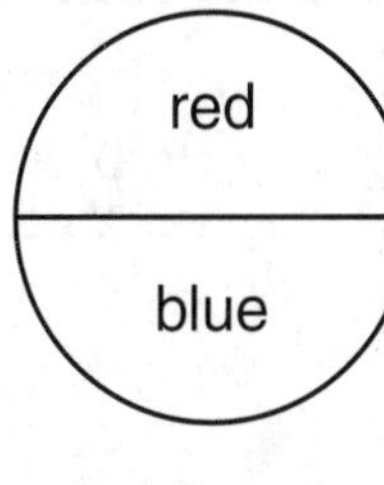

spinner 1

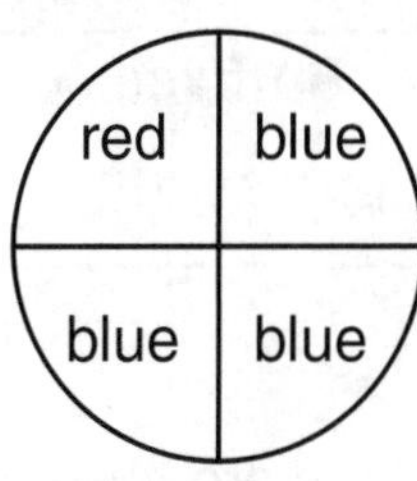

spinner 2

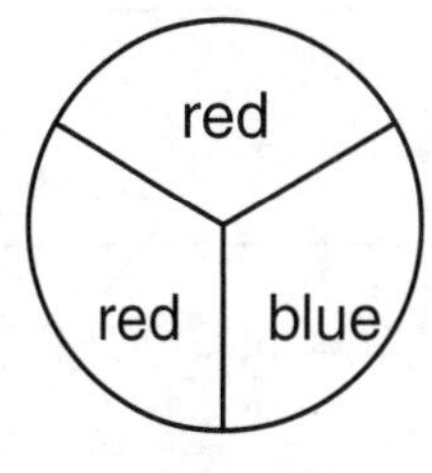

spinner 3

1. Color the spinners. Write the fraction for each color on each spinner.

   spinner 1 red: _______ blue: _______ spinner 2 red: _______ blue: _______

   spinner 3 red: _______ blue: _______

2. Which spinner shows equal chances of landing on red or on blue? ________________
3. Which spinner shows a greater chance of landing on red? ________________
4. Which spinner shows a greater chance of landing on blue? ________________

Name ______________________________ Practice 150

Math Practice: Fractions

Write the fraction. Ana landed on red 3 out of 10 spins.	Write the fraction. Deanna landed on blue 4 out of 5 spins.	Write the fraction. Fred landed on red 2 out of 3 spins.

Draw a spinner with 5 sections. Use red and blue to color the spinner. Make the spinner more likely to land on blue than red.	Draw a spinner with 5 sections. Use red and blue to color the spinner. Make the spinner more likely to land on red than blue.

Language Practice: Suffixes

Suffixes are added to the end of the word. Suffixes change the meaning of the word.

Suffixes		
less: without	*ar, er,* or *or*: one who	*ory*, *ary*, or *ery*: place where

Add the appropriate ending to each word.

1. ______________________ : store for baked goods (bake)
2. ______________________ : one who teaches (teach)
3. ______________________ : without meat (meat)
4. ______________________ : a journalist (report)
5. ______________________ : store selling food and other items (grocer)
6. ______________________ : one who sings (sing)
7. ______________________ : one who takes pictures (photograph)
8. ______________________ : without a single penny (penny)

Name _______________ Practice 151

Math Practice: Fractions

Circle the larger fraction.	Circle the larger fraction.	Circle the larger fraction.
$\frac{2}{3}$ $\frac{5}{6}$	$\frac{1}{2}$ $\frac{7}{8}$	$\frac{2}{4}$ $\frac{1}{5}$

How many minutes are in $\frac{1}{4}$ of an hour?	How many minutes are in $\frac{1}{3}$ of an hour?
There are ______ minutes.	There are ______ minutes.

Language Practice: Dictionary Skills

All the words in a dictionary are in alphabetical order. Each page of a dictionary has two guide words at the top of the page. The guide words make it easier to find a specific word.

Write each word on the correct page of the dictionary.

check	fit	snug	so	five	chart	snow	chase	fix

fist fixed	charm checker	snowball soccer
____________	____________	____________
____________	____________	____________
____________	____________	____________

Name ______________________________ Practice 152

Math Practice: Fractions

Simplify the fraction.	Simplify the fraction.	Simplify the fraction.
$\frac{6}{8} =$	$\frac{5}{10} =$	$\frac{4}{8} =$

Solve.	Solve.
A recipe calls for $\frac{3}{9}$ cup of butter. Kevin only has measuring cups for $\frac{1}{2}$, $\frac{1}{3}$, and $\frac{1}{4}$. Which cup should he use? He should use the ______________ measuring cup.	Jolie needs to put $\frac{4}{6}$ gallon of gas in the lawn mower. She only has canisters that measure $\frac{1}{3}$, $\frac{2}{3}$, or $\frac{1}{4}$. Which canister should she use? She should use the ______________ canister.

Language Practice: Homographs

Homographs are words that have the same spelling but have different meanings.

Examples: He is up to bat.  She saw a flying bat. 

Complete each sentence with the correct homograph.

yard	can	gum	bark

1. Benji will not ______________ at strangers.
2. I ______________ do the magic trick.
3. A tree's ______________ is like our skin.
4. A ______________ is 36 inches or 3 feet.
5. The tooth is held in place by the ______________.
6. Vinny likes to play ball in the back ______________.
7. Put the garbage in the ______________.
8. May I have a piece of ______________?

Name _______________ Practice 153

Math Practice: Fractions

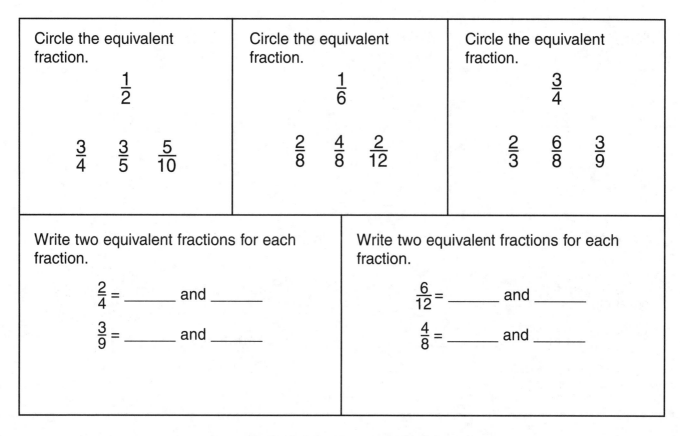

Circle the equivalent fraction. $\frac{1}{2}$	Circle the equivalent fraction. $\frac{1}{6}$	Circle the equivalent fraction. $\frac{3}{4}$
$\frac{3}{4}$ $\frac{3}{5}$ $\frac{5}{10}$	$\frac{2}{8}$ $\frac{4}{8}$ $\frac{2}{12}$	$\frac{2}{3}$ $\frac{6}{8}$ $\frac{3}{9}$

Write two equivalent fractions for each fraction.	Write two equivalent fractions for each fraction.
$\frac{2}{4}$ = ______ and ______	$\frac{6}{12}$ = ______ and ______
$\frac{3}{9}$ = ______ and ______	$\frac{4}{8}$ = ______ and ______

Language Practice: Clipped Words

Clipped words are words that have been shortened by every day use.

Example: *Limo* is short for limousine.

Circle all of the clipped words used in the story. Write the longer version for each clipped word on the lines.

Dear Uncle Donald,

Yesterday, we drove to the gym to see a display on different inventions. We saw an early Ford auto, a bike with a big front wheel, and an old-fashioned stove! We also saw photos of the Wright Brother's plane and of the first phone!

Your niece,

Dolly

1. ____________________
2. ____________________
3. ____________________
4. ____________________
5. ____________________
6. ____________________

Name ______________________________ Practice 154

Math Practice: Decimals

Circle the number in the *tenths* place.	Circle the number in the *tenths* place.	Circle the number in the *tenths* place.
.91	.36	.09

Write each number in standard form.	Write each number in standard form.
eight-tenths: __________	four-tenths: __________
nine-tenths: __________	two-tenths: __________

Language Practice: Root Words

Root words are also known as base words. *Suffixes* are added to the base word to change its meaning.

Root Words		Suffixes
dent, don = tooth	*ortho* = straight	*ist* = one who studies or works with
opt = eye	*ped, pod* = foot	*ian, ic, ical* = relating to

Underline the root word and its suffixes. Write the meaning of the underlined word on the line.

1. Kerry goes to the orthodontist. ______________________
2. Dr. Stone is a podiatrist. ______________________
3. Matthew wants to be an optician. ______________________
4. Dr. Bone was my dentist. ______________________
5. Flip books are optical illusions. ______________________

Bonus: What does *pedestrian* mean? ______________________

Name ______________________________ Practice 155

Math Practice: Decimals

In which place is the 4?	In which place is the 4?	In which place is the 4?
.94	.40	.74
tenths hundredths	tenths hundredths	tenths hundredths

Put the decimals in order from smallest to greatest.	Put the decimals in order from smallest to greatest.
.84 .11 .26 .89	.03 .93 .30 .39
____, ____, ____, ____	____, ____, ____, ____

Language Practice: Root Words

Root words are also known as based words. *Suffixes* are added to the base word to change its meaning.

Prefixes	Root Words	Suffixes
auto = self *tele* = distance	*graph* = write, written *photo* = light *scope* = see, watch	*graph* = write *graphy* = study of *metry* = measure

Write the word next to its definition.

1. ______________________________ : a famous person's signature.
2. ______________________________ : to measure a distance
3. ______________________________ : study of light
4. ______________________________ : see distance
5. ______________________________ : lens used to take pictures of far-away objects
6. ______________________________ : write from a long distance

Name ______________________________ Practice 156

Math Practice: Decimals

Write the decimal for each number word. four-tenths __________	Write the decimal for each number word. one and eight-tenths __________	Write the decimal for each number word. three and four-tenths __________

Write the decimal for each number word. five-hundredths __________ fifty-six tenths __________	Write the decimal for each number word. three-hundredths __________ nine-hundredths __________

Language Practice: Acronyms

An *acronym* is a word formed from the first letter, or letters, of words in a phrase. The acronym is written in all capital letters. No periods are used.

Example: NATO **N**orth **A**tlantic **T**reaty **O**rganization

Underline the first letter in each word. Write the acronym for each set of words on the line provided.

1. sealed with a kiss ____________________
2. as soon as possible ____________________
3. read only memory ____________________
4. disc operating system ____________________
5. National Aeronautics & Space Administration ____________________
6. mothers against drunk driving ____________________

Name ______________________________ Practice 157

Math Practice: Decimals

Use the < or > sign.

.41 ◯ .14

.57 ◯ .75

Use the < or > sign.

.26 ◯ .06

.37 ◯ .70

Use the < or > sign.

.86 ◯ .68

.90 ◯ .09

Add.

$$\begin{array}{r} .41 \\ +\ .57 \\ \hline \end{array} \qquad \begin{array}{r} .03 \\ +\ .83 \\ \hline \end{array}$$

Add.

$$\begin{array}{r} .47 \\ +\ .42 \\ \hline \end{array} \qquad \begin{array}{r} .60 \\ +\ .06 \\ \hline \end{array}$$

Language Practice: Initialisms

An *initialism* is like an acronym, but it cannot be pronounced like a word.

Example: Internal Revenue Service IRS

Underline the first letter in each word. Write the acronym for each set of words on the line.

1. compact disc ______________________
2. post script ______________________
3. recreational vehicle ______________________
4. National Football League ______________________
5. Central Intelligence Agency ______________________
6. unidentified flying object ______________________
7. intelligence quotient ______________________

Name

Practice 158

Math Practice: Decimals

Subtract.	Subtract.	Subtract.
$\begin{array}{r} .33 \\ -\ .03 \\ \hline \end{array}$ $\quad$ $\begin{array}{r} .81 \\ -\ .01 \\ \hline \end{array}$	$\begin{array}{r} .68 \\ -\ .68 \\ \hline \end{array}$ $\quad$ $\begin{array}{r} .50 \\ -\ .20 \\ \hline \end{array}$	$\begin{array}{r} .47 \\ -\ .40 \\ \hline \end{array}$ $\quad$ $\begin{array}{r} .95 \\ -\ .85 \\ \hline \end{array}$

Solve and then write < or >.	Solve and then write < or >.
$.48 - .18 \ \bigcirc \ .25 - .05$	$.74 - .71 \ \bigcirc \ .30 - .10$

Language Practice: Homophones

Homophones are groups of words that sound the same but have different meanings and spellings. Circle the homophone that goes with each picture.

Name ______________________________ Practice 159

Math Practice: Decimals

Add. .31 + .13	Subtract. .88 − .78	Add. .55 + .22

Circle the largest decimal. Draw a line under the smallest decimal. .36 .01 .47 .11 .09	Circle the largest decimal. Draw a line under the smallest decimal. .29 .80 .41 .08 .62

Language Practice: Quotation Marks

Quotation marks (" ") are used to show what a person is saying or has said. The first word in the quotation also begins with a capital letter.

Example: Josie said, *"Grandma, guess what I learned in class?"*

Read each sentence and add the missing quotation marks (" ").

1. Mrs. Greer said, People blink 20,000 times a day.
2. James asked, Are our bodies mostly water?
3. You use 15 muscles each time you smile, stated Iris.
4. How long is the small intestine? questioned Rosie.
5. My temperature is 99°. Am I sick? asked Penny.
6. Most people have more than 100,000 hairs on their heads, said Mr. Adams.
7. Gino asked, Is a sneeze faster than a fastball?
8. How many times does my heart beat each day? asked Vera.

Name ______________________________ Practice 160

Math Practice: Decimals

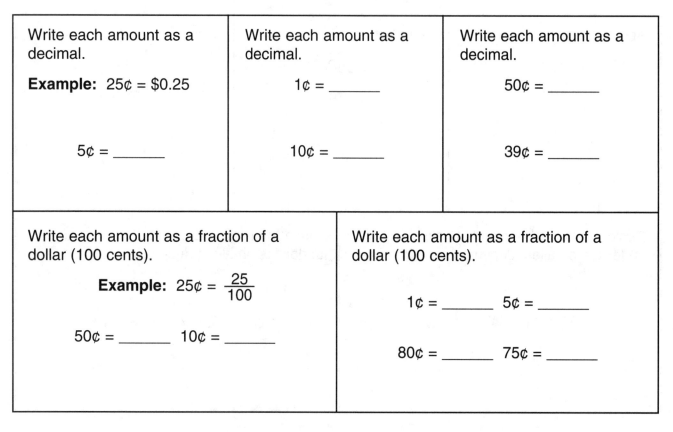

<table>
<tr>
<td>Write each amount as a decimal.

Example: 25¢ = $0.25

5¢ = ______</td>
<td>Write each amount as a decimal.

1¢ = ______

10¢ = ______</td>
<td>Write each amount as a decimal.

50¢ = ______

39¢ = ______</td>
</tr>
<tr>
<td colspan="2">Write each amount as a fraction of a dollar (100 cents).

Example: 25¢ = $\frac{25}{100}$

50¢ = ______ 10¢ = ______</td>
<td>Write each amount as a fraction of a dollar (100 cents).

1¢ = ______ 5¢ = ______

80¢ = ______ 75¢ = ______</td>
</tr>
</table>

Language Practice: Quotation Marks

Quotation marks (“ ”) are used to show what a person is saying or has said.

Examples: Jimmy said, *“Let’s go to the movies!”*
(*Let’s go to the movies* is what Jimmy said.)

Read the story and add the missing quotation marks.

Today we are going to learn about President William H. Taft, said Mrs. Fox. Who knows anything about President Taft?

I do, said Kaylene. William H. Taft was the 27th president of the United States.

That’s right! said Mrs. Fox.

Mrs. Fox, President Taft’s favorite sport was baseball. When he was president he started the tradition of having the president throw out the first ball on the first day of baseball season, added Harry.

Name

Practice 161

Math Practice: Money

Rewrite in standard form.	Rewrite in standard form.	Rewrite in standard form.
$\frac{\$239}{100}$ ________	$\frac{\$875}{100}$ ________	$\frac{\$351}{100}$ ________

Rewrite as a fraction.	Rewrite as a fraction.
\$3.46 ______	\$2.99 ______
\$1.84 ______	\$8.17 ______

Language Practice: Similes

Similes are a way of comparing two items using the words "like" or "as."

Example: *Martina is as busy as a bee.*

Busy as a bee is the simile.

It means that Martina is always doing something.

Write the letter of each simile on the line next to its definition.

1. ________ : not having any bumps.
2. ________ : never stops talking
3. ________ : not soft or spongy
4. ________ : a messy eater
5. ________ : not waking up
6. ________ : not flexible
7. ________ : being extremely cold
8. ________ : eating tiny bits of food

A. sleep like a log
B. eats like a bird
C. eats like a pig
D. chatters like a monkey
E. as cold as ice
F. as stiff as a board
G. as flat as a pancake
H. as hard as a rock

Name _______________ Practice 162

Math Practice: Money

Rewrite each amount as a fraction.	Rewrite each amount as a fraction.	Rewrite each amount as a fraction.
$1.42 ______ $3.06 ______	$.58 ______ $5.19 ______	$6.01 ______ $4.85 ______

Rewrite the amount of money in standard form.	Rewrite the amount of money in standard form.
one and seventy-three hundredths __________	seven and six-hundredths __________

Language Practice: Similes

Similes are a way of comparing two items using the words "like" or "as."

Example: *His voice is as clear as a bell.*
Clear as a bell is the simile.
It means the man's words are easy to understand.

Complete each simile with the correct word or phrase.

bear	cats and dogs	China shop	doorpost	grass	honey	mouse

1. Grandpa is as deaf as a ______________________________!
2. Faith is like a bull in a ______________________________.
3. Maxwell's eyes are as green as the ______________________________.
4. Umi and Mac are always fighting like ______________________________.
5. Natasha is as hungry as a ______________________________.
6. Kono is as quiet as a ______________________________.
7. Webb is as sweet as ______________________________.

Name

Math Practice: Multiplication

Multiply.	Multiply.	Multiply.
14 x 2 23 x 1	99 x 0 31 x 3	42 x 2 11 x 9

Rewrite the problem vertically and then solve.	Rewrite the problem vertically and then solve.
12 x 4 = ______	10 x 6 = ______

Language Practice: Homographs

Homographs are words that have the same spelling but have different meanings.

Example: The *ball* is round.
Cinderella went to the *ball*.

Read each clue. Complete the crossword puzzle.

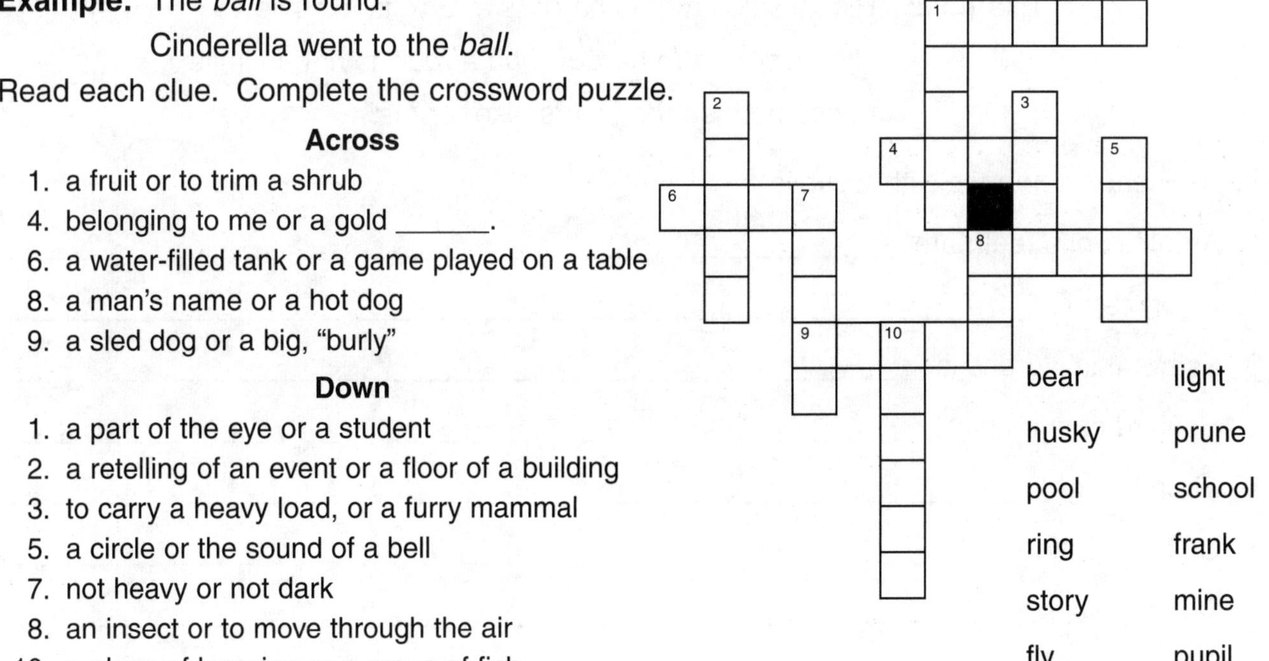

bear
light
husky
prune
pool
school
ring
frank
story
mine
fly
pupil

Across

1. a fruit or to trim a shrub
4. belonging to me or a gold ______.
6. a water-filled tank or a game played on a table
8. a man's name or a hot dog
9. a sled dog or a big, "burly"

Down

1. a part of the eye or a student
2. a retelling of an event or a floor of a building
3. to carry a heavy load, or a furry mammal
5. a circle or the sound of a bell
7. not heavy or not dark
8. an insect or to move through the air
10. a place of learning or a group of fish

Name ______________________ Practice 164

Math Practice: Metric Measurement

Rename each number.	Rename each number.	Rename each number.
300 cm = _______ m 500 cm = _______ m	100 cm = _______ m 200 cm = _______ m	800 cm = _______ m 600 cm = _______ sm

Write what you would use (cm or m) to measure a ladybug.	Write what you would use (cm or m) to measure a giraffe.
 ______	 ______

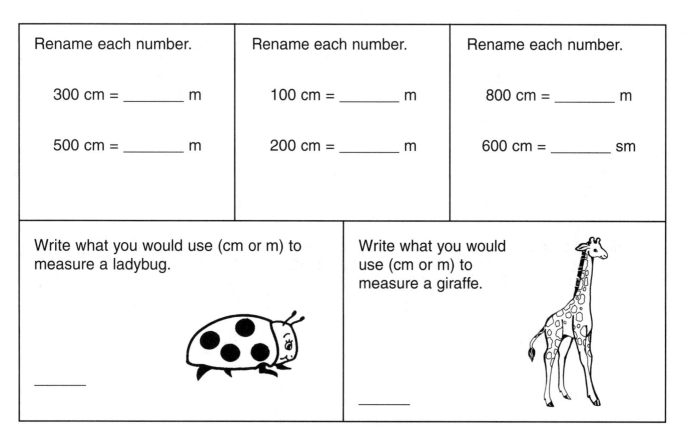

Language Practice: Similes

Similes are a way of comparing two items using the words "like" or "as."

Example: "His muscles are as hard *as a rock*" is a simile.
"His muscles are harder *than a rock*" is not a simile.
It does not use the words "like" or "as."

Complete each sentence with a simile.

1. An alligator's teeth are______________________________.
2. A lion can run ______________________________.
3. Esmeralda's dress is ______________________________.
4. Howard can jump ______________________________.
5. Ebony sings______________________________.
6. Colby wrestles______________________________.
7. Tabitha plays the piano ______________________________.
8. Walton and Reginald are______________________________.

Name ______________________ Practice 165

Math Practice: Multiplication

Multiply.	Multiply.	Multiply.
22 x 3 19 x 1	30 x 2 48 x 0	14 x 2 10 x 9

Write the missing factors.	Write the missing factors.
10 x ______ = 20	11 x ______ = 66
4 x ______ = 20	12 x ______ = 36

Language Practice: *Compound Sentence*

Joining two or more sentences together with a conjunction makes a *compound sentence.*

Example: Angelo read the newspaper. Angelo read the magazine.
Compound sentence: Angelo read the newspaper and the magazine.

Rewrite each pair of sentences as one compound sentence. Use the conjunctions in the box.

but	nor	so	yet

1. Raine wanted to go shopping. Raine didn't have any money.

____

2. I bought new soccer shoes. I have not joined a soccer team.

____

3. Dan fixed the flat tire. Henry rode the bike home.

____

4. Petra does not like cats. Petra does not like dogs.

____

Name ______________________________ Practice 166

Math Practice: Multiplication

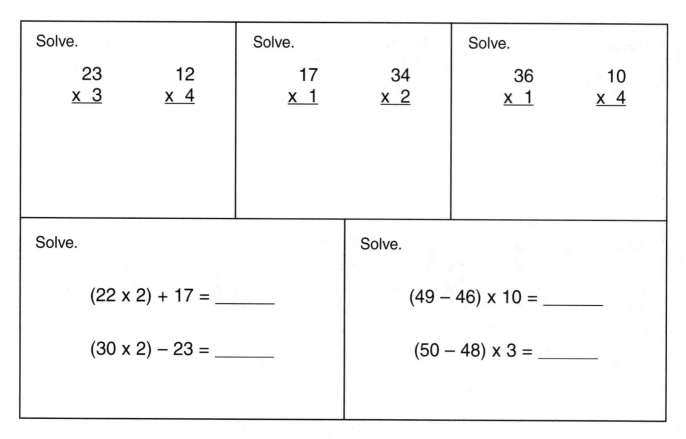

Solve.	Solve.	Solve.
23 x 3 12 x 4	17 x 1 34 x 2	36 x 1 10 x 4

Solve.	Solve.
(22 x 2) + 17 = ______	(49 – 46) x 10 = ______
(30 x 2) – 23 = ______	(50 – 48) x 3 = ______

Language Practice: Comprehension

The Arctic Region

People are often surprised at how many different animals live in the Arctic Region. That is because the Arctic, located at the North Pole, is one of the coldest regions on Earth. Reindeer and caribou roam the Arctic in large herds. Bears, foxes and hares also live there.

1. Where is the Arctic Region?______________________________

2. Why is it surprising that animals live there?______________________________

   ____

3. Which animals roam the Arctic Region in herds? ______________________________

   ____

Name ______________________________ Practice 167

Math Practice: Multiplication

Multiply and add. (36 x 3) + (48 x 7) = ? ________	Multiply and add. (65 x 3) + (2 x 69) = ? ________	Multiply and add. (67 x 5) + (94 x 7) = ? ________

Solve. Milton's car can travel 82 miles on one gallon of gas. His car holds 7 gallons. How many miles can Milton travel? Milton can travel ______ miles.	Solve. Josefina has 158 special coins. Each coin is worth $5.00. What is the value of Josefina's collection? The value of the collection is ______________.

Language Practice: Possessive Pronouns

A *possessive pronoun* shows ownership. An *'s* is not added to the end of the pronoun.

Example: Robert's book. It is *his*.
The possessive pronoun is *his*.
It takes the place of the possessive noun *Robert's*.

Read each sentence and underline the possessive noun. Write the correct possessive pronoun on the line.

Possessive Pronouns:	mine	yours	hers	his	its	our	their	whose

Example: The new computer is *Jamila's*. *hers*

1. The soccer balls are Kevin's. ______________
2. The locker is Mimi's. ______________
3. We picked the fruit from Mr. and Mrs. Padilla's trees. ______________
4. The cardboard dog house is Buster's home. ______________
5. This is my family's photo album. ______________

Name ______________________________________ Practice 168

Math Practice: Multiplication

Multiply.	Multiply.	Multiply.
304 x 2 441 x 2	203 x 3 410 x 2	101 x 8 222 x 4

Solve.	Solve.
Harper has 4 popsicle sticks. Jeff has 12 times as many popsicle sticks as Harper. How many popsicle sticks does Jeff have? Jeff has ______ popsicle sticks.	Raine climbed 11 stairs in a minute. How many stairs can Raine climb in 9 minutes? Raine can climb ______ stairs.

Language Practice: Comprehension

A *fact* is a true statement that can be backed up by research. An *opinion* expresses how a person feels about a topic.

Examples: *Fact* → Wolves are the largest members of the canine family.

Opinion → Wolves should be kept as house pets.

Read the paragraph. Underline the sentences that are opinions.

Wolves

Wolves live in large groups called "packs." Each pack has between 8 and 15 members. Packs are a great way for all animals to live. Wolves will eat just about any animal that they can catch. It is too bad the wolves will eat bunnies and sheep. Wolves can run for hours at speeds as fast as 25 miles an hour. When wolves in a pack see a prey, they can chase the prey until it is exhausted. A wolf can eat as much as 30 pounds of meat in one meal. Then the wolf will not eat again for weeks.

Name ______________________ Practice 169

Math Practice: Multiplication

Group the factors another way. Solve. $4 \times (6 \times 3)$	Group the factors another way. Solve. $5 \times (2 \times 6)$	Group the factors another way. Solve. $7 \times (4 \times 4)$

Write the missing factors and products.	Write the missing factors and products.
3 x 6 = ______ x 2 = ______	2 x 5 = ______ x 8 = ______
4 x 0 = ______ x 9 = ______	4 x 5 = ______ x 3 = ______

Language Practice: Word Categories

Write each word in the correct category. Some of the words can belong in more than one category. Use each word only one time.

collection	day	drawing	flash	glass	moon	night	oil
paint	pane	picture	porthole	sketch	stained	sun	

Window	Art	Light
1.______	1.______	1.______
2.______	2.______	2.______
3.______	3.______	3.______
4.______	4.______	4.______
5.______	5.______	5.______

Name

Math Practice: Multiplication

Multiply. 81 x 2	Multiply. 16 x 3	Multiply. 15 x 2
Solve. 17 x 3	Solve. 14 x 4	

Language Practice: Acronyms

An *acronym* is formed from the first (or first few) letters of words in a phase. The acronym is written in all capital letters. No periods are used.

Example: SCUBA **S**elf **c**ontained **u**nderwater **b**reathing **a**pparatus

Read each sentence. Underline the words that can be written as an acronym. Write the acronym on the line.

1. When addressing an envelope, be sure to include the Zone Improvement Place code. ______________
2. How much Random Access Memory does the computer have? ______________
3. I forgot my Personal Identification Number! ______________
4. My mother belongs to the National Organization for Women. ______________
5. For our spring vacation, we went to visit the Experimental Prototype Community of Tomorrow. ______________
6. Mr. Givens has information on the Disk Operating System. ______________
7. Most of the new computers have Read Only Memory. ______________

Name ______ Practice 171

Math Practice: Multiplication

Multiply.	Multiply.	Multiply.
534 x 2	229 x 3	482 x 2

Choose the operation.	Choose the operation.
+ − x	+ − x
Baxter has 8 pockets. In each pocket there are 6 pennies. How many pennies does Baxter have in all?	Taylor had 39 red marbles and 27 blue marbles. How many marbles does Taylor have in all?
__________ pennies	__________ marbles

Language Practice: Questioning Pronouns

Questioning pronouns ask questions. *What*, *who*, *which*, and *whom* are questioning pronouns.

Complete each sentence with the correct questioning pronoun.

1. ____________________ went to the practice last night?
2. ____________________ did the concert master do during the rehearsal?
3. ____________________ instrument would you like to play?
4. To ____________________ does this instrument's case belong?
5. ____________________ time does the concert begin?
6. ____________________ is the guest conductor?
7. ____________________ will the musicians wear?
8. ____________________ piece of music do you like the best?
9. For ____________________ are you saving these seats?
10. ____________________ would like to get refreshments?

Name

Math Practice: Multiplication

Multiply.	Multiply.	Multiply.
2,345 x 2	3,250 x 2	4,021 x 4

Round each number to the nearest ten and then multiply.

8 →
 x 12 → ____

15 →
 x 14 → ____

Round each number to the nearest ten and then multiply.

11 →
 x 9 → ____

13 →
 x 13 → ____

Language Practice: Dictionary Skills

Each page of a dictionary has two guide words at the top of the page. The guide words make it easier to find a specific word.

Write each word on the correct page of the dictionary.

fisherman	bronze	diva	man	claw
bumblebee	look	cactus	duck	minus
democratic	employer	gage	lounge	indigo

brocade — **dispute**	**dissolve** — **goat**	**iguana** — **mirror**
____	____	____
____	____	____
____	____	____
____	____	____
____	____	____

Name ____ Practice 173

Math Practice: Customary Measurement

Write the number of inches.	Write the number of feet in each yard.	Write the number of inches in each yard.
1 foot = ______ inches	1 yard = ______ feet	1 yard = ______ inches
2 feet = ______ inches	2 yards = ______ feet	2 yards = ______ inches

Complete the chart.

Inches	6"		18"		30"	
Feet		1'		2'		3'

Complete the chart.

Feet	1'	2'	3'	4'		
Yards	$\frac{1}{3}$			$\frac{11}{3}$	$\frac{12}{3}$	2

Language Practice: Metaphors

Metaphors describe a noun (person, place, or thing), or describe an action (verb), without using the words "like" or "as."

Example: She has a *computer for a brain.*
Computer for a brain is the metaphor.
It means she is really smart at doing something.

Underline the metaphor in each sentence.

1. Lyndon runs faster than a gazelle.
2. Jeffrey's hair is straighter than a ruler.
3. Ramiro plays chess better than a chess master.
4. Ms. Benton was buried under a mountain of paperwork.
5. Katherine is a fountain of information.
6. Hope thinks she is better than sliced bread!
7. Norman's bark is worse than his bite.
8. Orson's stomach was a bottomless pit.

Name ______________________________ Practice 174

Math Practice: Customary Measurement

Rename the measurement.	Rename the measurement.	Rename the measurement.
18 inches ____ foot ____ inches	24 inches ____ feet ____ inches	42 inches ____ feet ____ inches

Use division to solve the problem.	Use division to solve the problem.
$\frac{1}{3}$ of 24 inches 24 ÷ 3 = ______ $\frac{1}{3}$ of 24 inches = ______ inches	$\frac{1}{5}$ of 40 inches 40 ÷ 5 = ______ $\frac{1}{5}$ of 40 inches = ______ inches

Language Practice: Metaphors

Metaphors describe a noun (person, place or thing), or describe an action (verb), without using the words "*like*" or "*as.*"

Example: *An iceberg is warmer* than my room!
An iceberg is warmer is the metaphor.
It means my room is really cold.

Find the metaphor in each sentence. Write the meaning of the metaphor on the line.

Example: Meredith dug a hole *all the way to China.*
Meredith dug an extremely deep hole.

1. A snail runs faster than Yolanda.

____

2. Jerrell's face turned greener than the grass.

____

3. I can see the wheels turning in Marvel's mind.

____

Name ______________________

Math Practice: Multiplying by Multiples of Ten

Multiply.	Multiply.	Multiply.
10 x 100 = ______	30 x 30 = ______	10 x 50 = ______
20 x 10 = ______	40 x 10 = ______	10 x 600 = ______

Solve.	**Solve.**
Cyril has 20 dimes. How much money does Cyril have?	Eleni has 10 half dollars. How much money does Eleni have in all?
Cyril has __________ in all.	Eleni has __________ in all.

Language Practice: Proofreading

Proofreading is rereading a piece of writing, finding the mistakes, and then correcting them. Read the paragraph and circle the mistakes. Write the word correctly on the line.

The Trampoline

As a young boy growing up in the 1920s, Geroge Nissen waz ______________
fascinated by the "bouncing tables" used in circuses and bye ______________
acrobats. ______________

while in high school, George Nissen set about designing a ______________
"bouncing table" that wuld be safe, easy to use, and easy to store. ______________
he went to town dumps and scrounged around four springs, old ______________
rubber inner tubes, and scrap iron to use inn building different ______________
models of a "bouncing table." ______________

he later named his perfected invention "trampoline" from the ______________
spanish word *trampolin,* which meant "diving board." ______________

Name ______

Practice 176

Math Practice: Multiplying by Multiples of Ten

Multiply.	Multiply.	Multiply.
20 x 1,000 20 x 100	30 x 10 30 x 100	50 x 10 50 x 1,000

Solve.	Solve.
There are 10 ant farms with 100 ants on each farm. How many ants are there in all?	There are 20 bags of seeds with 1,000 seeds in each bag. How many seeds are there in all?
There are ______ ants in all.	There are ______ seeds in all.

Language Practice: Idioms

Idioms are phrases that have special meanings. Read each sentence and underline the phrase that can be rewritten with an idiom. Write the letter of the idiomatic phrase on the line.

A. swallowed the story hook, line, and sinker	D. works for chicken feed
B. has quite a sweet tooth	E. blowing his own horn
C. put her foot down	F. was tickled pink

Example: A Christy **believed** Uncle Roscoe's fishing story.

1. _____ Howard is always talking about himself.

2. _____ Cullen's mother finally told him "no."

3. _____ Justin can not resist eating candy.

4. _____ Elvira does not earn very much money but she loves the work.

5. _____ Carmine greatly enjoyed the singing telegram.

Name ______________________________ Practice 177

Math Practice: Multiplication

Multiply.	Multiply.	Multiply.
(2 x 6) x 9 = ______ (3 x 5) x 5 = ______	(10 x 2) x 5 = ______ (11 x 4) x 3 = ______	(6 x 1) x 6 = ______ (0 x 100) x 1,000 = ______

Write the problem and then solve it.	Write the problem and then solve it.
Neil has 17 books. Joanne has twice as many books than Neil. How many books does Joanne have? Joanne has ______ books.	John has $0.91. Bettina has three times the amount of money that John has. How much money does Bettina have? Bettina has ___________ .

Language Practice: Demonstrative (Pointing) Pronouns

Demonstrative pronouns point out, or identify, a noun and indicate the specific item that a person is talking about. The demonstrative pronouns are *that*, *these*, *this*, and *those*.

Read each sentence and underline the words that can be replaced with a demonstrative pronoun. Write the demonstrative pronoun on the line.

Example: *The roses are beautiful!* These

1. What happened to the red car? ______________
2. Who cleaned all of the windows? ______________
3. The purple shoes are mine! ______________
4. The bedroom is a mess! ______________
5. Who ate all of the walnuts? ______________
6. The painting is a masterpiece. ______________
7. Have you ever seen a dancing monkey before? ______________
8. The eyeglasses belong to Carmella. ______________

Name

Practice 178

Math Practice: Dividing by 10

Divide.	Divide.	Divide.
$10\overline{)30}$ $10\overline{)20}$	$10\overline{)40}$ $10\overline{)60}$	$10\overline{)70}$ $10\overline{)80}$

Solve.	Solve.
Check the answer by multiplying the divisor by the quotient.	Check Check the answer by multiplying the divisor by the quotient.
$10\overline{)10}$	$10\overline{)50}$

Language Practice: Reading Temperature

Temperature is measured with a thermometer. A *Fahrenheit* or *Celsius* degree is the form in which temperature is reported.

Read the facts below and answer *yes* or *no* to the questions that follow.

98.6° F ⟶ is normal body temperature.
32° F ⟶ is the temperature at which water freezes.
80° F ⟶ is an average summer temperature in some places.
212° F ⟶ is the temperature at which water boils.
22° F ⟶ is an average winter temperature in some places.

1. If a child had a temperature of 100.3˚, would that be considered a fever? ________
2. If it is 32° outside, should you wear a jacket? ________
3. Could a child go swimming outdoors if it is 40˚ outside? ________
4. Would hot chocolate be boiling if it were 100˚? ________
5. Could it be 90˚ in the summer? ________

Name ______________________ Practice 179

Math Practice: Line Segments

A *line segment* is part of a line. Write the name of the line segment two different ways.

A B

______ and ______

A *line segment* is part of a line. Write the name of the line segment two different ways.

D E

______ and ______

A *line segment* is part of a line. Write the name of the line segment two different ways.

M N

______ and ______

A *line* is straight and continues on forever in both directions. Write the name of the line two different ways.

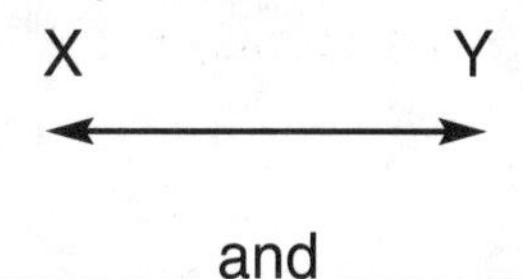

______ and ______

Write the name of the line two different ways.

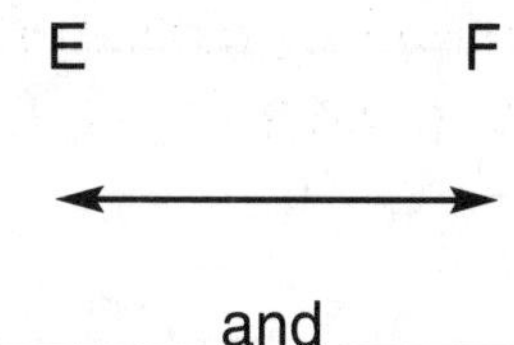

______ and ______

Language Practice: Irregular Verbs

Read each verb. Write *present* or *past* on the line provided.

1. blow ______________
2. blew ______________
3. come ______________
4. came ______________
5. did ______________
6. do ______________
7. fight ______________
8. fought ______________
9. fly ______________
10. flew ______________
11. sang ______________
12. sing ______________
13. began ______________
14. begin ______________
15. made ______________
16. make ______________
17. give ______________
18. gave ______________

Underline the verb. Write the correct form of the verb on the line.

1. He blow out the candles. ______________________
2. I make the skirt yesterday. ______________________
3. Gabriel fly to Miami. ______________________
4. She give the gift to me. ______________________
5. Who sing at the game? ______________________

Name _______________ Practice 180

Math Practice: Line Segments

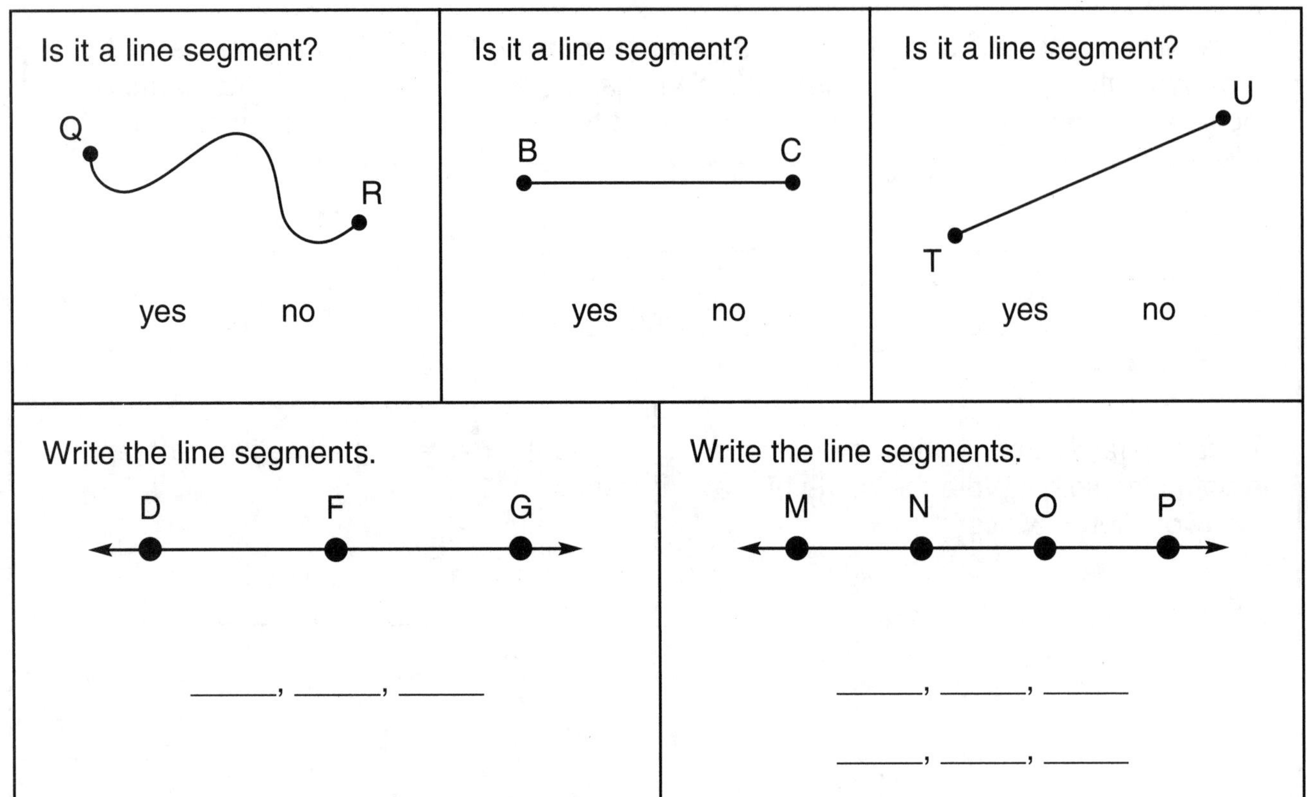
Is it a line segment?
Q
R
yes no
Is it a line segment?
B C
yes no
Is it a line segment?
U
T
yes no
Write the line segments.
D F G
____, ____, ____
Write the line segments.
M N O P
____, ____, ____
____, ____, ____

Language Practice: Irregular Verbs

Complete each sentence with the correct verb tense.

1. (fly, flew) The birds ________________ south each winter.
2. (sing, sang) We ________________ four songs at church yesterday.
3. (grow, grew) The pine tree ________________ three feet last year.
4. (choose, chose) Which toy did you ________________ ?
5. (give, gave) Who ________________ the gift to Mr. Gallagher?
6. (make, made) Did you ________________ your bed this morning?
7. (tell, told) Stanley will ________________ a ghost story.
8. (fight, fought) Did any of your relatives ________________ in the war?
9. (blow, blew) The wind ________________ the wind chimes.
10. (begin, began) The play ________________ two hours ago.

Name ______ Practice 181

Math Practice: Angles

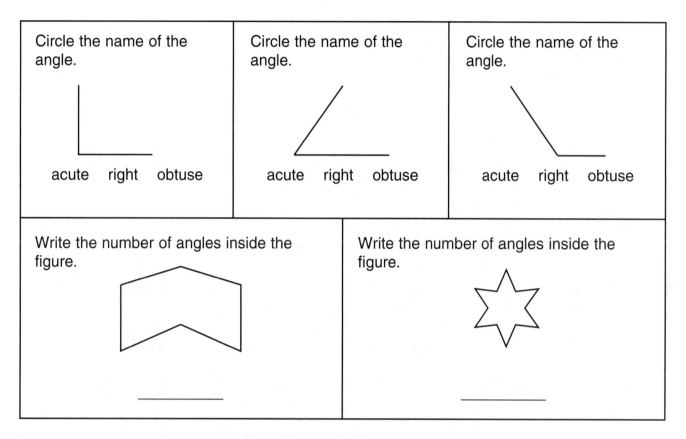

Circle the name of the angle.	Circle the name of the angle.	Circle the name of the angle.
acute right obtuse	acute right obtuse	acute right obtuse

Write the number of angles inside the figure.	Write the number of angles inside the figure.
______	______

Language Practice: Irregular Verbs

Read each sentence and circle the verb. Write *present* or *past* on the line provided.

1. Joey flew to England. ______
2. Jennifer threw ten strikeouts. ______
3. Benjamin brought the birthday cake. ______
4. Did you remember to take out the garbage? ______
5. Rick sold twenty boxes of chocolate. ______
6. The tournament has begun. ______
7. Which shirt is Chelsea wearing? ______
8. Who made the delicious pancakes? ______
9. The green plant grows in the sunshine. ______
10. Speak to the children about the mess. ______

Name ______________________ Practice 182

Math Practice: Plane Figures

Write the name of the plane figure.	Write the name of the plane figure.	Write the name of the plane figure.
______________	______________	______________

Draw the plane figures.	Draw the plane figures.
diamond rhombus hexagon	trapezoid oval circle

Language Practice: Analogies

Analogies show a relationship between two things.

Example: *Typewriter is to writer as pencil is to student.*
This analogy shows a specific object a person would use.

Complete each analogy.

chef	gardener	nurse	painter	pilot	teacher

1. Camera is to photographer as chalk is to ______________________.
2. Stethoscope is to doctor as plane is to ______________________.
3. Gavel is to judge as rake is to ______________________.
4. Telephone is to operator as food is to ______________________.
5. Calculator is to accountant as pot is to ______________________.
6. Music is to singer as brush is to ______________________.

Name ______________________________ Practice 183

Math Practice: Congruence

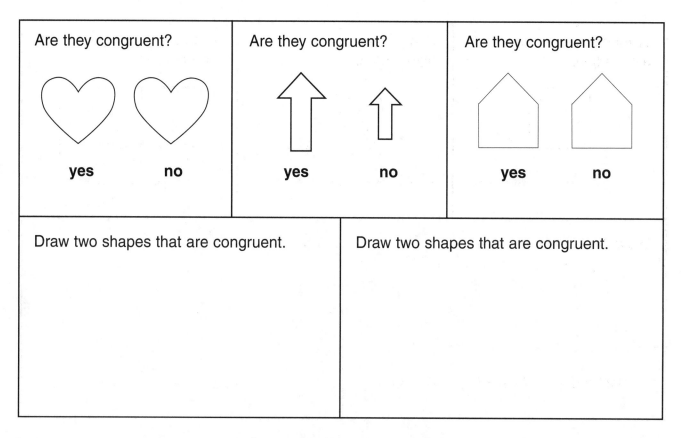

Are they congruent?	Are they congruent?	Are they congruent?
yes no	yes no	yes no

Draw two shapes that are congruent.	Draw two shapes that are congruent.

Language Practice: Analogies

Analogies show a relationship between two things.

Example: *Cat is to meow as turkey is to gobble.*
This analogy is comparing the action of two animals.

bark	fly	gallop	growl	hoot	hop

Complete each analogy.

1. Fish is to swim as bird is to ______________________.
2. Snake is to crawl as frog is to ______________________.
3. Kangaroo is to jump as horse is to ______________________.
4. Mouse is to squeak as dog is to ______________________.
5. Bird is to cheep as owl is to ______________________.
6. Crow is to caw as bear is to ______________________.

Complete the analogy.

Lion is to ______________ as monkey is to ______________.

Name ________________________________ Practice 184

Math Practice: Symmetry

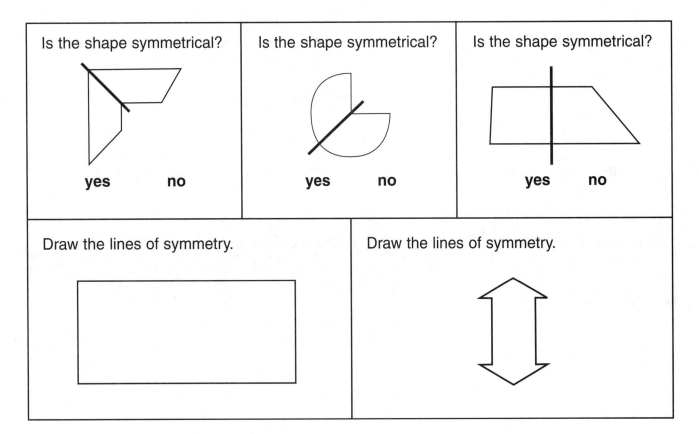

Is the shape symmetrical?	Is the shape symmetrical?	Is the shape symmetrical?
yes no	yes no	yes no

Draw the lines of symmetry.	Draw the lines of symmetry.

Language Practice: Analogies

Analogies show a relationship between two things.

Example: *Small is to little as chilly is to cold.*
This analogy is comparing synonyms.

Complete each analogy.

caps	couch	icy	joyful	rehearse	windy

1. Big is to huge as blustery is to ________________.
2. Hot is to burning as cold is to ________________.
3. Jump is to hop as practice is to ________________.
4. Chair is to seat as sofa is to ________________.
5. Sneakers are to tennis shoes as hats are to ________________.
6. Afraid is to scared as happy is to ________________.

Complete the analogy.

Nest is to ________________ as cave is to ________________.

Name ______________________________ Practice 185

Math Practice: Solid Figures

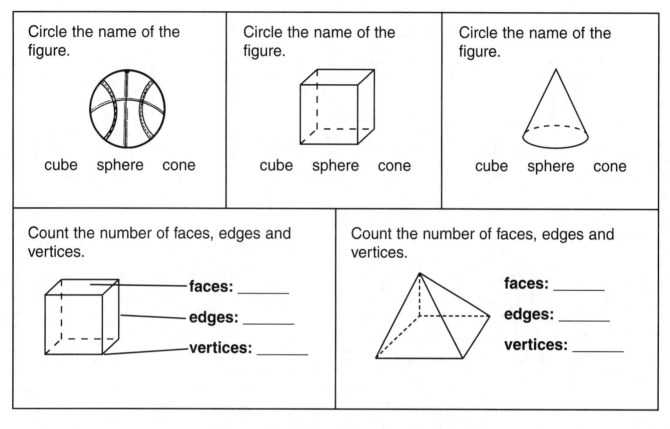

<table>
<tr>
<td>Circle the name of the figure.

cube sphere cone</td>
<td>Circle the name of the figure.
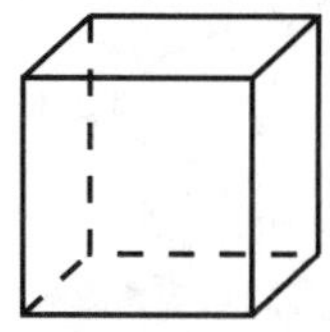
cube sphere cone</td>
<td>Circle the name of the figure.
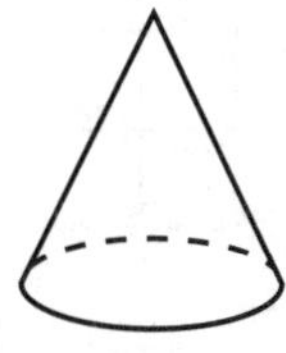
cube sphere cone</td>
</tr>
<tr>
<td>Count the number of faces, edges and vertices.
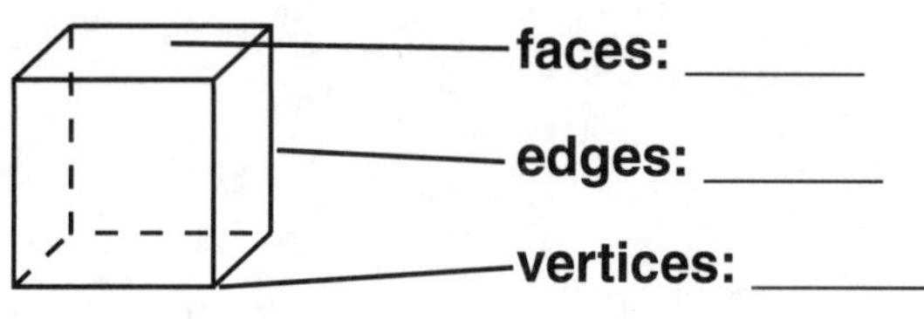
faces: ______
edges: ______
vertices: ______</td>
<td colspan="2">Count the number of faces, edges and vertices.
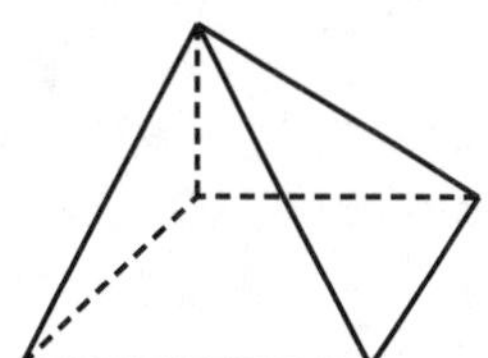
faces: ______
edges: ______
vertices: ______</td>
</tr>
</table>

Language Practice: Analogies

Analogies show a relationship between two things.

Example: *Toe is to foot as inch is to yard.*
This analogy is comparing part of an object to the whole object.

Complete each analogy.

beach	hand	music	notepad	pizza	year

1. Crayon is to box as paper is to ______________________________.
2. Star is to sky as sand is to ______________________________.
3. Letter is to alphabet as note is to ______________________________.
4. Day is to month as month is to ______________________________.
5. Eye is to face as finger is to ______________________________.

Complete the analogy.

Feather is to ____________________ as leaf is to ____________________.

Name ______________________________ Practice 186

Math Practice: Volume

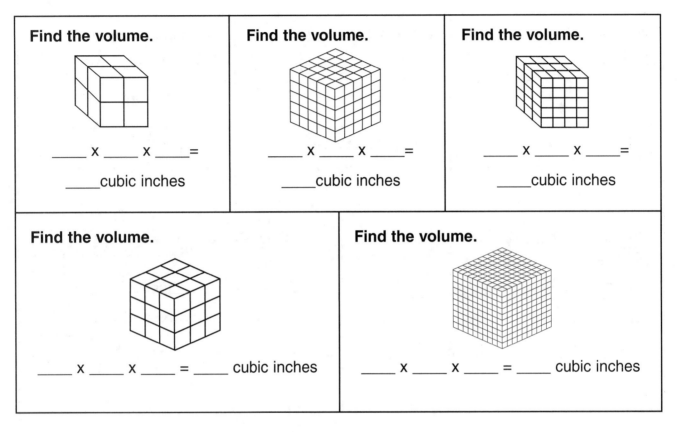

Find the volume.	Find the volume.	Find the volume.
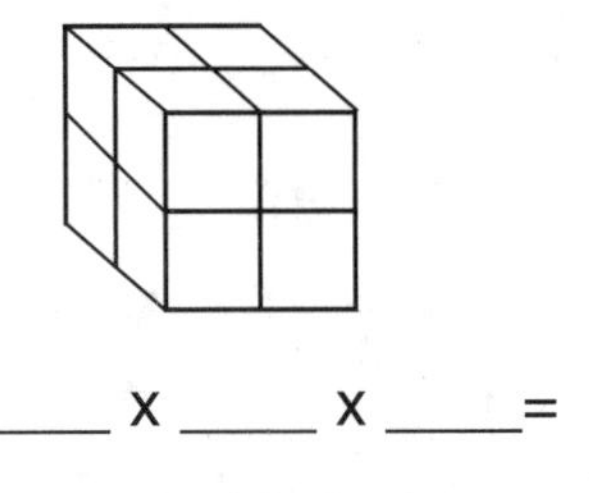 ____ x ____ x ____= ____cubic inches	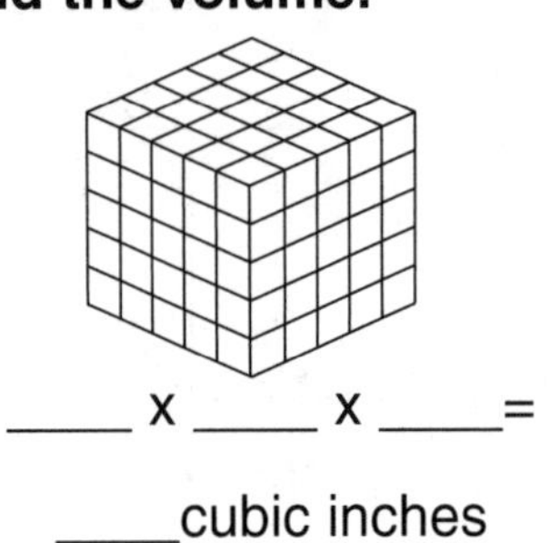 ____ x ____ x ____= ____cubic inches	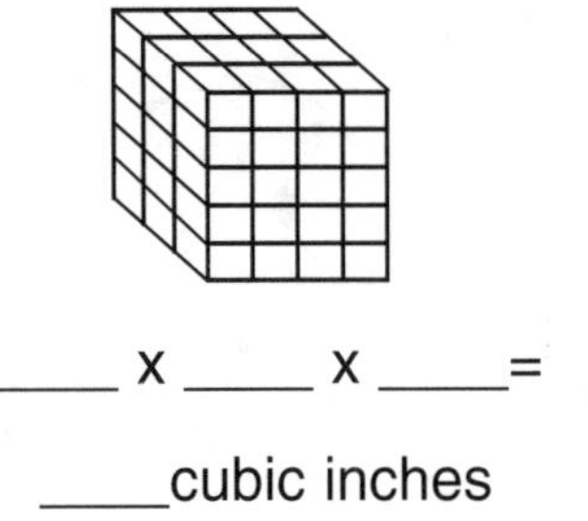 ____ x ____ x ____= ____cubic inches

Find the volume.	Find the volume.
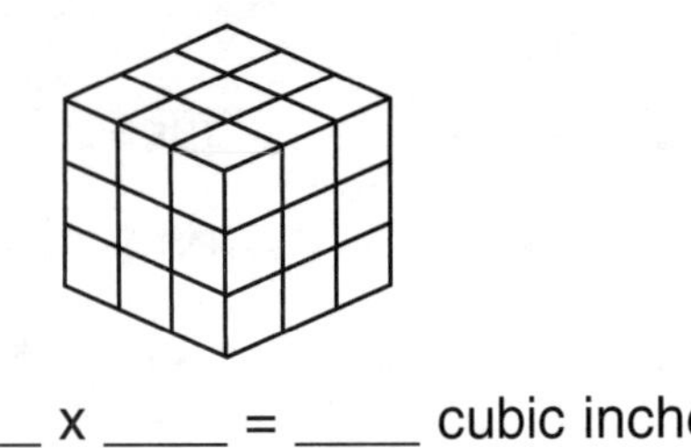 ____ x ____ x ____ = ____ cubic inches	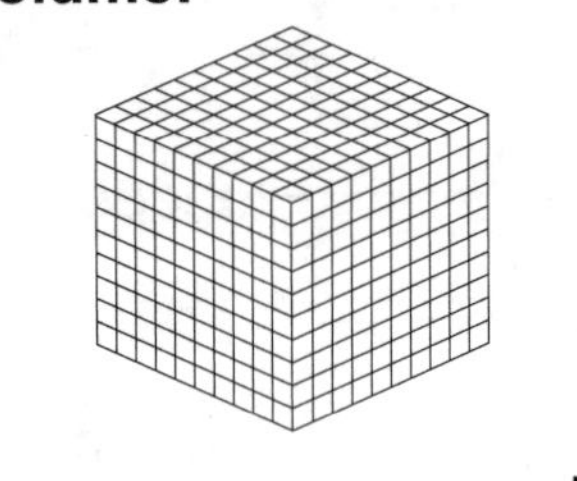 ____ x ____ x ____ = ____ cubic inches

Language Practice: Analogies

Analogies show a relationship between two things.

Example: *Sharp is to dull as light is to dark.*
This analogy is comparing antonyms.

Complete each analogy.

little	neat	slow	straight	wet	white

1. Up is to down as big is to ______________________________.
2. Awake is to sleep as dry is to ______________________________.
3. Loud is to quiet as messy is to ______________________________.
4. Hot is to cold as black is to ______________________________.
5. Tall is to short as curly is to______________________________.
6. Run is to walk as fast is to ______________________________.

Complete the analogy.

Hard is to ____________________ as lost is to ____________________.

Name

Math Practice: Ordered Pairs

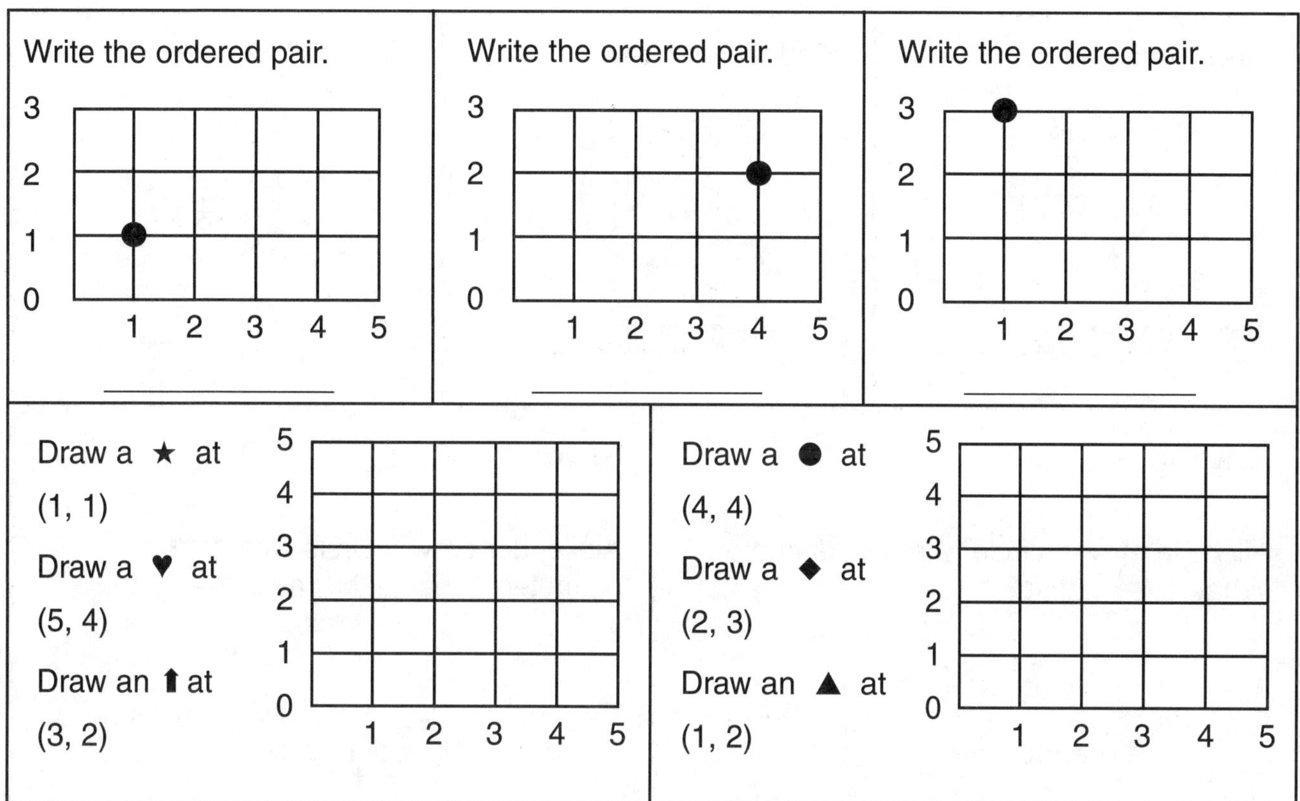
Write the ordered pair.
Write the ordered pair.
Write the ordered pair.
3
2
1
0
1 2 3 4 5
Draw a ★ at (1, 1)
Draw a ♥ at (5, 4)
Draw an ⬆ at (3, 2)
Draw a ● at (4, 4)
Draw a ◆ at (2, 3)
Draw an ▲ at (1, 2)
5
4
3
2
1
0

Language Practice: Sequencing

Write the steps for making a peanut butter and jelly sandwich. (You may not need all 10 steps.)

Step 1: ____________________

Step 2: ____________________

Step 3: ____________________

Step 4: ____________________

Step 5: ____________________

Step 6: ____________________

Step 7: ____________________

Step 8: ____________________

Step 9: ____________________

Step 10: ____________________

Math Practice: Circles

Find the diameter.

2"

The diameter is ______.

Find the diameter.

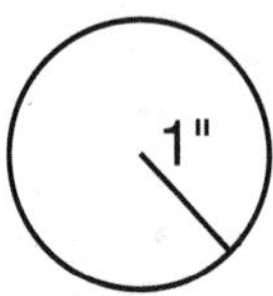

The diameter is ______.

Find the diameter.

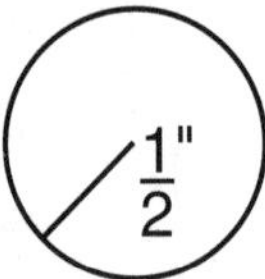

The diameter is ______.

Solve.

Michelle drew a circle with a 4" diameter. What is the radius?

The radius is ______.

Solve.

Alexander drew a circle with a 12" diameter. What is the radius?

The radius is ______.

Language Practice: Analogies

Analogies show a relationship between two things.

Example: *Chair is to sit as bed is to sleep.*
This analogy shows how items are used.

Complete each analogy.

climb	cut	drink	drive	sweep	watch

1. Glasses are to see as knife is to ________________________.
2. Oven is to bake as television is to ________________________.
3. Book is to read as broom is to ________________________.
4. Bike is to ride as ladder is to ________________________.
5. Piano is to play as car is to ________________________.
6. Radio is to listen as water is to ________________________.

Complete the analogy.

Pencil is to ____________________ as food is to ____________________.

Name ______ Practice 189

Math Practice: Multiplication

Estimate the product: Multiply the front numbers. Write zeros for the other numbers and multiply.	Estimate the product: Multiply the front numbers. Write zeros for the other numbers and multiply.	Estimate the product: Multiply the front numbers. Write zeros for the other numbers and multiply.
245 x 3 = ________	216 x 4 = ________	309 x 2 = ________

Solve.	Solve.
Each box contains about 323 candies. There are 5 boxes. About how many candies are there?	About 128 people can sit on each row of seats. There are 9 rows of seats. About how many people are there?
There are about __________ candies.	There are about __________ people.

Language Practice: Prefixes

Prefixes are added to the beginning of a word. Prefixes change the meaning of the word.

mid = middle	*mini* = small	*multi* = many

Write the meaning of each word on the line provided.

1. midair: ______________________
2. midbrain: ______________________
3. midnight: ______________________
4. midpoint: ______________________
5. midsummer: ______________________
6. midtown: ______________________
7. midweek: ______________________
8. midyear: ______________________
9. minibike: ______________________
10. minicar: ______________________
11. miniskirt: ______________________
12. multicolored: ______________________
13. multipurpose: ______________________
14. multivitamin: ______________________

Bonus: Write the word that means "many languages." ______________________

Name ____________________ Practice 190

Math Practice: Division with Remainders

Divide. Write the remainder.	Divide. Write the remainder.	Divide. Write the remainder.
$3\overline{)16}$	$4\overline{)11}$	$5\overline{)19}$
The remainder is ______.	The remainder is ______.	The remainder is ______.

Solve.	Solve.
Cal had 100 cows and 8 pastures. He puts an equal number of cows in each pasture. How many cows are left over?	Sal had 42 horses and 9 barns. She put an equal number of horses in each barn. How many horses are left over?
There are ______ cows left.	There are ______ horse left.

Language Practice: Prefixes

anti = against   *dis* = not

Write the meaning of each word on the line.

1. antiwar: ____________________
2. antimusic: ____________________
3. antitoxin: ____________________
4. antifreeze: ____________________
5. antipollution: ____________________
6. antipoverty: ____________________
7. antitrust: ____________________
8. distrust: ____________________
9. dislike: ____________________
10. disassemble: ____________________
11. disbelieve: ____________________
12. discomfort: ____________________
13. disconnect: ____________________
14. disorder: ____________________

Bonus: Write the word that means "not tasty." ____________________

Name

Practice 191

Math Practice: Division with Remainders

Divide. Write the remainder.	Divide. Write the remainder.	Divide. Write the remainder.
$6\overline{)81}$	$2\overline{)5}$	$8\overline{)75}$
R = ______	R = ______	R = ______

Solve.	Solve.
Herman has 75 pairs of socks divided equally among 9 drawers. How many socks are in each drawer?	Shelly has 83 belts divided equally among 9 hooks. How many belts are on each hook?
There are ______ socks in each drawer.	There are ______ belts on each hook.
The remainder is ______.	The remainder is ______.

Language Practice: Commas

Commas are used before a conjunction.
Commonly used conjunctions are: *and*, *or*, *but*, and *for*.

Example: Presley played in the yard, *and* swung on the swing.

Read each sentence. Write the missing comma.

1. He is always late for school in trouble or sitting in the principal's office.
2. Charlie would like to play the game but he has to go to the track meet.
3. Leeza enjoys running but she is not able to run long distances.
4. Did you forget your homework or did Brandy turn it in for you?

Write a sentence that uses a conjunction. Remember to use a comma.

____

____

____

____

Name ______________________ Practice 192

Math Practice: Division with Remainders

Divide. Write the remainder. $8\overline{)65}$ R = ______	Divide. Write the remainder. $9\overline{)27}$ R = ______	Divide. Write the remainder. $10\overline{)16}$ R = ______

Solve.	Solve.
Angela had 74 pictures. She put an equal number of pictures into 3 albums. How many pictures are in each album? There ______ are pictures in each album. The remainder is ______.	Andrew had 44 baseball cards. He put an equal number of cards onto 7 trading sheets. How many cards are on each trading sheet? There are ______ cards on each sheet. The remainder is ______.

Language Practice: Homographs

Homographs are words that have the same spelling but have different meanings.

Examples: The rooster's *crow* woke us up. The *crow* is in the field.

Write the homograph next to its definition.

date	fan	toast

1. ______________________ a wish for happiness
2. ______________________ something that moves the air
3. ______________________ the day, the month, and the year
4. ______________________ an admirer
5. ______________________ a type of fruit
6. ______________________ a slice of bread browned on both sides

Name ____ **Practice 193**

Math Practice: Division with Remainders

Divide. Write the remainder.	Divide. Write the remainder.	Divide. Write the remainder.
$3\overline{)157}$	$6\overline{)389}$	$4\overline{)58}$
R = ______	R = ______	R = ______

Solve. Check the answer by multiplying the quotient by the divisor and adding the remainder.	Solve. Check the answer by multiplying the quotient by the divisor and adding the remainder.
$9\overline{)154}$	$8\overline{)239}$

Language Practice: Their, They're, and There

Deciding which *their*, *they're*, or *there* to use can be confusing. Remember the following:

- **Their:** shows ownership.
  Example: *Their* dog is always chasing cats.
- **They're:** a contraction of *they* and *are*.
  Example: *They're* (they are) best friends.
- **There:** tells a location
  Example: The picnic is over *there*.

Read each sentence. Write the correct form of *there* on the line.

1. ____________________________ bikes are in the driveway.
2. Mom parked the car over ____________________________.
3. Every night they walk ____________________________ dogs.
4. ____________________________ coming to the celebration.

5. I thought I left my book ____________________________ .
6. ____________________________ is Steven!

Name ______________________________ Practice 194

Math Practice: Division with Remainders

Divide. Write the remainder. $5\overline{)171}$ R = ______	Divide. Write the remainder. $6\overline{)642}$ R = ______	Divide. Write the remainder. $5\overline{)236}$ R = ______

Solve. There are 189 candles divided equally among 8 boxes. How many candles are in each box? There are ______ candles in each box. There are ______ candles left over.	Solve. There are 583 matches divided equally among 6 boxes. How many matches are in each box? There are ______ matches in each box. There is ______ match left over.

Language Practice: Possessives

Possessives show "ownership." To make a noun possessive, add an **'s** to the end of it.

Example: *Phil's* cameras (The cameras belongs to Phil.)

Rewrite each phrase as a possessive phrase. The first one has already been done for you.

1. the hammer belongs to Amanda ______ *Amanda's hammer* ______
2. the television belongs to Hannah ______________________
3. the river in Yosemite ______________________
4. the mountains in Argentina ______________________
5. the speech of the President ______________________
6. the bone belongs to Baxter ______________________
7. the painting is by van Gogh ______________________
8. the banana belongs to the monkey ______________________

Name ______ **Practice 195**

Math Practice: Averages

Find the average. 19, 35 The average is ______ .	Find the average. 86, 28 The average is ______ .	Find the average. 55, 47 The average is ______ .

Solve. Warren bowling scores were 176, 194, and 149. What is Warren's bowling average? Warren's bowling average is ______ .	Solve. Gracie's bowling scores were 143, 138, and 112. What is Grace's bowling average? Grace's bowling average is ______ .

Language Practice: Possessive and Plural Nouns

A *possessive noun* shows ownership.

Example: The Johnsons' car is blue.

A *plural noun* means more than one.

Example: The Johnsons have a car.

Underline the possessive or plural noun. Write the possessive or plural on the line.

1. The Kramers have a big house. ____________________
2. The Kramers' house is next door. ____________________
3. Lizards live in under the rock. ____________________
4. The lizards' rocks are big and flat. ____________________
5. The computers are always crashing! ____________________
6. The computers' mouse pads are missing! ____________________
7. The telephones are brand new. ____________________
8. The telephones' chimes sound pretty. ____________________

Name

Practice 196

Math Practice: Multiplication

Multiply.	Multiply.	Multiply.
\$82.79 x 6	\$21.43 x 1	\$49.33 x 2

Solve.	Use the information to the left to solve the following problem.
The 4H Club held a bake sale and sold 230 cupcakes. Each cupcake sold for 10¢. How much money did the 4H club make?	The 4H Club spent \$3.14 buying the mixes and frosting. What is the 4H club's profit from the bake sale?
The 4H Club made ______ .	The profit is ______ .

Language Practice: Possessive Pronouns

A *possessive pronoun* shows ownership. An ***'s*** is not added to the end of the pronoun.

Example: Shirley's dog ⟶ Her dog

The *possessive pronoun* is *her.*

It takes the place of the possessive noun *Shirley's.*

Read each sentence and underline the possessive noun. Write the correct possessive pronoun on the line.

her	his	its	our	their

1. Raymond's cat is stuck in the tree. ______________
2. The bird's cage needs to be cleaned. ______________
3. My family's ranch has many heads of cattle. ______________
4. Lena's glasses are on top of her head. ______________
5. Tom's and Lily's homework is always late. ______________

Name ______________________________ Practice 197

Math Practice: Division

Divide.	Divide.	Divide.
$4\overline{)142}$	$6\overline{)731}$	$9\overline{)566}$

Solve.	Solve.
There are 858 people on the tour. How many 9-seat tour buses are needed?	How many pairs of $8 sunglasses can be bought with $138?
______ tour buses are needed.	______ pairs of sunglasses

Language Practice: More Possessive Pronouns

A *possessive pronoun* shows ownership. An 's is not added to the end of the pronoun.

Example: This book is *mine*. (It *belongs to me*.)
The possessive pronoun is *mine*.
It shows that I possess the book. It is mine.

The following are possessive pronouns. Use each in a sentence to show possession. Underline the possessive pronoun.

hers (belongs to her)	*yours* (belongs to you)
theirs (belongs to them)	*ours* (belongs to us)

1. ______________________________
2. ______________________________
3. ______________________________
4. ______________________________

Name

Practice 198

Math Practice: Division

Divide. $7\overline{)225}$	Divide. $1\overline{)491}$	Divide. $8\overline{)573}$

Solve.

The concert tickets cost $8 each. The choir has $825. How many tickets can they buy?

The choir club can buy ______ tickets.

Solve.

Each night a different number of people (653, 375, 491, 702) attend the concert. What is the average number of attendance?

The average number is ______.

Language Practice: Research Report

When writing a research report, it is important to use your own words.

Money

Example: Feathers, beads, stones, and shells were once used as money.
Instead of money, people used feathers, beads, stones, and shells.

Rewrite each sentence using your own words.

1. In Burma, their coins were called "flower silver" because of the flower design on each piece of silver.

   ____

2. In Mexico, cacao (chocolate) beans were used for money.

   ____

3. At one time, Ethiopians used bars of rock salt for money.

   ____

4. Coins were first made during the 17th century.

   ____

Name ____________________ Practice 199

Math Practice: Division

Divide.	Divide.	Divide.
$6\overline{)2,498}$	$9\overline{)2,546}$	$7\overline{)4,189}$

Solve.	Solve.
There are 6,731 fruity O's in 3 boxes. About how many fruity O's are in each box?	A camel drinks 9 gallons of water each minute. About how many minutes will it take for the camel to drink 8,822 gallons of water?
There are about ______ fruity O's.	It will take about ______ minutes.

Language Practice: Research Report

Read the paragraph. Answer each question with a complete sentence.

Paper Money

In China, people used heavy coins as money. Because people became tired of carrying the heavy coins, merchants began taking the coins and giving the customer a handwritten receipt in exchange. During the 11th century, the government began issuing printed receipts (paper money) with a fixed monetary value.

1. What did the Chinese people use as money? ______________________________
2. How did the idea for using paper money come about? ______________________________

____

Use the information from questions 1 and 2 to write a two-sentence summary about paper money.

____

____

Name ______________________________ Practice 200

Math Practice: Division

Divide.	Divide.	Divide.
$9\overline{)5{,}491}$	$7\overline{)5{,}276}$	$5\overline{)1{,}891}$

Solve.	Solve.
A farmer had 3,200 corn plants in his field. If each row yielded 80 plants, how many rows did the farmer have in his field? ____________	Each sheared sheep produces 7 pounds of wool. How many sheep were sheared to produce 1,540 pounds of wool? ____________

Language Practice: Proofreading

Proofreading is rereading a piece of writing, finding the mistakes, and then correcting them. Read the paragraph and circle the mistakes. Write the word correctly on the line.

United States Currency

at one time, the early settlers in Maryland and Virginia used tobacco leafs as a form of currency. The first paper u.s. dollar was known as the continental Currency bill. In 1837, a small bank in Ypsilanti, michigan, issued an $3 bill.

Now, both coins and paper bills is used in the U.S. Sometimes the paper bill are called "greenbacks" cause of the green ink used in making the bills.

1. ____________
2. ____________
3. ____________
4. ____________
5. ____________
6. ____________
7. ____________
8. ____________

Name _______________ Practice 201

Math Practice: Number Sense

Write the missing sign. (+, –, x, ÷) 95 ◯ 4 = 380	Write the missing sign. (+, –, x, ÷) 9 ◯ 1 = 9	Write the missing sign. (+, –, x, ÷) 529 ◯ 142 = 671

Find the average for 639, 854, 473, 882. The average is ______.	Estimate the answer. 544 bags of popcorn were sold for 77¢ each. How much money was made? <$400 >$400

Language Practice: Research Report

Dewey Decimal System

The Dewey Decimal System was named after its inventor, John Dewey. John Dewey used a system of numbers to organize books in a library. Write the category number where each book could be found.

000 General Works (Encyclopedias, Almanacs)
100 Philosophy and Psychology
200 Religion and Myths
300 Social Sciences (Law, Education, Folk Lore)
400 Philology (Languages, Dictionaries, Grammar)
500 Pure Science (Math, Chemistry, Biology, Botany)
600 Applied Science (Medicine, Agriculture, T.V.)
700 Fine Arts (Painting, Music, Photography)
800 Literature (Novels, Poetry, Plays)
900 History, Geography, Biography

1. *Poems for Winter* _______
2. *Understanding People* _______
3. *My Life* by Michael Jordan _______
4. *Chemistry is Easy!* _______
5. *German-French Dictionary* _______
6. *Old Farmer's Almanac* _______
7. *Who's Who in the Movies* _______
8. *Greek and Roman Myths* _______
9. *Ansel Adams Photographs* _______
10. *Dalton's Medical Manual* _______

Name ______________________________ Practice 202

Math Practice: Division

Divide.	Divide.	Divide.
$4\overline{)1,223}$	$7\overline{)1,628}$	$5\overline{)7,564}$

Choose the operation.	Choose the operation.
Amanda needs to sell 3,679 candy bars within the next week. How many candy bars does she need to sell each day?	Each book in the set of encyclopedias costs $3.99. If there are 26 books in the set, how much does the set cost?
add subtract multiply divide	add subtract multiply divide

Language Practice: Research Report

When doing research, a variety of sources of information should be used. Some sources of information are the following:

encyclopedias, dictionaries, thesauruses, magazines, newspapers, card catalog, and Internet

Write the resource that can be used to find the following information.

1. ______________________: to find the day's weather
2. ______________________: to check the spelling of a word
3. ______________________: to find a synonym for a word
4. ______________________: to find out the meaning of a word
5. ______________________: to find the most up-to-date information on NASA
6. ______________________: to find out the sports scores from the previous day's game
7. ______________________: to find out book titles and authors for a certain topics
8. ______________________: to find out general information on a state
9. ______________________: to find out a recent interview of an athlete

Page 5

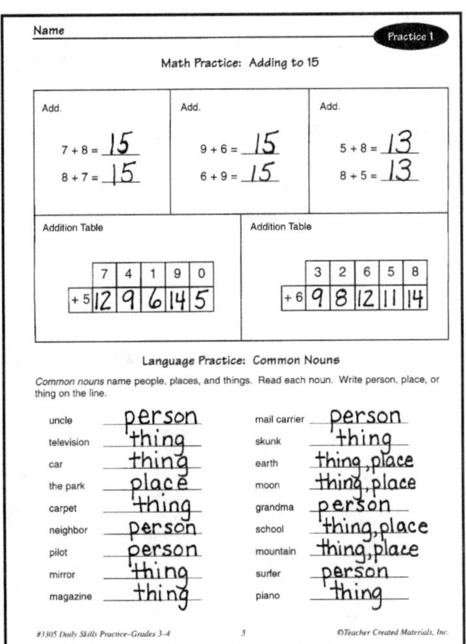

Name ______ Practice 1

Math Practice: Adding to 15

Add.	Add.	Add.
7 + 8 = 15	9 + 6 = 15	5 + 8 = 13
8 + 7 = 15	6 + 9 = 15	8 + 5 = 13

Addition Table

	7	4	1	9	0
+ 5	12	9	6	14	5

Addition Table

	3	2	6	5	8
+ 6	9	8	12	11	14

Language Practice: Common Nouns

Common nouns name people, places, and things. Read each noun. Write person, place, or thing on the line.

uncle	person	mail carrier	person
television	thing	skunk	thing
car	thing	earth	thing, place
the park	place	moon	thing, place
carpet	thing	grandma	person
neighbor	person	school	thing, place
pilot	person	mountain	thing, place
mirror	thing	surfer	person
magazine	thing	piano	thing

#3305 Daily Skills Practice–Grades 3–4 5 ©Teacher Created Materials, Inc.

Page 6

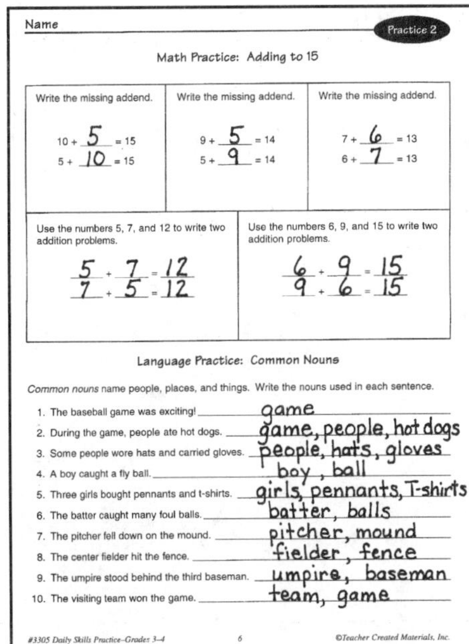

Name ______ Practice 2

Math Practice: Adding to 15

Write the missing addend.	Write the missing addend.	Write the missing addend.
10 + 5 = 15	9 + 5 = 14	7 + 6 = 13
5 + 10 = 15	5 + 9 = 14	6 + 7 = 13

Use the numbers 5, 7, and 12 to write two addition problems.	Use the numbers 6, 9, and 15 to write two addition problems.
5 + 7 = 12	6 + 9 = 15
7 + 5 = 12	9 + 6 = 15

Language Practice: Common Nouns

Common nouns name people, places, and things. Write the nouns used in each sentence.

1. The baseball game was exciting! game
2. During the game, people ate hot dogs. game, people, hot dogs
3. Some people wore hats and carried gloves. people, hats, gloves
4. A boy caught a fly ball. boy, ball
5. Three girls bought pennants and t-shirts. girls, pennants, T-shirts
6. The batter caught many foul balls. batter, balls
7. The pitcher fell down on the mound. pitcher, mound
8. The center fielder hit the fence. fielder, fence
9. The umpire stood behind the third baseman. umpire, baseman
10. The visiting team won the game. team, game

#3305 Daily Skills Practice–Grades 3–4 6 ©Teacher Created Materials, Inc.

Page 7

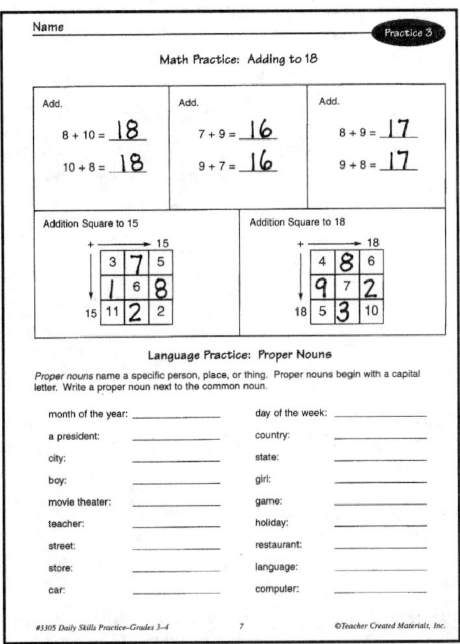

Name ______ Practice 3

Math Practice: Adding to 18

Add.	Add.	Add.
8 + 10 = 18	7 + 9 = 16	8 + 9 = 17
10 + 8 = 18	9 + 7 = 16	9 + 8 = 17

Addition Square to 15

3	7	5
1	6	8
11	2	2

Addition Square to 18

4	8	6
9	7	2
5	3	10

Language Practice: Proper Nouns

Proper nouns name a specific person, place, or thing. Proper nouns begin with a capital letter. Write a proper noun next to the common noun.

month of the year:	______	day of the week:	______
a president:	______	country:	______
city:	______	state:	______
boy:	______	girl:	______
movie theater:	______	game:	______
teacher:	______	holiday:	______
street:	______	restaurant:	______
store:	______	language:	______
car:	______	computer:	______

#3305 Daily Skills Practice–Grades 3–4 7 ©Teacher Created Materials, Inc.

Page 8

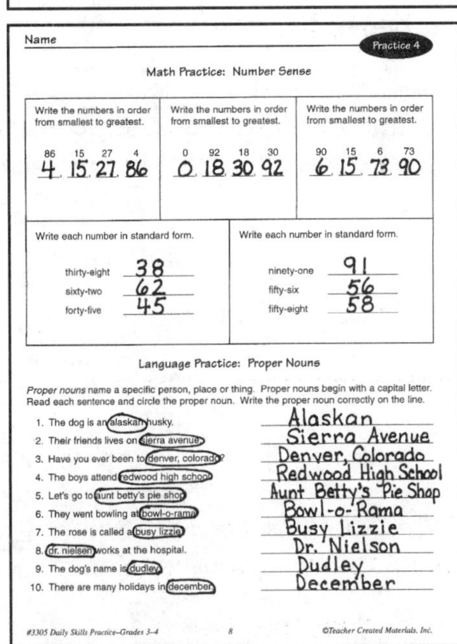

Name ______ Practice 4

Math Practice: Number Sense

Write the numbers in order from smallest to greatest.	Write the numbers in order from smallest to greatest.	Write the numbers in order from smallest to greatest.
86 15 27 4	0 92 18 30	90 15 6 73
4 15 27 86	0 18 30 92	6 15 73 90

Write each number in standard form.		Write each number in standard form.	
thirty-eight	38	ninety-one	91
sixty-two	62	fifty-six	56
forty-five	45	fifty-eight	58

Language Practice: Proper Nouns

Proper nouns name a specific person, place or thing. Proper nouns begin with a capital letter. Read each sentence and circle the proper noun. Write the proper noun correctly on the line.

1. The dog is an alaskan husky. Alaskan
2. Their friends lives on sierra avenue. Sierra Avenue
3. Have you ever been to denver, colorado? Denver, Colorado
4. The boys attend redwood high school. Redwood High School
5. Let's go to aunt betty's pie shop. Aunt Betty's Pie Shop
6. They went bowling at bowl-o-rama. Bowl-o-Rama
7. The rose is called a busy lizzie. Busy Lizzie
8. dr. nielsen works at the hospital. Dr. Nielson
9. The dog's name is dudley. Dudley
10. There are many holidays in december. December

#3305 Daily Skills Practice–Grades 3–4 8 ©Teacher Created Materials, Inc.

Page 9

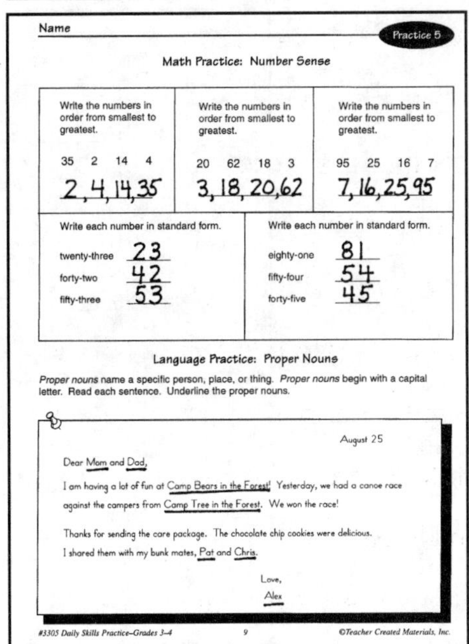

Name ______ Practice 5

Math Practice: Number Sense

Write the numbers in order from smallest to greatest.	Write the numbers in order from smallest to greatest.	Write the numbers in order from smallest to greatest.
35 2 14 4	20 62 18 3	95 25 16 7
2, 4, 14, 35	3, 18, 20, 62	7, 16, 25, 95

Write each number in standard form.		Write each number in standard form.	
twenty-three	23	eighty-one	81
forty-two	42	fifty-four	54
fifty-three	53	forty-five	45

Language Practice: Proper Nouns

Proper nouns name a specific person, place, or thing. *Proper nouns* begin with a capital letter. Read each sentence. Underline the proper nouns.

August 25

Dear Mom and Dad,

I am having a lot of fun at Camp Bears in the Forest! Yesterday, we had a canoe race against the campers from Camp Tree in the Forest. We won the race!

Thanks for sending the care package. The chocolate chip cookies were delicious. I shared them with my bunk mates, Pat and Chris.

Love,

Alex

#3305 Daily Skills Practice–Grades 3–4 9 ©Teacher Created Materials, Inc.

Page 10

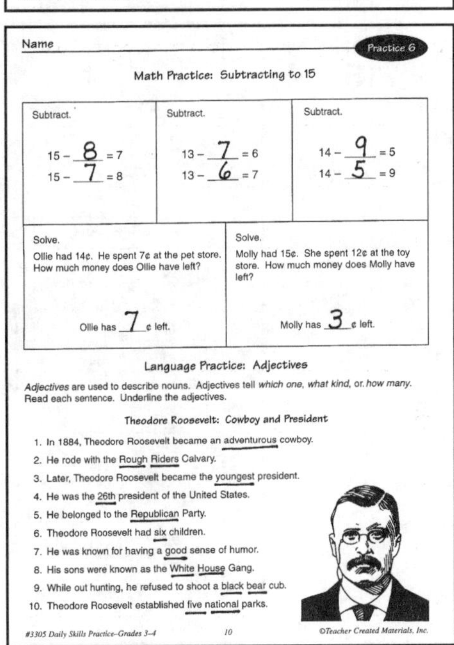

Name ______ Practice 6

Math Practice: Subtracting to 15

Subtract.	Subtract.	Subtract.
15 – 8 = 7	13 – 7 = 6	14 – 9 = 5
15 – 7 = 8	13 – 6 = 7	14 – 5 = 9

Solve.	Solve.
Ollie had 14¢. He spent 7¢ at the pet store. How much money does Ollie have left?	Molly had 15¢. She spent 12¢ at the toy store. How much money does Molly have left?
Ollie has 7 ¢ left.	Molly has 3 ¢ left.

Language Practice: Adjectives

Adjectives are used to describe nouns. Adjectives tell *which one, what kind,* or *how many.* Read each sentence. Underline the adjectives.

Theodore Roosevelt: Cowboy and President

1. In 1884, Theodore Roosevelt became an adventurous cowboy.
2. He rode with the Rough Riders Calvary.
3. Later, Theodore Roosevelt became the youngest president.
4. He was the 26th president of the United States.
5. He belonged to the Republican Party.
6. Theodore Roosevelt had six children.
7. He was known for having a good sense of humor.
8. His sons were known as the White House Gang.
9. While out hunting, he refused to shoot a black bear cub.
10. Theodore Roosevelt established five national parks.

#3305 Daily Skills Practice–Grades 3–4 10 ©Teacher Created Materials, Inc.

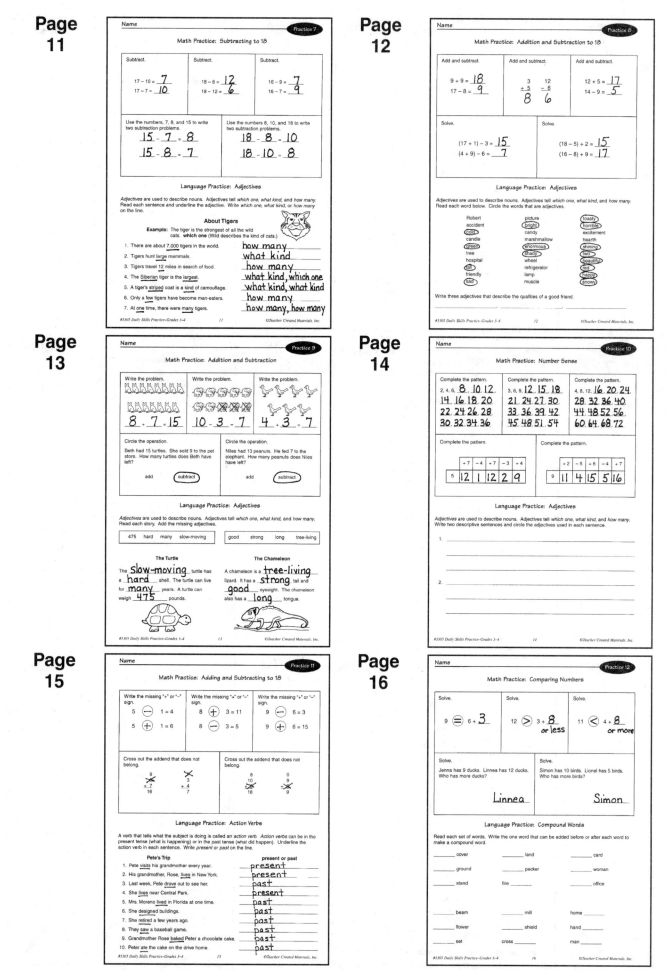

Page 11

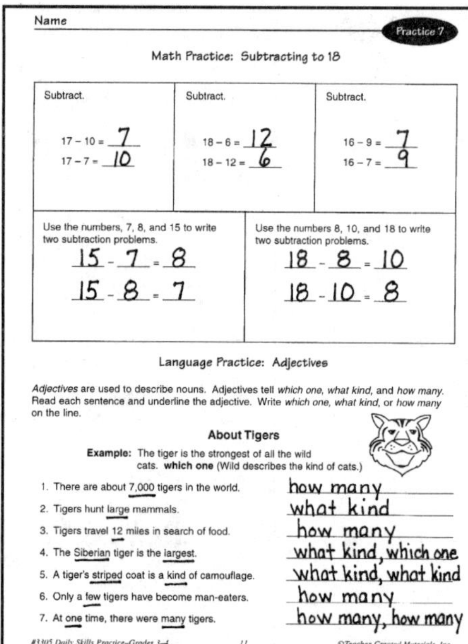
Name

Practice 7

Math Practice: Subtracting to 18

Subtract.	Subtract.	Subtract.
17 − 10 = 7 17 − 7 = 10	18 − 6 = 12 18 − 12 = 6	16 − 9 = 7 16 − 7 = 9

Use the numbers, 7, 8, and 15 to write two subtraction problems.	Use the numbers 8, 10, and 18 to write two subtraction problems.
15 − 7 = 8 15 − 8 = 7	18 − 8 = 10 18 − 10 = 8

Language Practice: Adjectives

Adjectives are used to describe nouns. Adjectives tell *which one, what kind,* and *how many.* Read each sentence and underline the adjective. Write *which one, what kind,* or *how many* on the line.

About Tigers

Example: The tiger is the strongest of all the wild cats. **which one** (Wild describes the kind of cats.)

1. There are about 7,000 tigers in the world. how many
2. Tigers hunt large mammals. what kind
3. Tigers travel 12 miles in search of food. how many
4. The Siberian tiger is the largest. what kind, which one
5. A tiger's striped coat is a kind of camouflage. what kind, what kind
6. Only a few tigers have become man-eaters. how many
7. At one time, there were many tigers. how many, how many

#3305 Daily Skills Practice—Grades 3–4 11 ©Teacher Created Materials, Inc.

Page 12

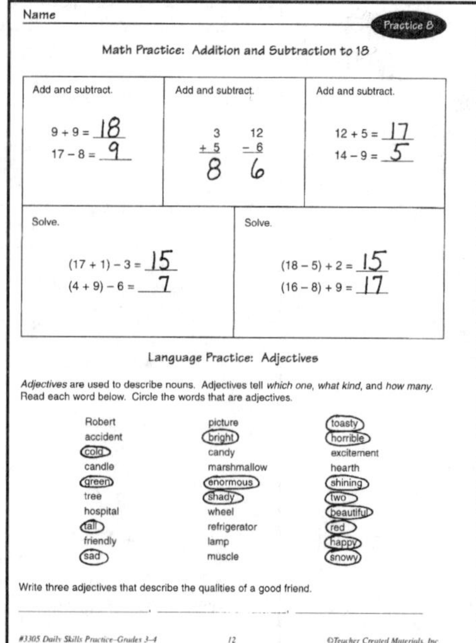
Name

Practice 8

Math Practice: Addition and Subtraction to 18

Add and subtract.	Add and subtract.	Add and subtract.
9 + 9 = 18 17 − 8 = 9	3 + 5 = 8 12 − 6 = 6	12 + 5 = 17 14 − 9 = 5

Solve.	Solve.
(17 + 1) − 3 = 15 (4 + 9) − 6 = 7	(18 − 5) + 2 = 15 (16 − 8) + 9 = 17

Language Practice: Adjectives

Adjectives are used to describe nouns. Adjectives tell *which one, what kind,* and *how many.* Read each word below. Circle the words that are adjectives.

Robert	picture	(toasty)
accident	(bright)	(horrible)
(cold)	candy	excitement
candle	marshmallow	hearth
(green)	(enormous)	(shining)
tree	(shady)	(two)
hospital	wheel	(beautiful)
(tall)	refrigerator	(red)
friendly	lamp	(happy)
(sad)	muscle	(snowy)

Write three adjectives that describe the qualities of a good friend.

________, ________, ________

#3305 Daily Skills Practice—Grades 3–4 12 ©Teacher Created Materials, Inc.

Page 13

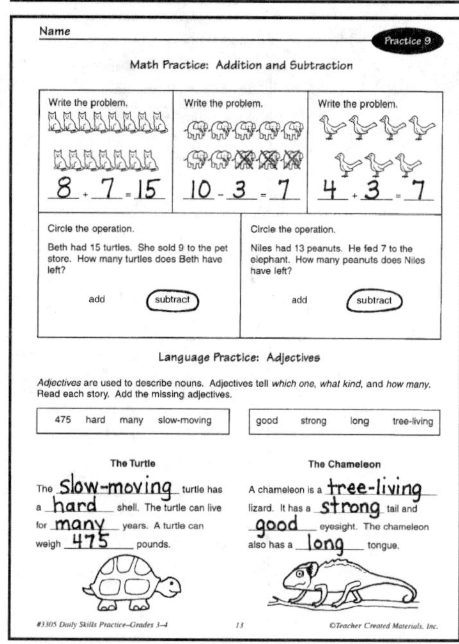
Name

Practice 9

Math Practice: Addition and Subtraction

Write the problem.	Write the problem.	Write the problem.
8 + 7 = 15	10 − 3 = 7	4 + 3 = 7

Circle the operation.	Circle the operation.
Beth had 15 turtles. She sold 9 to the pet store. How many turtles does Beth have left? add (subtract)	Niles had 13 peanuts. He fed 7 to the elephant. How many peanuts does Niles have left? add (subtract)

Language Practice: Adjectives

Adjectives are used to describe nouns. Adjectives tell *which one, what kind,* and *how many.* Read each story. Add the missing adjectives.

475 hard many slow-moving

good strong long tree-living

The Turtle

The slow-moving turtle has a hard shell. The turtle can live for many years. A turtle can weigh 475 pounds.

The Chameleon

A chameleon is a tree-living lizard. It has a strong tail and good eyesight. The chameleon also has a long tongue.

#3305 Daily Skills Practice—Grades 3–4 13 ©Teacher Created Materials, Inc.

Page 14

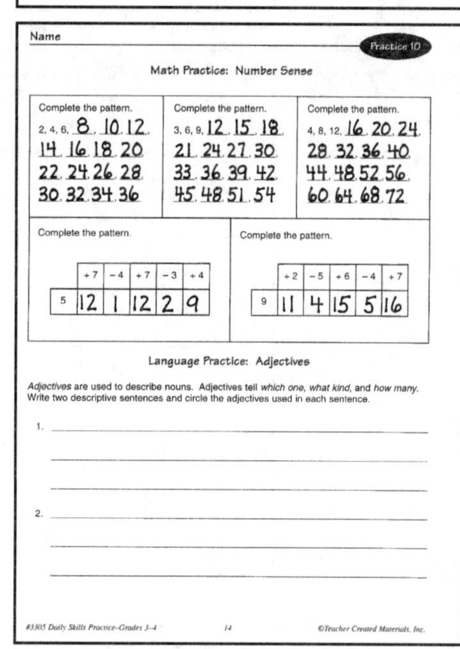
Name

Practice 10

Math Practice: Number Sense

Complete the pattern.	Complete the pattern.	Complete the pattern.
2, 4, 6, 8, 10, 12, 14, 16, 18, 20, 22, 24, 26, 28, 30, 32, 34, 36	3, 6, 9, 12, 15, 18, 21, 24, 27, 30, 33, 36, 39, 42, 45, 48, 51, 54	4, 8, 12, 16, 20, 24, 28, 32, 36, 40, 44, 48, 52, 56, 60, 64, 68, 72

Complete the pattern.

	+7	−4	+7	−3	+4
5	12	1	12	2	9

Complete the pattern.

	+2	−5	+6	−4	+7
9	11	4	15	5	16

Language Practice: Adjectives

Adjectives are used to describe nouns. Adjectives tell *which one, what kind,* and *how many.* Write two descriptive sentences and circle the adjectives used in each sentence.

1. ____________________

2. ____________________

#3305 Daily Skills Practice—Grades 3–4 14 ©Teacher Created Materials, Inc.

Page 15

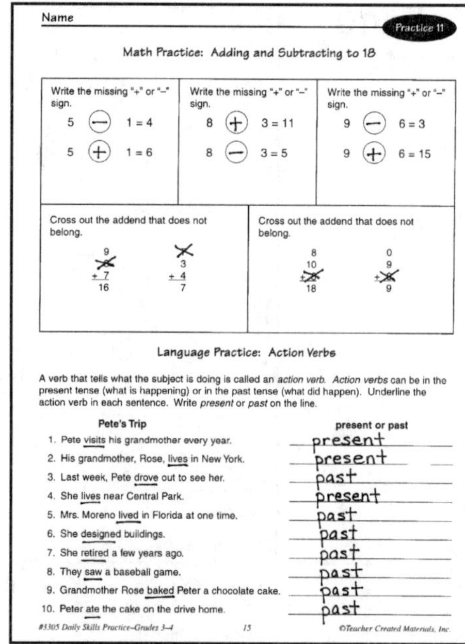
Name

Practice 11

Math Practice: Adding and Subtracting to 18

Write the missing "+" or "−" sign.	Write the missing "+" or "−" sign.	Write the missing "+" or "−" sign.
5 (−) 1 = 4 5 (+) 1 = 6	8 (+) 3 = 11 8 (−) 3 = 5	9 (−) 6 = 3 9 (+) 6 = 15

Cross out the addend that does not belong.	Cross out the addend that does not belong.
9, ~~X~~, + 7 = 16 ; ~~X~~, 3, + 4 = 7	8, 10, + ~~X~~ = 18 ; 0, 9, + ~~X~~ = 9

Language Practice: Action Verbs

A verb that tells what the subject is doing is called an *action verb. Action verbs* can be in the present tense (what is happening) or in the past tense (what did happen). Underline the action verb in each sentence. Write *present* or *past* on the line.

Pete's Trip	present or past
1. Pete visits his grandmother every year.	present
2. His grandmother, Rose, lives in New York.	present
3. Last week, Pete drove out to see her.	past
4. She lives near Central Park.	present
5. Mrs. Moreno lived in Florida at one time.	past
6. She designed buildings.	past
7. She retired a few years ago.	past
8. They saw a baseball game.	past
9. Grandmother Rose baked Peter a chocolate cake.	past
10. Peter ate the cake on the drive home.	past

#3305 Daily Skills Practice—Grades 3–4 15 ©Teacher Created Materials, Inc.

Page 16

Name

Practice 12

Math Practice: Comparing Numbers

Solve.	Solve.	Solve.
9 (=) 6 + 3	12 (>) 3 + 8 or less	11 (<) 4 + 8 or more

Solve.	Solve.
Jenna has 9 ducks. Linnea has 12 ducks. Who has more ducks? Linnea	Simon has 10 birds. Lionel has 5 birds. Who has more birds? Simon

Language Practice: Compound Words

Read each set of words. Write the one word that can be added before or after each word to make a compound word.

______ cover	______ land	______ card
______ ground	______ pecker	______ woman
______ stand	fire ______	______ office
______ beam	______ mill	home ______
______ flower	______ shield	hand ______
______ set	cross ______	man ______

#3305 Daily Skills Practice—Grades 3–4 16 ©Teacher Created Materials, Inc.

Page 17

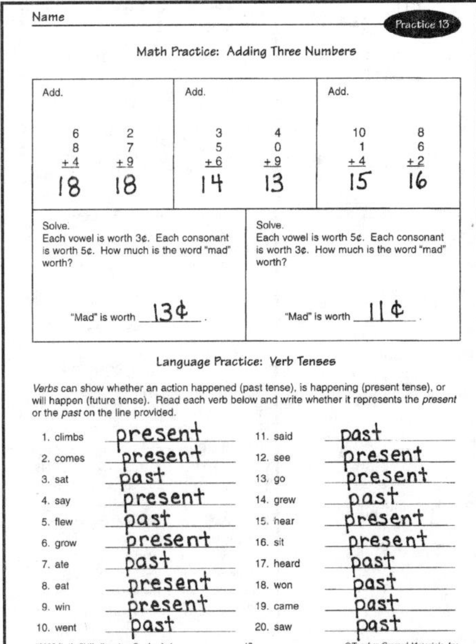

Name Practice 13

Math Practice: Adding Three Numbers

Add.	Add.	Add.
6 + 8 + 4 = 18; 2 + 7 + 9 = 18	3 + 5 + 6 = 14; 4 + 0 + 9 = 13	10 + 1 + 4 = 15; 8 + 6 + 2 = 16

Solve.	Solve.
Each vowel is worth 3¢. Each consonant is worth 5¢. How much is the word "mad" worth? "Mad" is worth 13¢.	Each vowel is worth 5¢. Each consonant is worth 3¢. How much is the word "mad" worth? "Mad" is worth 11¢.

Language Practice: Verb Tenses

Verbs can show whether an action happened (past tense), is happening (present tense), or will happen (future tense). Read each verb below and write whether it represents the *present* or the *past* on the line provided.

1. climbs present
2. comes present
3. sat past
4. say present
5. flew past
6. grow present
7. ate past
8. eat present
9. win present
10. went past
11. said past
12. see present
13. go present
14. grew past
15. hear present
16. sit present
17. heard past
18. won past
19. came past
20. saw past

#3305 Daily Skills Practice–Grades 3–4 17 ©Teacher Created Materials, Inc.

Page 18

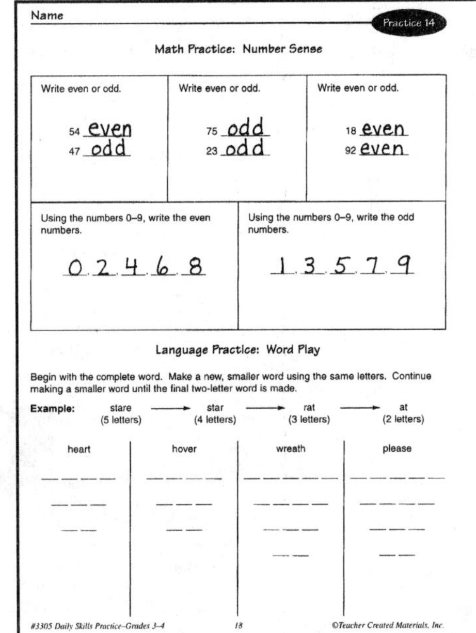

Name Practice 14

Math Practice: Number Sense

Write even or odd.	Write even or odd.	Write even or odd.
54 even; 47 odd	75 odd; 23 odd	18 even; 92 even

Using the numbers 0–9, write the even numbers.	Using the numbers 0–9, write the odd numbers.
0 2 4 6 8	1 3 5 7 9

Language Practice: Word Play

Begin with the complete word. Make a new, smaller word using the same letters. Continue making a smaller word until the final two-letter word is made.

Example: stare (5 letters) → star (4 letters) → rat (3 letters) → at (2 letters)

heart hover wreath please

#3305 Daily Skills Practice–Grades 3–4 18 ©Teacher Created Materials, Inc.

Page 19

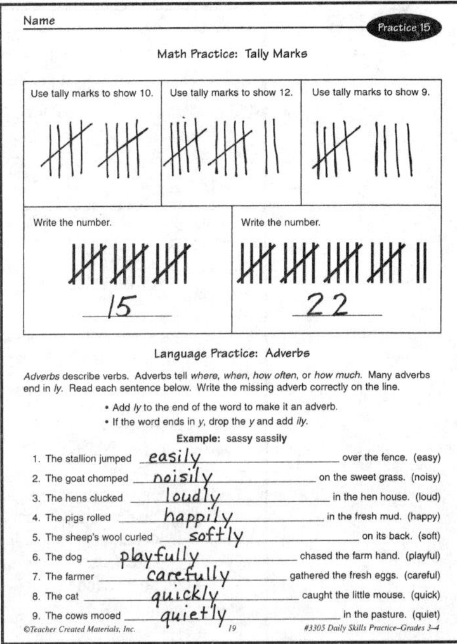

Name Practice 15

Math Practice: Tally Marks

Use tally marks to show 10.	Use tally marks to show 12.	Use tally marks to show 9.

Write the number.	Write the number.
15	22

Language Practice: Adverbs

Adverbs describe verbs. Adverbs tell *where, when, how often,* or *how much.* Many adverbs end in *ly.* Read each sentence below. Write the missing adverb correctly on the line.

- Add *ly* to the end of the word to make it an adverb.
- If the word ends in *y,* drop the *y* and add *ily.*

Example: sassy sassily

1. The stallion jumped easily over the fence. (easy)
2. The goat chomped noisily on the sweet grass. (noisy)
3. The hens clucked loudly in the hen house. (loud)
4. The pigs rolled happily in the fresh mud. (happy)
5. The sheep's wool curled softly on its back. (soft)
6. The dog playfully chased the farm hand. (playful)
7. The farmer carefully gathered the fresh eggs. (careful)
8. The cat quickly caught the little mouse. (quick)
9. The cows mooed quietly in the pasture. (quiet)

©Teacher Created Materials, Inc. 19 #3305 Daily Skills Practice–Grades 3–4

Page 20

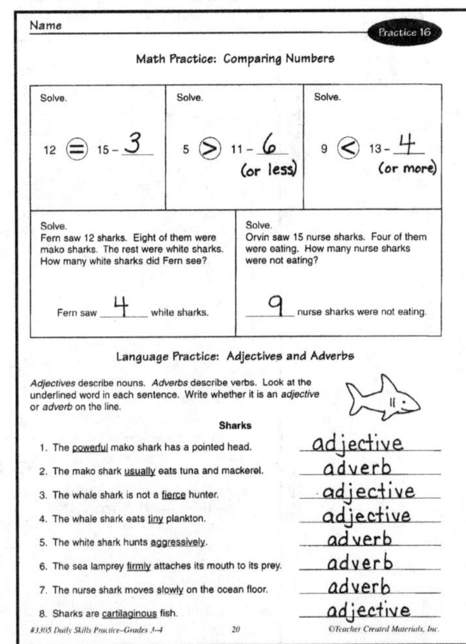

Name Practice 16

Math Practice: Comparing Numbers

Solve.	Solve.	Solve.
12 = 15 – 3	5 > 11 – 6 (or less)	9 < 13 – 4 (or more)

Solve.	Solve.
Fern saw 12 sharks. Eight of them were mako sharks. The rest were white sharks. How many white sharks did Fern see? Fern saw 4 white sharks.	Orvin saw 15 nurse sharks. Four of them were eating. How many nurse sharks were not eating? 9 nurse sharks were not eating.

Language Practice: Adjectives and Adverbs

Adjectives describe nouns. *Adverbs* describe verbs. Look at the underlined word in each sentence. Write whether it is an *adjective* or *adverb* on the line.

Sharks

1. The powerful mako shark has a pointed head. adjective
2. The mako shark usually eats tuna and mackerel. adverb
3. The whale shark is not a fierce hunter. adjective
4. The whale shark eats tiny plankton. adjective
5. The white shark hunts aggressively. adverb
6. The sea lamprey firmly attaches its mouth to its prey. adverb
7. The nurse shark moves slowly on the ocean floor. adverb
8. Sharks are cartilaginous fish. adjective

#3305 Daily Skills Practice–Grades 3–4 20 ©Teacher Created Materials, Inc.

Page 21

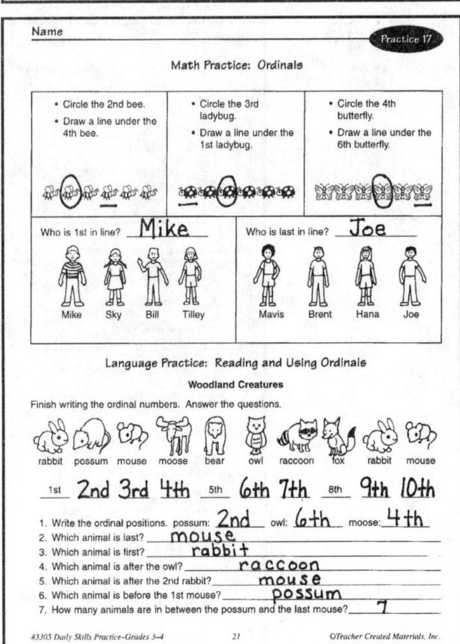

Name Practice 17

Math Practice: Ordinals

• Circle the 2nd bee. • Draw a line under the 4th bee.	• Circle the 3rd ladybug. • Draw a line under the 1st ladybug.	• Circle the 4th butterfly. • Draw a line under the 6th butterfly.

Who is 1st in line? Mike	Who is last in line? Joe
Mike Sky Bill Tilley	Mavis Brent Hana Joe

Language Practice: Reading and Using Ordinals

Woodland Creatures

Finish writing the ordinal numbers. Answer the questions.

rabbit possum mouse moose bear owl raccoon fox rabbit mouse

1st 2nd 3rd 4th 5th 6th 7th 8th 9th 10th

1. Write the ordinal positions. possum: 2nd owl: 6th moose: 4th
2. Which animal is last? mouse
3. Which animal is first? rabbit
4. Which animal is after the owl? raccoon
5. Which animal is after the 2nd rabbit? mouse
6. Which animal is before the 1st mouse? possum
7. How many animals are in between the possum and the last mouse? 7

#3305 Daily Skills Practice–Grades 3–4 21 ©Teacher Created Materials, Inc.

Page 22

Name Practice 18

Math Practice: Number Sense

Write the number that is 2 more.	Write the number that is 5 more.	Write the number that is 10 more.
26 28	39 44	86 96
78 80	95 100	13 23
50 52	47 52	0 10
63 65	55 60	43 53

Write each number in standard form.	Write each number in standard form.
eighty-seven 87	seventy-three 73
ninety-five 95	fifteen 15
thirty-six 36	fifty-two 52

Language Practice: Reading and Using Ordinals

Read each sentence and underline the ordinal number. Write the ordinal number on the line.

Example: Margot lives on thirty-third street. 33rd

1. Gilbert is seventeenth in line. 17th
2. Levi climbed to the fortieth step. 40th
3. Who's office is on the twenty-ninth floor? 29th
4. Kay is on her eighty-fifth tour of Egypt. 85th
5. Mona's song is ninety-first on the music hit list. 91st
6. Jerome bought his fifty-sixth baseball card. 56th
7. We have watched our seventy-second TV commercial. 72nd
8. Our home is the fourth brown house on the street. 4th

#3305 Daily Skills Practice–Grades 3–4 22 ©Teacher Created Materials, Inc.

Page 23

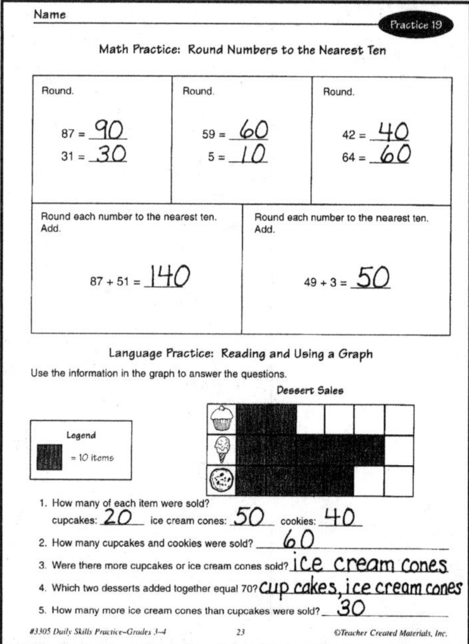

Name ______ Practice 19

Math Practice: Round Numbers to the Nearest Ten

Round.	Round.	Round.
87 = 90 31 = 30	59 = 60 5 = 10	42 = 40 64 = 60

Round each number to the nearest ten. Add.	Round each number to the nearest ten. Add.
87 + 51 = 140	49 + 3 = 50

Language Practice: Reading and Using a Graph

Use the information in the graph to answer the questions.

Dessert Sales

Legend: ■ = 10 items

1. How many of each item were sold? cupcakes: 20 ice cream cones: 50 cookies: 40
2. How many cupcakes and cookies were sold? 60
3. Were there more cupcakes or ice cream cones sold? ice cream cones
4. Which two desserts added together equal 70? cup cakes, ice cream cones
5. How many more ice cream cones than cupcakes were sold? 30

#3305 Daily Skills Practice–Grades 3–4 23 ©Teacher Created Materials, Inc.

Page 24

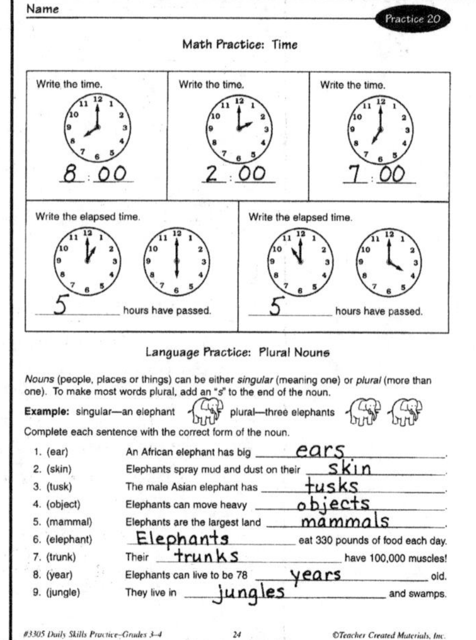

Name ______ Practice 20

Math Practice: Time

Write the time.	Write the time.	Write the time.
8 : 00	2 : 00	7 : 00

Write the elapsed time.	Write the elapsed time.
5 hours have passed.	5 hours have passed.

Language Practice: Plural Nouns

Nouns (people, places or things) can be either *singular* (meaning one) or *plural* (more than one). To make most words plural, add an "*s*" to the end of the noun.

Example: singular—an elephant plural—three elephants

Complete each sentence with the correct form of the noun.

1. (ear) An African elephant has big ears.
2. (skin) Elephants spray mud and dust on their skin.
3. (tusk) The male Asian elephant has tusks.
4. (object) Elephants can move heavy objects.
5. (mammal) Elephants are the largest land mammals.
6. (elephant) Elephants eat 330 pounds of food each day.
7. (trunk) Their trunks have 100,000 muscles!
8. (year) Elephants can live to be 78 years old.
9. (jungle) They live in jungles and swamps.

#3305 Daily Skills Practice–Grades 3–4 24 ©Teacher Created Materials, Inc.

Page 25

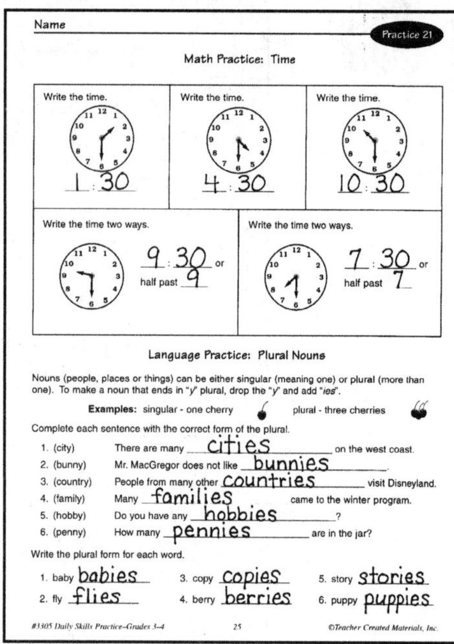

Name ______ Practice 21

Math Practice: Time

Write the time.	Write the time.	Write the time.
1 : 30	4 : 30	10 : 30

Write the time two ways.	Write the time two ways.
9 : 30 or half past 9	7 : 30 or half past 7

Language Practice: Plural Nouns

Nouns (people, places or things) can be either singular (meaning one) or plural (more than one). To make a noun that ends in "*y*" plural, drop the "*y*" and add "*ies*".

Examples: singular - one cherry plural - three cherries

Complete each sentence with the correct form of the plural.

1. (city) There are many cities on the west coast.
2. (bunny) Mr. MacGregor does not like bunnies.
3. (country) People from many other countries visit Disneyland.
4. (family) Many families came to the winter program.
5. (hobby) Do you have any hobbies?
6. (penny) How many pennies are in the jar?

Write the plural form for each word.

1. baby babies 2. fly flies 3. copy copies 4. berry berries 5. story stories 6. puppy puppies

#3305 Daily Skills Practice–Grades 3–4 25 ©Teacher Created Materials, Inc.

Page 26

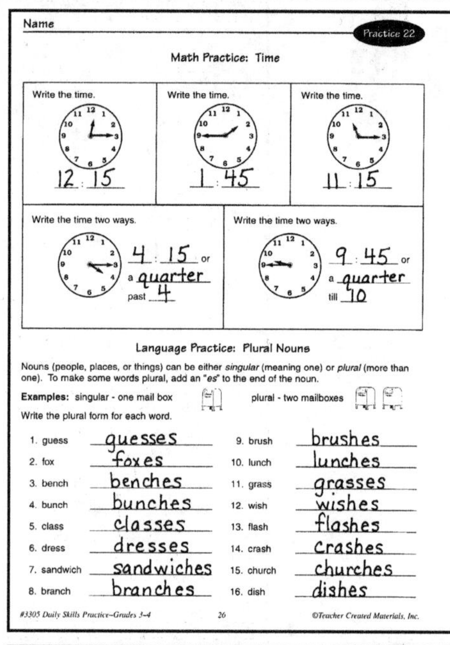

Name ______ Practice 22

Math Practice: Time

Write the time.	Write the time.	Write the time.
12 : 15	1 : 45	11 : 15

Write the time two ways.	Write the time two ways.
4 : 15 or a quarter past 4	9 : 45 or a quarter till 10

Language Practice: Plural Nouns

Nouns (people, places, or things) can be either *singular* (meaning one) or *plural* (more than one). To make some words plural, add an "*es*" to the end of the noun.

Examples: singular - one mail box plural - two mailboxes

Write the plural form for each word.

1. guess guesses
2. fox foxes
3. bench benches
4. bunch bunches
5. class classes
6. dress dresses
7. sandwich sandwiches
8. branch branches
9. brush brushes
10. lunch lunches
11. grass grasses
12. wish wishes
13. flash flashes
14. crash crashes
15. church churches
16. dish dishes

#3305 Daily Skills Practice–Grades 3–4 26 ©Teacher Created Materials, Inc.

Page 27

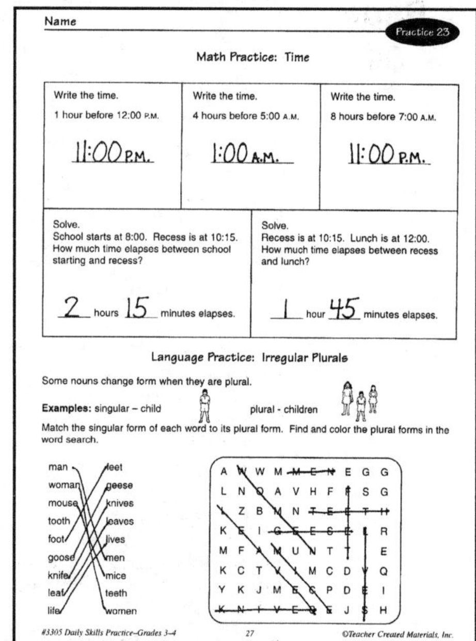

Name ______ Practice 23

Math Practice: Time

Write the time. 1 hour before 12:00 P.M.	Write the time. 4 hours before 5:00 A.M.	Write the time. 8 hours before 7:00 A.M.
11:00 P.M.	1:00 A.M.	11:00 P.M.

Solve. School starts at 8:00. Recess is at 10:15. How much time elapses between school starting and recess?	Solve. Recess is at 10:15. Lunch is at 12:00. How much time elapses between recess and lunch?
2 hours 15 minutes elapses.	1 hour 45 minutes elapses.

Language Practice: Irregular Plurals

Some nouns change form when they are plural.

Examples: singular – child plural - children

Match the singular form of each word to its plural form. Find and color the plural forms in the word search.

man, woman, mouse, tooth, foot, goose, knife, leaf, life — feet, geese, knives, leaves, lives, men, mice, teeth, women

A	W	M	M	E	N	E	G	G
L	N	O	A	V	H	F	S	G
I	Z	B	M	N	T	E	E	T	H
K	E	I	G	E	E	S	E	R
M	F	A	M	U	N	T	T	E
K	C	T	V	L	M	C	D	V	Q
Y	K	J	M	E	P	D	E	I
K	N	I	V	E	S	J	S	H

#3305 Daily Skills Practice–Grades 3–4 27 ©Teacher Created Materials, Inc.

Page 28

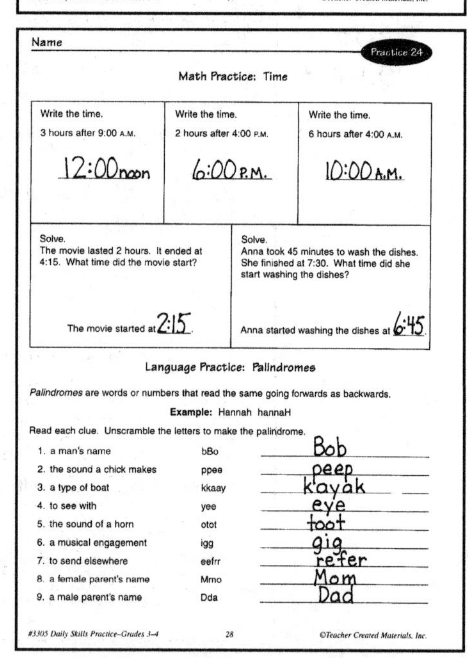

Name ______ Practice 24

Math Practice: Time

Write the time. 3 hours after 9:00 A.M.	Write the time. 2 hours after 4:00 P.M.	Write the time. 6 hours after 4:00 A.M.
12:00 noon	6:00 P.M.	10:00 A.M.

Solve. The movie lasted 2 hours. It ended at 4:15. What time did the movie start?	Solve. Anna took 45 minutes to wash the dishes. She finished at 7:30. What time did she start washing the dishes?
The movie started at 2:15.	Anna started washing the dishes at 6:45.

Language Practice: Palindromes

Palindromes are words or numbers that read the same going forwards as backwards.

Example: Hannah hannaH

Read each clue. Unscramble the letters to make the palindrome.

1. a man's name bBo Bob
2. the sound a chick makes ppee peep
3. a type of boat kkaay kayak
4. to see with yee eye
5. the sound of a horn otot toot
6. a musical engagement igg gig
7. to send elsewhere eefrr refer
8. a female parent's name Mmo Mom
9. a male parent's name Dda Dad

#3305 Daily Skills Practice–Grades 3–4 28 ©Teacher Created Materials, Inc.

Page 29

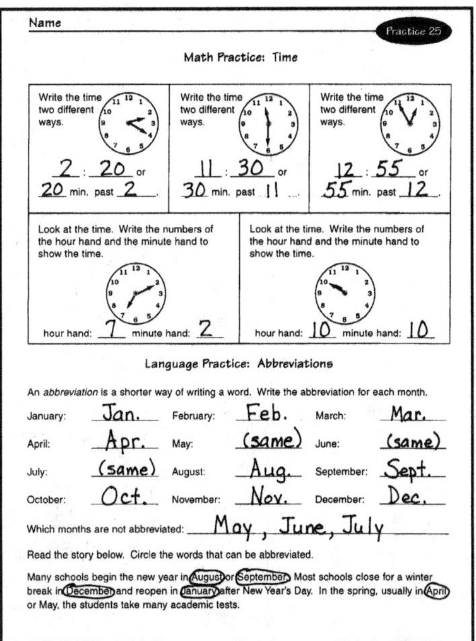

Name — Practice 25

Math Practice: Time

Write the time two different ways. 2 : 20 or 20 min. past 2	Write the time two different ways. 11 : 30 or 30 min. past 11	Write the time two different ways. 12 : 55 or 55 min. past 12

Look at the time. Write the numbers of the hour hand and the minute hand to show the time. hour hand: 7 minute hand: 2	Look at the time. Write the numbers of the hour hand and the minute hand to show the time. hour hand: 10 minute hand: 10

Language Practice: Abbreviations

An *abbreviation* is a shorter way of writing a word. Write the abbreviation for each month.

January: Jan.	February: Feb.	March: Mar.
April: Apr.	May: (same)	June: (same)
July: (same)	August: Aug.	September: Sept.
October: Oct.	November: Nov.	December: Dec.

Which months are not abbreviated: May, June, July

Read the story below. Circle the words that can be abbreviated.

Many schools begin the new year in August or September. Most schools close for a winter break in December and reopen in January after New Year's Day. In the spring, usually in April or May, the students take many academic tests.

#3305 Daily Skills Practice–Grades 3–4 29 ©Teacher Created Materials, Inc.

Page 30

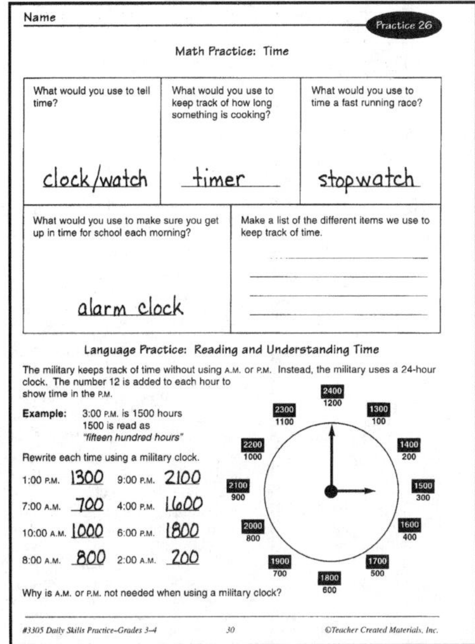

Name — Practice 26

Math Practice: Time

What would you use to tell time? clock/watch	What would you use to keep track of how long something is cooking? timer	What would you use to time a fast running race? stopwatch

What would you use to make sure you get up in time for school each morning? alarm clock	Make a list of the different items we use to keep track of time.

Language Practice: Reading and Understanding Time

The military keeps track of time without using A.M. or P.M. Instead, the military uses a 24-hour clock. The number 12 is added to each hour to show time in the P.M.

Example: 3:00 P.M. is 1500 hours
1500 is read as *"fifteen hundred hours"*

Rewrite each time using a military clock.

1:00 P.M. 1300	9:00 P.M. 2100
7:00 A.M. 700	4:00 P.M. 1600
10:00 A.M. 1000	6:00 P.M. 1800
8:00 A.M. 800	2:00 A.M. 200

Why is A.M. or P.M. not needed when using a military clock?

#3305 Daily Skills Practice–Grades 3–4 30 ©Teacher Created Materials, Inc.

Page 31

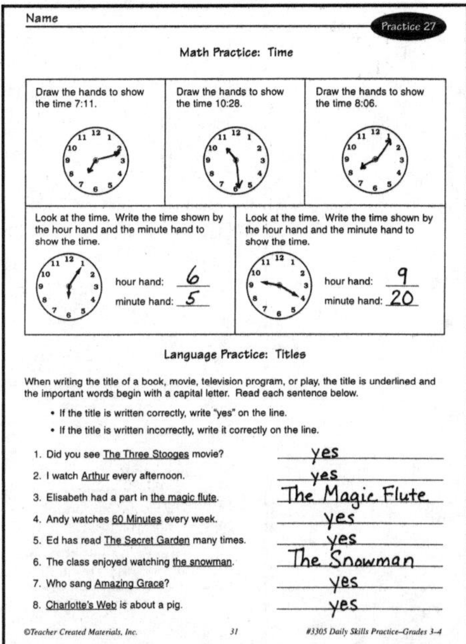

Name — Practice 27

Math Practice: Time

Draw the hands to show the time 7:11.	Draw the hands to show the time 10:28.	Draw the hands to show the time 8:06.

Look at the time. Write the time shown by the hour hand and the minute hand to show the time. hour hand: 6 minute hand: 5	Look at the time. Write the time shown by the hour hand and the minute hand to show the time. hour hand: 9 minute hand: 20

Language Practice: Titles

When writing the title of a book, movie, television program, or play, the title is underlined and the important words begin with a capital letter. Read each sentence below.

- If the title is written correctly, write "yes" on the line.
- If the title is written incorrectly, write it correctly on the line.

1. Did you see The Three Stooges movie? yes
2. I watch Arthur every afternoon. yes
3. Elisabeth had a part in the magic flute. The Magic Flute
4. Andy watches 60 Minutes every week. yes
5. Ed has read The Secret Garden many times. yes
6. The class enjoyed watching the snowman. The Snowman
7. Who sang Amazing Grace? yes
8. Charlotte's Web is about a pig. yes

©Teacher Created Materials, Inc. 31 #3305 Daily Skills Practice–Grades 3–4

Page 32

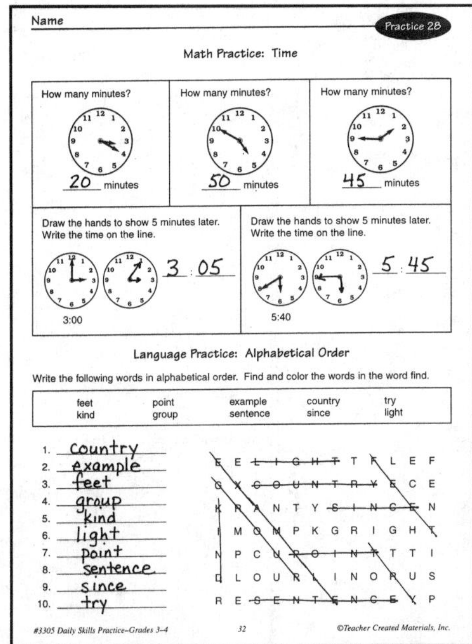

Name — Practice 28

Math Practice: Time

How many minutes? 20 minutes	How many minutes? 50 minutes	How many minutes? 45 minutes

Draw the hands to show 5 minutes later. Write the time on the line. 3:00 → 3 : 05	Draw the hands to show 5 minutes later. Write the time on the line. 5:40 → 5 : 45

Language Practice: Alphabetical Order

Write the following words in alphabetical order. Find and color the words in the word find.

feet kind	point group	example sentence	country since	try light

1. country
2. example
3. feet
4. group
5. kind
6. light
7. point
8. sentence
9. since
10. try

#3305 Daily Skills Practice–Grades 3–4 32 ©Teacher Created Materials, Inc.

Page 33

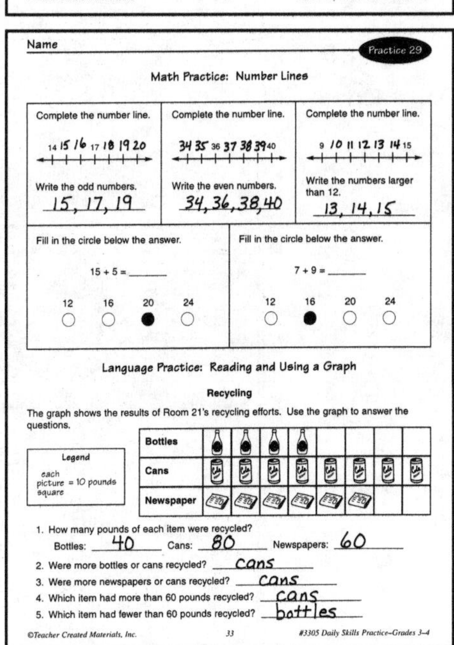

Name — Practice 29

Math Practice: Number Lines

Complete the number line. 14 15 16 17 18 19 20. Write the odd numbers. 15, 17, 19	Complete the number line. 34 35 36 37 38 39 40. Write the even numbers. 34, 36, 38, 40	Complete the number line. 9 10 11 12 13 14 15. Write the numbers larger than 12. 13, 14, 15

Fill in the circle below the answer. 15 + 5 = ___ 12 16 20 (filled) 24	Fill in the circle below the answer. 7 + 9 = ___ 12 16 (filled) 20 24

Language Practice: Reading and Using a Graph

Recycling

The graph shows the results of Room 21's recycling efforts. Use the graph to answer the questions.

Legend: each picture = 10 pounds square

Bottles, Cans, Newspaper

1. How many pounds of each item were recycled? Bottles: 40 Cans: 80 Newspapers: 60
2. Were more bottles or cans recycled? cans
3. Were more newspapers or cans recycled? cans
4. Which item had more than 60 pounds recycled? cans
5. Which item had fewer than 60 pounds recycled? bottles

©Teacher Created Materials, Inc. 33 #3305 Daily Skills Practice–Grades 3–4

Page 34

Name — Practice 30

Math Practice: Number Sense

Write the missing numbers. 24, 28, 32 / 32, 36, 40	Write the missing numbers. 42, 52, 62 / 96, 106, 116	Write the missing numbers. 10, 15, 20 / 8, 10, 12

Mystery Number: I am larger than 50 and smaller than 60. When you count by 5s you say my name. What number am I? 55	Mystery Number: I am an odd number. I am larger than 20 and smaller than 25. When you count by 3s you say my name. What number am I? 21

Language Practice: Abbreviations

An *abbreviation* is a shorter way of writing a word. Write the abbreviation for each day of the week.

Sunday: Sun.	Monday: Mon.	Friday: Fri.
Wednesday: Wed.	Thursday: Thurs.	
Saturday: Sat.	Tuesday: Tues.	

Read the story. Circle the words that can be abbreviated.

Every Monday Julian takes piano lessons from Mrs. Hall. On Thursday Julian has karate lessons. On Tuesday and Friday Julian has soccer practice with a soccer game on Saturday. On Sunday and Wednesday Julian can take it easy!

#3305 Daily Skills Practice–Grades 3–4 34 ©Teacher Created Materials, Inc.

Page 35

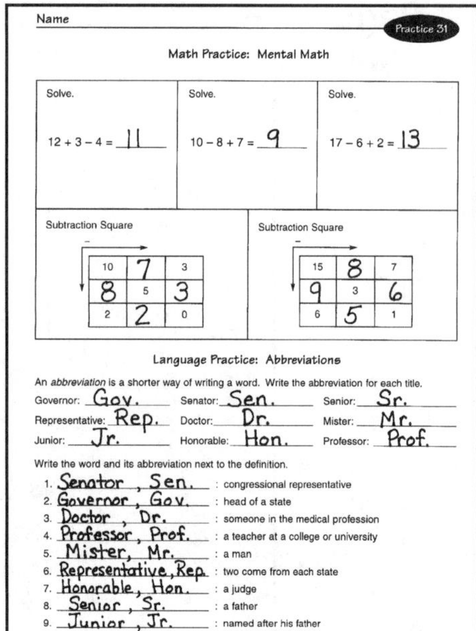

Name — Practice 31

Math Practice: Mental Math

Solve.	Solve.	Solve.
12 + 3 − 4 = 11	10 − 8 + 7 = 9	17 − 6 + 2 = 13

Subtraction Square

10	7	3
8	5	3
2	2	0

Subtraction Square

15	8	7
9	3	6
6	5	1

Language Practice: Abbreviations

An *abbreviation* is a shorter way of writing a word. Write the abbreviation for each title.

Governor: Gov. Senator: Sen. Senior: Sr.
Representative: Rep. Doctor: Dr. Mister: Mr.
Junior: Jr. Honorable: Hon. Professor: Prof.

Write the word and its abbreviation next to the definition.

1. Senator, Sen. : congressional representative
2. Governor, Gov. : head of a state
3. Doctor, Dr. : someone in the medical profession
4. Professor, Prof. : a teacher at a college or university
5. Mister, Mr. : a man
6. Representative, Rep. : two come from each state
7. Honorable, Hon. : a judge
8. Senior, Sr. : a father
9. Junior, Jr. : named after his father

#3305 Daily Skills Practice–Grades 3–4 35 ©Teacher Created Materials, Inc.

Page 36

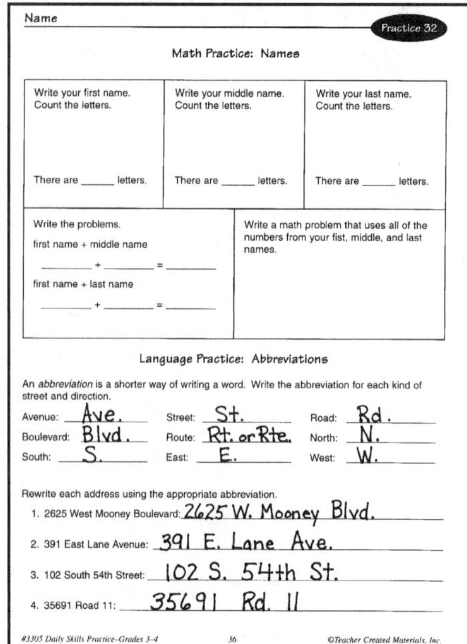

Name — Practice 32

Math Practice: Names

Write your first name. Count the letters.	Write your middle name. Count the letters.	Write your last name. Count the letters.
There are ____ letters.	There are ____ letters.	There are ____ letters.

Write the problems.
first name + middle name
____ + ____ = ____
first name + last name
____ + ____ = ____

Write a math problem that uses all of the numbers from your fist, middle, and last names.

Language Practice: Abbreviations

An *abbreviation* is a shorter way of writing a word. Write the abbreviation for each kind of street and direction.

Avenue: Ave. Street: St. Road: Rd.
Boulevard: Blvd. Route: Rt. or Rte. North: N.
South: S. East: E. West: W.

Rewrite each address using the appropriate abbreviation.

1. 2625 West Mooney Boulevard: 2625 W. Mooney Blvd.
2. 391 East Lane Avenue: 391 E. Lane Ave.
3. 102 South 54th Street: 102 S. 54th St.
4. 35691 Road 11: 35691 Rd. 11

#3305 Daily Skills Practice–Grades 3–4 36 ©Teacher Created Materials, Inc.

Page 37

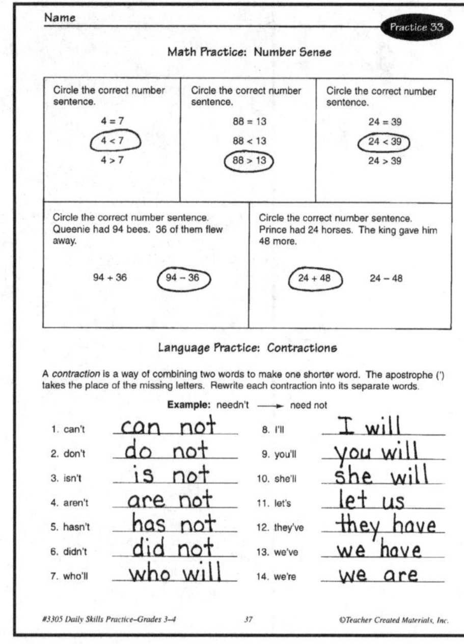

Name — Practice 33

Math Practice: Number Sense

Circle the correct number sentence.	Circle the correct number sentence.	Circle the correct number sentence.
4 = 7 / (4 < 7) / 4 > 7	88 = 13 / 88 < 13 / (88 > 13)	24 = 39 / (24 < 39) / 24 > 39

Circle the correct number sentence. Queenie had 94 bees. 36 of them flew away.
94 + 36 (94 − 36)

Circle the correct number sentence. Prince had 24 horses. The king gave him 48 more.
(24 + 48) 24 − 48

Language Practice: Contractions

A *contraction* is a way of combining two words to make one shorter word. The apostrophe (') takes the place of the missing letters. Rewrite each contraction into its separate words.

Example: needn't → need not

1. can't can not
2. don't do not
3. isn't is not
4. aren't are not
5. hasn't has not
6. didn't did not
7. who'll who will
8. I'll I will
9. you'll you will
10. she'll she will
11. let's let us
12. they've they have
13. we've we have
14. we're we are

#3305 Daily Skills Practice–Grades 3–4 37 ©Teacher Created Materials, Inc.

Page 38

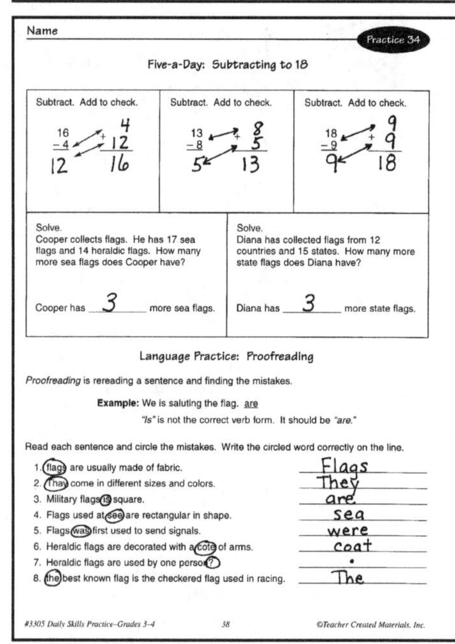

Name — Practice 34

Five-a-Day: Subtracting to 18

Subtract. Add to check.	Subtract. Add to check.	Subtract. Add to check.
16 − 4 = 12; 4 + 12 = 16	13 − 8 = 5; 8 + 5 = 13	18 − 9 = 9; 9 + 9 = 18

Solve.
Cooper collects flags. He has 17 sea flags and 14 heraldic flags. How many more sea flags does Cooper have?
Cooper has 3 more sea flags.

Solve.
Diana has collected flags from 12 countries and 15 states. How many more state flags does Diana have?
Diana has 3 more state flags.

Language Practice: Proofreading

Proofreading is rereading a sentence and finding the mistakes.

Example: We is saluting the flag. are
"Is" is not the correct verb form. It should be *"are."*

Read each sentence and circle the mistakes. Write the circled word correctly on the line.

1. (flags) are usually made of fabric. Flags
2. (Thay) come in different sizes and colors. They
3. Military flags (is) square. are
4. Flags used at (see) are rectangular in shape. sea
5. Flags (was) first used to send signals. were
6. Heraldic flags are decorated with a (cote) of arms. coat
7. Heraldic flags are used by one person(?) .
8. (the) best known flag is the checkered flag used in racing. The

#3305 Daily Skills Practice–Grades 3–4 38 ©Teacher Created Materials, Inc.

Page 39

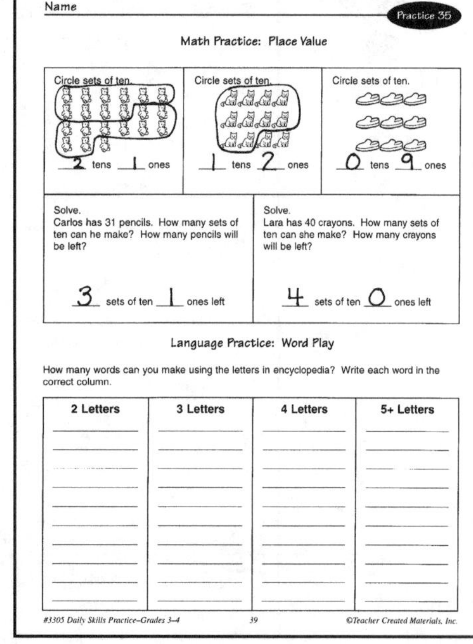

Name — Practice 35

Math Practice: Place Value

Circle sets of ten.	Circle sets of ten.	Circle sets of ten.
2 tens 1 ones	1 tens 2 ones	0 tens 9 ones

Solve.
Carlos has 31 pencils. How many sets of ten can he make? How many pencils will be left?
3 sets of ten 1 ones left

Solve.
Lara has 40 crayons. How many sets of ten can she make? How many crayons will be left?
4 sets of ten 0 ones left

Language Practice: Word Play

How many words can you make using the letters in encyclopedia? Write each word in the correct column.

2 Letters	3 Letters	4 Letters	5+ Letters

#3305 Daily Skills Practice–Grades 3–4 39 ©Teacher Created Materials, Inc.

Page 40

Name — Practice 36

Math Practice: Place Value

Write the number.	Write the number.	Write the number.
3 tens 2 ones = 32	4 tens 6 ones = 46	2 tens 9 ones = 29

Write < or >. Complete the sentence.
88 is greater than 81.

Write < or >. Complete the sentence.
26 is less than 79.

Language Practice: Contractions

A *contraction* is a way of combining two words into one shorter word. The *apostrophe* takes the place of the missing letters. Complete each sentence with the correct word or contraction.

1. wed we'd They were wed on Sunday morning.
2. Wed We'd We'd gone to the beautiful ceremony.
3. ill I'll Mrs. Crenshaw is very ill.
4. Ill I'll I'll take her some chicken soup.
5. well we'll The well is full of water.
6. Well We'll We'll go fill the pail.
7. shell she'll Benita found a conch shell.
8. Shell She'll She'll fill it with candy.
9. shed she'd Mom was working in the shed.
10. Shed She'd She'd been out there all day.

#3305 Daily Skills Practice–Grades 3–4 40 ©Teacher Created Materials, Inc.

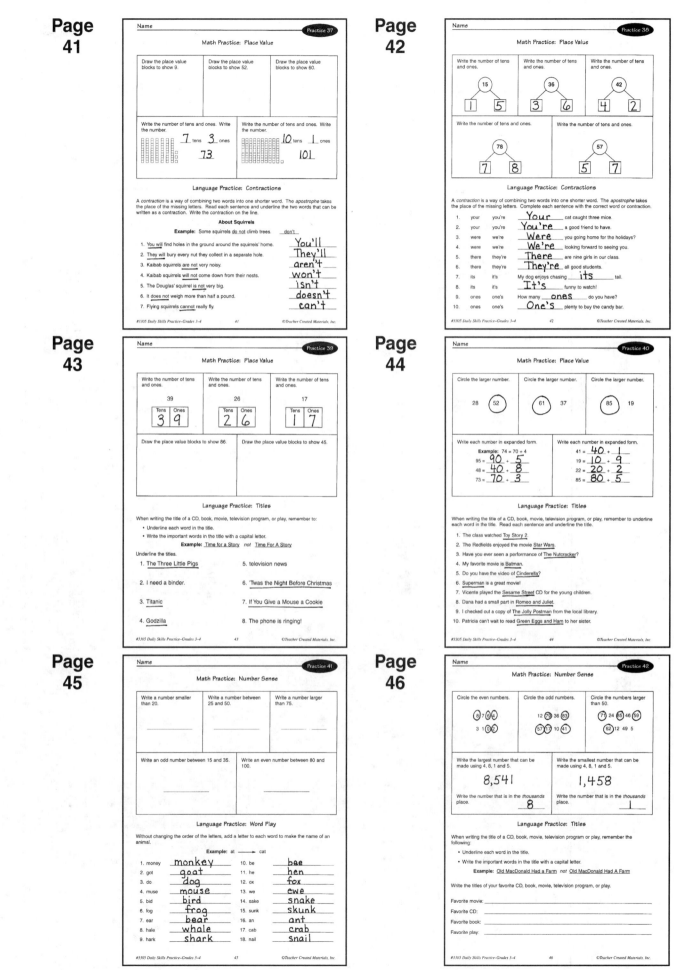

Page 41

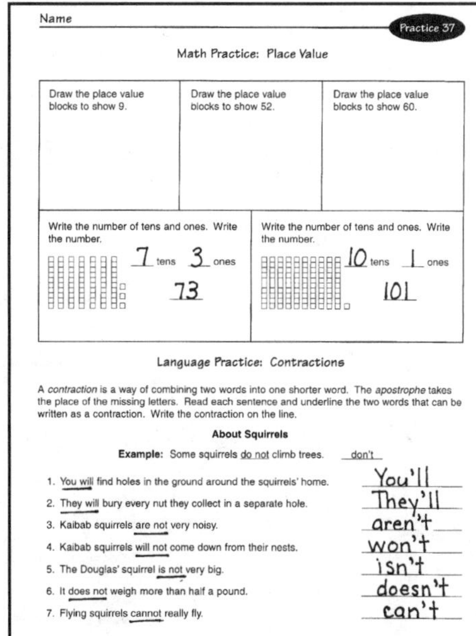

Name — Practice 37

Math Practice: Place Value

Draw the place value blocks to show 9. | Draw the place value blocks to show 52. | Draw the place value blocks to show 60.

Write the number of tens and ones. Write the number. 7 tens 3 ones — 73

Write the number of tens and ones. Write the number. 10 tens 1 ones — 101

Language Practice: Contractions

A *contraction* is a way of combining two words into one shorter word. The *apostrophe* takes the place of the missing letters. Read each sentence and underline the two words that can be written as a contraction. Write the contraction on the line.

About Squirrels

Example: Some squirrels do not climb trees. don't

1. You will find holes in the ground around the squirrels' home. You'll
2. They will bury every nut they collect in a separate hole. They'll
3. Kaibab squirrels are not very noisy. aren't
4. Kaibab squirrels will not come down from their nests. won't
5. The Douglas' squirrel is not very big. isn't
6. It does not weigh more than half a pound. doesn't
7. Flying squirrels cannot really fly. can't

#3305 Daily Skills Practice–Grades 3–4 — 41 — ©Teacher Created Materials, Inc.

Page 42

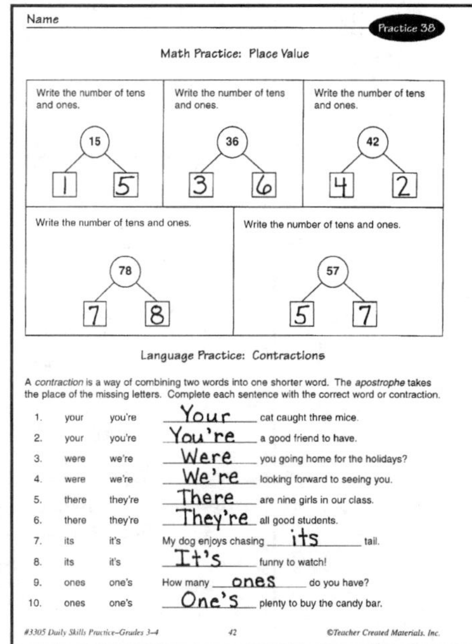

Name — Practice 38

Math Practice: Place Value

Write the number of tens and ones. 15: 1, 5 | 36: 3, 6 | 42: 4, 2

Write the number of tens and ones. 78: 7, 8 | 57: 5, 7

Language Practice: Contractions

A *contraction* is a way of combining two words into one shorter word. The *apostrophe* takes the place of the missing letters. Complete each sentence with the correct word or contraction.

1. your you're Your cat caught three mice.
2. your you're You're a good friend to have.
3. were we're Were you going home for the holidays?
4. were we're We're looking forward to seeing you.
5. there they're There are nine girls in our class.
6. there they're They're all good students.
7. its it's My dog enjoys chasing its tail.
8. its it's It's funny to watch!
9. ones one's How many ones do you have?
10. ones one's One's plenty to buy the candy bar.

#3305 Daily Skills Practice–Grades 3–4 — 42 — ©Teacher Created Materials, Inc.

Page 43

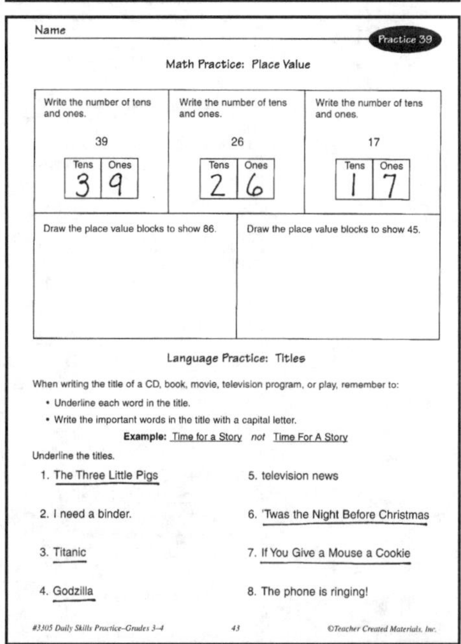

Name — Practice 39

Math Practice: Place Value

Write the number of tens and ones. 39: Tens 3, Ones 9 | 26: Tens 2, Ones 6 | 17: Tens 1, Ones 7

Draw the place value blocks to show 86. | Draw the place value blocks to show 45.

Language Practice: Titles

When writing the title of a CD, book, movie, television program, or play, remember to:

- Underline each word in the title.
- Write the important words in the title with a capital letter.

Example: Time for a Story *not* Time For A Story

Underline the titles.

1. The Three Little Pigs
2. I need a binder.
3. Titanic
4. Godzilla
5. television news
6. 'Twas the Night Before Christmas
7. If You Give a Mouse a Cookie
8. The phone is ringing!

#3305 Daily Skills Practice–Grades 3–4 — 43 — ©Teacher Created Materials, Inc.

Page 44

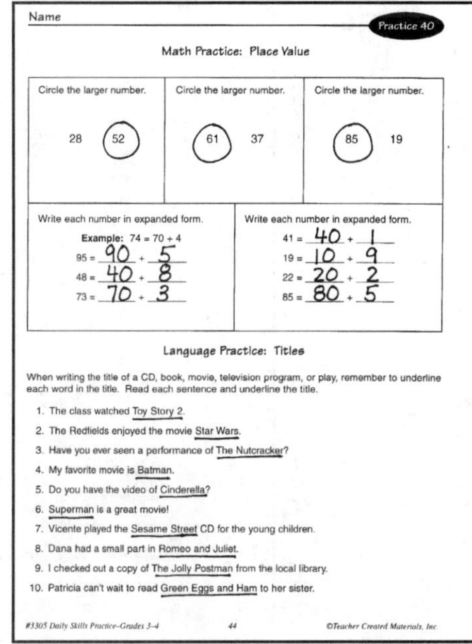

Name — Practice 40

Math Practice: Place Value

Circle the larger number. 28 (52) | (61) 37 | (85) 19

Write each number in expanded form. Example: 74 = 70 + 4; 95 = 90 + 5; 48 = 40 + 8; 73 = 70 + 3

Write each number in expanded form. 41 = 40 + 1; 19 = 10 + 9; 22 = 20 + 2; 85 = 80 + 5

Language Practice: Titles

When writing the title of a CD, book, movie, television program, or play, remember to underline each word in the title. Read each sentence and underline the title.

1. The class watched Toy Story 2.
2. The Redfields enjoyed the movie Star Wars.
3. Have you ever seen a performance of The Nutcracker?
4. My favorite movie is Batman.
5. Do you have the video of Cinderella?
6. Superman is a great movie!
7. Vicente played the Sesame Street CD for the young children.
8. Dana had a small part in Romeo and Juliet.
9. I checked out a copy of The Jolly Postman from the local library.
10. Patricia can't wait to read Green Eggs and Ham to her sister.

#3305 Daily Skills Practice–Grades 3–4 — 44 — ©Teacher Created Materials, Inc.

Page 45

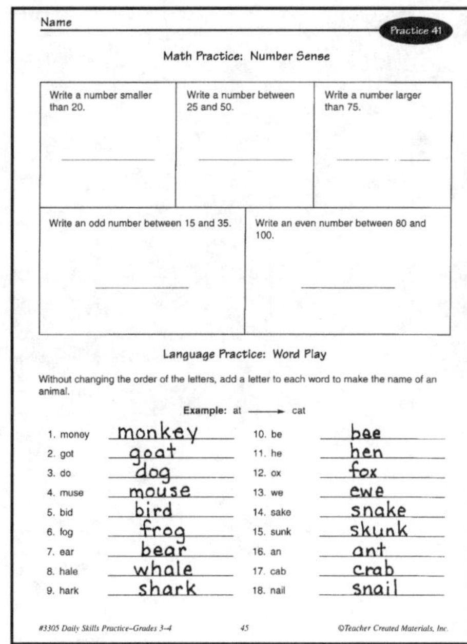

Name — Practice 41

Math Practice: Number Sense

Write a number smaller than 20. | Write a number between 25 and 50. | Write a number larger than 75.

Write an odd number between 15 and 35. | Write an even number between 80 and 100.

Language Practice: Word Play

Without changing the order of the letters, add a letter to each word to make the name of an animal.

Example: at ⟶ cat

1. money monkey
2. got goat
3. do dog
4. muse mouse
5. bid bird
6. fog frog
7. ear bear
8. hale whale
9. hark shark
10. be bee
11. he hen
12. ox fox
13. we ewe
14. sake snake
15. sunk skunk
16. an ant
17. cab crab
18. nail snail

#3305 Daily Skills Practice–Grades 3–4 — 45 — ©Teacher Created Materials, Inc.

Page 46

Name — Practice 42

Math Practice: Number Sense

Circle the even numbers. (8) 7 (6) (4) 3 1 (0) (2)

Circle the odd numbers. 12 (79) 36 (83) (57) (17) 10 (41)

Circle the numbers larger than 50. (71) 24 (85) 46 (59) (62) 12 49 5

Write the largest number that can be made using 4, 8, 1 and 5. 8,541

Write the number that is in the *thousands* place. 8

Write the smallest number that can be made using 4, 8, 1 and 5. 1,458

Write the number that is in the *thousands* place. 1

Language Practice: Titles

When writing the title of a CD, book, movie, television program or play, remember the following:

- Underline each word in the title.
- Write the important words in the title with a capital letter.

Example: Old MacDonald Had a Farm *not* Old MacDonald Had A Farm

Write the titles of your favorite CD, book, movie, television program, or play.

Favorite movie: ______

Favorite CD: ______

Favorite book: ______

Favorite play: ______

#3305 Daily Skills Practice–Grades 3–4 — 46 — ©Teacher Created Materials, Inc.

Page 47

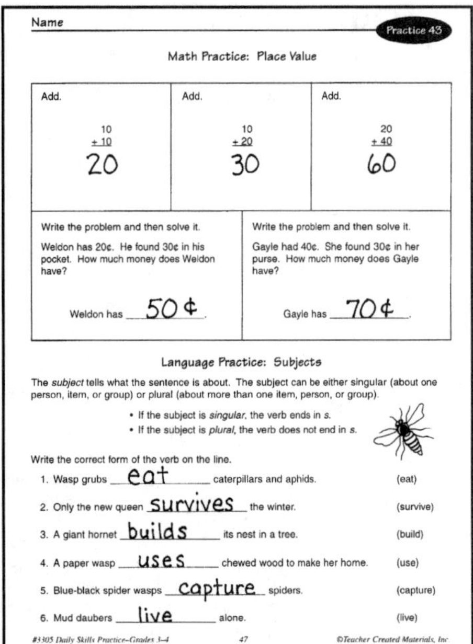

Name ________ Practice 43

Math Practice: Place Value

Add.	Add.	Add.
10 + 10 = 20	10 + 20 = 30	20 + 40 = 60

Write the problem and then solve it.	Write the problem and then solve it.
Weldon has 20¢. He found 30¢ in his pocket. How much money does Weldon have? Weldon has 50¢.	Gayle had 40¢. She found 30¢ in her purse. How much money does Gayle have? Gayle has 70¢.

Language Practice: Subjects

The *subject* tells what the sentence is about. The subject can be either singular (about one person, item, or group) or plural (about more than one item, person, or group).

- If the subject is *singular*, the verb ends in *s*.
- If the subject is *plural*, the verb does not end in *s*.

Write the correct form of the verb on the line.

1. Wasp grubs eat caterpillars and aphids. (eat)
2. Only the new queen survives the winter. (survive)
3. A giant hornet builds its nest in a tree. (build)
4. A paper wasp uses chewed wood to make her home. (use)
5. Blue-black spider wasps capture spiders. (capture)
6. Mud daubers live alone. (live)

#3305 Daily Skills Practice–Grades 3–4 47 ©Teacher Created Materials, Inc

Page 48

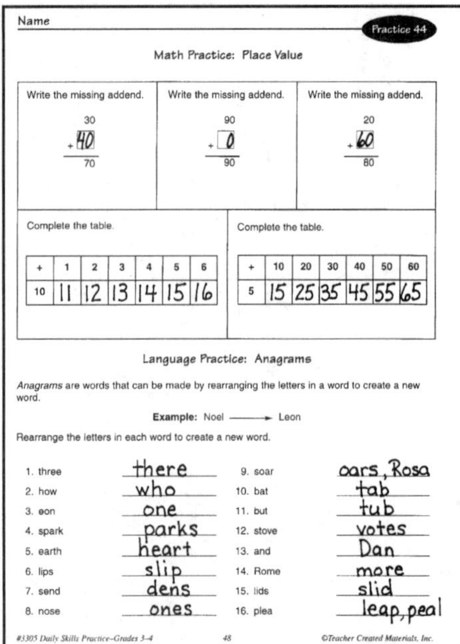

Name ________ Practice 44

Math Practice: Place Value

Write the missing addend.	Write the missing addend.	Write the missing addend.
30 + 40 = 70	90 + 0 = 90	20 + 60 = 80

Complete the table.

+	1	2	3	4	5	6
10	11	12	13	14	15	16

Complete the table.

+	10	20	30	40	50	60
5	15	25	35	45	55	65

Language Practice: Anagrams

Anagrams are words that can be made by rearranging the letters in a word to create a new word.

Example: Noel ⟶ Leon

Rearrange the letters in each word to create a new word.

1. three there
2. how who
3. eon one
4. spark parks
5. earth heart
6. lips slip
7. send dens
8. nose ones
9. soar oars, Rosa
10. bat tab
11. but tub
12. stove votes
13. and Dan
14. Rome more
15. lids slid
16. plea leap, peal

#3305 Daily Skills Practice–Grades 3–4 48 ©Teacher Created Materials, Inc.

Page 49

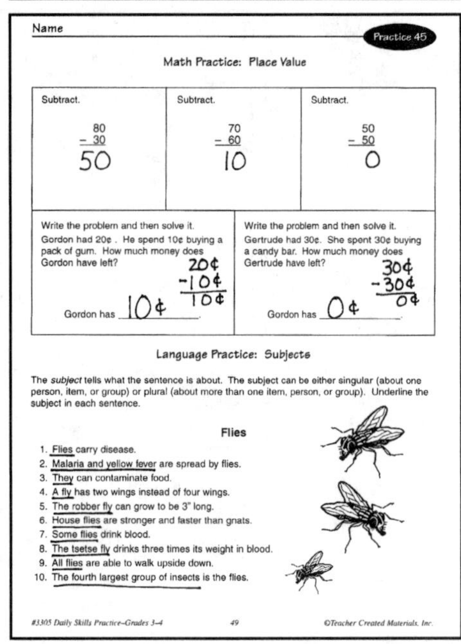

Name ________ Practice 45

Math Practice: Place Value

Subtract.	Subtract.	Subtract.
80 − 30 = 50	70 − 60 = 10	50 − 50 = 0

Write the problem and then solve it.	Write the problem and then solve it.
Gordon had 20¢. He spend 10¢ buying a pack of gum. How much money does Gordon have left? 20¢ − 10¢ = 10¢. Gordon has 10¢	Gertrude had 30¢. She spent 30¢ buying a candy bar. How much money does Gertrude have left? 30¢ − 30¢ = 0¢. Gordon has 0¢

Language Practice: Subjects

The *subject* tells what the sentence is about. The subject can be either singular (about one person, item, or group) or plural (about more than one item, person, or group). Underline the subject in each sentence.

Flies

1. Flies carry disease.
2. Malaria and yellow fever are spread by flies.
3. They can contaminate food.
4. A fly has two wings instead of four wings.
5. The robber fly can grow to be 3" long.
6. House flies are stronger and faster than gnats.
7. Some flies drink blood.
8. The tsetse fly drinks three times its weight in blood.
9. All flies are able to walk upside down.
10. The fourth largest group of insects is the flies.

#3305 Daily Skills Practice–Grades 3–4 49 ©Teacher Created Materials, Inc.

Page 50

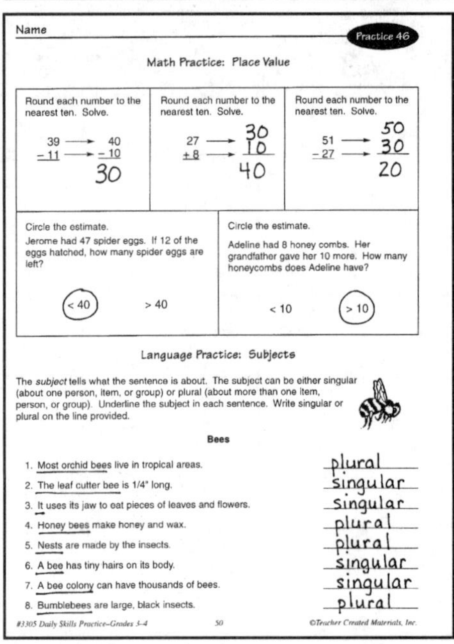

Name ________ Practice 46

Math Practice: Place Value

Round each number to the nearest ten. Solve.	Round each number to the nearest ten. Solve.	Round each number to the nearest ten. Solve.
39 ⟶ 40; − 11 ⟶ − 10; 30	27 ⟶ 30; + 8 ⟶ 10; 40	51 ⟶ 50; − 27 ⟶ 30; 20

Circle the estimate.	Circle the estimate.
Jerome had 47 spider eggs. If 12 of the eggs hatched, how many spider eggs are left? (< 40) > 40	Adeline had 8 honey combs. Her grandfather gave her 10 more. How many honeycombs does Adeline have? < 10 (> 10)

Language Practice: Subjects

The *subject* tells what the sentence is about. The subject can be either singular (about one person, item, or group) or plural (about more than one item, person, or group). Underline the subject in each sentence. Write singular or plural on the line provided.

Bees

1. Most orchid bees live in tropical areas. plural
2. The leaf cutter bee is 1/4" long. singular
3. It uses its jaw to eat pieces of leaves and flowers. singular
4. Honey bees make honey and wax. plural
5. Nests are made by the insects. plural
6. A bee has tiny hairs on its body. singular
7. A bee colony can have thousands of bees. singular
8. Bumblebees are large, black insects. plural

#3305 Daily Skills Practice–Grades 3–4 50 ©Teacher Created Materials, Inc.

Page 51

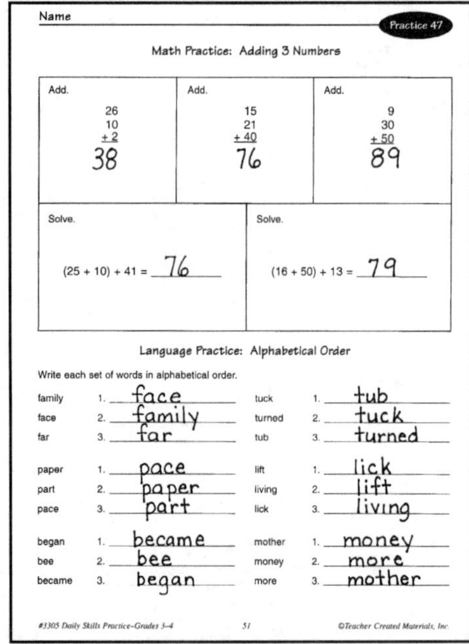

Name ________ Practice 47

Math Practice: Adding 3 Numbers

Add.	Add.	Add.
26 + 10 + 2 = 38	15 + 21 + 40 = 76	9 + 30 + 50 = 89

Solve.	Solve.
(25 + 10) + 41 = 76	(16 + 50) + 13 = 79

Language Practice: Alphabetical Order

Write each set of words in alphabetical order.

family	1. face	tuck	1. tub
face	2. family	turned	2. tuck
far	3. far	tub	3. turned
paper	1. pace	lift	1. lick
part	2. paper	living	2. lift
pace	3. part	lick	3. living
began	1. became	mother	1. money
bee	2. bee	money	2. more
became	3. began	more	3. mother

#3305 Daily Skills Practice–Grades 3–4 51 ©Teacher Created Materials, Inc.

Page 52

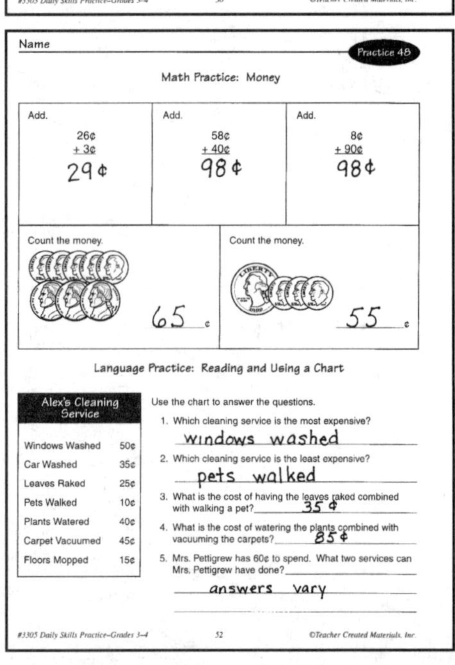

Name ________ Practice 48

Math Practice: Money

Add.	Add.	Add.
26¢ + 3¢ = 29¢	58¢ + 40¢ = 98¢	8¢ + 90¢ = 98¢

Count the money.	Count the money.
65¢	55¢

Language Practice: Reading and Using a Chart

Alex's Cleaning Service	
Windows Washed	50¢
Car Washed	35¢
Leaves Raked	25¢
Pets Walked	10¢
Plants Watered	40¢
Carpet Vacuumed	45¢
Floors Mopped	15¢

Use the chart to answer the questions.

1. Which cleaning service is the most expensive? windows washed
2. Which cleaning service is the least expensive? pets walked
3. What is the cost of having the leaves raked combined with walking a pet? 35¢
4. What is the cost of watering the plants combined with vacuuming the carpets? 85¢
5. Mrs. Pettigrew has 60¢ to spend. What two services can Mrs. Pettigrew have done? answers vary

#3305 Daily Skills Practice–Grades 3–4 52 ©Teacher Created Materials, Inc.

Page 53

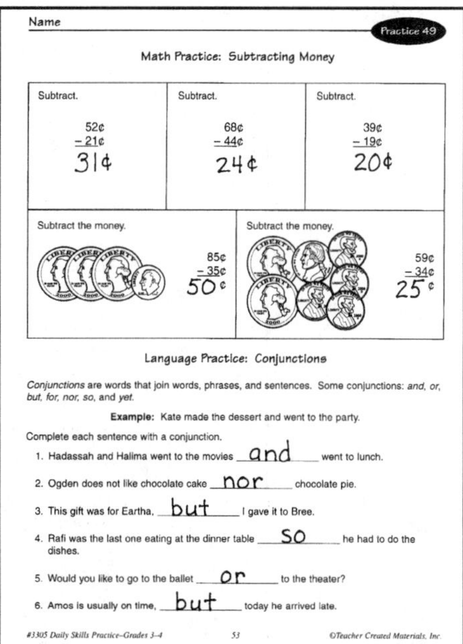

Name _______________ Practice 49

Math Practice: Subtracting Money

Subtract.	Subtract.	Subtract.
52¢ − 21¢ = 31¢	68¢ − 44¢ = 24¢	39¢ − 19¢ = 20¢

Subtract the money.	Subtract the money.
85¢ − 35¢ = 50¢	59¢ − 34¢ = 25¢

Language Practice: Conjunctions

Conjunctions are words that join words, phrases, and sentences. Some conjunctions: *and, or, but, for, nor, so,* and *yet.*

Example: Kate made the dessert and went to the party.

Complete each sentence with a conjunction.

1. Hadassah and Halima went to the movies __and__ went to lunch.
2. Ogden does not like chocolate cake __nor__ chocolate pie.
3. This gift was for Eartha, __but__ I gave it to Bree.
4. Rafi was the last one eating at the dinner table __so__ he had to do the dishes.
5. Would you like to go to the ballet __or__ to the theater?
6. Amos is usually on time, __but__ today he arrived late.

#3305 Daily Skills Practice–Grades 3–4 53 ©Teacher Created Materials, Inc.

Page 54

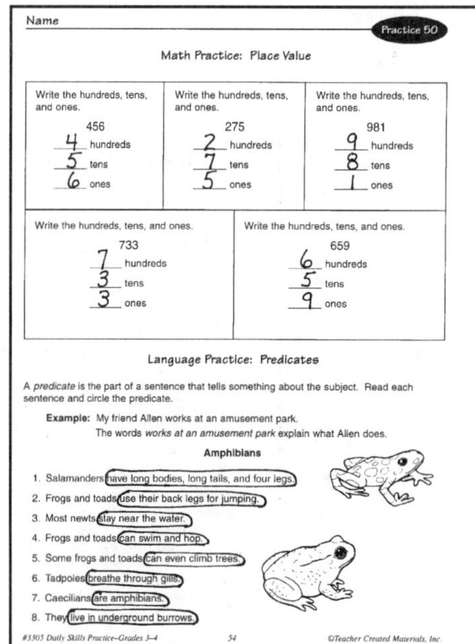

Name _______________ Practice 50

Math Practice: Place Value

Write the hundreds, tens, and ones.	Write the hundreds, tens, and ones.	Write the hundreds, tens, and ones.
456: 4 hundreds, 5 tens, 6 ones	275: 2 hundreds, 7 tens, 5 ones	981: 9 hundreds, 8 tens, 1 ones

Write the hundreds, tens, and ones.	Write the hundreds, tens, and ones.
733: 7 hundreds, 3 tens, 3 ones	659: 6 hundreds, 5 tens, 9 ones

Language Practice: Predicates

A *predicate* is the part of a sentence that tells something about the subject. Read each sentence and circle the predicate.

Example: My friend Allen works at an amusement park.
The words *works at an amusement park* explain what Allen does.

Amphibians

1. Salamanders (have long bodies, long tails, and four legs.)
2. Frogs and toads (use their back legs for jumping.)
3. Most newts (stay near the water.)
4. Frogs and toads (can swim and hop.)
5. Some frogs and toads (can even climb trees.)
6. Tadpoles (breathe through gills.)
7. Caecilians (are amphibians.)
8. They (live in underground burrows.)

#3305 Daily Skills Practice–Grades 3–4 54 ©Teacher Created Materials, Inc.

Page 55

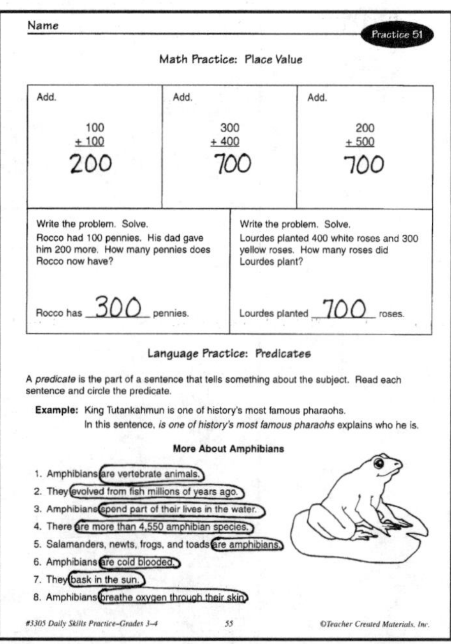

Name _______________ Practice 51

Math Practice: Place Value

Add.	Add.	Add.
100 + 100 = 200	300 + 400 = 700	200 + 500 = 700

Write the problem. Solve.	Write the problem. Solve.
Rocco had 100 pennies. His dad gave him 200 more. How many pennies does Rocco now have? Rocco has __300__ pennies.	Lourdes planted 400 white roses and 300 yellow roses. How many roses did Lourdes plant? Lourdes planted __700__ roses.

Language Practice: Predicates

A *predicate* is the part of a sentence that tells something about the subject. Read each sentence and circle the predicate.

Example: King Tutankahmun is one of history's most famous pharaohs.
In this sentence, *is one of history's most famous pharaohs* explains who he is.

More About Amphibians

1. Amphibians (are vertebrate animals.)
2. They (evolved from fish millions of years ago.)
3. Amphibians (spend part of their lives in the water.)
4. There (are more than 4,550 amphibian species.)
5. Salamanders, newts, frogs, and toads (are amphibians.)
6. Amphibians (are cold blooded.)
7. They (bask in the sun.)
8. Amphibians (breathe oxygen through their skin.)

#3305 Daily Skills Practice–Grades 3–4 55 ©Teacher Created Materials, Inc.

Page 56

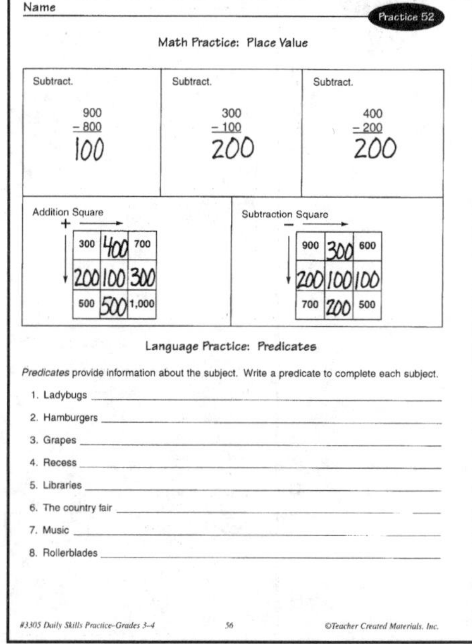

Name _______________ Practice 52

Math Practice: Place Value

Subtract.	Subtract.	Subtract.
900 − 800 = 100	300 − 100 = 200	400 − 200 = 200

Addition Square (+)

300	400	700
200	100	300
500	500	1,000

Subtraction Square (−)

900	300	600
200	100	100
700	200	500

Language Practice: Predicates

Predicates provide information about the subject. Write a predicate to complete each subject.

1. Ladybugs ____________
2. Hamburgers ____________
3. Grapes ____________
4. Recess ____________
5. Libraries ____________
6. The country fair ____________
7. Music ____________
8. Rollerblades ____________

#3305 Daily Skills Practice–Grades 3–4 56 ©Teacher Created Materials, Inc.

Page 57

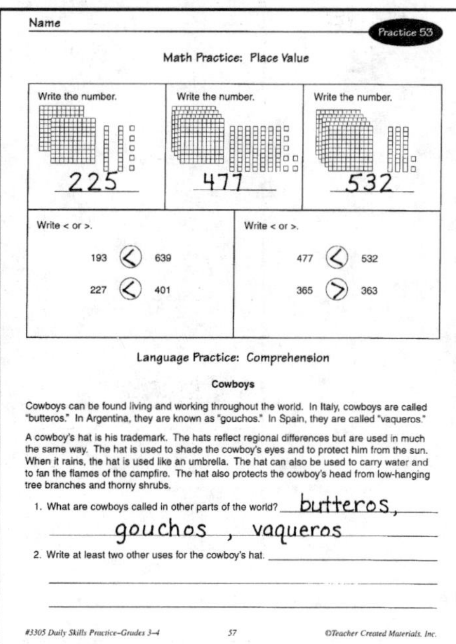

Name _______________ Practice 53

Math Practice: Place Value

Write the number.	Write the number.	Write the number.
225	477	532

Write < or >.	Write < or >.
193 < 639	477 < 532
227 < 401	365 > 363

Language Practice: Comprehension

Cowboys

Cowboys can be found living and working throughout the world. In Italy, cowboys are called "butteros." In Argentina, they are known as "gouchos." In Spain, they are called "vaqueros."

A cowboy's hat is his trademark. The hats reflect regional differences but are used in much the same way. The hat is used to shade the cowboy's eyes and to protect him from the sun. When it rains, the hat is used like an umbrella. The hat can also be used to carry water and to fan the flames of the campfire. The hat also protects the cowboy's head from low-hanging tree branches and thorny shrubs.

1. What are cowboys called in other parts of the world? __butteros, gouchos, vaqueros__
2. Write at least two other uses for the cowboy's hat. ____________

#3305 Daily Skills Practice–Grades 3–4 57 ©Teacher Created Materials, Inc.

Page 58

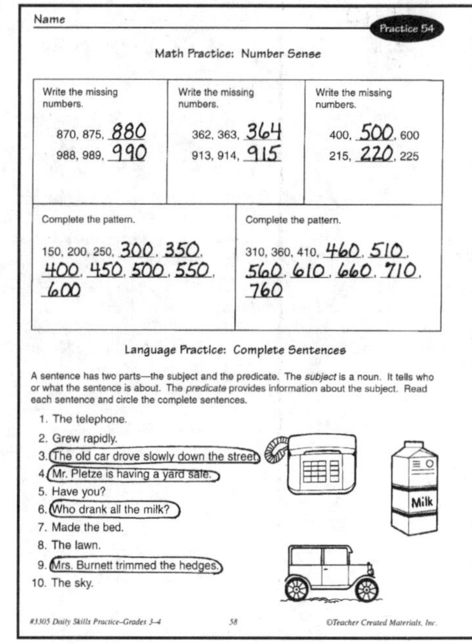

Name _______________ Practice 54

Math Practice: Number Sense

Write the missing numbers.	Write the missing numbers.	Write the missing numbers.
870, 875, 880	362, 363, 364	400, 500, 600
988, 989, 990	913, 914, 915	215, 220, 225

Complete the pattern.	Complete the pattern.
150, 200, 250, 300, 350, 400, 450, 500, 550, 600	310, 360, 410, 460, 510, 560, 610, 660, 710, 760

Language Practice: Complete Sentences

A sentence has two parts—the subject and the predicate. The *subject* is a noun. It tells who or what the sentence is about. The *predicate* provides information about the subject. Read each sentence and circle the complete sentences.

1. The telephone.
2. Grew rapidly.
3. (The old car drove slowly down the street.)
4. (Mr. Pletze is having a yard sale.)
5. Have you?
6. (Who drank all the milk?)
7. Made the bed.
8. The lawn.
9. (Mrs. Burnett trimmed the hedges.)
10. The sky.

#3305 Daily Skills Practice–Grades 3–4 58 ©Teacher Created Materials, Inc.

Page 59

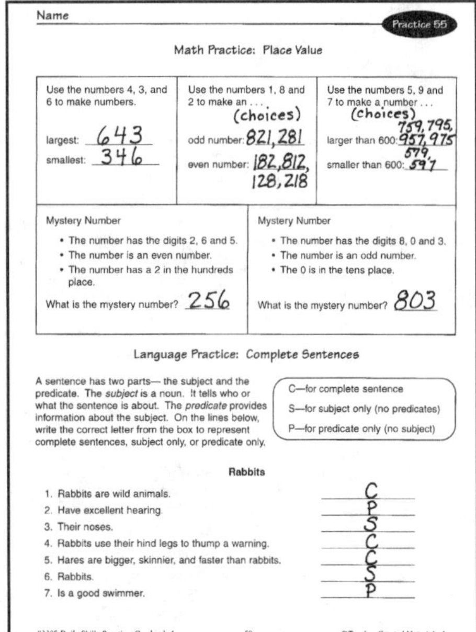

Name ________ Practice 55

Math Practice: Place Value

Use the numbers 4, 3, and 6 to make numbers.	Use the numbers 1, 8 and 2 to make an . . . (choices)	Use the numbers 5, 9 and 7 to make a number . . . (choices)
largest: 643 smallest: 346	odd number: 821, 281 even number: 182, 812, 128, 218	larger than 600: 759, 795, 957, 975 smaller than 600: 579, 597

Mystery Number	Mystery Number
• The number has the digits 2, 6 and 5. • The number is an even number. • The number has a 2 in the hundreds place. What is the mystery number? 256	• The number has the digits 8, 0 and 3. • The number is an odd number. • The 0 is in the tens place. What is the mystery number? 803

Language Practice: Complete Sentences

A sentence has two parts— the subject and the predicate. The *subject* is a noun. It tells who or what the sentence is about. The *predicate* provides information about the subject. On the lines below, write the correct letter from the box to represent complete sentences, subject only, or predicate only.

C—for complete sentence
S—for subject only (no predicates)
P—for predicate only (no subject)

Rabbits

1. Rabbits are wild animals. C
2. Have excellent hearing. P
3. Their noses. S
4. Rabbits use their hind legs to thump a warning. C
5. Hares are bigger, skinnier, and faster than rabbits. C
6. Rabbits. S
7. Is a good swimmer. P

#3305 Daily Skills Practice–Grades 3–4 59 ©Teacher Created Materials, Inc

Page 60

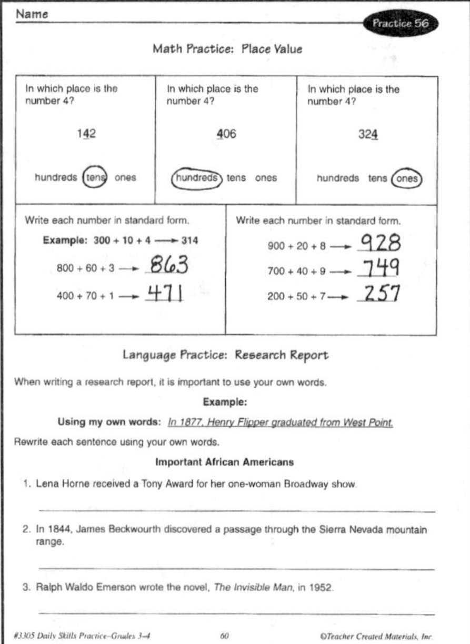

Name ________ Practice 56

Math Practice: Place Value

In which place is the number 4?	In which place is the number 4?	In which place is the number 4?
142 hundreds (tens) ones	406 (hundreds) tens ones	324 hundreds tens (ones)

Write each number in standard form.	Write each number in standard form.
Example: 300 + 10 + 4 ⟶ 314 800 + 60 + 3 ⟶ 863 400 + 70 + 1 ⟶ 471	900 + 20 + 8 ⟶ 928 700 + 40 + 9 ⟶ 749 200 + 50 + 7 ⟶ 257

Language Practice: Research Report

When writing a research report, it is important to use your own words.

Example:

Using my own words: In 1877, Henry Flipper graduated from West Point.

Rewrite each sentence using your own words.

Important African Americans

1. Lena Horne received a Tony Award for her one-woman Broadway show.
2. In 1844, James Beckwourth discovered a passage through the Sierra Nevada mountain range.
3. Ralph Waldo Emerson wrote the novel, *The Invisible Man*, in 1952.

#3305 Daily Skills Practice–Grades 3–4 60 ©Teacher Created Materials, Inc

Page 61

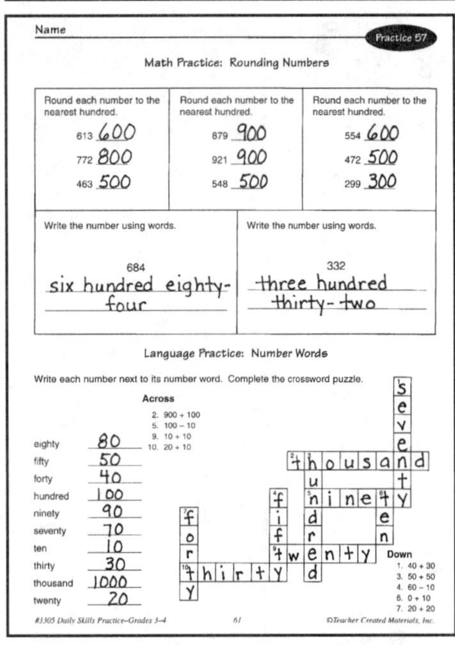

Name ________ Practice 57

Math Practice: Rounding Numbers

Round each number to the nearest hundred.	Round each number to the nearest hundred.	Round each number to the nearest hundred.
613 600 772 800 463 500	879 900 921 900 548 500	554 600 472 500 299 300

Write the number using words.	Write the number using words.
684 six hundred eighty-four	332 three hundred thirty-two

Language Practice: Number Words

Write each number next to its number word. Complete the crossword puzzle.

eighty 80
fifty 50
forty 40
hundred 100
ninety 90
seventy 70
ten 10
thirty 30
thousand 1000
twenty 20

Across
2. 900 + 100
5. 100 – 10
9. 10 + 10
10. 20 + 10

Down
1. 40 + 30
3. 50 + 50
4. 60 – 10
6. 0 + 10
7. 20 + 20

#3305 Daily Skills Practice–Grades 3–4 61 ©Teacher Created Materials, Inc.

Page 62

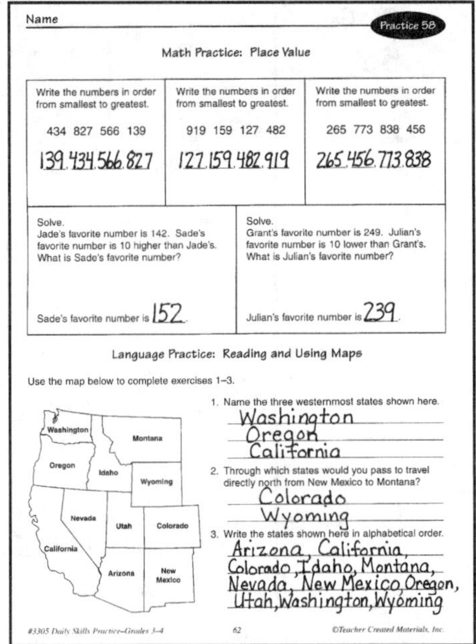

Name ________ Practice 58

Math Practice: Place Value

Write the numbers in order from smallest to greatest.	Write the numbers in order from smallest to greatest.	Write the numbers in order from smallest to greatest.
434 827 566 139 139, 434, 566, 827	919 159 127 482 127, 159, 482, 919	265 773 838 456 265, 456, 773, 838

Solve.	Solve.
Jade's favorite number is 142. Sade's favorite number is 10 higher than Jade's. What is Sade's favorite number? Sade's favorite number is 152.	Grant's favorite number is 249. Julian's favorite number is 10 lower than Grant's. What is Julian's favorite number? Julian's favorite number is 239.

Language Practice: Reading and Using Maps

Use the map below to complete exercises 1–3.

1. Name the three westernmost states shown here. Washington, Oregon, California
2. Through which states would you pass to travel directly north from New Mexico to Montana? Colorado, Wyoming
3. Write the states shown here in alphabetical order. Arizona, California, Colorado, Idaho, Montana, Nevada, New Mexico, Oregon, Utah, Washington, Wyoming

#3305 Daily Skills Practice–Grades 3–4 62 ©Teacher Created Materials, Inc.

Page 63

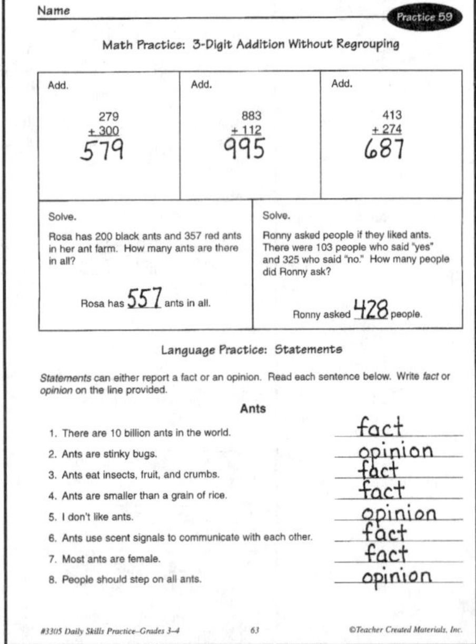

Name ________ Practice 59

Math Practice: 3-Digit Addition Without Regrouping

Add.	Add.	Add.
279 + 300 = 579	883 + 112 = 995	413 + 274 = 687

Solve.	Solve.
Rosa has 200 black ants and 357 red ants in her ant farm. How many ants are there in all? Rosa has 557 ants in all.	Ronny asked people if they liked ants. There were 103 people who said "yes" and 325 who said "no." How many people did Ronny ask? Ronny asked 428 people.

Language Practice: Statements

Statements can either report a fact or an opinion. Read each sentence below. Write *fact* or *opinion* on the line provided.

Ants

1. There are 10 billion ants in the world. fact
2. Ants are stinky bugs. opinion
3. Ants eat insects, fruit, and crumbs. fact
4. Ants are smaller than a grain of rice. fact
5. I don't like ants. opinion
6. Ants use scent signals to communicate with each other. fact
7. Most ants are female. fact
8. People should step on all ants. opinion

#3305 Daily Skills Practice–Grades 3–4 63 ©Teacher Created Materials, Inc.

Page 64

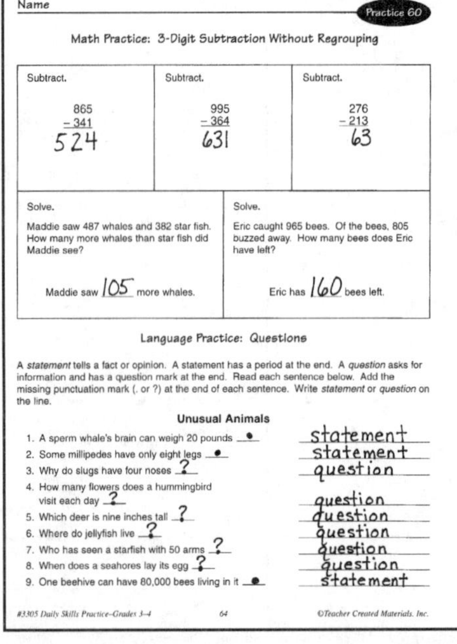

Name ________ Practice 60

Math Practice: 3-Digit Subtraction Without Regrouping

Subtract.	Subtract.	Subtract.
865 – 341 = 524	995 – 364 = 631	276 – 213 = 63

Solve.	Solve.
Maddie saw 487 whales and 382 star fish. How many more whales than star fish did Maddie see? Maddie saw 105 more whales.	Eric caught 965 bees. Of the bees, 805 buzzed away. How many bees does Eric have left? Eric has 160 bees left.

Language Practice: Questions

A *statement* tells a fact or opinion. A statement has a period at the end. A *question* asks for information and has a question mark at the end. Read each sentence below. Add the missing punctuation mark (. or ?) at the end of each sentence. Write *statement* or *question* on the line.

Unusual Animals

1. A sperm whale's brain can weigh 20 pounds . statement
2. Some millipedes have only eight legs . statement
3. Why do slugs have four noses ? question
4. How many flowers does a hummingbird visit each day ? question
5. Which deer is nine inches tall ? question
6. Where do jellyfish live ? question
7. Who has seen a starfish with 50 arms ? question
8. When does a seahores lay its egg ? question
9. One beehive can have 80,000 bees living in it . statement

#3305 Daily Skills Practice–Grades 3–4 64 ©Teacher Created Materials, Inc.

Page 65

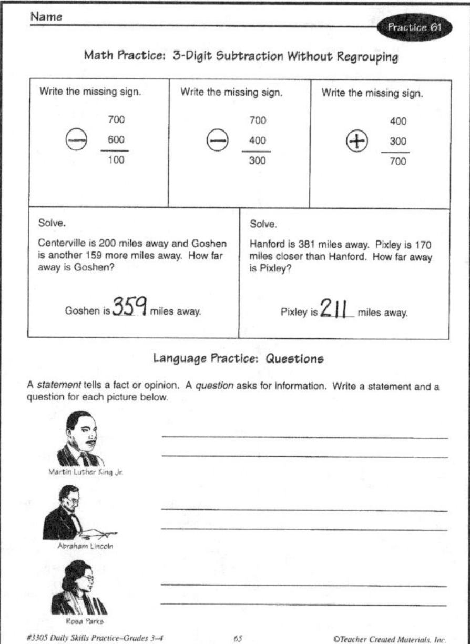

Name ______ Practice 61

Math Practice: 3-Digit Subtraction Without Regrouping

Write the missing sign.	Write the missing sign.	Write the missing sign.
− 700 / 600 / 100	− 700 / 400 / 300	+ 400 / 300 / 700

Solve.	Solve.
Centerville is 200 miles away and Goshen is another 159 more miles away. How far away is Goshen? Goshen is 359 miles away.	Hanford is 381 miles away. Pixley is 170 miles closer than Hanford. How far away is Pixley? Pixley is 211 miles away.

Language Practice: Questions

A *statement* tells a fact or opinion. A *question* asks for information. Write a statement and a question for each picture below.

Martin Luther King Jr.

Abraham Lincoln

Rosa Parks

#3305 Daily Skills Practice–Grades 3–4 65 ©Teacher Created Materials, Inc.

Page 66

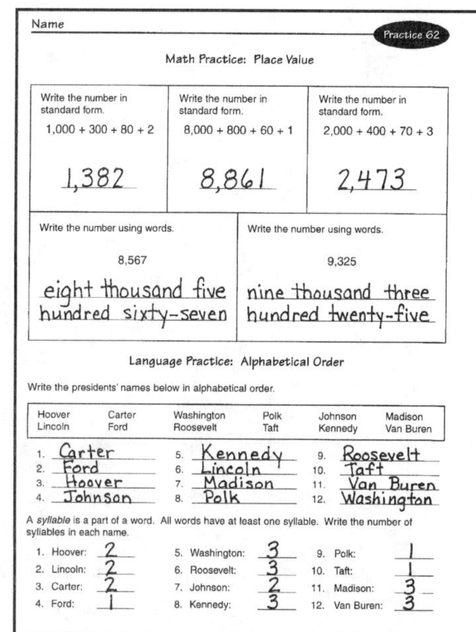

Name ______ Practice 62

Math Practice: Place Value

Write the number in standard form. 1,000 + 300 + 80 + 2	Write the number in standard form. 8,000 + 800 + 60 + 1	Write the number in standard form. 2,000 + 400 + 70 + 3
1,382	8,861	2,473

Write the number using words. 8,567	Write the number using words. 9,325
eight thousand five hundred sixty-seven	nine thousand three hundred twenty-five

Language Practice: Alphabetical Order

Write the presidents' names below in alphabetical order.

Hoover Lincoln	Carter Ford	Washington Roosevelt	Polk Taft	Johnson Kennedy	Madison Van Buren

1. Carter
2. Ford
3. Hoover
4. Johnson
5. Kennedy
6. Lincoln
7. Madison
8. Polk
9. Roosevelt
10. Taft
11. Van Buren
12. Washington

A *syllable* is a part of a word. All words have at least one syllable. Write the number of syllables in each name.

1. Hoover: 2
2. Lincoln: 2
3. Carter: 2
4. Ford: 1
5. Washington: 3
6. Roosevelt: 3
7. Johnson: 2
8. Kennedy: 3
9. Polk: 1
10. Taft: 1
11. Madison: 3
12. Van Buren: 3

#3305 Daily Skills Practice–Grades 3–4 66 ©Teacher Created Materials, Inc.

Page 67

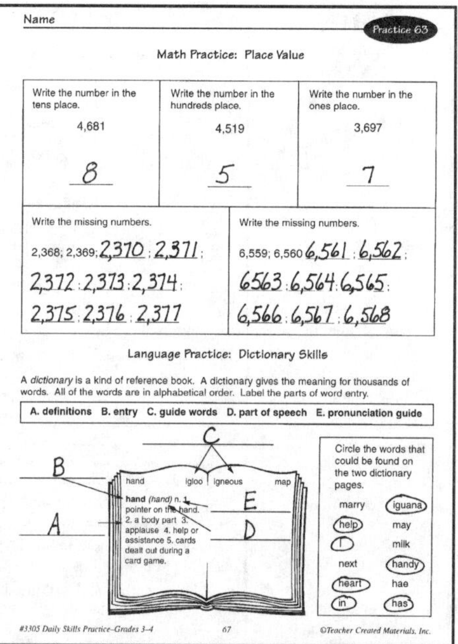

Name ______ Practice 63

Math Practice: Place Value

Write the number in the tens place. 4,681	Write the number in the hundreds place. 4,519	Write the number in the ones place. 3,697
8	5	7

Write the missing numbers.	Write the missing numbers.
2,368; 2,369; 2,370; 2,371; 2,372; 2,373; 2,374; 2,375; 2,376; 2,377	6,559; 6,560; 6,561; 6,562; 6563; 6,564; 6,565; 6,566; 6,567; 6,568

Language Practice: Dictionary Skills

A *dictionary* is a kind of reference book. A dictionary gives the meaning for thousands of words. All of the words are in alphabetical order. Label the parts of word entry.

A. definitions B. entry C. guide words D. part of speech E. pronunciation guide

Circle the words that could be found on the two dictionary pages.

marry, iguana, help, may, I, milk, next, handy, heart, hae, in, has

#3305 Daily Skills Practice–Grades 3–4 67 ©Teacher Created Materials, Inc.

Page 68

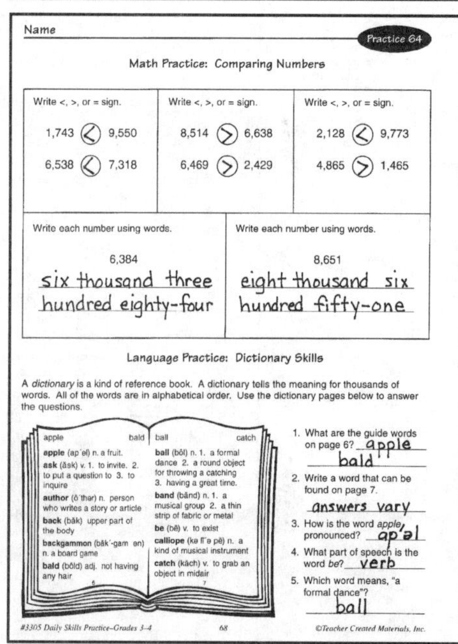

Name ______ Practice 64

Math Practice: Comparing Numbers

Write <, >, or = sign.	Write <, >, or = sign.	Write <, >, or = sign.
1,743 < 9,550	8,514 > 6,638	2,128 < 9,773
6,538 < 7,318	6,469 > 2,429	4,865 > 1,465

Write each number using words. 6,384	Write each number using words. 8,651
six thousand three hundred eighty-four	eight thousand six hundred fifty-one

Language Practice: Dictionary Skills

A *dictionary* is a kind of reference book. A dictionary tells the meaning for thousands of words. All of the words are in alphabetical order. Use the dictionary pages below to answer the questions.

apple bald
ball catch
apple (ap' el) n. a fruit.
ask (äsk) v. 1. to invite. 2. to put a question to 3. to inquire
author (ô' ther) n. person who writes a story or article
back (băk) upper part of the body
backgammon (băk' gam en) n. a board game
bald (bôld) adj. not having any hair
ball (bôl) n. 1. a formal dance 2. a round object for throwing a catching 3. having a great time.
band (bănd) n. 1. a musical group 2. a thin strip of fabric or metal
be (bē) v. to exist
calliope (kə lī' ə pē) n. a kind of musical instrument
catch (kăch) v. to grab an object in midair

1. What are the guide words on page 6? apple bald
2. Write a word that can be found on page 7. answers vary
3. How is the word *apple*, pronounced? ap'əl
4. What part of speech is the word *be*? verb
5. Which word means, "a formal dance"? ball

#3305 Daily Skills Practice–Grades 3–4 68 ©Teacher Created Materials, Inc.

Page 69

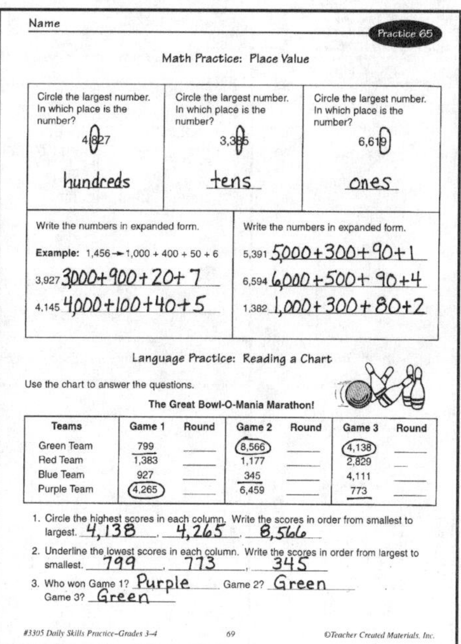

Name ______ Practice 65

Math Practice: Place Value

Circle the largest number. In which place is the number? 4,827	Circle the largest number. In which place is the number? 3,395	Circle the largest number. In which place is the number? 6,619
hundreds	tens	ones

Write the numbers in expanded form.	Write the numbers in expanded form.
Example: 1,456 → 1,000 + 400 + 50 + 6	5,391 5,000+300+90+1
3,927 3,000+900+20+7	6,594 6,000+500+90+4
4,145 4,000+100+40+5	1,382 1,000+300+80+2

Language Practice: Reading a Chart

Use the chart to answer the questions.

The Great Bowl-O-Mania Marathon!

Teams	Game 1	Round	Game 2	Round	Game 3	Round
Green Team	799		8,566		4,138	
Red Team	1,383		1,177		2,829	
Blue Team	927		345		4,111	
Purple Team	4,265		6,459		773	

1. Circle the highest scores in each column. Write the scores in order from smallest to largest. 4,138, 4,265, 8,566
2. Underline the lowest scores in each column. Write the scores in order from largest to smallest. 799, 773, 345
3. Who won Game 1? Purple Game 2? Green Game 3? Green

#3305 Daily Skills Practice–Grades 3–4 69 ©Teacher Created Materials, Inc.

Page 70

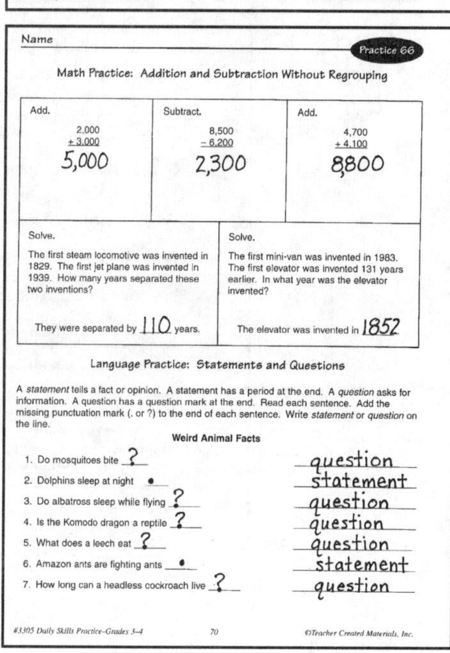

Name ______ Practice 66

Math Practice: Addition and Subtraction Without Regrouping

Add.	Subtract.	Add.
2,000 + 3,000 = 5,000	8,500 − 6,200 = 2,300	4,700 + 4,100 = 8800

Solve.	Solve.
The first steam locomotive was invented in 1829. The first jet plane was invented in 1939. How many years separated these two inventions? They were separated by 110 years.	The first mini-van was invented in 1983. The first elevator was invented 131 years earlier. In what year was the elevator invented? The elevator was invented in 1852

Language Practice: Statements and Questions

A *statement* tells a fact or opinion. A statement has a period at the end. A *question* asks for information. A question has a question mark at the end. Read each sentence. Add the missing punctuation mark (. or ?) to the end of each sentence. Write *statement* or *question* on the line.

Weird Animal Facts

1. Do mosquitoes bite ? question
2. Dolphins sleep at night . statement
3. Do albatross sleep while flying ? question
4. Is the Komodo dragon a reptile ? question
5. What does a leech eat ? question
6. Amazon ants are fighting ants . statement
7. How long can a headless cockroach live ? question

#3305 Daily Skills Practice–Grades 3–4 70 ©Teacher Created Materials, Inc.

Page 71

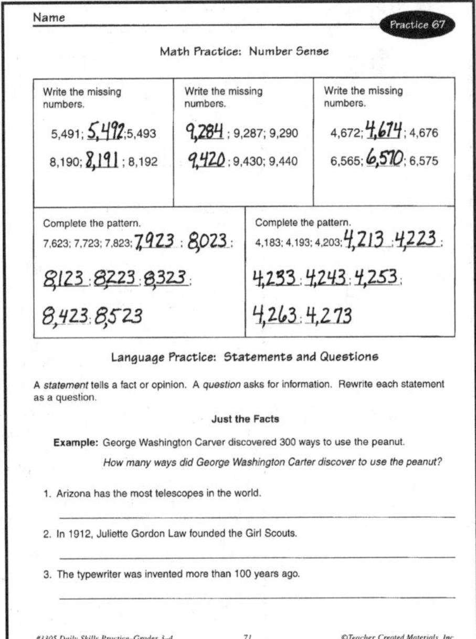

Name ______ Practice 67

Math Practice: Number Sense

Write the missing numbers.	Write the missing numbers.	Write the missing numbers.
5,491; 5,492; 5,493 8,190; 8,191; 8,192	9,284; 9,287; 9,290 9,420; 9,430; 9,440	4,672; 4,674; 4,676 6,565; 6,570; 6,575

Complete the pattern.	Complete the pattern.
7,623; 7,723; 7,823; 7,923; 8,023; 8,123; 8,223; 8,323; 8,423; 8,523	4,183; 4,193; 4,203; 4,213; 4,223; 4,233; 4,243; 4,253; 4,263; 4,273

Language Practice: Statements and Questions

A *statement* tells a fact or opinion. A *question* asks for information. Rewrite each statement as a question.

Just the Facts

Example: George Washington Carver discovered 300 ways to use the peanut.

How many ways did George Washington Carter discover to use the peanut?

1. Arizona has the most telescopes in the world.
2. In 1912, Juliette Gordon Law founded the Girl Scouts.
3. The typewriter was invented more than 100 years ago.

#3305 Daily Skills Practice–Grades 3–4 71 ©Teacher Created Materials, Inc.

Page 72

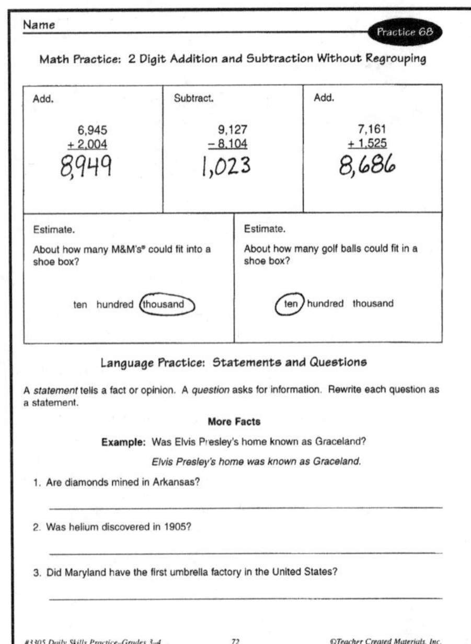

Name ______ Practice 68

Math Practice: 2 Digit Addition and Subtraction Without Regrouping

Add.	Subtract.	Add.
6,945 + 2,004 8,949	9,127 − 8,104 1,023	7,161 + 1,525 8,686

Estimate.	Estimate.
About how many M&M's® could fit into a shoe box? ten hundred (thousand)	About how many golf balls could fit in a shoe box? (ten) hundred thousand

Language Practice: Statements and Questions

A *statement* tells a fact or opinion. A *question* asks for information. Rewrite each question as a statement.

More Facts

Example: Was Elvis Presley's home known as Graceland?

Elvis Presley's home was known as Graceland.

1. Are diamonds mined in Arkansas?
2. Was helium discovered in 1905?
3. Did Maryland have the first umbrella factory in the United States?

#3305 Daily Skills Practice–Grades 3–4 72 ©Teacher Created Materials, Inc.

Page 73

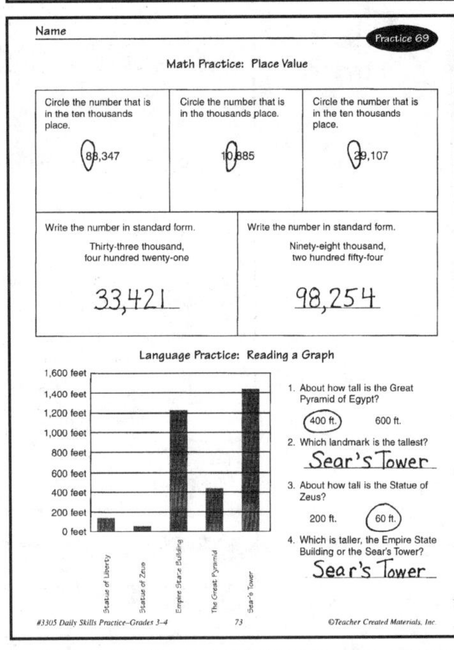

Name ______ Practice 69

Math Practice: Place Value

Circle the number that is in the ten thousands place.	Circle the number that is in the thousands place.	Circle the number that is in the ten thousands place.
(8)8,347	1(0),885	(2)9,107

Write the number in standard form.	Write the number in standard form.
Thirty-three thousand, four hundred twenty-one 33,421	Ninety-eight thousand, two hundred fifty-four 98,254

Language Practice: Reading a Graph

1. About how tall is the Great Pyramid of Egypt? (400 ft.) 600 ft.
2. Which landmark is the tallest? Sear's Tower
3. About how tall is the Statue of Zeus? 200 ft. (60 ft.)
4. Which is taller, the Empire State Building or the Sear's Tower? Sear's Tower

#3305 Daily Skills Practice–Grades 3–4 73 ©Teacher Created Materials, Inc.

Page 74

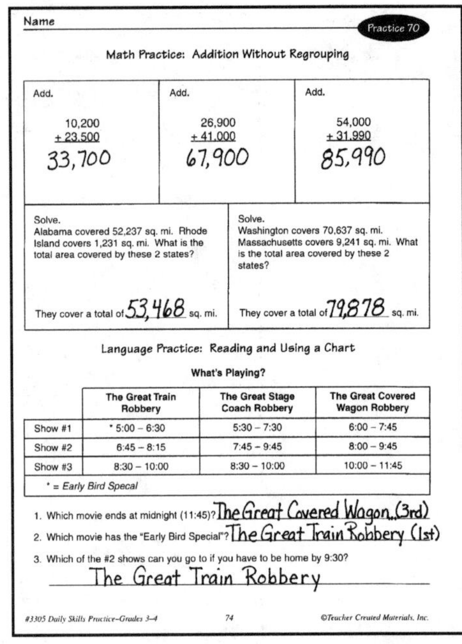

Name ______ Practice 70

Math Practice: Addition Without Regrouping

Add.	Add.	Add.
10,200 + 23,500 33,700	26,900 + 41,000 67,900	54,000 + 31,990 85,990

Solve.	Solve.
Alabama covered 52,237 sq. mi. Rhode Island covers 1,231 sq. mi. What is the total area covered by these 2 states? They cover a total of 53,468 sq. mi.	Washington covers 70,637 sq. mi. Massachusetts covers 9,241 sq. mi. What is the total area covered by these 2 states? They cover a total of 79,878 sq. mi.

Language Practice: Reading and Using a Chart

What's Playing?

	The Great Train Robbery	The Great Stage Coach Robbery	The Great Covered Wagon Robbery
Show #1	* 5:00 – 6:30	5:30 – 7:30	6:00 – 7:45
Show #2	6:45 – 8:15	7:45 – 9:45	8:00 – 9:45
Show #3	8:30 – 10:00	8:30 – 10:00	10:00 – 11:45

* = *Early Bird Special*

1. Which movie ends at midnight (11:45)? The Great Covered Wagon (3rd)
2. Which movie has the "Early Bird Special"? The Great Train Robbery (1st)
3. Which of the #2 shows can you go to if you have to be home by 9:30? The Great Train Robbery

#3305 Daily Skills Practice–Grades 3–4 74 ©Teacher Created Materials, Inc.

Page 75

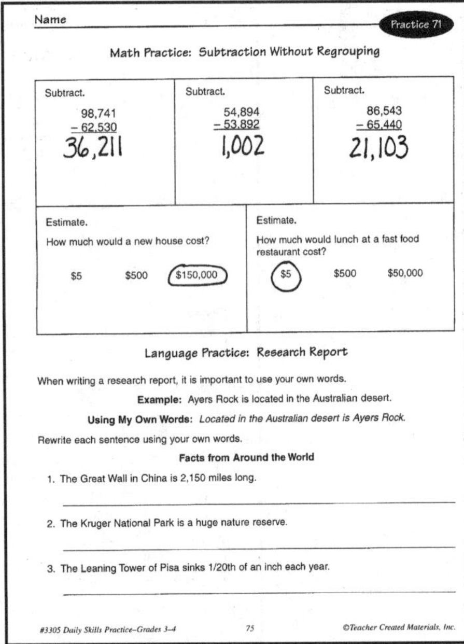

Name ______ Practice 71

Math Practice: Subtraction Without Regrouping

Subtract.	Subtract.	Subtract.
98,741 − 62,530 36,211	54,894 − 53,892 1,002	86,543 − 65,440 21,103

Estimate.	Estimate.
How much would a new house cost? $5 $500 ($150,000)	How much would lunch at a fast food restaurant cost? ($5) $500 $50,000

Language Practice: Research Report

When writing a research report, it is important to use your own words.

Example: Ayers Rock is located in the Australian desert.

Using My Own Words: *Located in the Australian desert is Ayers Rock.*

Rewrite each sentence using your own words.

Facts from Around the World

1. The Great Wall in China is 2,150 miles long.
2. The Kruger National Park is a huge nature reserve.
3. The Leaning Tower of Pisa sinks 1/20th of an inch each year.

#3305 Daily Skills Practice–Grades 3–4 75 ©Teacher Created Materials, Inc.

Page 76

Name ______ Practice 72

Math Practice: Subtraction Without Regrouping

Subtract.	Subtract.	Subtract.
36,182 − 14,031 22,151	42,892 − 31,642 11,250	45,577 − 35,157 10,420

Write the number using numbers and words.	Write the number using numbers and words.
82,657 82 thousands, 6 hundreds, 5 tens, 7 ones	23,496 23 thousands, 4 hundreds, 9 tens, 6 ones

Language Practice: Alphabetical Order

Make a list of games and toys.	Rewrite the list in alphabetical order.
1.	1.
2.	2.
3.	3.
4.	4.
5.	5.
6.	6.
7.	7.
8.	8.
9.	9.
10.	10.

#3305 Daily Skills Practice–Grades 3–4 76 ©Teacher Created Materials, Inc.

Page 77

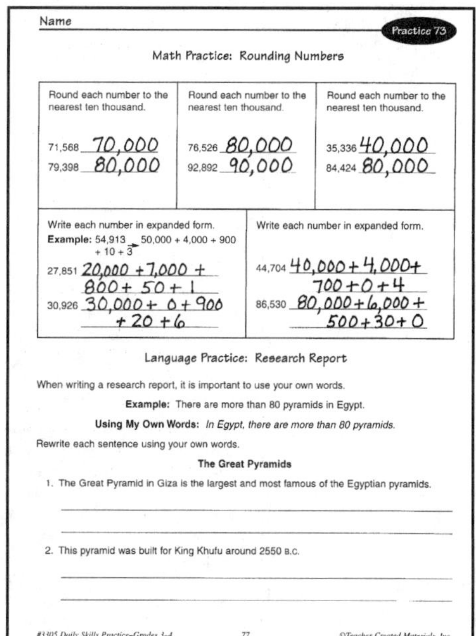

Name Practice 73

Math Practice: Rounding Numbers

Round each number to the nearest ten thousand.	Round each number to the nearest ten thousand.	Round each number to the nearest ten thousand.
71,568 70,000 79,398 80,000	76,526 80,000 92,892 90,000	35,336 40,000 84,424 80,000

Write each number in expanded form.	Write each number in expanded form.
Example: 54,913 = 50,000 + 4,000 + 900 + 10 + 3 27,851 20,000 + 7,000 + 800 + 50 + 1 30,926 30,000 + 0 + 900 + 20 + 6	44,704 40,000 + 4,000 + 700 + 0 + 4 86,530 80,000 + 6,000 + 500 + 30 + 0

Language Practice: Research Report

When writing a research report, it is important to use your own words.

Example: There are more than 80 pyramids in Egypt.

Using My Own Words: *In Egypt, there are more than 80 pyramids.*

Rewrite each sentence using your own words.

The Great Pyramids

1. The Great Pyramid in Giza is the largest and most famous of the Egyptian pyramids.
2. This pyramid was built for King Khufu around 2550 B.C.

#3305 Daily Skills Practice–Grades 3–4 77 ©Teacher Created Materials, Inc.

Page 78

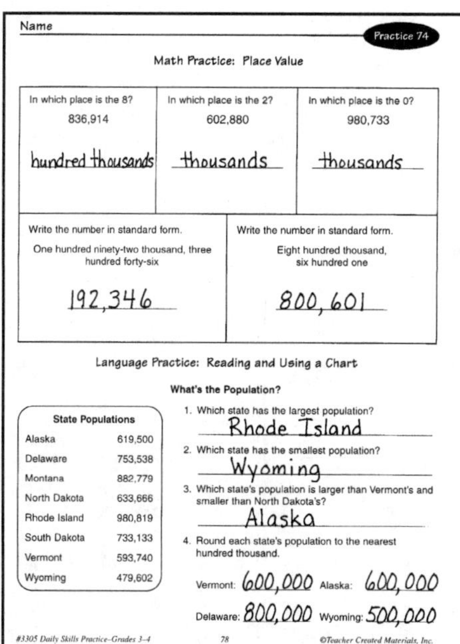

Name Practice 74

Math Practice: Place Value

In which place is the 8? 836,914	In which place is the 2? 602,880	In which place is the 0? 980,733
hundred thousands	thousands	thousands

Write the number in standard form. One hundred ninety-two thousand, three hundred forty-six	Write the number in standard form. Eight hundred thousand, six hundred one
192,346	800,601

Language Practice: Reading and Using a Chart

What's the Population?

State Populations	
Alaska	619,500
Delaware	753,538
Montana	882,779
North Dakota	633,666
Rhode Island	980,819
South Dakota	733,133
Vermont	593,740
Wyoming	479,602

1. Which state has the largest population? Rhode Island
2. Which state has the smallest population? Wyoming
3. Which state's population is larger than Vermont's and smaller than North Dakota's? Alaska
4. Round each state's population to the nearest hundred thousand.
   Vermont: 600,000 Alaska: 600,000
   Delaware: 800,000 Wyoming: 500,000

#3305 Daily Skills Practice–Grades 3–4 78 ©Teacher Created Materials, Inc.

Page 79

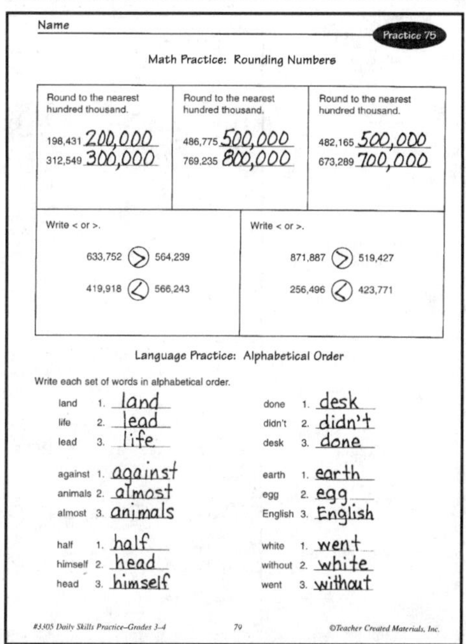

Name Practice 75

Math Practice: Rounding Numbers

Round to the nearest hundred thousand.	Round to the nearest hundred thousand.	Round to the nearest hundred thousand.
198,431 200,000 312,549 300,000	486,775 500,000 769,235 800,000	482,165 500,000 673,289 700,000

Write < or >.	Write < or >.
633,752 > 564,239 419,918 < 566,243	871,887 > 519,427 256,496 < 423,771

Language Practice: Alphabetical Order

Write each set of words in alphabetical order.

land life lead	1. land 2. lead 3. life	done didn't desk	1. desk 2. didn't 3. done
against animals almost	1. against 2. almost 3. animals	earth egg English	1. earth 2. egg 3. English
half himself head	1. half 2. head 3. himself	white without went	1. went 2. white 3. without

#3305 Daily Skills Practice–Grades 3–4 79 ©Teacher Created Materials, Inc.

Page 80

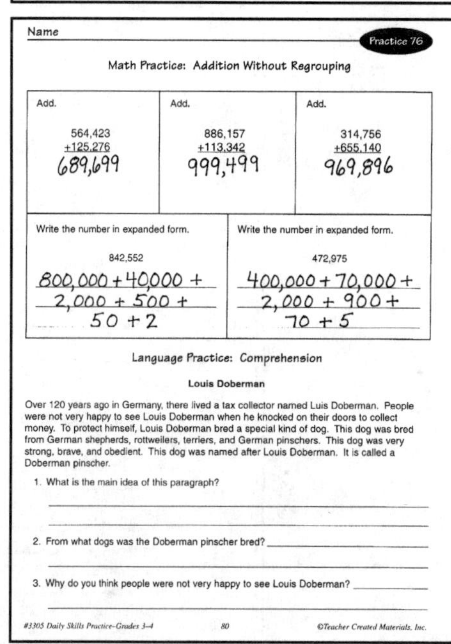

Name Practice 76

Math Practice: Addition Without Regrouping

Add.	Add.	Add.
564,423 +125,276 689,699	886,157 +113,342 999,499	314,756 +655,140 969,896

Write the number in expanded form.	Write the number in expanded form.
842,552 800,000 + 40,000 + 2,000 + 500 + 50 + 2	472,975 400,000 + 70,000 + 2,000 + 900 + 70 + 5

Language Practice: Comprehension

Louis Doberman

Over 120 years ago in Germany, there lived a tax collector named Luis Doberman. People were not very happy to see Louis Doberman when he knocked on their doors to collect money. To protect himself, Louis Doberman bred a special kind of dog. This dog was bred from German shepherds, rottweilers, terriers, and German pinschers. This dog was very strong, brave, and obedient. This dog was named after Louis Doberman. It is called a Doberman pinscher.

1. What is the main idea of this paragraph?
2. From what dogs was the Doberman pinscher bred?
3. Why do you think people were not very happy to see Louis Doberman?

#3305 Daily Skills Practice–Grades 3–4 80 ©Teacher Created Materials, Inc.

Page 81

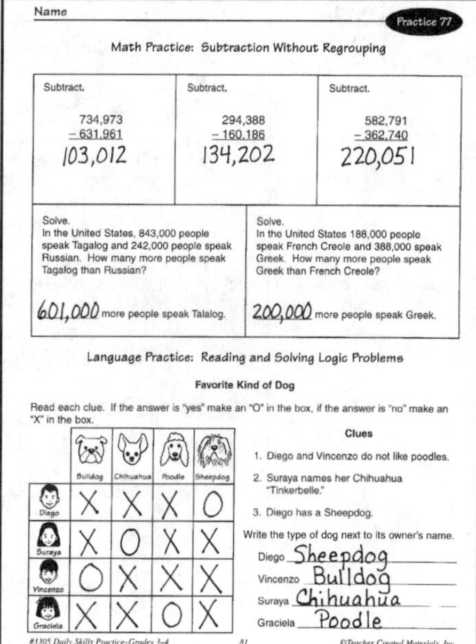

Name Practice 77

Math Practice: Subtraction Without Regrouping

Subtract.	Subtract.	Subtract.
734,973 – 631,961 103,012	294,388 – 160,186 134,202	582,791 – 362,740 220,051

Solve. In the United States, 843,000 people speak Tagalog and 242,000 people speak Russian. How many more people speak Tagalog than Russian?	Solve. In the United States 188,000 people speak French Creole and 388,000 people speak Greek. How many more people speak Greek than French Creole?
601,000 more people speak Talalog.	200,000 more people speak Greek.

Language Practice: Reading and Solving Logic Problems

Favorite Kind of Dog

Read each clue. If the answer is "yes" make an "O" in the box, if the answer is "no" make an "X" in the box.

	Bulldog	Chihuahua	Poodle	Sheepdog
Diego	X	X	X	O
Suraya	X	O	X	X
Vincenzo	O	X	X	X
Graciela	X	X	O	X

Clues

1. Diego and Vincenzo do not like poodles.
2. Suraya names her Chihuahua "Tinkerbelle."
3. Diego has a Sheepdog.

Write the type of dog next to its owner's name.

Diego Sheepdog
Vincenzo Bulldog
Suraya Chihuahua
Graciela Poodle

#3305 Daily Skills Practice–Grades 3–4 81 ©Teacher Created Materials, Inc.

Page 82

Name Practice 78

Math Practice: Time

How many minutes in one hour?	How many minutes in half an hour?	How many minutes in a quarter of an hour?
60 minutes	30 minutes	15 minutes

How many minutes in 2 hours?	How many minutes in $1\frac{1}{2}$ hours?
120 minutes	90 minutes

Language Practice: Articles

Articles are used with nouns. Articles tell how the noun is being used. There are three articles. They are: **a**, **an**, and **the**.

- Use *a* before nouns that begin with a consonant.
- Use *an* before nouns that begin with a vowel (a, e, i, o, u).

Write the article for each sentence.

1. (an, the) Reba sat under an apple tree.
2. (a, an) Her dog is an Akita.
3. (a, an) She had a picnic basket with her.
4. (an, the) In the basket were sandwiches.
5. (an, the) Reba and her dog ate the sandwiches.
6. (a, the) Reba drank the juice.
7. (a, an) Before leaving, Reba picked an apple.

a an the

#3305 Daily Skills Practice–Grades 3–4 82 ©Teacher Created Materials, Inc.

Page 83

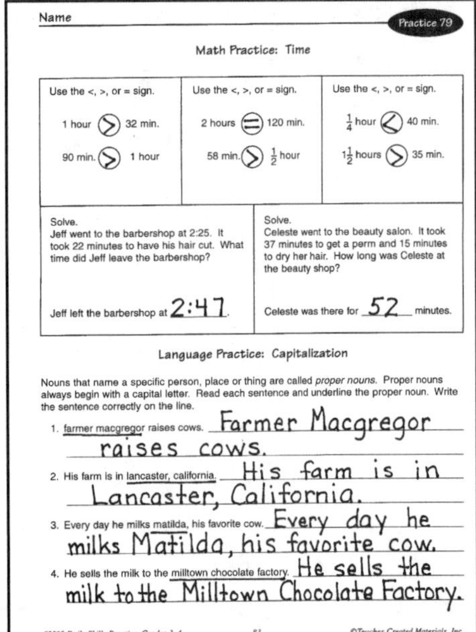

Name ______ Practice 79

Math Practice: Time

Use the <, >, or = sign.	Use the <, >, or = sign.	Use the <, >, or = sign.
1 hour (>) 32 min.	2 hours (=) 120 min.	$\frac{1}{4}$ hour (<) 40 min.
90 min. (>) 1 hour	58 min. (>) $\frac{1}{2}$ hour	$1\frac{1}{2}$ hours (>) 35 min.

Solve. Jeff went to the barbershop at 2:25. It took 22 minutes to have his hair cut. What time did Jeff leave the barbershop?	Solve. Celeste went to the beauty salon. It took 37 minutes to get a perm and 15 minutes to dry her hair. How long was Celeste at the beauty shop?
Jeff left the barbershop at 2:47.	Celeste was there for 52 minutes.

Language Practice: Capitalization

Nouns that name a specific person, place or thing are called *proper nouns*. Proper nouns always begin with a capital letter. Read each sentence and underline the proper noun. Write the sentence correctly on the line.

1. farmer macgregor raises cows. Farmer Macgregor raises cows.
2. His farm is in lancaster, california. His farm is in Lancaster, California.
3. Every day he milks matilda, his favorite cow. Every day he milks Matilda, his favorite cow.
4. He sells the milk to the milltown chocolate factory. He sells the milk to the Milltown Chocolate Factory.

#3305 Daily Skills Practice—Grades 3–4 83 ©Teacher Created Materials, Inc.

Page 84

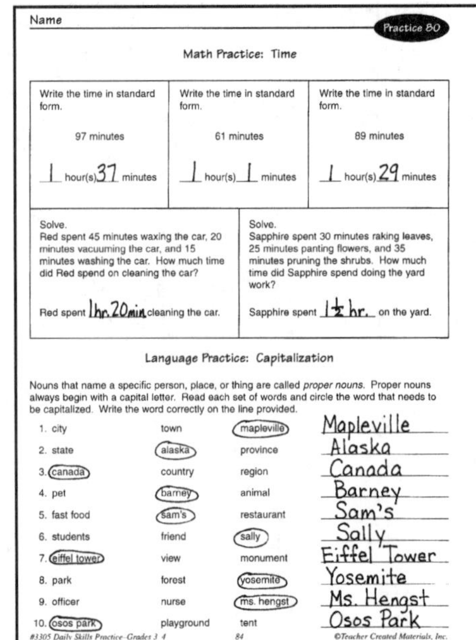

Name ______ Practice 80

Math Practice: Time

Write the time in standard form. 97 minutes	Write the time in standard form. 61 minutes	Write the time in standard form. 89 minutes
1 hour(s) 37 minutes	1 hour(s) 1 minutes	1 hour(s) 29 minutes

Solve. Red spent 45 minutes waxing the car, 20 minutes vacuuming the car, and 15 minutes washing the car. How much time did Red spend on cleaning the car?	Solve. Sapphire spent 30 minutes raking leaves, 25 minutes panting flowers, and 35 minutes pruning the shrubs. How much time did Sapphire spend doing the yard work?
Red spent 1hr. 20min. cleaning the car.	Sapphire spent $1\frac{1}{2}$ hr. on the yard.

Language Practice: Capitalization

Nouns that name a specific person, place or thing are called *proper nouns*. Proper nouns always begin with a capital letter. Read each set of words and circle the word that needs to be capitalized. Write the word correctly on the line provided.

1. city town (mapleville) Mapleville
2. state (alaska) province Alaska
3. (canada) country region Canada
4. pet (barney) animal Barney
5. fast food (sam's) restaurant Sam's
6. students friend (sally) Sally
7. (eiffel tower) view monument Eiffel Tower
8. park forest (yosemite) Yosemite
9. officer nurse (ms. hengst) Ms. Hengst
10. (osos park) playground tent Osos Park

#3305 Daily Skills Practice—Grades 3–4 84 ©Teacher Created Materials, Inc.

Page 85

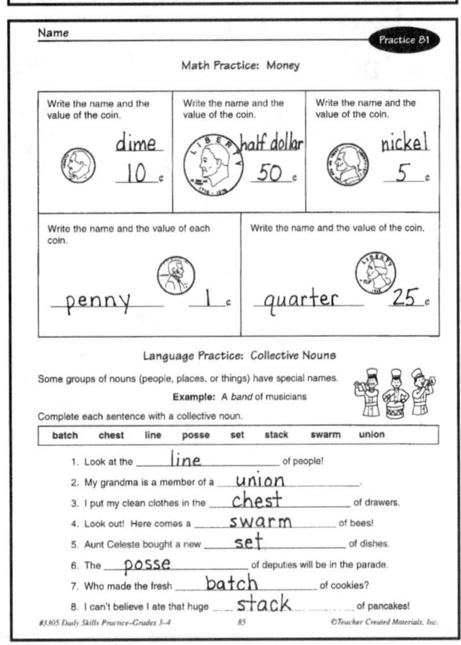

Name ______ Practice 81

Math Practice: Money

Write the name and the value of the coin.	Write the name and the value of the coin.	Write the name and the value of the coin.
dime 10¢	half dollar 50¢	nickel 5¢

Write the name and the value of each coin.	Write the name and the value of the coin.
penny 1¢	quarter 25¢

Language Practice: Collective Nouns

Some groups of nouns (people, places, or things) have special names.

Example: A *band* of musicians

Complete each sentence with a collective noun.

batch	chest	line	posse	set	stack	swarm	union

1. Look at the line of people!
2. My grandma is a member of a union.
3. I put my clean clothes in the chest of drawers.
4. Look out! Here comes a swarm of bees!
5. Aunt Celeste bought a new set of dishes.
6. The posse of deputies will be in the parade.
7. Who made the fresh batch of cookies?
8. I can't believe I ate that huge stack of pancakes!

#3305 Daily Skills Practice—Grades 3–4 85 ©Teacher Created Materials, Inc.

Page 86

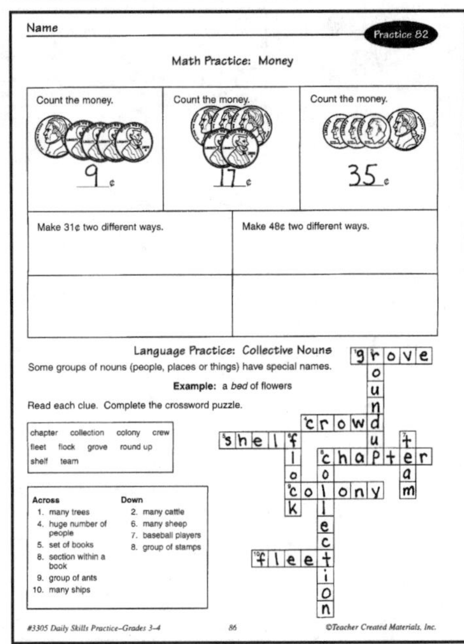

Name ______ Practice 82

Math Practice: Money

Count the money.	Count the money.	Count the money.
9¢	17¢	35¢

Make 31¢ two different ways.	Make 48¢ two different ways.

Language Practice: Collective Nouns

Some groups of nouns (people, places or things) have special names.

Example: a *bed* of flowers

Read each clue. Complete the crossword puzzle.

chapter collection colony crew fleet flock grove round up shelf team

Across
1. many trees — grove
4. huge number of people — crowd
5. set of books — shelf
8. section within a book — chapter
9. group of ants — colony
10. many ships — fleet

Down
2. many cattle — round up
6. many sheep — flock
7. baseball players — team
8. group of stamps — collection

#3305 Daily Skills Practice—Grades 3–4 86 ©Teacher Created Materials, Inc.

Page 87

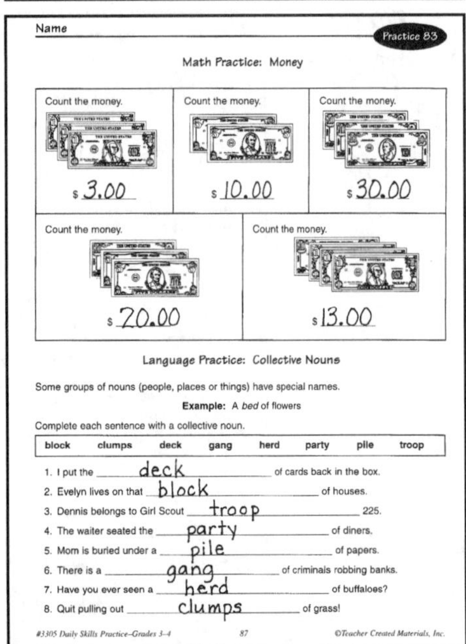

Name ______ Practice 83

Math Practice: Money

Count the money.	Count the money.	Count the money.
\$3.00	\$10.00	\$30.00

Count the money.	Count the money.
\$20.00	\$13.00

Language Practice: Collective Nouns

Some groups of nouns (people, places, or things) have special names.

Example: A *bed* of flowers

Complete each sentence with a collective noun.

block	clumps	deck	gang	herd	party	pile	troop

1. I put the deck of cards back in the box.
2. Evelyn lives on that block of houses.
3. Dennis belongs to Girl Scout troop 225.
4. The waiter seated the party of diners.
5. Mom is buried under a pile of papers.
6. There is a gang of criminals robbing banks.
7. Have you ever seen a herd of buffaloes?
8. Quit pulling out clumps of grass!

#3305 Daily Skills Practice—Grades 3–4 87 ©Teacher Created Materials, Inc.

Page 88

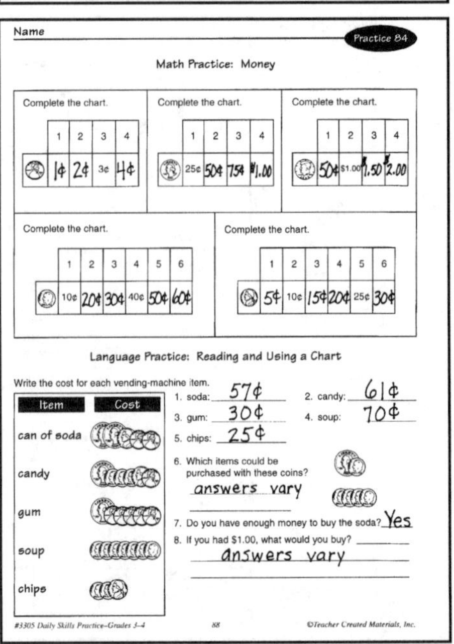

Name ______ Practice 84

Math Practice: Money

Complete the chart.

	1	2	3	4
penny	1¢	2¢	3¢	4¢

Complete the chart.

	1	2	3	4
quarter	25¢	50¢	75¢	\$1.00

Complete the chart.

	1	2	3	4
half dollar	50¢	\$1.00	\$1.50	\$2.00

Complete the chart.

	1	2	3	4	5	6
dime	10¢	20¢	30¢	40¢	50¢	60¢

Complete the chart.

	1	2	3	4	5	6
nickel	5¢	10¢	15¢	20¢	25¢	30¢

Language Practice: Reading and Using a Chart

Write the cost for each vending-machine item.

Item	Cost
can of soda	
candy	
gum	
soup	
chips	

1. soda: 57¢ 2. candy: 61¢
3. gum: 30¢ 4. soup: 70¢
5. chips: 25¢
6. Which items could be purchased with these coins? answers vary
7. Do you have enough money to buy the soda? Yes
8. If you had \$1.00, what would you buy? answers vary

#3305 Daily Skills Practice—Grades 3–4 88 ©Teacher Created Materials, Inc.

Page 89

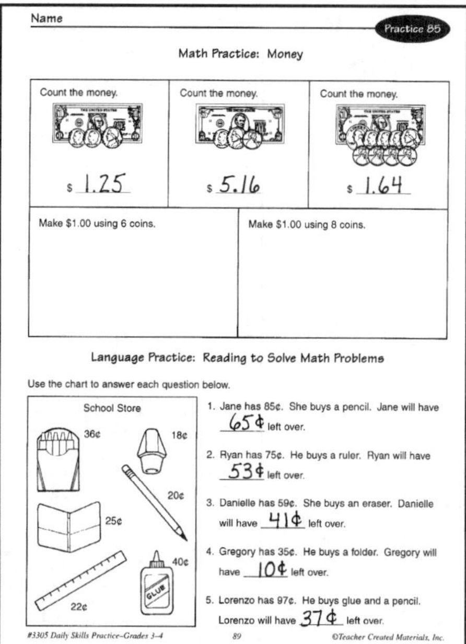

Name ______ Practice 85

Math Practice: Money

Count the money.	Count the money.	Count the money.
$ 1.25	$ 5.16	$ 1.64

Make $1.00 using 6 coins.	Make $1.00 using 8 coins.

Language Practice: Reading to Solve Math Problems

Use the chart to answer each question below.

School Store: 36¢, 18¢, 20¢, 25¢, 40¢, 22¢

1. Jane has 85¢. She buys a pencil. Jane will have 65¢ left over.
2. Ryan has 75¢. He buys a ruler. Ryan will have 53¢ left over.
3. Danielle has 59¢. She buys an eraser. Danielle will have 41¢ left over.
4. Gregory has 35¢. He buys a folder. Gregory will have 10¢ left over.
5. Lorenzo has 97¢. He buys glue and a pencil. Lorenzo will have 37¢ left over.

#3305 Daily Skills Practice–Grades 3–4 89 ©Teacher Created Materials, Inc.

Page 90

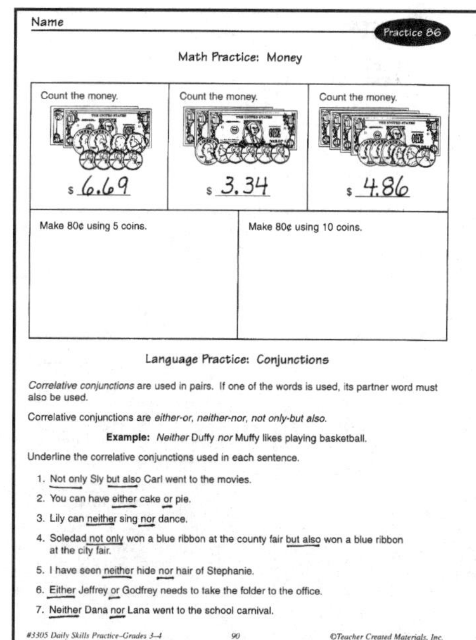

Name ______ Practice 86

Math Practice: Money

Count the money.	Count the money.	Count the money.
$ 6.69	$ 3.34	$ 4.86

Make 80¢ using 5 coins.	Make 80¢ using 10 coins.

Language Practice: Conjunctions

Correlative conjunctions are used in pairs. If one of the words is used, its partner word must also be used.

Correlative conjunctions are *either-or, neither-nor, not only-but also.*

Example: *Neither* Duffy *nor* Muffy likes playing basketball.

Underline the correlative conjunctions used in each sentence.

1. Not only Sly but also Carl went to the movies.
2. You can have either cake or pie.
3. Lily can neither sing nor dance.
4. Soledad not only won a blue ribbon at the county fair but also won a blue ribbon at the city fair.
5. I have seen neither hide nor hair of Stephanie.
6. Either Jeffrey or Godfrey needs to take the folder to the office.
7. Neither Dana nor Lana went to the school carnival.

#3305 Daily Skills Practice–Grades 3–4 90 ©Teacher Created Materials, Inc.

Page 91

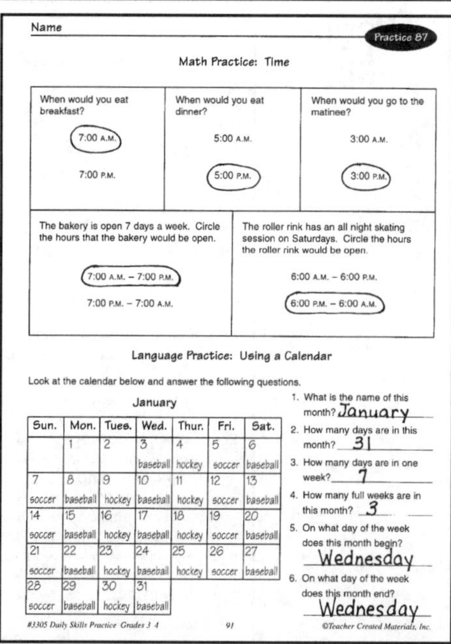

Name ______ Practice 87

Math Practice: Time

When would you eat breakfast?	When would you eat dinner?	When would you go to the matinee?
(7:00 A.M.) 7:00 P.M.	5:00 A.M. (5:00 P.M.)	3:00 A.M. (3:00 P.M.)

The bakery is open 7 days a week. Circle the hours that the bakery would be open.	The roller rink has an all night skating session on Saturdays. Circle the hours the roller rink would be open.
(7:00 A.M. – 7:00 P.M.) 7:00 P.M. – 7:00 A.M.	6:00 A.M. – 6:00 P.M. (6:00 P.M. – 6:00 A.M.)

Language Practice: Using a Calendar

Look at the calendar below and answer the following questions.

January

Sun.	Mon.	Tues.	Wed.	Thur.	Fri.	Sat.
	1	2	3 baseball	4 hockey	5 soccer	6 baseball
7 soccer	8 baseball	9 hockey	10 baseball	11 hockey	12 soccer	13 baseball
14 soccer	15 baseball	16 hockey	17 baseball	18 hockey	19 soccer	20 baseball
21 soccer	22 baseball	23 hockey	24 baseball	25 hockey	26 soccer	27 baseball
28 soccer	29 baseball	30 hockey	31 baseball			

1. What is the name of this month? January
2. How many days are in this month? 31
3. How many days are in one week? 7
4. How many full weeks are in this month? 3
5. On what day of the week does this month begin? Wednesday
6. On what day of the week does this month end? Wednesday

#3305 Daily Skills Practice Grades 3–4 91 ©Teacher Created Materials, Inc.

Page 92

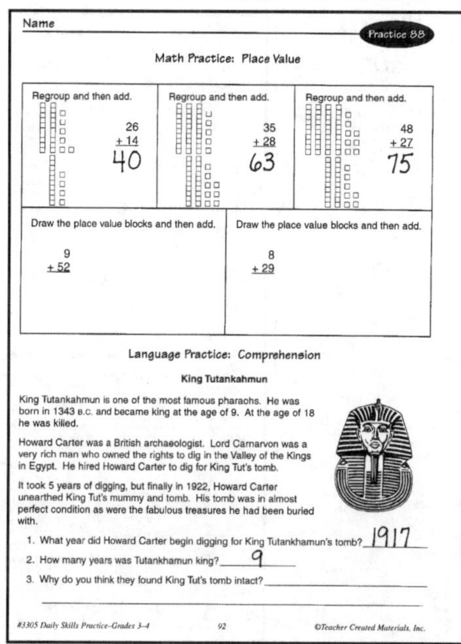

Name ______ Practice 88

Math Practice: Place Value

Regroup and then add.	Regroup and then add.	Regroup and then add.
26 + 14 = 40	35 + 28 = 63	48 + 27 = 75

Draw the place value blocks and then add.	Draw the place value blocks and then add.
9 + 52	8 + 29

Language Practice: Comprehension

King Tutankahmun

King Tutankahmun is one of the most famous pharaohs. He was born in 1343 B.C. and became king at the age of 9. At the age of 18 he was killed.

Howard Carter was a British archaeologist. Lord Carnarvon was a very rich man who owned the rights to dig in the Valley of the Kings in Egypt. He hired Howard Carter to dig for King Tut's tomb.

It took 5 years of digging, but finally in 1922, Howard Carter unearthed King Tut's mummy and tomb. His tomb was in almost perfect condition as were the fabulous treasures he had been buried with.

1. What year did Howard Carter begin digging for King Tutankhamun's tomb? 1917
2. How many years was Tutankhamun king? 9
3. Why do you think they found King Tut's tomb intact? ______

#3305 Daily Skills Practice–Grades 3–4 92 ©Teacher Created Materials, Inc.

Page 93

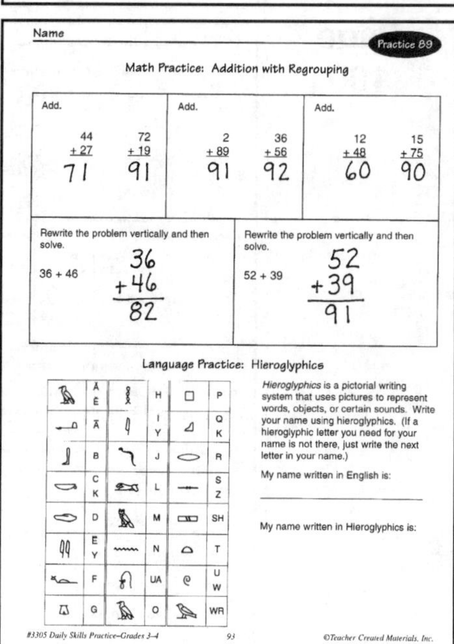

Name ______ Practice 89

Math Practice: Addition with Regrouping

Add.	Add.	Add.
44 + 27 = 71; 72 + 19 = 91	2 + 89 = 91; 36 + 56 = 92	12 + 48 = 60; 15 + 75 = 90

Rewrite the problem vertically and then solve.	Rewrite the problem vertically and then solve.
36 + 46: 36 + 46 = 82	52 + 39: 52 + 39 = 91

Language Practice: Hieroglyphics

Hieroglyphics is a pictorial writing system that uses pictures to represent words, objects, or certain sounds. Write your name using hieroglyphics. (If a hieroglyphic letter you need for your name is not there, just write the next letter in your name.)

My name written in English is: ______

My name written in Hieroglyphics is: ______

#3305 Daily Skills Practice–Grades 3–4 93 ©Teacher Created Materials, Inc.

Page 94

Name ______ Practice 90

Math Practice: Addition with Regrouping

Add.	Add.	Add.
27¢ + 27¢ = 54¢	36¢ + 9¢ = 45¢	75 + 8 = 83¢

Solve. Marigold has 19¢. Her sister gives her 26¢. How much money does Marigold have? Marigold has 45¢.	Solve. Marvin has 37¢. His brother gives him 37¢. How much money does Marvin have? Marvin has 74¢.

Language Practice: Comparatives

When comparing 2 items, add "*er*" to the end of the descriptive adjective or adverb. If the descriptive word ends in "*y*", drop the "*y*" and add "*ier*."

Example: Justine is *tall.* ("*Tall*" refers to one person.)

Justine is *taller* than Muffy. ("*Taller*" is comparing the size of one person to another.)

Read each sentence and write the correct form of the descriptive word on the line.

1. The Empire State Building is taller than my house. (tall)
2. A tiger can run faster than a turtle. (fast)
3. It is colder today. (cold)
4. A ladybug is tinier than a butterfly. (tiny)
5. The doorbell rings louder than the telephone. (loud)
6. Ernie's room is always messier than Norman's room. (messy)
7. The campfire is warmer than the flashlight. (warm)

#3305 Daily Skills Practice–Grades 3–4 94 ©Teacher Created Materials, Inc.

Page 95

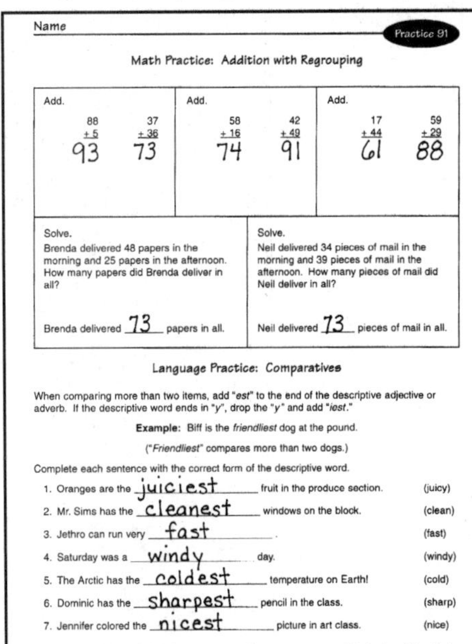

Name ______ Practice 91

Math Practice: Addition with Regrouping

Add.		Add.		Add.	
88 + 5 = 93	37 + 36 = 73	58 + 16 = 74	42 + 49 = 91	17 + 44 = 61	59 + 29 = 88

Solve.
Brenda delivered 48 papers in the morning and 25 papers in the afternoon. How many papers did Brenda deliver in all?
Brenda delivered 73 papers in all.

Solve.
Neil delivered 34 pieces of mail in the morning and 39 pieces of mail in the afternoon. How many pieces of mail did Neil deliver in all?
Neil delivered 73 pieces of mail in all.

Language Practice: Comparatives

When comparing more than two items, add "*est*" to the end of the descriptive adjective or adverb. If the descriptive word ends in "*y*", drop the "*y*" and add "*iest*."

Example: Biff is the *friendliest* dog at the pound.
("*Friendliest*" compares more than two dogs.)

Complete each sentence with the correct form of the descriptive word.

1. Oranges are the juiciest fruit in the produce section. (juicy)
2. Mr. Sims has the cleanest windows on the block. (clean)
3. Jethro can run very fast. (fast)
4. Saturday was a windy day. (windy)
5. The Arctic has the coldest temperature on Earth! (cold)
6. Dominic has the sharpest pencil in the class. (sharp)
7. Jennifer colored the nicest picture in art class. (nice)

#3305 Daily Skills Practice–Grades 3–4 95 ©Teacher Created Materials, Inc.

Page 96

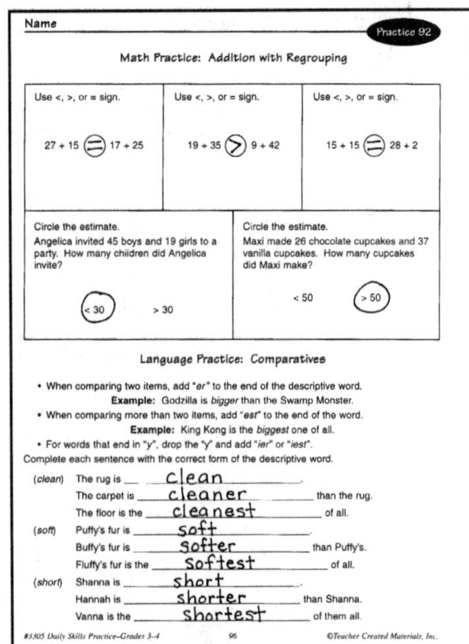

Name ______ Practice 92

Math Practice: Addition with Regrouping

Use <, >, or = sign.	Use <, >, or = sign.	Use <, >, or = sign.
27 + 15 (=) 17 + 25	19 + 35 (>) 9 + 42	15 + 15 (=) 28 + 2

Circle the estimate.
Angelica invited 45 boys and 19 girls to a party. How many children did Angelica invite?
(< 30) > 30

Circle the estimate.
Maxi made 26 chocolate cupcakes and 37 vanilla cupcakes. How many cupcakes did Maxi make?
< 50 (> 50)

Language Practice: Comparatives

- When comparing two items, add "*er*" to the end of the descriptive word.
  Example: Godzilla is *bigger* than the Swamp Monster.
- When comparing more than two items, add "*est*" to the end of the word.
  Example: King Kong is the *biggest* one of all.
- For words that end in "*y*", drop the "*y*" and add "*ier*" or "*iest*".

Complete each sentence with the correct form of the descriptive word.

(*clean*) The rug is clean.
The carpet is cleaner than the rug.
The floor is the cleanest of all.
(*soft*) Puffy's fur is soft.
Buffy's fur is softer than Puffy's.
Fluffy's fur is the softest of all.
(*short*) Shanna is short.
Hannah is shorter than Shanna.
Vanna is the shortest of them all.

#3305 Daily Skills Practice–Grades 3–4 96 ©Teacher Created Materials, Inc.

Page 97

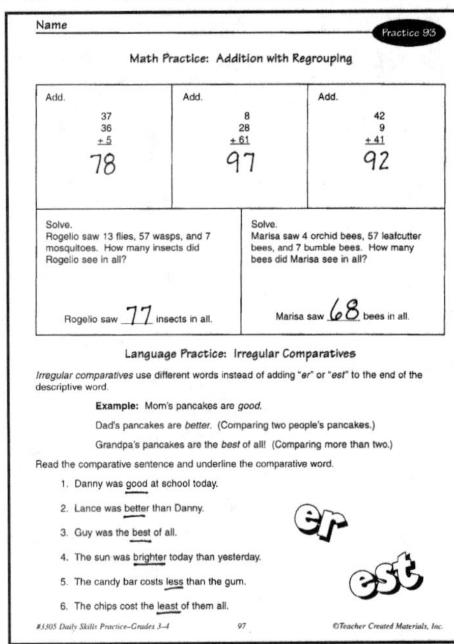

Name ______ Practice 93

Math Practice: Addition with Regrouping

Add.	Add.	Add.
37 + 36 + 5 = 78	8 + 28 + 61 = 97	42 + 9 + 41 = 92

Solve.
Rogelio saw 13 flies, 57 wasps, and 7 mosquitoes. How many insects did Rogelio see in all?
Rogelio saw 77 insects in all.

Solve.
Marisa saw 4 orchid bees, 57 leafcutter bees, and 7 bumble bees. How many bees did Marisa see in all?
Marisa saw 68 bees in all.

Language Practice: Irregular Comparatives

Irregular comparatives use different words instead of adding "*er*" or "*est*" to the end of the descriptive word.

Example: Mom's pancakes are *good.*
Dad's pancakes are *better.* (Comparing two people's pancakes.)
Grandpa's pancakes are the *best* of all! (Comparing more than two.)

Read the comparative sentence and underline the comparative word.

1. Danny was good at school today.
2. Lance was better than Danny.
3. Guy was the best of all.
4. The sun was brighter today than yesterday.
5. The candy bar costs less than the gum.
6. The chips cost the least of them all.

er est

#3305 Daily Skills Practice–Grades 3–4 97 ©Teacher Created Materials, Inc.

Page 98

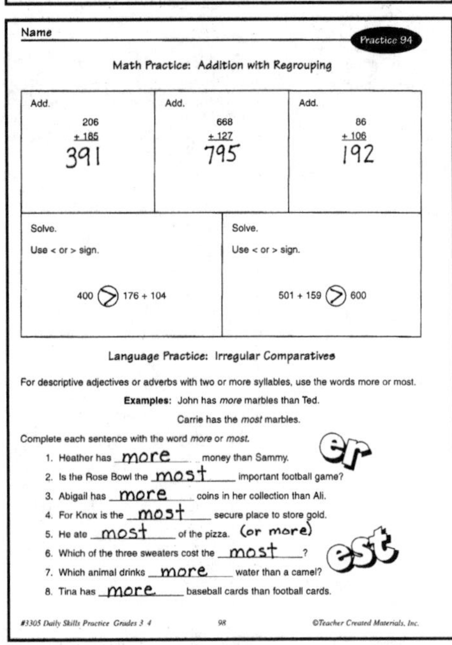

Name ______ Practice 94

Math Practice: Addition with Regrouping

Add.	Add.	Add.
206 + 185 = 391	668 + 127 = 795	86 + 106 = 192

Solve.
Use < or > sign.
400 (>) 176 + 104

Solve.
Use < or > sign.
501 + 159 (>) 600

Language Practice: Irregular Comparatives

For descriptive adjectives or adverbs with two or more syllables, use the words more or most.

Examples: John has *more* marbles than Ted.
Carrie has the *most* marbles.

Complete each sentence with the word *more* or *most.*

1. Heather has more money than Sammy.
2. Is the Rose Bowl the most important football game?
3. Abigail has more coins in her collection than Ali.
4. For Knox is the most secure place to store gold.
5. He ate most of the pizza. (or more)
6. Which of the three sweaters cost the most?
7. Which animal drinks more water than a camel?
8. Tina has more baseball cards than football cards.

er est

#3305 Daily Skills Practice–Grades 3–4 98 ©Teacher Created Materials, Inc.

Page 99

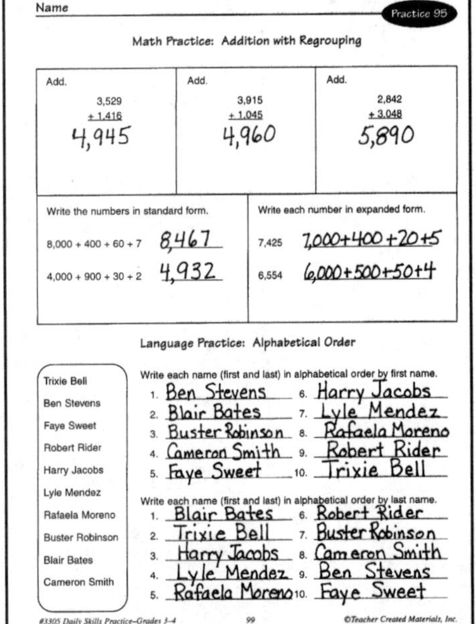

Name ______ Practice 95

Math Practice: Addition with Regrouping

Add.	Add.	Add.
3,529 + 1,416 = 4,945	3,915 + 1,045 = 4,960	2,842 + 3,048 = 5,890

Write the numbers in standard form.
8,000 + 400 + 60 + 7 = 8,467
4,000 + 900 + 30 + 2 = 4,932

Write each number in expanded form.
7,425 = 7,000+400+20+5
6,554 = 6,000+500+50+4

Language Practice: Alphabetical Order

Trixie Bell, Ben Stevens, Faye Sweet, Robert Rider, Harry Jacobs, Lyle Mendez, Rafaela Moreno, Buster Robinson, Blair Bates, Cameron Smith

Write each name (first and last) in alphabetical order by first name.

1. Ben Stevens
2. Blair Bates
3. Buster Robinson
4. Cameron Smith
5. Faye Sweet
6. Harry Jacobs
7. Lyle Mendez
8. Rafaela Moreno
9. Robert Rider
10. Trixie Bell

Write each name (first and last) in alphabetical order by last name.

1. Blair Bates
2. Trixie Bell
3. Harry Jacobs
4. Lyle Mendez
5. Rafaela Moreno
6. Robert Rider
7. Buster Robinson
8. Cameron Smith
9. Ben Stevens
10. Faye Sweet

#3305 Daily Skills Practice–Grades 3–4 99 ©Teacher Created Materials, Inc.

Page 100

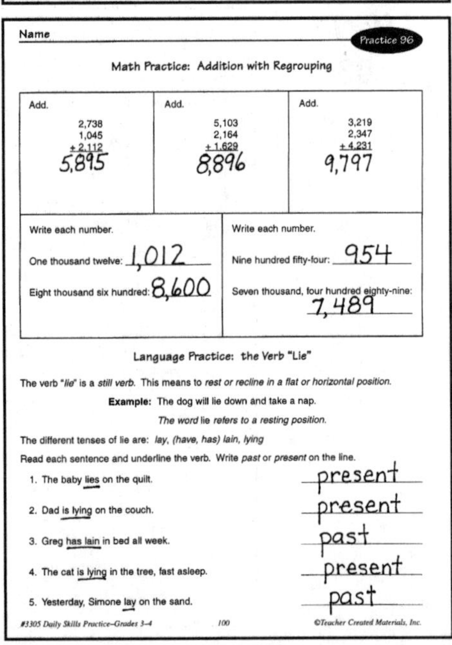

Name ______ Practice 96

Math Practice: Addition with Regrouping

Add.	Add.	Add.
2,738 + 1,045 + 2,112 = 5,895	5,103 + 2,164 + 1,629 = 8,896	3,219 + 2,347 + 4,231 = 9,797

Write each number.
One thousand twelve: 1,012
Eight thousand six hundred: 8,600

Write each number.
Nine hundred fifty-four: 954
Seven thousand, four hundred eighty-nine: 7,489

Language Practice: the Verb "Lie"

The verb "*lie*" is a *still verb*. This means to *rest or recline in a flat or horizontal position.*

Example: The dog will lie down and take a nap.
The word lie refers to a resting position.

The different tenses of lie are: *lay, (have, has) lain, lying*

Read each sentence and underline the verb. Write *past* or *present* on the line.

1. The baby lies on the quilt. present
2. Dad is lying on the couch. present
3. Greg has lain in bed all week. past
4. The cat is lying in the tree, fast asleep. present
5. Yesterday, Simone lay on the sand. past

#3305 Daily Skills Practice–Grades 3–4 100 ©Teacher Created Materials, Inc.

Page 101

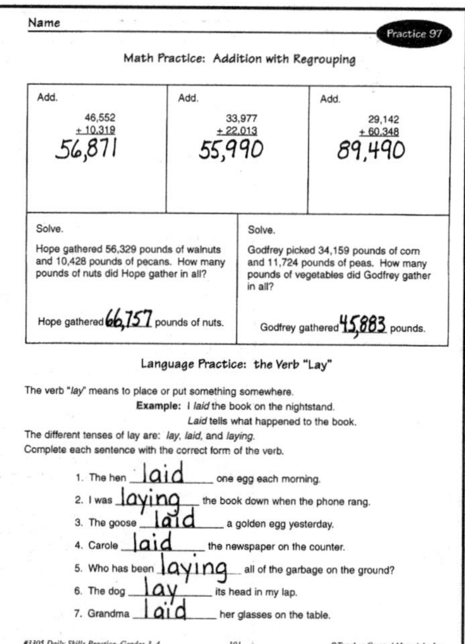

Name Practice 97

Math Practice: Addition with Regrouping

Add.	Add.	Add.
46,552 + 10,319 56,871	33,977 + 22,013 55,990	29,142 + 60,348 89,490

Solve.	Solve.
Hope gathered 56,329 pounds of walnuts and 10,428 pounds of pecans. How many pounds of nuts did Hope gather in all? Hope gathered 66,757 pounds of nuts.	Godfrey picked 34,159 pounds of corn and 11,724 pounds of peas. How many pounds of vegetables did Godfrey gather in all? Godfrey gathered 45,883 pounds.

Language Practice: the Verb "Lay"

The verb "*lay*" means to place or put something somewhere.

Example: I *laid* the book on the nightstand.
Laid tells what happened to the book.

The different tenses of lay are: *lay, laid,* and *laying.*

Complete each sentence with the correct form of the verb.

1. The hen laid one egg each morning.
2. I was laying the book down when the phone rang.
3. The goose laid a golden egg yesterday.
4. Carole laid the newspaper on the counter.
5. Who has been laying all of the garbage on the ground?
6. The dog lay its head in my lap.
7. Grandma laid her glasses on the table.

#3305 Daily Skills Practice–Grades 3–4 101 ©Teacher Created Materials, Inc.

Page 102

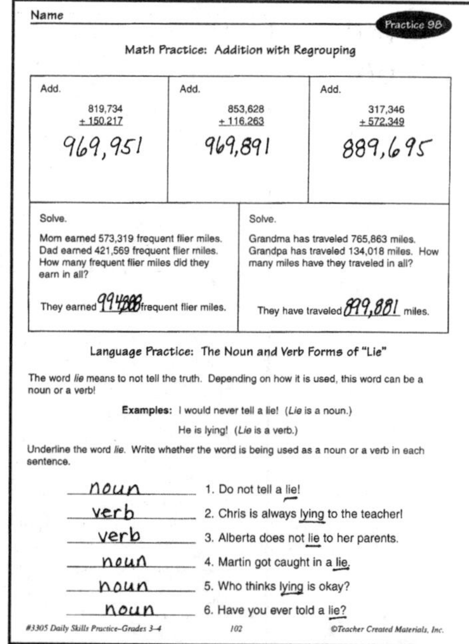

Name Practice 98

Math Practice: Addition with Regrouping

Add.	Add.	Add.
819,734 + 150,217 969,951	853,628 + 116,263 969,891	317,346 + 572,349 889,695

Solve.	Solve.
Mom earned 573,319 frequent flier miles. Dad earned 421,569 frequent flier miles. How many frequent flier miles did they earn in all? They earned 994,888 frequent flier miles.	Grandma has traveled 765,863 miles. Grandpa has traveled 134,018 miles. How many miles have they traveled in all? They have traveled 899,881 miles.

Language Practice: The Noun and Verb Forms of "Lie"

The word *lie* means to not tell the truth. Depending on how it is used, this word can be a noun or a verb!

Examples: I would never tell a lie! (*Lie* is a noun.)
He is lying! (*Lie* is a verb.)

Underline the word *lie.* Write whether the word is being used as a noun or a verb in each sentence.

noun 1. Do not tell a lie!
verb 2. Chris is always lying to the teacher!
verb 3. Alberta does not lie to her parents.
noun 4. Martin got caught in a lie.
noun 5. Who thinks lying is okay?
noun 6. Have you ever told a lie?

#3305 Daily Skills Practice–Grades 3–4 102 ©Teacher Created Materials, Inc.

Page 103

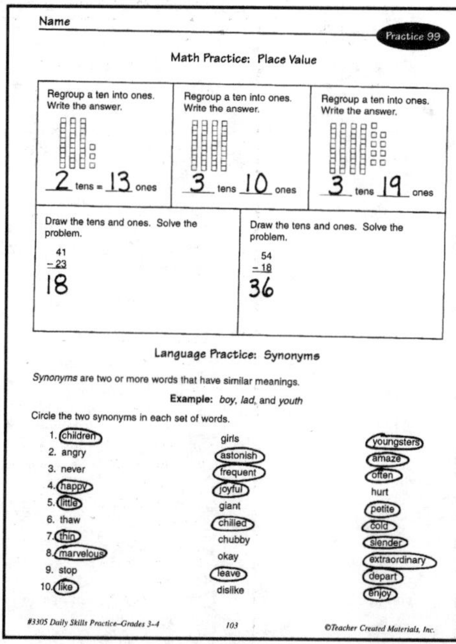

Name Practice 99

Math Practice: Place Value

Regroup a ten into ones. Write the answer.	Regroup a ten into ones. Write the answer.	Regroup a ten into ones. Write the answer.
2 tens = 13 ones	3 tens 10 ones	3 tens 19 ones

Draw the tens and ones. Solve the problem.	Draw the tens and ones. Solve the problem.
41 − 23 18	54 − 18 36

Language Practice: Synonyms

Synonyms are two or more words that have similar meanings.

Example: *boy, lad,* and *youth*

Circle the two synonyms in each set of words.

1. children	girls	youngsters
2. angry	astonish	amaze
3. never	frequent	often
4. happy	joyful	hurt
5. little	giant	petite
6. thaw	chilled	cold
7. thin	chubby	slender
8. marvelous	okay	extraordinary
9. stop	leave	depart
10. like	dislike	enjoy

#3305 Daily Skills Practice–Grades 3–4 103 ©Teacher Created Materials, Inc.

Page 104

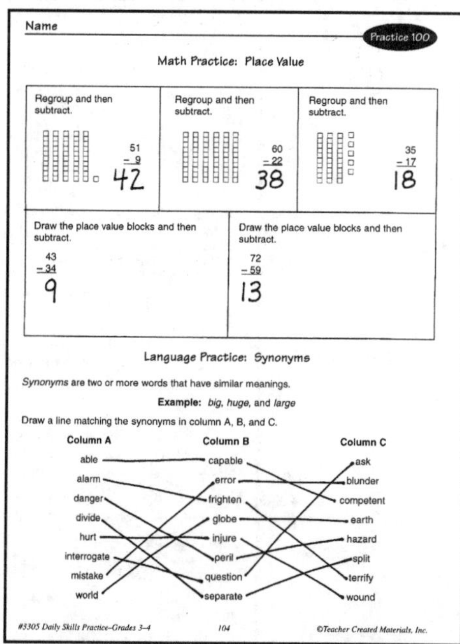

Name Practice 100

Math Practice: Place Value

Regroup and then subtract.	Regroup and then subtract.	Regroup and then subtract.
51 − 9 42	60 − 22 38	35 − 17 18

Draw the place value blocks and then subtract.	Draw the place value blocks and then subtract.
43 − 34 9	72 − 59 13

Language Practice: Synonyms

Synonyms are two or more words that have similar meanings.

Example: *big, huge,* and *large*

Draw a line matching the synonyms in column A, B, and C.

Column A	Column B	Column C
able	capable	ask
alarm	error	blunder
danger	frighten	competent
divide	globe	earth
hurt	injure	hazard
interrogate	peril	split
mistake	question	terrify
world	separate	wound

#3305 Daily Skills Practice–Grades 3–4 104 ©Teacher Created Materials, Inc.

Page 105

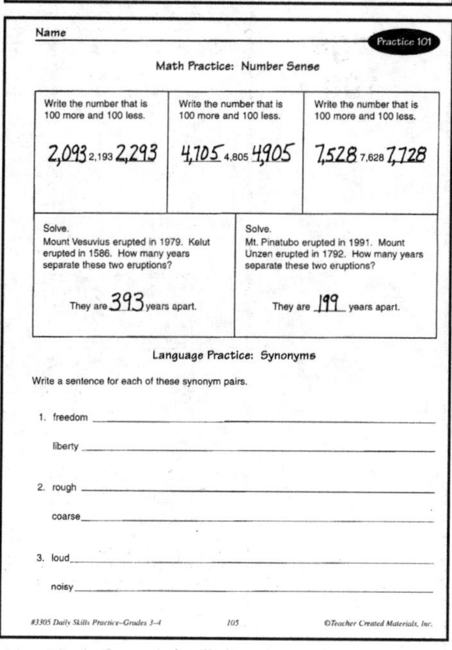

Name Practice 101

Math Practice: Number Sense

Write the number that is 100 more and 100 less.	Write the number that is 100 more and 100 less.	Write the number that is 100 more and 100 less.
2,093 2,193 2,293	4,705 4,805 4,905	7,528 7,628 7,728

Solve.	Solve.
Mount Vesuvius erupted in 1979. Kelut erupted in 1586. How many years separate these two eruptions? They are 393 years apart.	Mt. Pinatubo erupted in 1991. Mount Unzen erupted in 1792. How many years separate these two eruptions? They are 199 years apart.

Language Practice: Synonyms

Write a sentence for each of these synonym pairs.

1. freedom ______
   liberty ______
2. rough ______
   coarse ______
3. loud ______
   noisy ______

#3305 Daily Skills Practice–Grades 3–4 105 ©Teacher Created Materials, Inc.

Page 106

Name Practice 102

Math Practice: Subtraction with Regrouping

Subtract.	Subtract.	Subtract.
94 − 58 = 36 92 − 76 = 16	37 − 8 = 29 25 − 19 = 6	43 − 26 = 17 71 − 34 = 37

Solve.	Solve.
Lola had 82¢. She spent 45¢ at the bookstore. How much money does Lola have left? Lola has 37¢ left.	Mayer had 63¢. He spent 44¢ at the comic book store. How much money does Mayer have left? Mayer has 19¢ left.

Language Practice: Synonyms

Synonyms are two or more words that have similar meanings.

Example: *end, finish,* and *complete*

Read each sentence. Write a synonym on the line for the word in italics.

Example: We will have to *depart* soon. go

1. Weddings are a *happy* occasion. ______
2. Abby made a *hasty* departure from the party. ______
3. Herman will *close* the door quietly. ______
4. Veva bought a new *vehicle.* ______
5. Gabriel is a very *helpful* person. ______
6. Mary and her dad go to the library *frequently.* ______
7. Jamie and Heather are quite a *duo*! ______
8. Don't be so *reckless*! ______

#3305 Daily Skills Practice–Grades 3–4 106 ©Teacher Created Materials, Inc.

Page 107

Name ______ Practice 103

Math Practice: Subtraction with Regrouping

Subtract.	Subtract.	Subtract.
465 − 48 = 417; 383 − 34 = 349	290 − 81 = 209; 985 − 76 = 909	897 − 88 = 809; 856 − 47 = 809

Complete the pattern.	Complete the pattern.
464, 474, 484, 494, 504, 514, 524, 534, 544, 554, 564	901, 891, 881, 871, 861, 851, 841, 831, 821, 811, 801

Language Practice: Synonyms

Synonyms are two or more words that have similar meanings.

Example: *anger, rage,* and *fury*

Read each clue, look at the list on the right, and complete the crossword puzzle.

Across	Down
2. difficult	1. large
5. rear	3. old
7. all	6. sudden
8. help	9. yell
9. end	10. chubby
11. work	

abrupt	enormous	plump
ancient	every	shout
assist	hard	stop
back	job	

#3305 Daily Skills Practice–Grades 3–4 107 ©Teacher Created Materials, Inc.

Page 108

Name ______ Practice 104

Math Practice: Subtraction with Regrouping

Subtract.	Subtract.	Subtract.
$8.14 − 1.83 = $6.31	$7.31 − 4.28 = $3.03	$3.67 − .00 = $3.67

Cross out the unnecessary piece of information.	Cross out the unnecessary piece of information.
Jenny spent 69¢. Jenny had $1.25. ~~Jenny likes pennies the best.~~ How much money does Jenny have left? 56¢	Wells had 75¢. ~~He does not collect silver dollars.~~ Wells spent 37¢. How much money does Wells have left? 38¢

Language Practice: Antonyms

Antonyms are two words that have opposite meanings.

Example: *soft* and *hard*

Draw a line matching each pair of antonyms.

achieve	awake	answer	bad
asleep	back	beautiful	break
come	bent	chilly	copy
down	fail	clean	dirty
fat	freeze	fix	hero
front	go	good	noisy
melt	thin	original	question
play	up	quiet	ugly
straight	work	villain	warm

#3305 Daily Skills Practice–Grades 3–4 108 ©Teacher Created Materials, Inc.

Page 109

Name ______ Practice 105

Math Practice: Subtraction with Regrouping

Subtract.	Subtract.	Subtract.
2,682 − 1,376 = 1,306	6,875 − 5,228 = 1,647	4,531 − 3,104 = 1,427

Solve.	Solve.
Albert had $5,680. He spent $2,226 buying a tree house. How much money does Albert have left? Albert has $3,454 left.	Ronniese had 9,131 pennies in her piggy bank. She rolled 9,050 of the pennies. How many pennies does Ronniese have left? Ronniese has 61 pennies left.

Language Practice: Antonyms

Antonyms are two words that have opposite meanings.

Example: *hot* and *cold*

Draw a line matching each pair of synonyms. Find and color the antonyms in the word search.

hard	tiny
heavy	yes
huge	easy
inside	forget
no	married
poor	light
remember	rich
single	odd
even	she
he	outside

#3305 Daily Skills Practice–Grades 3–4 109 ©Teacher Created Materials, Inc.

Page 110

Name ______ Practice 106

Math Practice: Subtraction with Regrouping

Subtract.	Subtract.	Subtract.
7,963 − 4,344 = 3,619	6,584 − 5,409 = 1,175	5,224 − 3,107 = 2,117

Solve.	Solve.
Matthew Henson was born in 1866 and died in 1955. How old was Matthew Henson when he died? Matthew Henson was 89 years old.	Frederick Douglass was born in 1817 and died in 1895. How old was Frederick Douglass when he died? Frederick Douglass was 78 years old.

Language Practice: Antonyms

Antonyms are two words that have opposite meanings. Write the antonyms for each clue in the correct space in the crossword puzzle.

above, add, before, child, difficult, false, fast, earth, fresh, laugh, never, night, smart, together

Across	Down
2. sky	1. adult
4. day	3. stale
5. subtract	4. always
6. alone	5. below
7. after	8. slow
9. dumb	11. true
10. easy	12. cry

#3305 Daily Skills Practice–Grades 3–4 110 ©Teacher Created Materials, Inc.

Page 111

Name ______ Practice 107

Math Practice: Subtraction with Regrouping

Subtract.	Subtract.	Subtract.
$68.26 − 11.38 = $56.88	$83.45 − 70.99 = $12.46	$41.75 − 30.78 = $10.97

Solve.	Solve.
Melanie had $20.00. She spent $11.83 buying a board game. How much change was Melanie given? Melanie was given $8.17 in change.	Ted had $20.00. He spent $10.25 buying an out door game. How much change was Ted given? Ted was given $9.75 in change.

Language Practice: Idioms

Idioms are phrases that have special meanings.

Example: The new movie is *not your cup of tea.* This doesn't mean the movie has anything to do with tea. Instead, it means it isn't something that you would like to see.

Draw a line matching the idiom used in each sentence to its meaning.

1. Justin is always *on the ball.*	not doing anything
2. Dom needs to get to class *on the double.*	acting or looking the same
3. Gordon is skating *on thin ice.*	needs to hurry
4. Quit sitting there *like a bump on a log!*	ready to go
5. Abigail and Ali are *like two peas in a pod!*	in good shape
6. Grandma likes to keep herself *as fit as a fiddle.*	getting into trouble

#3305 Daily Skills Practice–Grades 3–4 111 ©Teacher Created Materials, Inc.

Page 112

Name ______ Practice 108

Math Practice: Money

Subtract.	Subtract.	Subtract.
$35.64 − $23.89 = $11.75	$59.61 − $42.95 = $16.66	$47.74 − $30.76 = $16.98

Solve.	Solve.
Sharnelle's house number is 3197. Vance's house number is 364 lower than Sharnelle's. What is Vance's house number? Vance's house number is 2,833.	Bert needs to drive his truck to its next destination 5,145 miles away. He has already driven 3,728 miles. How many miles does Bert have left to drive? Bert has 1,417 miles left to drive.

Language Practice: Run-On Sentences

Run-on sentences are two sentences written as one sentence without punctuation. Read each sentence. Rewrite it correctly on the lines.

Reptile Facts

Example: Reptiles are vertebrate animals waterproof scales cover their bodies.
Reptiles are vertebrate animals. Waterproof scales cover their bodies.

1. Crocodiles and alligators are the largest reptiles they hunt other animals for their food.
Crocodiles and alligators are the largest reptiles. They hunt other animals for their food.
2. Most reptiles hatch from eggs the baby reptile looks like its parents.
Most reptiles hatch from eggs. The baby reptile looks like its parents.

#3305 Daily Skills Practice–Grades 3–4 112 ©Teacher Created Materials, Inc.

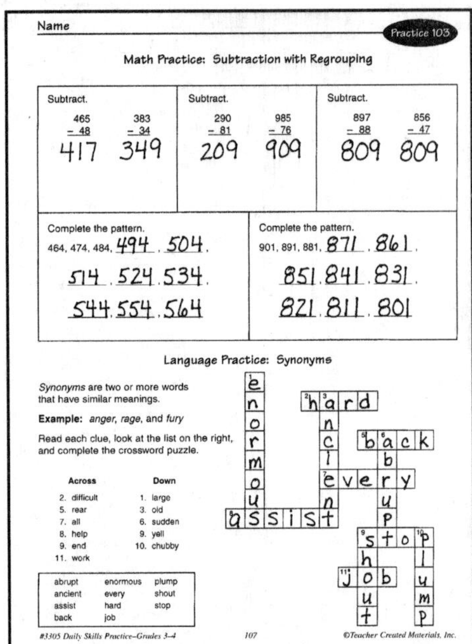

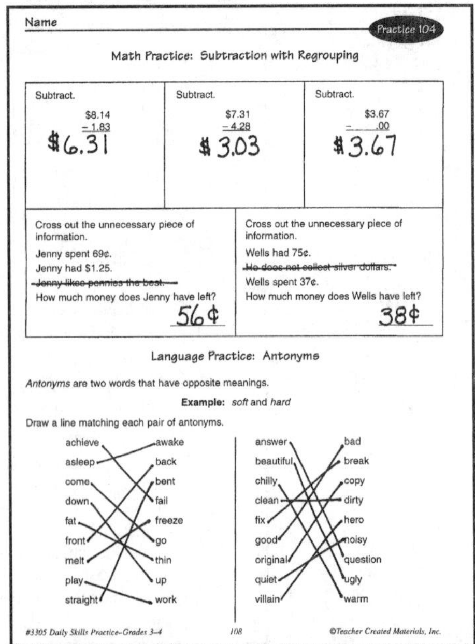

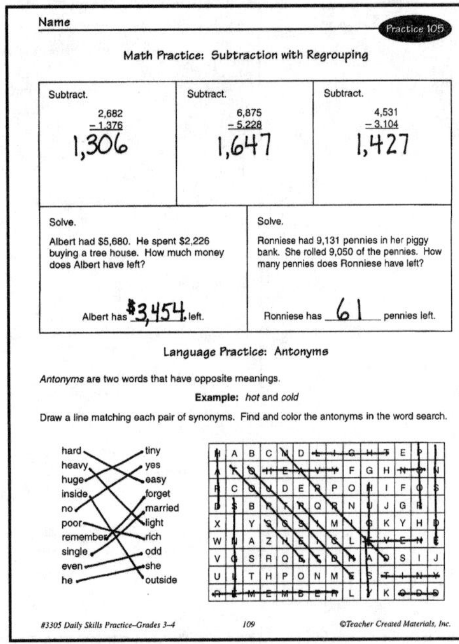

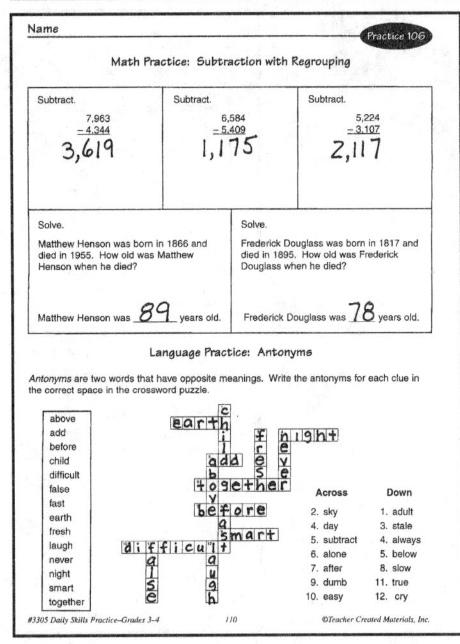

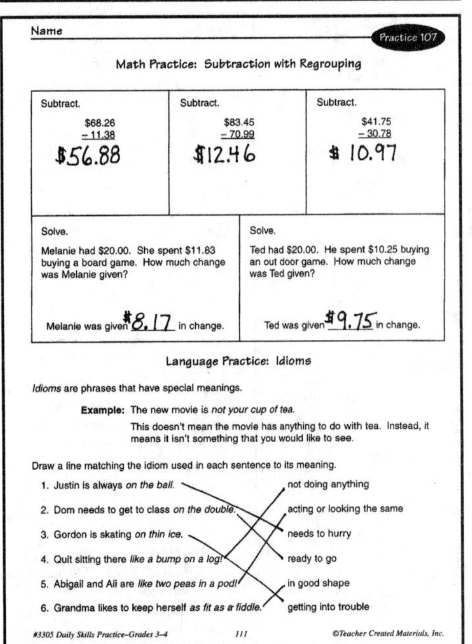

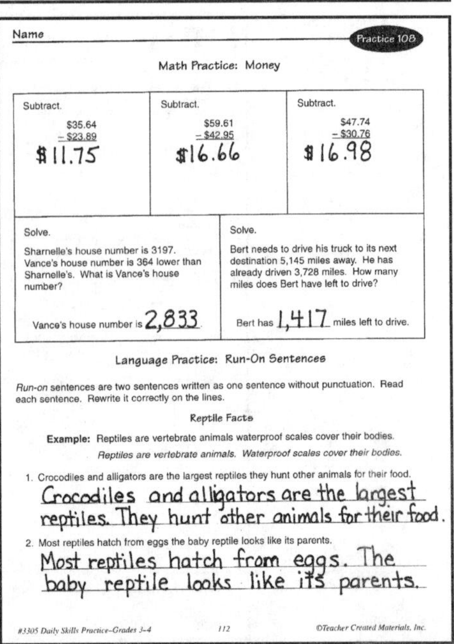

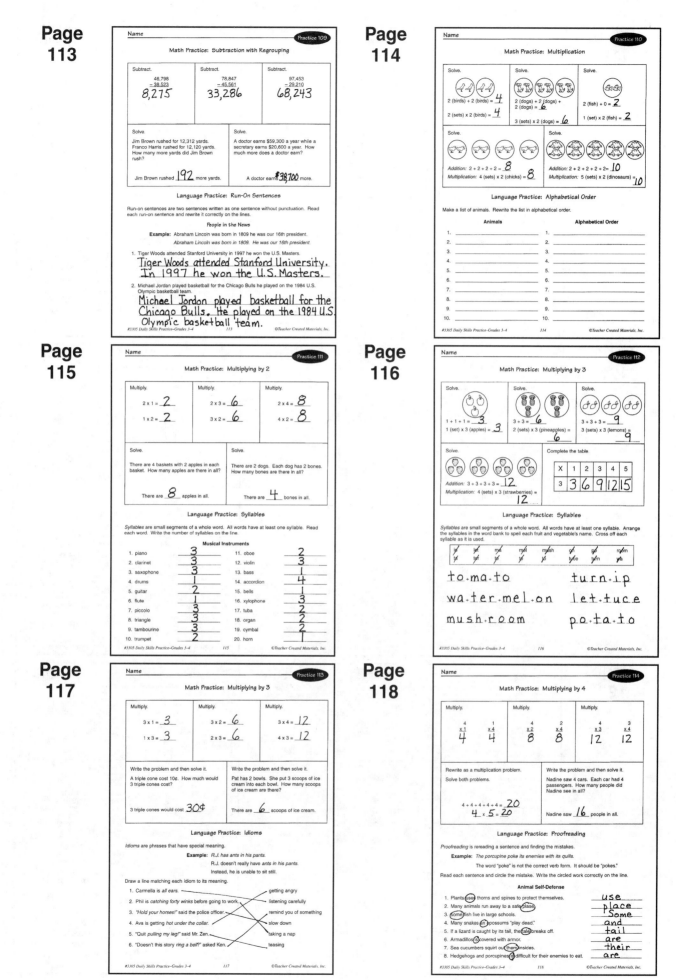

Page 113

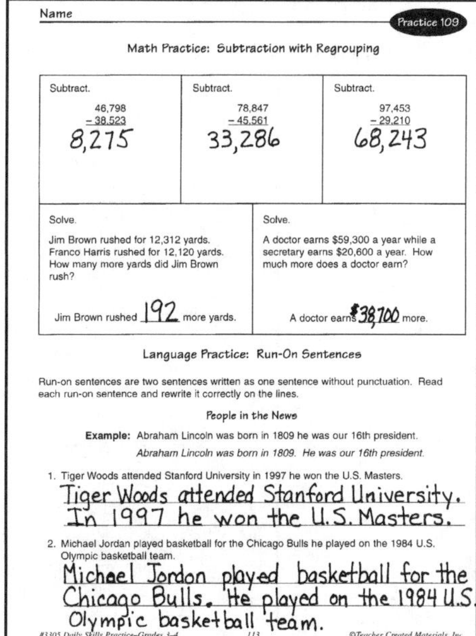

Name ______ Practice 109

Math Practice: Subtraction with Regrouping

Subtract.	Subtract.	Subtract.
46,798 − 38,523 = 8,275	78,847 − 45,561 = 33,286	97,453 − 29,210 = 68,243

Solve.	Solve.
Jim Brown rushed for 12,312 yards. Franco Harris rushed for 12,120 yards. How many more yards did Jim Brown rush? Jim Brown rushed 192 more yards.	A doctor earns $59,300 a year while a secretary earns $20,600 a year. How much more does a doctor earn? A doctor earns $38,700 more.

Language Practice: Run-On Sentences

Run-on sentences are two sentences written as one sentence without punctuation. Read each run-on sentence and rewrite it correctly on the lines.

People in the News

Example: Abraham Lincoln was born in 1809 he was our 16th president.
Abraham Lincoln was born in 1809. He was our 16th president.

1. Tiger Woods attended Stanford University in 1997 he won the U.S. Masters.
Tiger Woods attended Stanford University. In 1997 he won the U.S. Masters.
2. Michael Jordan played basketball for the Chicago Bulls he played on the 1984 U.S. Olympic basketball team.
Michael Jordan played basketball for the Chicago Bulls. He played on the 1984 U.S. Olympic basketball team.

#3305 Daily Skills Practice–Grades 3–4 113 ©Teacher Created Materials, Inc.

Page 114

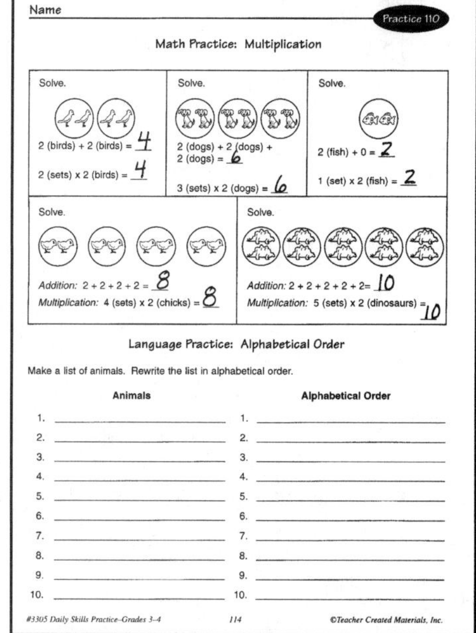

Name ______ Practice 110

Math Practice: Multiplication

Solve.	Solve.	Solve.
2 (birds) + 2 (birds) = 4 2 (sets) x 2 (birds) = 4	2 (dogs) + 2 (dogs) + 2 (dogs) = 6 3 (sets) x 2 (dogs) = 6	2 (fish) + 0 = 2 1 (set) x 2 (fish) = 2

Solve.	Solve.
Addition: 2 + 2 + 2 + 2 = 8 *Multiplication:* 4 (sets) x 2 (chicks) = 8	*Addition:* 2 + 2 + 2 + 2 + 2 = 10 *Multiplication:* 5 (sets) x 2 (dinosaurs) = 10

Language Practice: Alphabetical Order

Make a list of animals. Rewrite the list in alphabetical order.

Animals	Alphabetical Order
1.	1.
2.	2.
3.	3.
4.	4.
5.	5.
6.	6.
7.	7.
8.	8.
9.	9.
10.	10.

#3305 Daily Skills Practice–Grades 3–4 114 ©Teacher Created Materials, Inc.

Page 115

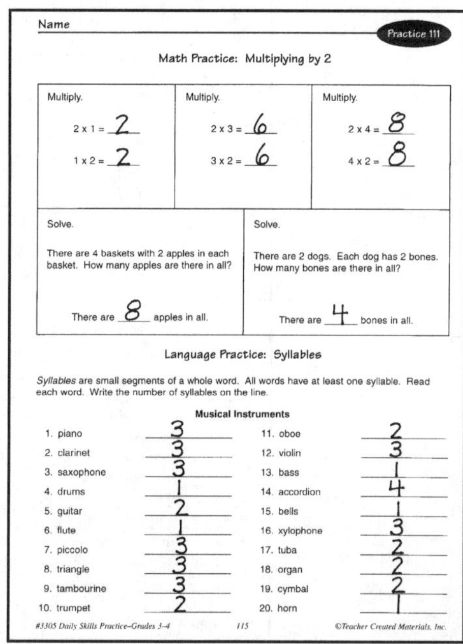

Name ______ Practice 111

Math Practice: Multiplying by 2

Multiply.	Multiply.	Multiply.
2 x 1 = 2 1 x 2 = 2	2 x 3 = 6 3 x 2 = 6	2 x 4 = 8 4 x 2 = 8

Solve.	Solve.
There are 4 baskets with 2 apples in each basket. How many apples are there in all? There are 8 apples in all.	There are 2 dogs. Each dog has 2 bones. How many bones are there in all? There are 4 bones in all.

Language Practice: Syllables

Syllables are small segments of a whole word. All words have at least one syllable. Read each word. Write the number of syllables on the line.

Musical Instruments

1. piano	3	11. oboe	2
2. clarinet	3	12. violin	3
3. saxophone	3	13. bass	1
4. drums	1	14. accordion	4
5. guitar	2	15. bells	1
6. flute	1	16. xylophone	3
7. piccolo	3	17. tuba	2
8. triangle	3	18. organ	2
9. tambourine	3	19. cymbal	2
10. trumpet	2	20. horn	1

#3305 Daily Skills Practice–Grades 3–4 115 ©Teacher Created Materials, Inc.

Page 116

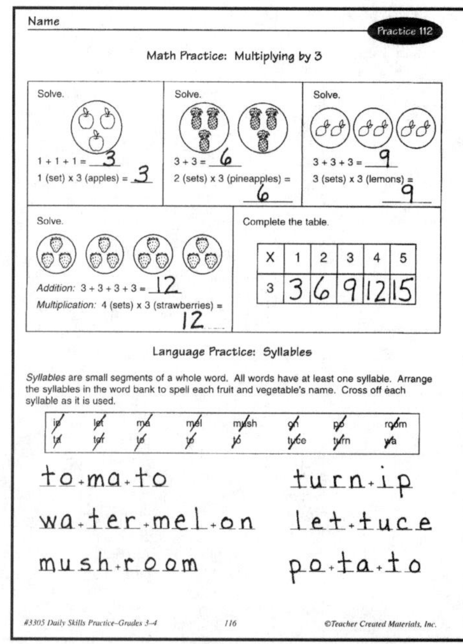

Name ______ Practice 112

Math Practice: Multiplying by 3

Solve.	Solve.	Solve.
1 + 1 + 1 = 3 1 (set) x 3 (apples) = 3	3 + 3 = 6 2 (sets) x 3 (pineapples) = 6	3 + 3 + 3 = 9 3 (sets) x 3 (lemons) = 9

Solve.

Addition: 3 + 3 + 3 + 3 = 12
Multiplication: 4 (sets) x 3 (strawberries) = 12

Complete the table.

X	1	2	3	4	5
3	3	6	9	12	15

Language Practice: Syllables

Syllables are small segments of a whole word. All words have at least one syllable. Arrange the syllables in the word bank to spell each fruit and vegetable's name. Cross off each syllable as it is used.

to-ma-to turn-ip
wa-ter-mel-on let-tuce
mush-room po-ta-to

#3305 Daily Skills Practice–Grades 3–4 116 ©Teacher Created Materials, Inc.

Page 117

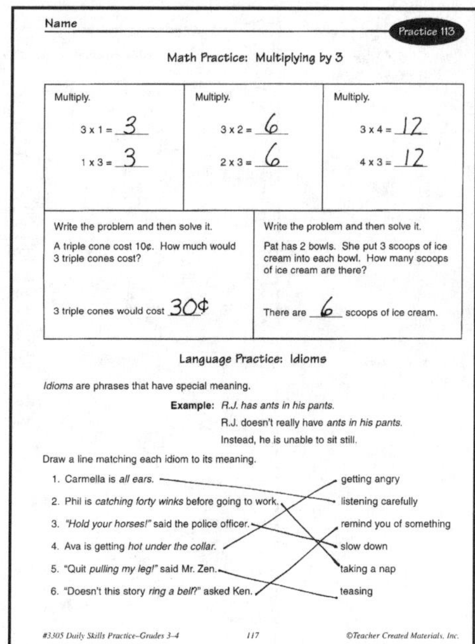

Name ______ Practice 113

Math Practice: Multiplying by 3

Multiply.	Multiply.	Multiply.
3 x 1 = 3 1 x 3 = 3	3 x 2 = 6 2 x 3 = 6	3 x 4 = 12 4 x 3 = 12

Write the problem and then solve it.	Write the problem and then solve it.
A triple cone cost 10¢. How much would 3 triple cones cost? 3 triple cones would cost 30¢	Pat has 2 bowls. She put 3 scoops of ice cream into each bowl. How many scoops of ice cream are there? There are 6 scoops of ice cream.

Language Practice: Idioms

Idioms are phrases that have special meaning.

Example: *R.J. has ants in his pants.*
R.J. doesn't really have *ants in his pants*.
Instead, he is unable to sit still.

Draw a line matching each idiom to its meaning.

1. Carmella is *all ears.* — getting angry
2. Phil is *catching forty winks* before going to work. — listening carefully
3. *"Hold your horses!"* said the police officer. — remind you of something
4. Ava is getting *hot under the collar.* — slow down
5. "Quit *pulling my leg!*" said Mr. Zen. — taking a nap
6. "Doesn't this story *ring a bell?*" asked Ken. — teasing

#3305 Daily Skills Practice–Grades 3–4 117 ©Teacher Created Materials, Inc.

Page 118

Name ______ Practice 114

Math Practice: Multiplying by 4

Multiply.	Multiply.	Multiply.
4 x 1 = 4; 1 x 4 = 4	4 x 2 = 8; 2 x 4 = 8	4 x 3 = 12; 3 x 4 = 12

Rewrite as a multiplication problem. Solve both problems.	Write the problem and then solve it.
4 + 4 + 4 + 4 + 4 = 20 4 x 5 = 20	Nadine saw 4 cars. Each car had 4 passengers. How many people did Nadine see in all? Nadine saw 16 people in all.

Language Practice: Proofreading

Proofreading is rereading a sentence and finding the mistakes.

Example: *The porcupine poke its enemies with its quills.*
The word "poke" is not the correct verb form. It should be "pokes."

Read each sentence and circle the mistake. Write the circled work correctly on the line.

Animal Self-Defense

1. Plants uses thorns and spines to protect themselves. — use
2. Many animals run away to a safe plase. — place
3. Some fish live in large schools. — Some
4. Many snakes an opossums "play dead." — and
5. If a lizard is caught by its tail, the tale breaks off. — tail
6. Armadillos is covered with armor. — are
7. Sea cucumbers squirt out them insides. — their
8. Hedgehogs and porcupines is difficult for their enemies to eat. — are

#3305 Daily Skills Practice–Grades 3–4 118 ©Teacher Created Materials, Inc.

Page 119

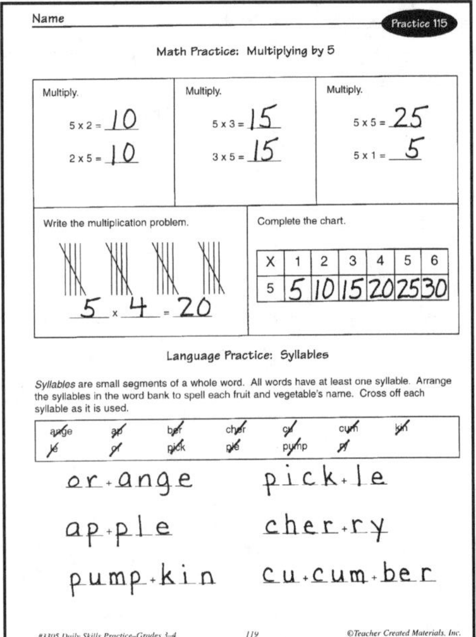

Name — Practice 115

Math Practice: Multiplying by 5

Multiply.	Multiply.	Multiply.
5 x 2 = 10 2 x 5 = 10	5 x 3 = 15 3 x 5 = 15	5 x 5 = 25 5 x 1 = 5

Write the multiplication problem.

5 x 4 = 20

Complete the chart.

X	1	2	3	4	5	6
5	5	10	15	20	25	30

Language Practice: Syllables

Syllables are small segments of a whole word. All words have at least one syllable. Arrange the syllables in the word bank to spell each fruit and vegetable's name. Cross off each syllable as it is used.

ange ap ber cher cu cum kin le or pick ple pump ry

or-ange pick-le
ap-ple cher-ry
pump-kin cu-cum-ber

#3305 Daily Skills Practice–Grades 3–4 119 ©Teacher Created Materials, Inc.

Page 120

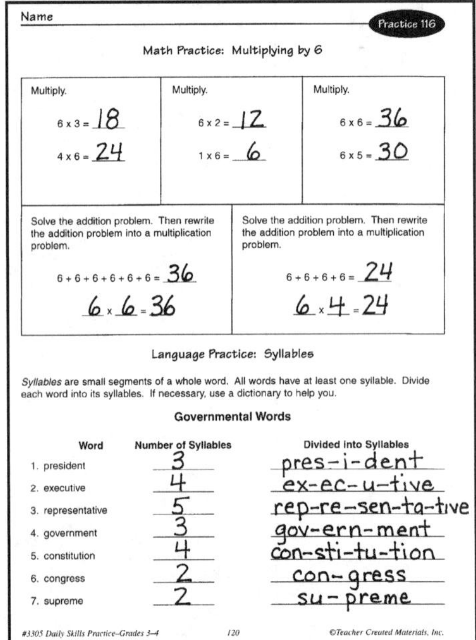

Name — Practice 116

Math Practice: Multiplying by 6

Multiply.	Multiply.	Multiply.
6 x 3 = 18 4 x 6 = 24	6 x 2 = 12 1 x 6 = 6	6 x 6 = 36 6 x 5 = 30

Solve the addition problem. Then rewrite the addition problem into a multiplication problem.

6 + 6 + 6 + 6 + 6 + 6 = 36
6 x 6 = 36

Solve the addition problem. Then rewrite the addition problem into a multiplication problem.

6 + 6 + 6 + 6 = 24
6 x 4 = 24

Language Practice: Syllables

Syllables are small segments of a whole word. All words have at least one syllable. Divide each word into its syllables. If necessary, use a dictionary to help you.

Governmental Words

Word	Number of Syllables	Divided into Syllables
1. president	3	pres-i-dent
2. executive	4	ex-ec-u-tive
3. representative	5	rep-re-sen-ta-tive
4. government	3	gov-ern-ment
5. constitution	4	con-sti-tu-tion
6. congress	2	con-gress
7. supreme	2	su-preme

#3305 Daily Skills Practice–Grades 3–4 120 ©Teacher Created Materials, Inc.

Page 121

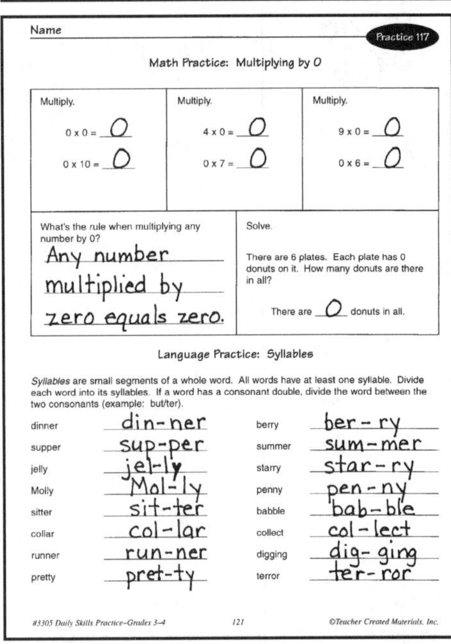

Name — Practice 117

Math Practice: Multiplying by 0

Multiply.	Multiply.	Multiply.
0 x 0 = 0 0 x 10 = 0	4 x 0 = 0 0 x 7 = 0	9 x 0 = 0 0 x 6 = 0

What's the rule when multiplying any number by 0?

Any number multiplied by zero equals zero.

Solve.

There are 6 plates. Each plate has 0 donuts on it. How many donuts are there in all?

There are 0 donuts in all.

Language Practice: Syllables

Syllables are small segments of a whole word. All words have at least one syllable. Divide each word into its syllables. If a word has a consonant double, divide the word between the two consonants (example: but/ter).

dinner	din-ner	berry	ber-ry
supper	sup-per	summer	sum-mer
jelly	jel-ly	starry	star-ry
Molly	Mol-ly	penny	pen-ny
sitter	sit-ter	babble	bab-ble
collar	col-lar	collect	col-lect
runner	run-ner	digging	dig-ging
pretty	pret-ty	terror	ter-ror

#3305 Daily Skills Practice–Grades 3–4 121 ©Teacher Created Materials, Inc.

Page 122

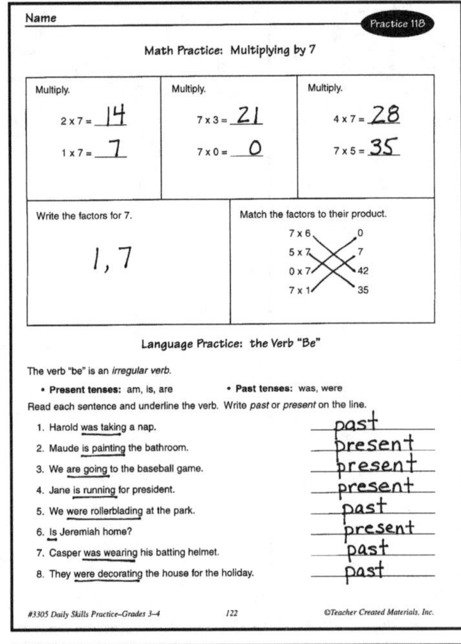

Name — Practice 118

Math Practice: Multiplying by 7

Multiply.	Multiply.	Multiply.
2 x 7 = 14 1 x 7 = 7	7 x 3 = 21 7 x 0 = 0	4 x 7 = 28 7 x 5 = 35

Write the factors for 7.

1, 7

Match the factors to their product.

7 x 6 — 42
5 x 7 — 35
0 x 7 — 0
7 x 1 — 7

Language Practice: the Verb "Be"

The verb "be" is an *irregular verb*.

- **Present tenses:** am, is, are
- **Past tenses:** was, were

Read each sentence and underline the verb. Write *past* or *present* on the line.

1. Harold was taking a nap. past
2. Maude is painting the bathroom. present
3. We are going to the baseball game. present
4. Jane is running for president. present
5. We were rollerblading at the park. past
6. Is Jeremiah home? present
7. Casper was wearing his batting helmet. past
8. They were decorating the house for the holiday. past

#3305 Daily Skills Practice–Grades 3–4 122 ©Teacher Created Materials, Inc.

Page 123

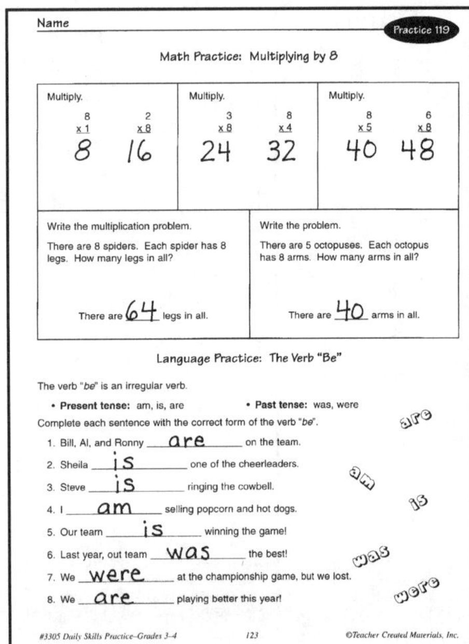

Name — Practice 119

Math Practice: Multiplying by 8

Multiply.	Multiply.	Multiply.
8 x 1 = 8 2 x 8 = 16	3 x 8 = 24 8 x 4 = 32	8 x 5 = 40 6 x 8 = 48

Write the multiplication problem.

There are 8 spiders. Each spider has 8 legs. How many legs in all?

There are 64 legs in all.

Write the problem.

There are 5 octopuses. Each octopus has 8 arms. How many arms in all?

There are 40 arms in all.

Language Practice: The Verb "Be"

The verb "be" is an irregular verb.

- **Present tense:** am, is, are
- **Past tense:** was, were

Complete each sentence with the correct form of the verb "be".

1. Bill, Al, and Ronny are on the team.
2. Sheila is one of the cheerleaders.
3. Steve is ringing the cowbell.
4. I am selling popcorn and hot dogs.
5. Our team is winning the game!
6. Last year, out team was the best!
7. We were at the championship game, but we lost.
8. We are playing better this year!

are am is was were

#3305 Daily Skills Practice–Grades 3–4 123 ©Teacher Created Materials, Inc.

Page 124

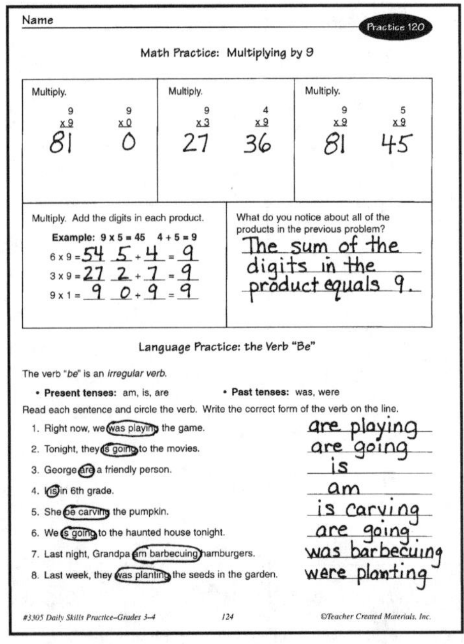

Name — Practice 120

Math Practice: Multiplying by 9

Multiply.	Multiply.	Multiply.
9 x 9 = 81 9 x 0 = 0	9 x 3 = 27 4 x 9 = 36	9 x 9 = 81 5 x 9 = 45

Multiply. Add the digits in each product.

Example: 9 x 5 = 45 4 + 5 = 9

6 x 9 = 54 5 + 4 = 9
3 x 9 = 27 2 + 7 = 9
9 x 1 = 9 0 + 9 = 9

What do you notice about all of the products in the previous problem?

The sum of the digits in the product equals 9.

Language Practice: the Verb "Be"

The verb "be" is an *irregular verb*.

- **Present tenses:** am, is, are
- **Past tenses:** was, were

Read each sentence and circle the verb. Write the correct form of the verb on the line.

1. Right now, we was playing the game. are playing
2. Tonight, they is going to the movies. are going
3. George are a friendly person. is
4. I is in 6th grade. am
5. She be carving the pumpkin. is carving
6. We is going to the haunted house tonight. are going
7. Last night, Grandpa am barbecuing hamburgers. was barbecuing
8. Last week, they was planting the seeds in the garden. were planting

#3305 Daily Skills Practice–Grades 3–4 124 ©Teacher Created Materials, Inc.

Page 125

Name ______ **Practice 121**

Math Practice: Division

Divide.	Divide.	Divide.
4 (apes) ÷ 2 (sets) = 2	6 (frogs) ÷ 2 (sets) = 3	8 (spiders) ÷ 2 (sets) = 4

Divide the lions into 2 equal sets. Write the division problem.	Divide the moose into 2 equal sets. Write the division problem.
12 ÷ 2 = 6	12 ÷ 2 = 6

Language Practice: Homophones

Homophones are groups of words that sound the same but have different meanings and spellings. Circle the homophone that goes with each picture.

blew (circled) / blue	hoes / hose (circled)	moose / mousse (circled)	gofer / gopher (circled)	prince / prints (circled)
one (circled) / won	fir (circled) / fur	wade / weighed (circled)	palette (circled) / pallet	pail (circled) / pale

Page 126

Name ______ **Practice 122**

Math Practice: Dividing by 2

Divide.	Divide.	Divide.
8 ÷ 2 = 4	12 ÷ 2 = 6	2 ÷ 2 = 1
4 ÷ 2 = 2	6 ÷ 2 = 3	10 ÷ 2 = 5

Solve.	Solve.
Cal has $6. Each piggy bank costs $2. How many piggy banks can Cal buy?	Kate has $8. Each book costs $2. How many books can Kate buy?
Cal can buy 3 piggy banks.	Kate can buy 4 books.

Language Practice: Compound Words

A *compound word* is made by combining two separate words into one new word. Write the answer to each clue in the crossword puzzle.

Across

2. placed over a chair or sofa
4. type of painting
6. no shoes
8. an architect's drawing
9. to tighten footwear

Down

1. used to open a door
5. used to tell time
7. kind of pants

barefoot	shoelace
blueprint	slipcover
doorknob	watercolor
overalls	wristwatch

Crossword answers: 1. doorknob; 2. slipcover; 4. watermelon; 5. wristwatch; 6. barefoot; 7. overalls; 8. blueprint; 9. shoelace

Page 127

Name ______ **Practice 123**

Math Practice: Dividing by 3

Divide.	Divide.	Divide.
6 (mice) ÷ 3 (sets) = 2	9 (hippos) ÷ 3 (sets) = 3	12 (pandas) ÷ 3 (sets) = 4

Divide the mice into 4 equal sets. Write the division problem.	Divide the bears into 3 equal sets. Write the division problem.
16 ÷ 4 = 4	3 ÷ 3 = 1

Language Practice: Reading to Solve Problems

Draw the picture for the problem. Write the division problem.

Grandma baked 12 cookies and divided them equally among the 3 grandchildren. 12÷3=4	Sylvester gathered 18 pebbles. He divided them equally among 3 jars. 18÷3=6
Josette picked 9 flowers. She divided them equally among 3 vases. 9÷3=3	Thomas caught 3 butterflies. He divided them equally among 3 nets. 3÷3=1

Page 128

Name ______ **Practice 124**

Math Practice: Dividing by 3

Divide.	Divide.	Divide.
3 ÷ 3 = 1	12 ÷ 3 = 4	21 ÷ 3 = 7
9 ÷ 3 = 3	15 ÷ 3 = 5	18 ÷ 3 = 6

Solve.	Solve.
Henny laid 12 eggs. Each basket can hold 3 eggs. How many baskets does Henny need?	Froggy laid 18 eggs. Each lily pad can hold 3 eggs. How many lily pads does Froggy need?
Henny needs 4 baskets.	Froggy needs 6 lily pads.

Language Practice: Compound Words

A *compound word* is made by combining two separate words into one new word. Make the compound words using the words in the word bank. Find and color each compound word in the word search.

apple	berry	blue	bread	butter	cake	cheese	corn
meal	melon	milk	nut	oat	pea	pine	water

1. watermelon
2. blueberry
3. cornbread
4. buttermilk
5. cheesecake
6. peanut
7. pineapple
8. oatmeal

P	W	A	T	E	R	M	E	L	O	N	A	P	P	L	H
G	E	E	L	O	P	P	I	N	E	A	P	P	L	E	O
R	A	A	I	C	E	C	R	E	A	M	T	G	A	E	T
C	O	R	N	B	R	E	A	D	H	T	O	M	L	S	D
N	D	B	L	U	E	B	E	R	R	Y	R	B	E	A	O
M	O	T	H	E	T	R	S	I	S	T	R	E	F	A	G
O	A	R	C	H	E	E	S	E	C	A	K	E	D	U	L
B	U	T	T	E	R	M	I	L	K	B	P	U	C	C	E

Page 129

Name ______ **Practice 125**

Math Practice: Dividing by 4

Divide.	Divide.	Divide.
12 ÷ 4 = 3	4 ÷ 4 = 1	20 ÷ 4 = 5
8 ÷ 4 = 2	16 ÷ 4 = 4	24 ÷ 4 = 6

Complete the chart.

÷	0	1	2	4
4	0	4	2	1

Write the missing factor.

16 ÷ 4 = 4 12 ÷ 3 = 4

20 ÷ 5 = 4 8 ÷ 2 = 4

Language Practice: Compound Words

A *compound word* is made by combining two separate words into one new word. Write the missing word to complete each set of compound words.

back board	frog man	bed bug
back side	gentle man	bed room
back field	weather man	bed spread
tooth pick	air line	paper back
tooth ache	air mail	bare back
tooth brush	air port	back bone

Page 130

Name ______ **Practice 126**

Math Practice: Dividing by 5

Divide.	Divide.	Divide.
15 ÷ 5 = 3	5 ÷ 5 = 1	25 ÷ 5 = 5
20 ÷ 5 = 4	10 ÷ 5 = 2	30 ÷ 5 = 6

Count by 5s to 50. Write the numbers.	Rewrite the division problem and then solve.
5 10 15 20 25 30 35 40 45 50	5)15 = 3 → 15÷5=3; 5)10 = 2 → 10÷5=2

Language Practice: Compound Words

A *compound word* is made by combining two separate words into one new word. Write eight compound word using the words provided in the box.

anchor	hair	ball	hay	bridge	leap	cracker	nut
crow	pin	cut	scare	draw	stack	frog	woman

pinball haystack

haircut leapfrog

anchorwoman nutcracker

scarecrow drawbridge

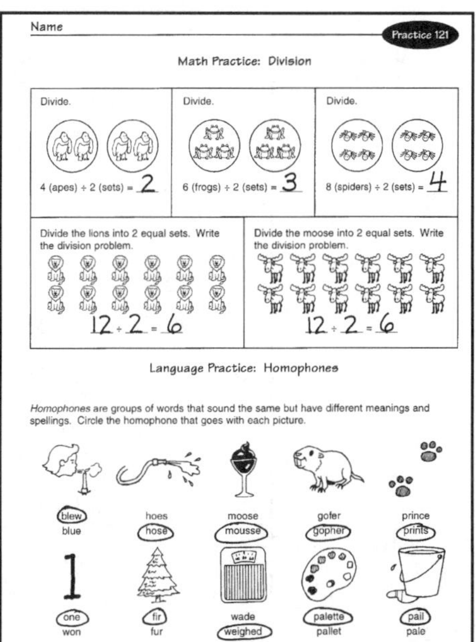

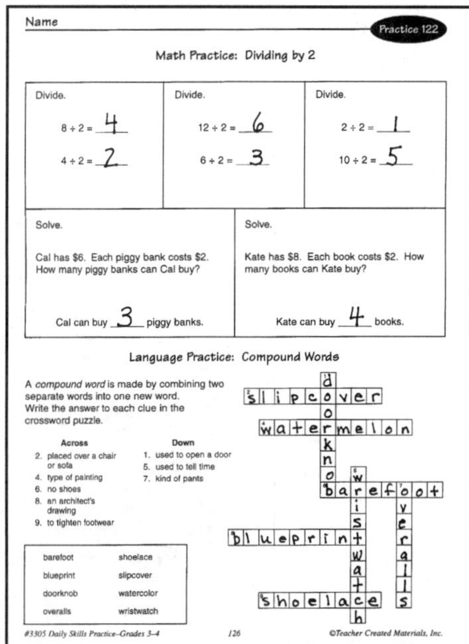

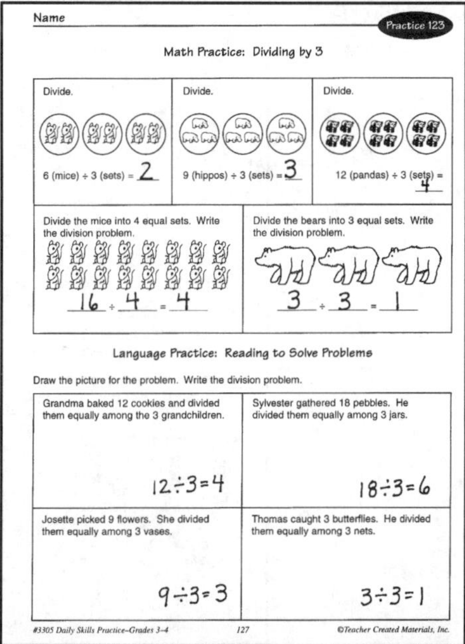

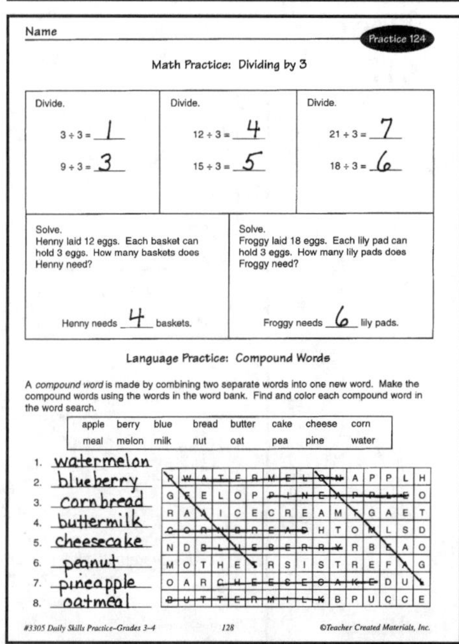

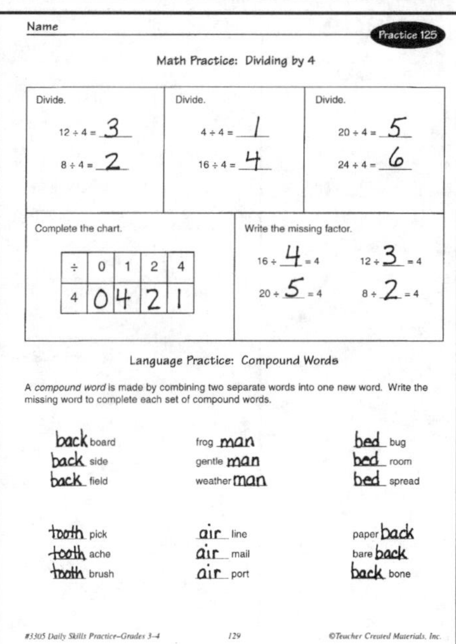

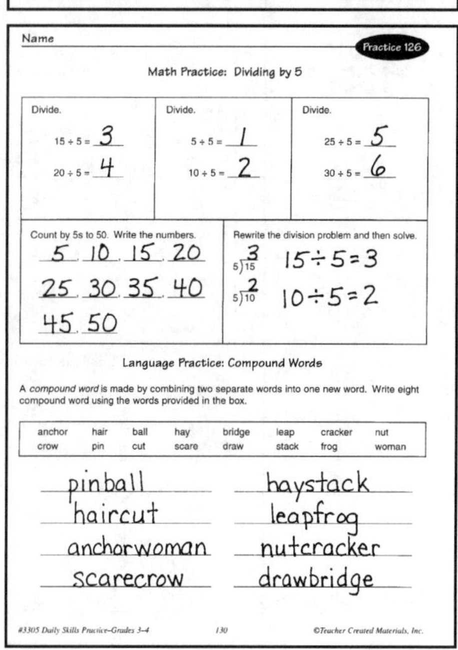

Page 131

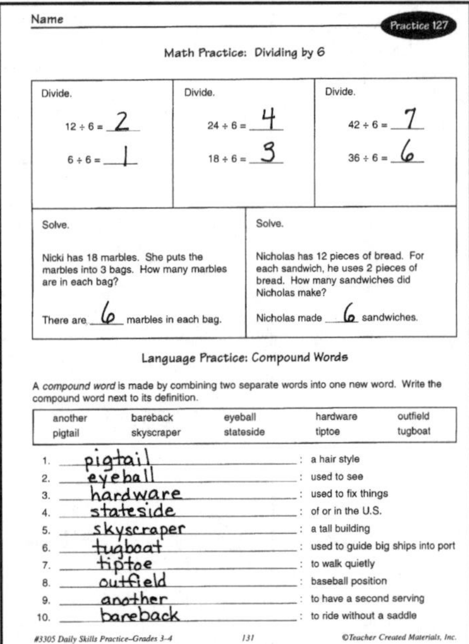

Name Practice 127

Math Practice: Dividing by 6

Divide.	Divide.	Divide.
12 ÷ 6 = 2	24 ÷ 6 = 4	42 ÷ 6 = 7
6 ÷ 6 = 1	18 ÷ 6 = 3	36 ÷ 6 = 6

Solve.

Nicki has 18 marbles. She puts the marbles into 3 bags. How many marbles are in each bag?

There are 6 marbles in each bag.

Solve.

Nicholas has 12 pieces of bread. For each sandwich, he uses 2 pieces of bread. How many sandwiches did Nicholas make?

Nicholas made 6 sandwiches.

Language Practice: Compound Words

A *compound word* is made by combining two separate words into one new word. Write the compound word next to its definition.

another	bareback	eyeball	hardware	outfield
pigtail	skyscraper	stateside	tiptoe	tugboat

1. pigtail : a hair style
2. eyeball : used to see
3. hardware : used to fix things
4. stateside : of or in the U.S.
5. skyscraper : a tall building
6. tugboat : used to guide big ships into port
7. tiptoe : to walk quietly
8. outfield : baseball position
9. another : to have a second serving
10. bareback : to ride without a saddle

#3305 Daily Skills Practice—Grades 3–4 131 ©Teacher Created Materials, Inc.

Page 132

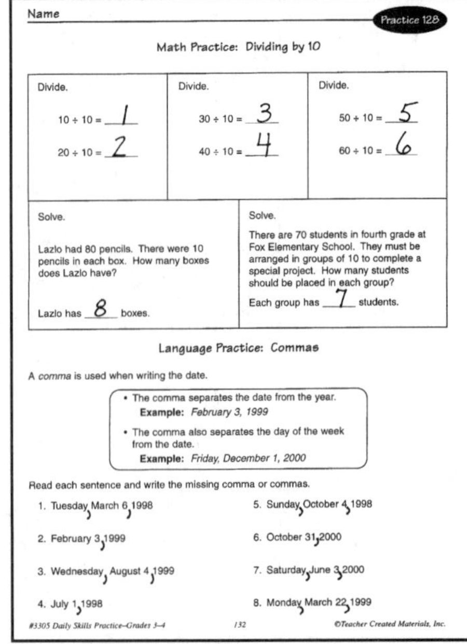

Name Practice 128

Math Practice: Dividing by 10

Divide.	Divide.	Divide.
10 ÷ 10 = 1	30 ÷ 10 = 3	50 ÷ 10 = 5
20 ÷ 10 = 2	40 ÷ 10 = 4	60 ÷ 10 = 6

Solve.

Lazlo had 80 pencils. There were 10 pencils in each box. How many boxes does Lazlo have?

Lazlo has 8 boxes.

Solve.

There are 70 students in fourth grade at Fox Elementary School. They must be arranged in groups of 10 to complete a special project. How many students should be placed in each group?

Each group has 7 students.

Language Practice: Commas

A *comma* is used when writing the date.

- The comma separates the date from the year. **Example:** *February 3, 1999*
- The comma also separates the day of the week from the date. **Example:** *Friday, December 1, 2000*

Read each sentence and write the missing comma or commas.

1. Tuesday, March 6, 1998
2. February 3, 1999
3. Wednesday, August 4, 1999
4. July 1, 1998
5. Sunday, October 4, 1998
6. October 31, 2000
7. Saturday, June 3, 2000
8. Monday, March 22, 1999

#3305 Daily Skills Practice—Grades 3–4 132 ©Teacher Created Materials, Inc.

Page 133

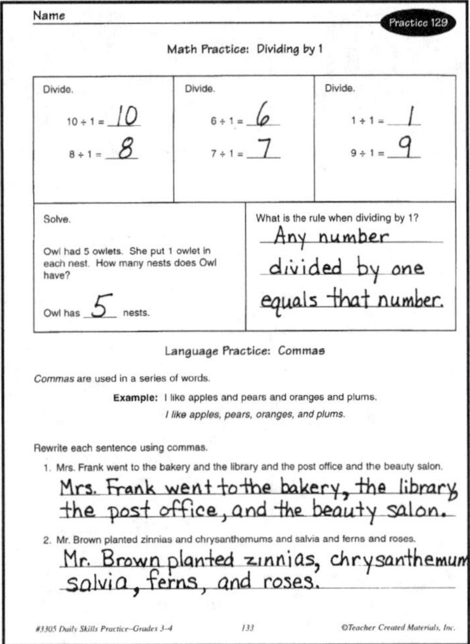

Name Practice 129

Math Practice: Dividing by 1

Divide.	Divide.	Divide.
10 ÷ 1 = 10	6 ÷ 1 = 6	1 ÷ 1 = 1
8 ÷ 1 = 8	7 ÷ 1 = 7	9 ÷ 1 = 9

Solve.

Owl had 5 owlets. She put 1 owlet in each nest. How many nests does Owl have?

Owl has 5 nests.

What is the rule when dividing by 1?

Any number divided by one equals that number.

Language Practice: Commas

Commas are used in a series of words.

Example: I like apples and pears and oranges and plums.
I like apples, pears, oranges, and plums.

Rewrite each sentence using commas.

1. Mrs. Frank went to the bakery and the library and the post office and the beauty salon.
   Mrs. Frank went to the bakery, the library, the post office, and the beauty salon.
2. Mr. Brown planted zinnias and chrysanthemums and salvia and ferns and roses.
   Mr. Brown planted zinnias, chrysanthemum, solvia, ferns, and roses.

#3305 Daily Skills Practice—Grades 3–4 133 ©Teacher Created Materials, Inc.

Page 134

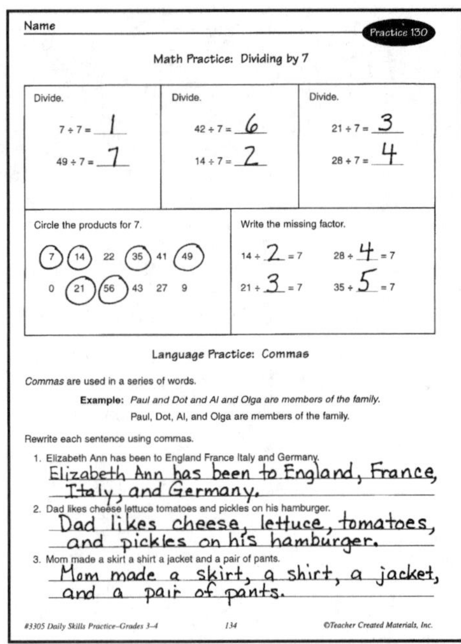

Name Practice 130

Math Practice: Dividing by 7

Divide.	Divide.	Divide.
7 ÷ 7 = 1	42 ÷ 7 = 6	21 ÷ 7 = 3
49 ÷ 7 = 7	14 ÷ 7 = 2	28 ÷ 7 = 4

Circle the products for 7.

(7) (14) 22 (35) 41 (49)
0 (21) (56) 43 27 9

Write the missing factor.

14 ÷ 2 = 7 28 ÷ 4 = 7
21 ÷ 3 = 7 35 ÷ 5 = 7

Language Practice: Commas

Commas are used in a series of words.

Example: *Paul and Dot and Al and Olga are members of the family.*
Paul, Dot, Al, and Olga are members of the family.

Rewrite each sentence using commas.

1. Elizabeth Ann has been to England France Italy and Germany.
   Elizabeth Ann has been to England, France, Italy, and Germany.
2. Dad likes cheese lettuce tomatoes and pickles on his hamburger.
   Dad likes cheese, lettuce, tomatoes, and pickles on his hamburger.
3. Mom made a skirt a shirt a jacket and a pair of pants.
   Mom made a skirt, a shirt, a jacket, and a pair of pants.

#3305 Daily Skills Practice—Grades 3–4 134 ©Teacher Created Materials, Inc.

Page 135

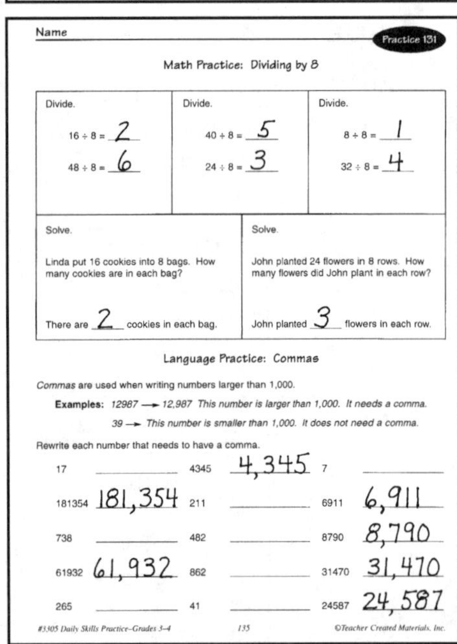

Name Practice 131

Math Practice: Dividing by 8

Divide.	Divide.	Divide.
16 ÷ 8 = 2	40 ÷ 8 = 5	8 ÷ 8 = 1
48 ÷ 8 = 6	24 ÷ 8 = 3	32 ÷ 8 = 4

Solve.

Linda put 16 cookies into 8 bags. How many cookies are in each bag?

There are 2 cookies in each bag.

Solve.

John planted 24 flowers in 8 rows. How many flowers did John plant in each row?

John planted 3 flowers in each row.

Language Practice: Commas

Commas are used when writing numbers larger than 1,000.

Examples: *12987 → 12,987 This number is larger than 1,000. It needs a comma.*
39 → This number is smaller than 1,000. It does not need a comma.

Rewrite each number that needs to have a comma.

17		4345	4,345	7	
181354	181,354	211		6911	6,911
738		482		8790	8,790
61932	61,932	862		31470	31,470
265		41		24587	24,587

#3305 Daily Skills Practice—Grades 3–4 135 ©Teacher Created Materials, Inc.

Page 136

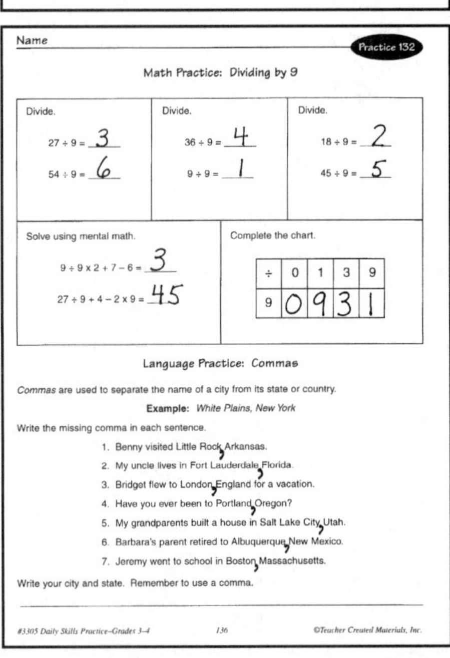

Name Practice 132

Math Practice: Dividing by 9

Divide.	Divide.	Divide.
27 ÷ 9 = 3	36 ÷ 9 = 4	18 ÷ 9 = 2
54 ÷ 9 = 6	9 ÷ 9 = 1	45 ÷ 9 = 5

Solve using mental math.

9 ÷ 9 x 2 + 7 – 6 = 3
27 ÷ 9 + 4 – 2 x 9 = 45

Complete the chart.

÷	0	1	3	9
9	0	9	3	1

Language Practice: Commas

Commas are used to separate the name of a city from its state or country.

Example: *White Plains, New York*

Write the missing comma in each sentence.

1. Benny visited Little Rock, Arkansas.
2. My uncle lives in Fort Lauderdale, Florida.
3. Bridget flew to London, England for a vacation.
4. Have you ever been to Portland, Oregon?
5. My grandparents built a house in Salt Lake City, Utah.
6. Barbara's parent retired to Albuquerque, New Mexico.
7. Jeremy went to school in Boston, Massachusetts.

Write your city and state. Remember to use a comma.

#3305 Daily Skills Practice—Grades 3–4 136 ©Teacher Created Materials, Inc.

Page 137

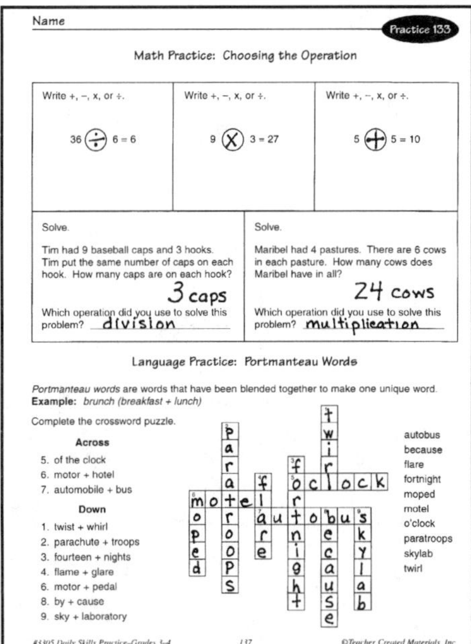

Name

Practice 133

Math Practice: Choosing the Operation

Write +, –, x, or ÷.	Write +, –, x, or ÷.	Write +, –, x, or ÷.
36 (÷) 6 = 6	9 (x) 3 = 27	5 (+) 5 = 10

Solve.	Solve.
Tim had 9 baseball caps and 3 hooks. Tim put the same number of caps on each hook. How many caps are on each hook? 3 caps Which operation did you use to solve this problem? division	Maribel had 4 pastures. There are 6 cows in each pasture. How many cows does Maribel have in all? 24 cows Which operation did you use to solve this problem? multiplication

Language Practice: Portmanteau Words

Portmanteau words are words that have been blended together to make one unique word.
Example: *brunch (breakfast + lunch)*

Complete the crossword puzzle.

Across
5. of the clock
6. motor + hotel
7. automobile + bus

Down
1. twist + whirl
2. parachute + troops
3. fourteen + nights
4. flame + glare
6. motor + pedal
8. by + cause
9. sky + laboratory

autobus, because, flare, fortnight, moped, motel, o'clock, paratroops, skylab, twirl

#3305 Daily Skills Practice–Grades 3–4 137 ©Teacher Created Materials, Inc.

Page 138

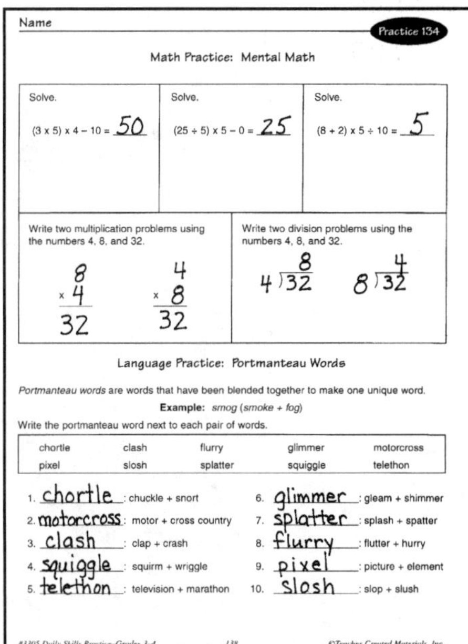

Name

Practice 134

Math Practice: Mental Math

Solve.	Solve.	Solve.
(3 x 5) x 4 – 10 = 50	(25 ÷ 5) x 5 – 0 = 25	(8 + 2) x 5 ÷ 10 = 5

Write two multiplication problems using the numbers 4, 8, and 32.	Write two division problems using the numbers 4, 8, and 32.
8 x 4 = 32; 4 x 8 = 32	32 ÷ 4 = 8; 32 ÷ 8 = 4

Language Practice: Portmanteau Words

Portmanteau words are words that have been blended together to make one unique word.
Example: *smog (smoke + fog)*

Write the portmanteau word next to each pair of words.

chortle	clash	flurry	glimmer	motorcross
pixel	slosh	splatter	squiggle	telethon

1. chortle: chuckle + snort
2. motorcross: motor + cross country
3. clash: clap + crash
4. squiggle: squirm + wriggle
5. telethon: television + marathon
6. glimmer: gleam + shimmer
7. splatter: splash + spatter
8. flurry: flutter + hurry
9. pixel: picture + element
10. slosh: slop + slush

#3305 Daily Skills Practice–Grades 3–4 138 ©Teacher Created Materials, Inc.

Page 139

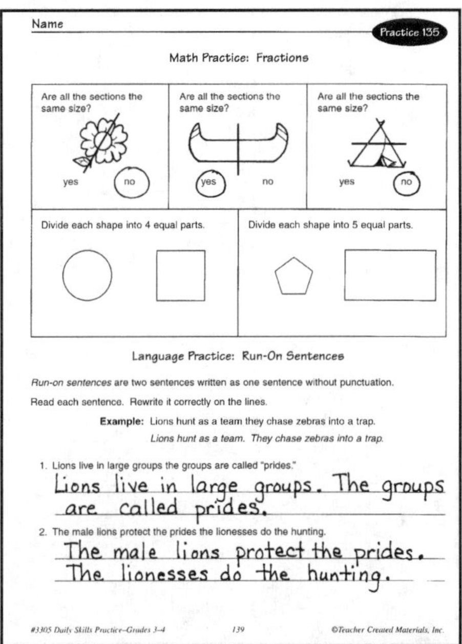

Name

Practice 135

Math Practice: Fractions

Are all the sections the same size?	Are all the sections the same size?	Are all the sections the same size?
yes (no)	(yes) no	yes (no)

Divide each shape into 4 equal parts.	Divide each shape into 5 equal parts.

Language Practice: Run-On Sentences

Run-on sentences are two sentences written as one sentence without punctuation.

Read each sentence. Rewrite it correctly on the lines.

Example: Lions hunt as a team they chase zebras into a trap.
Lions hunt as a team. They chase zebras into a trap.

1. Lions live in large groups the groups are called "prides."
Lions live in large groups. The groups are called prides.
2. The male lions protect the prides the lionesses do the hunting.
The male lions protect the prides. The lionesses do the hunting.

#3305 Daily Skills Practice–Grades 3–4 139 ©Teacher Created Materials, Inc.

Page 140

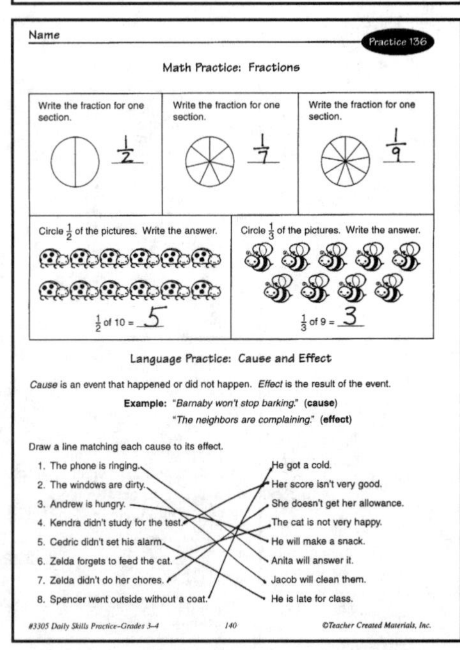

Name

Practice 136

Math Practice: Fractions

Write the fraction for one section.	Write the fraction for one section.	Write the fraction for one section.
1/2	1/7	1/9

Circle $\frac{1}{2}$ of the pictures. Write the answer.	Circle $\frac{1}{3}$ of the pictures. Write the answer.
$\frac{1}{2}$ of 10 = 5	$\frac{1}{3}$ of 9 = 3

Language Practice: Cause and Effect

Cause is an event that happened or did not happen. *Effect* is the result of the event.

Example: *"Barnaby won't stop barking."* **(cause)**
"The neighbors are complaining." **(effect)**

Draw a line matching each cause to its effect.

1. The phone is ringing.
2. The windows are dirty.
3. Andrew is hungry.
4. Kendra didn't study for the test.
5. Cedric didn't set his alarm.
6. Zelda forgets to feed the cat.
7. Zelda didn't do her chores.
8. Spencer went outside without a coat.

- He got a cold.
- Her score isn't very good.
- She doesn't get her allowance.
- The cat is not very happy.
- He will make a snack.
- Anita will answer it.
- Jacob will clean them.
- He is late for class.

#3305 Daily Skills Practice–Grades 3–4 140 ©Teacher Created Materials, Inc.

Page 141

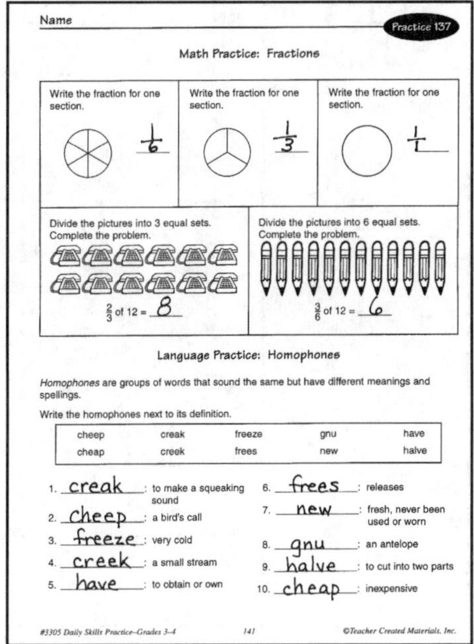

Name

Practice 137

Math Practice: Fractions

Write the fraction for one section.	Write the fraction for one section.	Write the fraction for one section.
1/6	1/3	1/1

Divide the pictures into 3 equal sets. Complete the problem.	Divide the pictures into 6 equal sets. Complete the problem.
$\frac{2}{3}$ of 12 = 8	$\frac{3}{6}$ of 12 = 6

Language Practice: Homophones

Homophones are groups of words that sound the same but have different meanings and spellings.

Write the homophones next to its definition.

cheep	creak	freeze	gnu	have
cheap	creek	frees	new	halve

1. creak: to make a squeaking sound
2. cheep: a bird's call
3. freeze: very cold
4. creek: a small stream
5. have: to obtain or own
6. frees: releases
7. new: fresh, never been used or worn
8. gnu: an antelope
9. halve: to cut into two parts
10. cheap: inexpensive

#3305 Daily Skills Practice–Grades 3–4 141 ©Teacher Created Materials, Inc.

Page 142

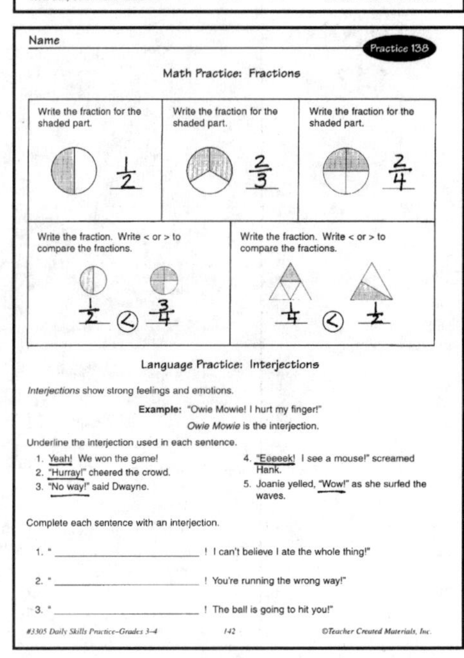

Name

Practice 138

Math Practice: Fractions

Write the fraction for the shaded part.	Write the fraction for the shaded part.	Write the fraction for the shaded part.
1/2	2/3	2/4

Write the fraction. Write < or > to compare the fractions.	Write the fraction. Write < or > to compare the fractions.
1/2 (<) 3/4	1/4 (<) 1/2

Language Practice: Interjections

Interjections show strong feelings and emotions.

Example: "Owie Mowie! I hurt my finger!"
Owie Mowie is the interjection.

Underline the interjection used in each sentence.

1. Yeah! We won the game!
2. "Hurray!" cheered the crowd.
3. "No way!" said Dwayne.
4. "Eeeeek! I see a mouse!" screamed Hank.
5. Joanie yelled, "Wow!" as she surfed the waves.

Complete each sentence with an interjection.

1. "________________! I can't believe I ate the whole thing!"
2. "________________! You're running the wrong way!"
3. "________________! The ball is going to hit you!"

#3305 Daily Skills Practice–Grades 3–4 142 ©Teacher Created Materials, Inc.

Page 143

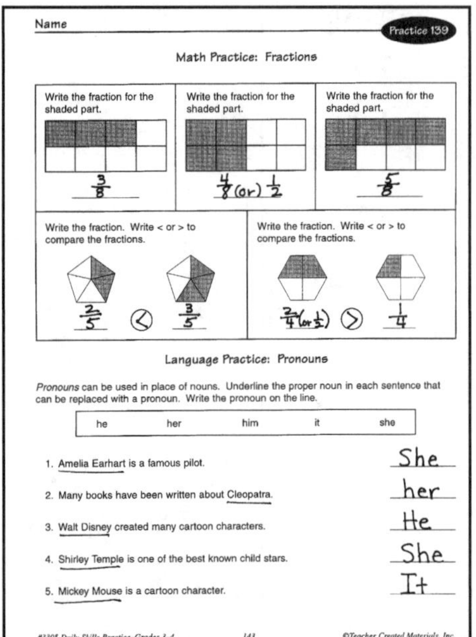

Name ______ Practice 139

Math Practice: Fractions

Write the fraction for the shaded part.	Write the fraction for the shaded part.	Write the fraction for the shaded part.
3/8	4/8 (or) 1/2	5/8

Write the fraction. Write < or > to compare the fractions.	Write the fraction. Write < or > to compare the fractions.
2/5 < 3/5	2/4 (or 1/2) > 1/4

Language Practice: Pronouns

Pronouns can be used in place of nouns. Underline the proper noun in each sentence that can be replaced with a pronoun. Write the pronoun on the line.

he	her	him	it	she

1. Amelia Earhart is a famous pilot. She
2. Many books have been written about Cleopatra. her
3. Walt Disney created many cartoon characters. He
4. Shirley Temple is one of the best known child stars. She
5. Mickey Mouse is a cartoon character. It

#3305 Daily Skills Practice—Grades 3–4 143 ©Teacher Created Materials, Inc.

Page 144

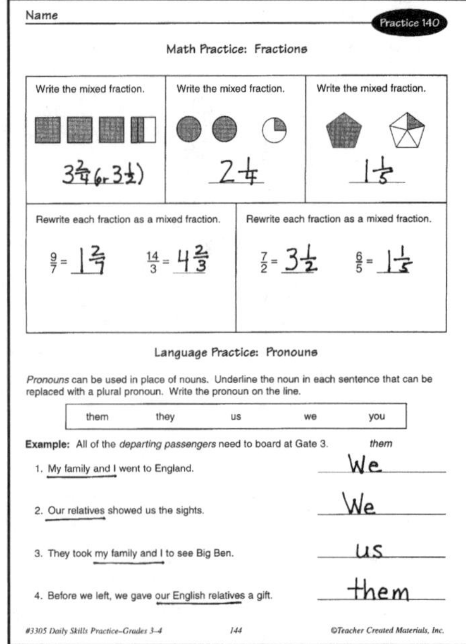

Name ______ Practice 140

Math Practice: Fractions

Write the mixed fraction.	Write the mixed fraction.	Write the mixed fraction.
3 2/4 (or 3 1/2)	2 1/4	1 1/5

Rewrite each fraction as a mixed fraction.	Rewrite each fraction as a mixed fraction.
9/7 = 1 2/7 14/3 = 4 2/3	7/2 = 3 1/2 6/5 = 1 1/5

Language Practice: Pronouns

Pronouns can be used in place of nouns. Underline the noun in each sentence that can be replaced with a plural pronoun. Write the pronoun on the line.

them	they	us	we	you

Example: All of the *departing passengers* need to board at Gate 3. *them*

1. My family and I went to England. We
2. Our relatives showed us the sights. We
3. They took my family and I to see Big Ben. us
4. Before we left, we gave our English relatives a gift. them

#3305 Daily Skills Practice—Grades 3–4 144 ©Teacher Created Materials, Inc.

Page 145

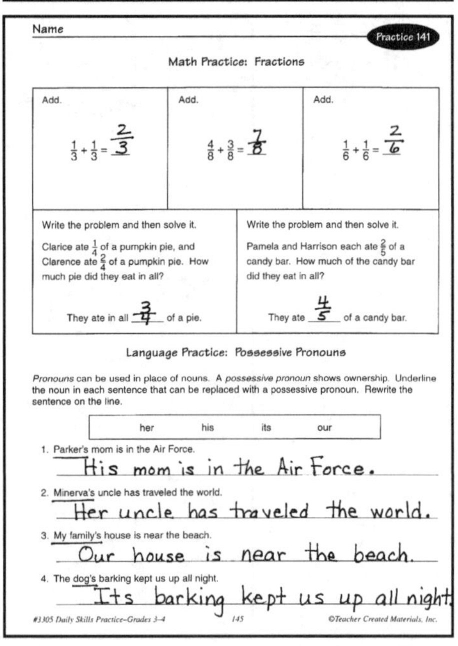

Name ______ Practice 141

Math Practice: Fractions

Add.	Add.	Add.
$\frac{1}{3} + \frac{1}{3} = \frac{2}{3}$	$\frac{4}{8} + \frac{3}{8} = \frac{7}{8}$	$\frac{1}{6} + \frac{1}{6} = \frac{2}{6}$

Write the problem and then solve it.	Write the problem and then solve it.
Clarice ate $\frac{1}{4}$ of a pumpkin pie, and Clarence ate $\frac{2}{4}$ of a pumpkin pie. How much pie did they eat in all? They ate in all 3/4 of a pie.	Pamela and Harrison each ate $\frac{2}{5}$ of a candy bar. How much of the candy bar did they eat in all? They ate 4/5 of a candy bar.

Language Practice: Possessive Pronouns

Pronouns can be used in place of nouns. A *possessive pronoun* shows ownership. Underline the noun in each sentence that can be replaced with a possessive pronoun. Rewrite the sentence on the line.

her	his	its	our

1. Parker's mom is in the Air Force. His mom is in the Air Force.
2. Minerva's uncle has traveled the world. Her uncle has traveled the world.
3. My family's house is near the beach. Our house is near the beach.
4. The dog's barking kept us up all night. Its barking kept us up all night.

#3305 Daily Skills Practice—Grades 3–4 145 ©Teacher Created Materials, Inc.

Page 146

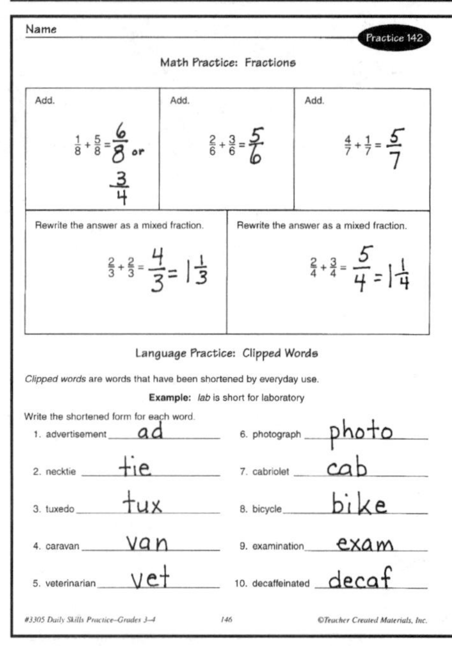

Name ______ Practice 142

Math Practice: Fractions

Add.	Add.	Add.
$\frac{1}{8} + \frac{5}{8} = \frac{6}{8}$ or $\frac{3}{4}$	$\frac{2}{6} + \frac{3}{6} = \frac{5}{6}$	$\frac{4}{7} + \frac{1}{7} = \frac{5}{7}$

Rewrite the answer as a mixed fraction.	Rewrite the answer as a mixed fraction.
$\frac{2}{3} + \frac{2}{3} = \frac{4}{3} = 1\frac{1}{3}$	$\frac{2}{4} + \frac{3}{4} = \frac{5}{4} = 1\frac{1}{4}$

Language Practice: Clipped Words

Clipped words are words that have been shortened by everyday use.

Example: *lab* is short for laboratory

Write the shortened form for each word.

1. advertisement ad
2. necktie tie
3. tuxedo tux
4. caravan van
5. veterinarian vet
6. photograph photo
7. cabriolet cab
8. bicycle bike
9. examination exam
10. decaffeinated decaf

#3305 Daily Skills Practice—Grades 3–4 146 ©Teacher Created Materials, Inc.

Page 147

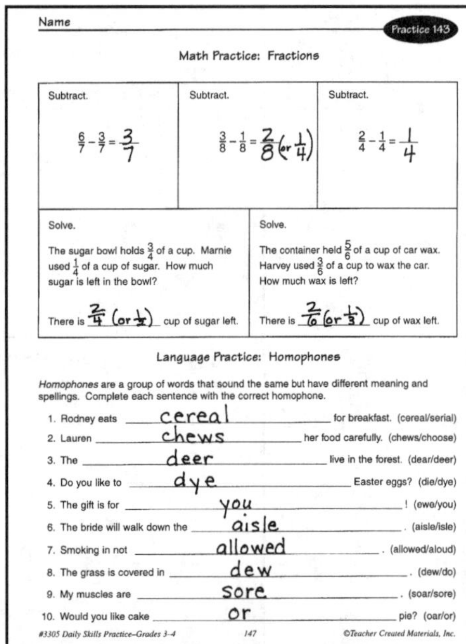

Name ______ Practice 143

Math Practice: Fractions

Subtract.	Subtract.	Subtract.
$\frac{6}{7} - \frac{3}{7} = \frac{3}{7}$	$\frac{3}{8} - \frac{1}{8} = \frac{2}{8}$ (or $\frac{1}{4}$)	$\frac{2}{4} - \frac{1}{4} = \frac{1}{4}$

Solve.	Solve.
The sugar bowl holds $\frac{3}{4}$ of a cup. Marnie used $\frac{1}{4}$ of a cup of sugar. How much sugar is left in the bowl? There is 2/4 (or 1/2) cup of sugar left.	The container held $\frac{5}{6}$ of a cup of car wax. Harvey used $\frac{3}{6}$ of a cup to wax the car. How much wax is left? There is 2/6 (or 1/3) cup of wax left.

Language Practice: Homophones

Homophones are a group of words that sound the same but have different meaning and spellings. Complete each sentence with the correct homophone.

1. Rodney eats cereal for breakfast. (cereal/serial)
2. Lauren chews her food carefully. (chews/choose)
3. The deer live in the forest. (dear/deer)
4. Do you like to dye Easter eggs? (die/dye)
5. The gift is for you! (ewe/you)
6. The bride will walk down the aisle. (aisle/isle)
7. Smoking in not allowed. (allowed/aloud)
8. The grass is covered in dew. (dew/do)
9. My muscles are sore. (soar/sore)
10. Would you like cake or pie? (oar/or)

#3305 Daily Skills Practice—Grades 3–4 147 ©Teacher Created Materials, Inc.

Page 148

Name ______ Practice 144

Math Practice: Fractions

Subtract.	Subtract.	Subtract.
$\frac{9}{10} - \frac{9}{10} = \frac{0}{0}$	$\frac{8}{9} - \frac{4}{9} = \frac{4}{9}$	$\frac{6}{7} - \frac{3}{7} = \frac{3}{7}$

Solve.	Solve.
Ben was given $\frac{5}{8}$ of a pie. He ate $\frac{2}{8}$ of the pie. How much pie was left? There was 3/8 pie left.	Julia had $\frac{18}{24}$ of the crayons. Her dog ate $\frac{6}{24}$ of the crayons. How many crayons does Julia have left? Julia has 12/24 or 1/2 crayons left.

Language Practice: Prepositions

Prepositions connect nouns or pronouns to the other words in the sentence. Prepositions tell where, when, or why something was done.

Example: *The dog is lying next to me.*

Next to me is the preposition.

It tells where the dog is lying.

Underline the preposition in each sentence. Write *where, when,* or *why* on the line.

1. My sister parked the car in the garage. where
2. The birthday party was at 3:00. when
3. We were late because our alarm clock broke. why
4. They had fun at the picnic. where
5. We went to the museum to see the art exhibit. where
6. They will bring the new TV on Wednesday. when

#3305 Daily Skills Practice—Grades 3–4 148 ©Teacher Created Materials, Inc.

Page 149

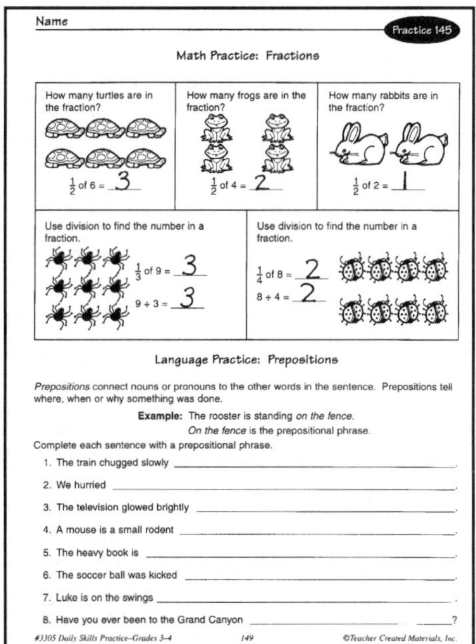

Name ______ Practice 145

Math Practice: Fractions

How many turtles are in the fraction?	How many frogs are in the fraction?	How many rabbits are in the fraction?
$\frac{1}{2}$ of 6 = 3	$\frac{1}{2}$ of 4 = 2	$\frac{1}{2}$ of 2 = 1

Use division to find the number in a fraction.	Use division to find the number in a fraction.
$\frac{1}{3}$ of 9 = 3 9 ÷ 3 = 3	$\frac{1}{4}$ of 8 = 2 8 ÷ 4 = 2

Language Practice: Prepositions

Prepositions connect nouns or pronouns to the other words in the sentence. Prepositions tell where, when or why something was done.

Example: The rooster is standing *on the fence*.
On the fence is the prepositional phrase.

Complete each sentence with a prepositional phrase.

1. The train chugged slowly ______.
2. We hurried ______.
3. The television glowed brightly ______.
4. A mouse is a small rodent ______.
5. The heavy book is ______.
6. The soccer ball was kicked ______.
7. Luke is on the swings ______.
8. Have you ever been to the Grand Canyon ______?

#3305 Daily Skills Practice–Grades 3–4 149 ©Teacher Created Materials, Inc.

Page 150

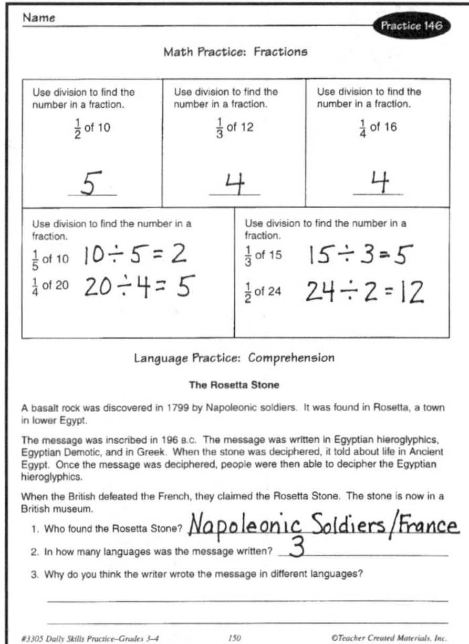

Name ______ Practice 146

Math Practice: Fractions

Use division to find the number in a fraction. $\frac{1}{2}$ of 10	Use division to find the number in a fraction. $\frac{1}{3}$ of 12	Use division to find the number in a fraction. $\frac{1}{4}$ of 16
5	4	4

Use division to find the number in a fraction.	Use division to find the number in a fraction.
$\frac{1}{5}$ of 10 10 ÷ 5 = 2 $\frac{1}{4}$ of 20 20 ÷ 4 = 5	$\frac{1}{3}$ of 15 15 ÷ 3 = 5 $\frac{1}{2}$ of 24 24 ÷ 2 = 12

Language Practice: Comprehension

The Rosetta Stone

A basalt rock was discovered in 1799 by Napoleonic soldiers. It was found in Rosetta, a town in lower Egypt.

The message was inscribed in 196 B.C. The message was written in Egyptian hieroglyphics, Egyptian Demotic, and in Greek. When the stone was deciphered, it told about life in Ancient Egypt. Once the message was deciphered, people were then able to decipher the Egyptian hieroglyphics.

When the British defeated the French, they claimed the Rosetta Stone. The stone is now in a British museum.

1. Who found the Rosetta Stone? Napoleonic Soldiers/France
2. In how many languages was the message written? 3
3. Why do you think the writer wrote the message in different languages?

#3305 Daily Skills Practice–Grades 3–4 150 ©Teacher Created Materials, Inc.

Page 151

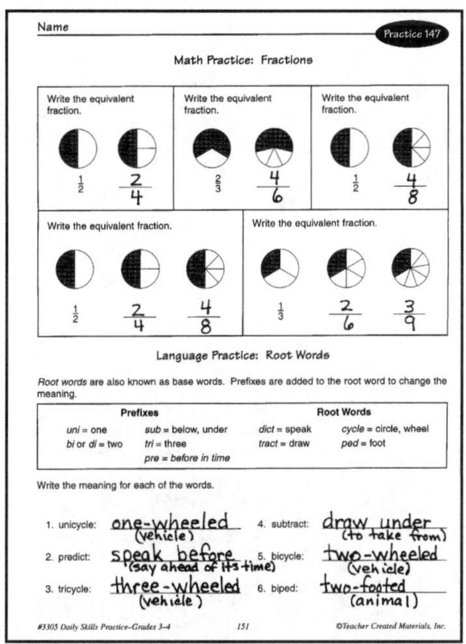

Name ______ Practice 147

Math Practice: Fractions

Write the equivalent fraction.	Write the equivalent fraction.	Write the equivalent fraction.
$\frac{1}{2}$ $\frac{2}{4}$	$\frac{2}{3}$ $\frac{4}{6}$	$\frac{1}{2}$ $\frac{4}{8}$

Write the equivalent fraction.	Write the equivalent fraction.
$\frac{1}{2}$ $\frac{2}{4}$ $\frac{4}{8}$	$\frac{1}{3}$ $\frac{2}{6}$ $\frac{3}{9}$

Language Practice: Root Words

Root words are also known as base words. Prefixes are added to the root word to change the meaning.

Prefixes		Root Words	
uni = one	*sub* = below, under	*dict* = speak	*cycle* = circle, wheel
bi or *di* = two	*tri* = three	*tract* = draw	*ped* = foot
	pre = before in time		

Write the meaning for each of the words.

1. unicycle: one-wheeled (vehicle)
2. predict: speak before (say ahead of its time)
3. tricycle: three-wheeled (vehicle)
4. subtract: draw under (to take from)
5. bicycle: two-wheeled (vehicle)
6. biped: two-footed (animal)

#3305 Daily Skills Practice–Grades 3–4 151 ©Teacher Created Materials, Inc.

Page 152

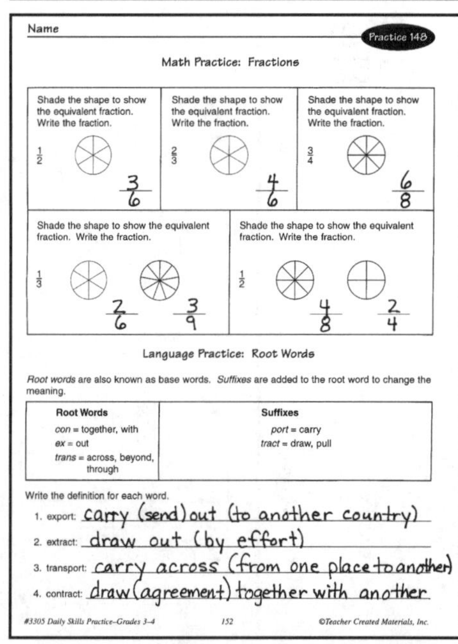

Name ______ Practice 148

Math Practice: Fractions

Shade the shape to show the equivalent fraction. Write the fraction.	Shade the shape to show the equivalent fraction. Write the fraction.	Shade the shape to show the equivalent fraction. Write the fraction.
$\frac{1}{2}$ $\frac{3}{6}$	$\frac{2}{3}$ $\frac{4}{6}$	$\frac{3}{4}$ $\frac{6}{8}$

Shade the shape to show the equivalent fraction. Write the fraction.	Shade the shape to show the equivalent fraction. Write the fraction.
$\frac{1}{3}$ $\frac{2}{6}$ $\frac{3}{9}$	$\frac{1}{2}$ $\frac{4}{8}$ $\frac{2}{4}$

Language Practice: Root Words

Root words are also known as base words. *Suffixes* are added to the root word to change the meaning.

Root Words	Suffixes
con = together, with *ex* = out *trans* = across, beyond, through	*port* = carry *tract* = draw, pull

Write the definition for each word.

1. export: carry (send) out (to another country)
2. extract: draw out (by effort)
3. transport: carry across (from one place to another)
4. contract: draw (agreement) together with another

#3305 Daily Skills Practice–Grades 3–4 152 ©Teacher Created Materials, Inc.

Page 153

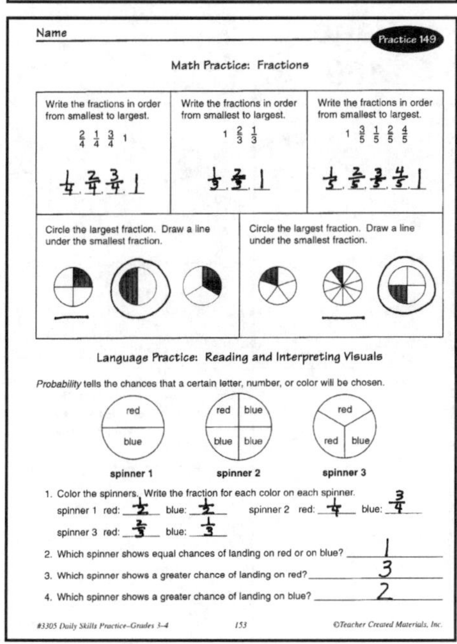

Name ______ Practice 149

Math Practice: Fractions

Write the fractions in order from smallest to largest. $\frac{2}{4}$ $\frac{1}{4}$ $\frac{3}{4}$ 1	Write the fractions in order from smallest to largest. 1 $\frac{2}{3}$ $\frac{1}{3}$	Write the fractions in order from smallest to largest. 1 $\frac{3}{5}$ $\frac{1}{5}$ $\frac{2}{5}$ $\frac{4}{5}$
$\frac{1}{4}$ $\frac{2}{4}$ $\frac{3}{4}$ 1	$\frac{1}{3}$ $\frac{2}{3}$ 1	$\frac{1}{5}$ $\frac{2}{5}$ $\frac{3}{5}$ $\frac{4}{5}$ 1

Circle the largest fraction. Draw a line under the smallest fraction.	Circle the largest fraction. Draw a line under the smallest fraction.

Language Practice: Reading and Interpreting Visuals

Probability tells the chances that a certain letter, number, or color will be chosen.

spinner 1: red, blue
spinner 2: red, blue, blue, blue
spinner 3: red, red, blue

1. Color the spinners. Write the fraction for each color on each spinner.
   spinner 1 red: $\frac{1}{2}$ blue: $\frac{1}{2}$ spinner 2 red: $\frac{1}{4}$ blue: $\frac{3}{4}$
   spinner 3 red: $\frac{2}{3}$ blue: $\frac{1}{3}$
2. Which spinner shows equal chances of landing on red or on blue? 1
3. Which spinner shows a greater chance of landing on red? 3
4. Which spinner shows a greater chance of landing on blue? 2

#3305 Daily Skills Practice–Grades 3–4 153 ©Teacher Created Materials, Inc.

Page 154

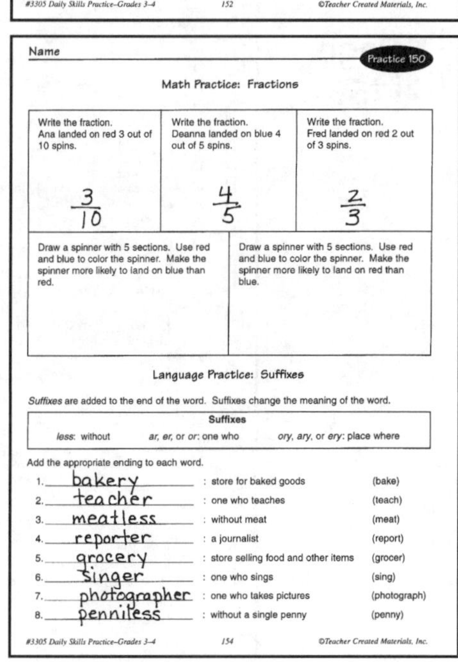

Name ______ Practice 150

Math Practice: Fractions

Write the fraction. Ana landed on red 3 out of 10 spins.	Write the fraction. Deanna landed on blue 4 out of 5 spins.	Write the fraction. Fred landed on red 2 out of 3 spins.
$\frac{3}{10}$	$\frac{4}{5}$	$\frac{2}{3}$

Draw a spinner with 5 sections. Use red and blue to color the spinner. Make the spinner more likely to land on blue than red.	Draw a spinner with 5 sections. Use red and blue to color the spinner. Make the spinner more likely to land on red than blue.

Language Practice: Suffixes

Suffixes are added to the end of the word. Suffixes change the meaning of the word.

Suffixes		
less: without	*ar, er,* or *or*: one who	*ory, ary,* or *ery*: place where

Add the appropriate ending to each word.

1. bakery : store for baked goods (bake)
2. teacher : one who teaches (teach)
3. meatless : without meat (meat)
4. reporter : a journalist (report)
5. grocery : store selling food and other items (grocer)
6. singer : one who sings (sing)
7. photographer : one who takes pictures (photograph)
8. penniless : without a single penny (penny)

#3305 Daily Skills Practice–Grades 3–4 154 ©Teacher Created Materials, Inc.

Page 155

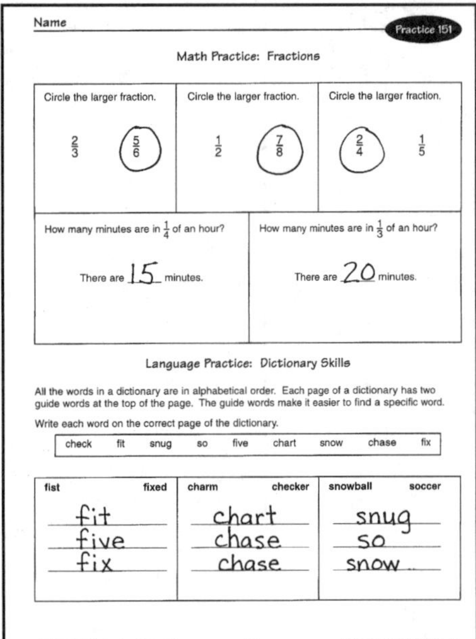

Name Practice 151

Math Practice: Fractions

Circle the larger fraction.	Circle the larger fraction.	Circle the larger fraction.
$\frac{2}{3}$ (circled: $\frac{5}{6}$)	$\frac{1}{2}$ (circled: $\frac{7}{8}$)	(circled: $\frac{2}{4}$) $\frac{1}{5}$

How many minutes are in $\frac{1}{4}$ of an hour?	How many minutes are in $\frac{1}{3}$ of an hour?
There are 15 minutes.	There are 20 minutes.

Language Practice: Dictionary Skills

All the words in a dictionary are in alphabetical order. Each page of a dictionary has two guide words at the top of the page. The guide words make it easier to find a specific word.

Write each word on the correct page of the dictionary.

check fit snug so five chart snow chase fix

fist fixed	charm checker	snowball soccer
fit	chart	snug
five	chase	so
fix	chase	snow

#3305 Daily Skills Practice–Grades 3–4 155 ©Teacher Created Materials, Inc.

Page 156

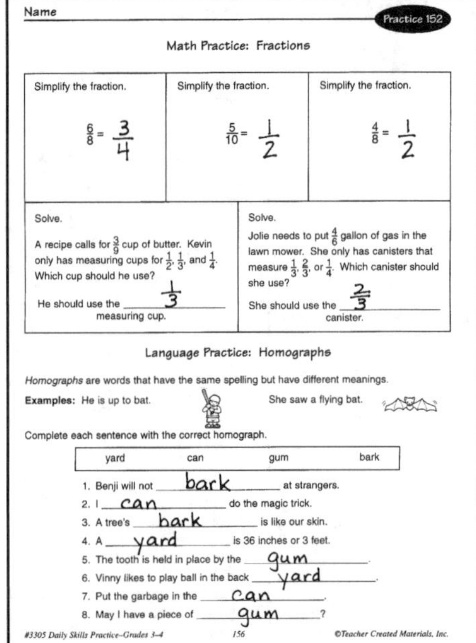

Name Practice 152

Math Practice: Fractions

Simplify the fraction.	Simplify the fraction.	Simplify the fraction.
$\frac{6}{8} = \frac{3}{4}$	$\frac{5}{10} = \frac{1}{2}$	$\frac{4}{8} = \frac{1}{2}$

Solve.	Solve.
A recipe calls for $\frac{2}{3}$ cup of butter. Kevin only has measuring cups for $\frac{1}{2}$, $\frac{1}{3}$, and $\frac{1}{4}$. Which cup should he use? He should use the $\frac{1}{3}$ measuring cup.	Jolie needs to put $\frac{4}{6}$ gallon of gas in the lawn mower. She only has canisters that measure $\frac{1}{3}$, $\frac{2}{3}$, or $\frac{1}{4}$. Which canister should she use? She should use the $\frac{2}{3}$ canister.

Language Practice: Homographs

Homographs are words that have the same spelling but have different meanings.

Examples: He is up to bat. She saw a flying bat.

Complete each sentence with the correct homograph.

yard can gum bark

1. Benji will not bark at strangers.
2. I can do the magic trick.
3. A tree's bark is like our skin.
4. A yard is 36 inches or 3 feet.
5. The tooth is held in place by the gum.
6. Vinny likes to play ball in the back yard.
7. Put the garbage in the can.
8. May I have a piece of gum?

#3305 Daily Skills Practice–Grades 3–4 156 ©Teacher Created Materials, Inc.

Page 157

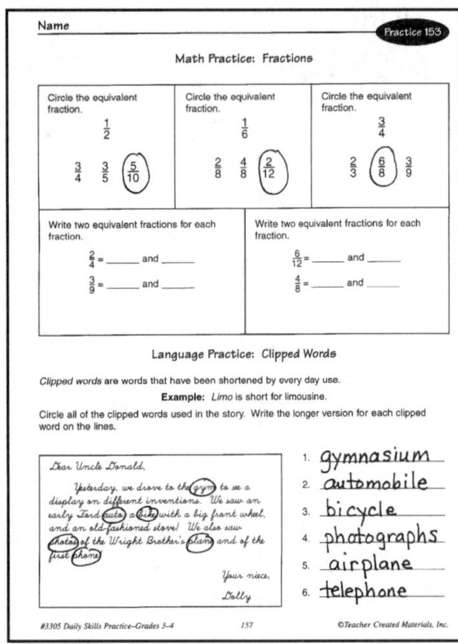

Name Practice 153

Math Practice: Fractions

Circle the equivalent fraction. $\frac{1}{2}$	Circle the equivalent fraction. $\frac{1}{6}$	Circle the equivalent fraction. $\frac{3}{4}$
$\frac{3}{4}$ $\frac{3}{5}$ (circled: $\frac{5}{10}$)	$\frac{2}{8}$ $\frac{4}{8}$ (circled: $\frac{2}{12}$)	$\frac{2}{3}$ (circled: $\frac{6}{8}$) $\frac{3}{9}$

Write two equivalent fractions for each fraction.	Write two equivalent fractions for each fraction.
$\frac{2}{4}$ = ____ and ____	$\frac{6}{12}$ = ____ and ____
$\frac{3}{9}$ = ____ and ____	$\frac{4}{8}$ = ____ and ____

Language Practice: Clipped Words

Clipped words are words that have been shortened by every day use.

Example: *Limo* is short for limousine.

Circle all of the clipped words used in the story. Write the longer version for each clipped word on the lines.

Dear Uncle Donald,

Yesterday, we drove to the gym to see a display on different inventions. We saw an early Ford auto, a bike with a big front wheel, and an old-fashioned stove! We also saw photos of the Wright Brother's plane and of the first phone.

Your niece,

Dolly

1. gymnasium
2. automobile
3. bicycle
4. photographs
5. airplane
6. telephone

#3305 Daily Skills Practice–Grades 3–4 157 ©Teacher Created Materials, Inc.

Page 158

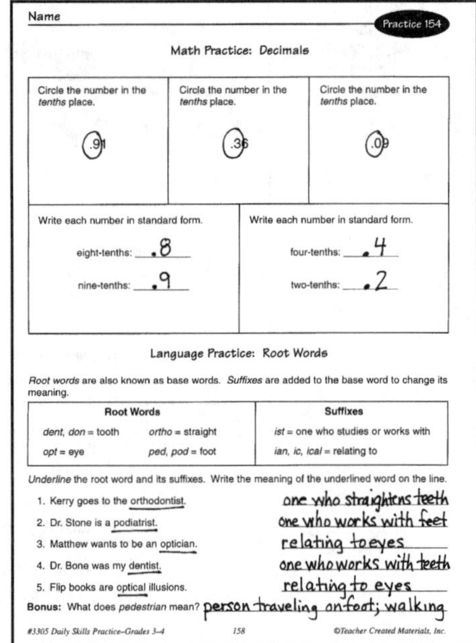

Name Practice 154

Math Practice: Decimals

Circle the number in the *tenths* place.	Circle the number in the *tenths* place.	Circle the number in the *tenths* place.
.91 (9 circled)	.36 (3 circled)	.09 (0 circled)

Write each number in standard form.	Write each number in standard form.
eight-tenths: .8	four-tenths: .4
nine-tenths: .9	two-tenths: .2

Language Practice: Root Words

Root words are also known as base words. *Suffixes* are added to the base word to change its meaning.

Root Words		Suffixes
dent, don = tooth	*ortho* = straight	*ist* = one who studies or works with
opt = eye	*ped, pod* = foot	*ian, ic, ical* = relating to

Underline the root word and its suffixes. Write the meaning of the underlined word on the line.

1. Kerry goes to the orthodontist. one who straightens teeth
2. Dr. Stone is a podiatrist. one who works with feet
3. Matthew wants to be an optician. relating to eyes
4. Dr. Bone was my dentist. one who works with teeth
5. Flip books are optical illusions. relating to eyes

Bonus: What does *pedestrian* mean? person traveling on foot; walking

#3305 Daily Skills Practice–Grades 3–4 158 ©Teacher Created Materials, Inc.

Page 159

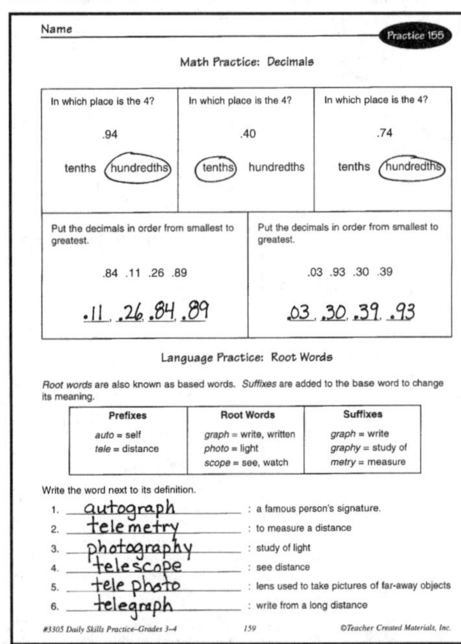

Name Practice 155

Math Practice: Decimals

In which place is the 4?	In which place is the 4?	In which place is the 4?
.94	.40	.74
tenths (circled: hundredths)	(circled: tenths) hundredths	tenths (circled: hundredths)

Put the decimals in order from smallest to greatest.	Put the decimals in order from smallest to greatest.
.84 .11 .26 .89	.03 .93 .30 .39
.11, .26, .84, .89	.03, .30, .39, .93

Language Practice: Root Words

Root words are also known as based words. *Suffixes* are added to the base word to change its meaning.

Prefixes	Root Words	Suffixes
auto = self *tele* = distance	*graph* = write, written *photo* = light *scope* = see, watch	*graph* = write *graphy* = study of *metry* = measure

Write the word next to its definition.

1. autograph : a famous person's signature.
2. telemetry : to measure a distance
3. photography : study of light
4. telescope : see distance
5. tele photo : lens used to take pictures of far-away objects
6. telegraph : write from a long distance

#3305 Daily Skills Practice–Grades 3–4 159 ©Teacher Created Materials, Inc.

Page 160

Name Practice 156

Math Practice: Decimals

Write the decimal for each number word.	Write the decimal for each number word.	Write the decimal for each number word.
four-tenths	one and eight-tenths	three and four-tenths
.4	1.8	3.4

Write the decimal for each number word.	Write the decimal for each number word.
five-hundredths .05	three-hundredths .03
fifty-six tenths .56	nine-hundredths .09

Language Practice: Acronyms

An *acronym* is a word formed from the first letter, or letters, of words in a phrase. The acronym is written in all capital letters. No periods are used.

Example: NATO North Atlantic Treaty Organization

Underline the first letter in each word. Write the acronym for each set of words on the line provided.

1. sealed with a kiss SWAK
2. as soon as possible ASAP
3. read only memory ROM
4. disc operating system DOS
5. National Aeronautics & Space Administration NASA
6. mothers against drunk driving MADD

#3305 Daily Skills Practice–Grades 3–4 160 ©Teacher Created Materials, Inc.

Page 161

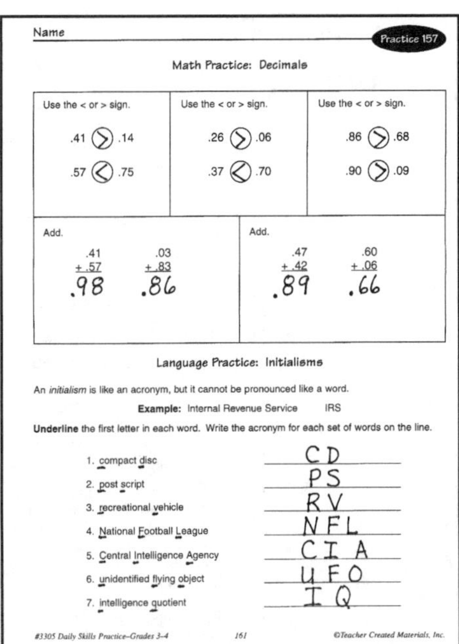

Name

Practice 157

Math Practice: Decimals

Use the < or > sign.	Use the < or > sign.	Use the < or > sign.
.41 > .14 .57 < .75	.26 > .06 .37 < .70	.86 > .68 .90 > .09

Add.	Add.
.41 + .57 = .98 .03 + .83 = .86	.47 + .42 = .89 .60 + .06 = .66

Language Practice: Initialisms

An *initialism* is like an acronym, but it cannot be pronounced like a word.

Example: Internal Revenue Service IRS

Underline the first letter in each word. Write the acronym for each set of words on the line.

1. compact disc — CD
2. post script — PS
3. recreational vehicle — RV
4. National Football League — NFL
5. Central Intelligence Agency — CIA
6. unidentified flying object — UFO
7. intelligence quotient — IQ

#3305 Daily Skills Practice–Grades 3–4 161 ©Teacher Created Materials, Inc.

Page 162

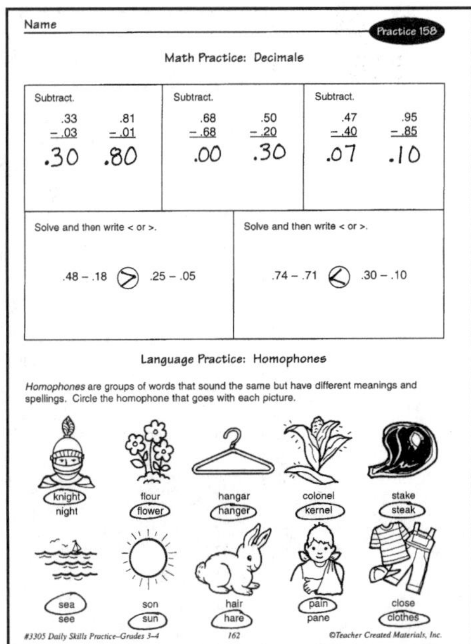

Name

Practice 158

Math Practice: Decimals

Subtract.	Subtract.	Subtract.
.33 − .03 = .30 .81 − .01 = .80	.68 − .68 = .00 .50 − .20 = .30	.47 − .40 = .07 .95 − .85 = .10

Solve and then write < or >.	Solve and then write < or >.
.48 – .18 > .25 – .05	.74 – .71 < .30 – .10

Language Practice: Homophones

Homophones are groups of words that sound the same but have different meanings and spellings. Circle the homophone that goes with each picture.

knight (circled) / night; flour / flower (circled); hangar / hanger (circled); colonel / kernel (circled); stake / steak (circled)

sea (circled) / see; son / sun (circled); hair / hare (circled); pain (circled) / pane; close / clothes (circled)

#3305 Daily Skills Practice–Grades 3–4 162 ©Teacher Created Materials, Inc.

Page 163

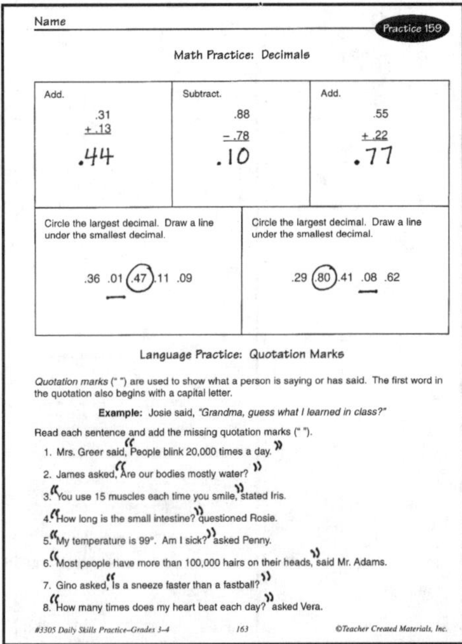

Name

Practice 159

Math Practice: Decimals

Add.	Subtract.	Add.
.31 + .13 = .44	.88 − .78 = .10	.55 + .22 = .77

Circle the largest decimal. Draw a line under the smallest decimal.	Circle the largest decimal. Draw a line under the smallest decimal.
.36 .01 (.47) .11 .09	.29 (.80) .41 .08 .62

Language Practice: Quotation Marks

Quotation marks (" ") are used to show what a person is saying or has said. The first word in the quotation also begins with a capital letter.

Example: Josie said, *"Grandma, guess what I learned in class?"*

Read each sentence and add the missing quotation marks (" ").

1. Mrs. Greer said, "People blink 20,000 times a day."
2. James asked, "Are our bodies mostly water?"
3. "You use 15 muscles each time you smile," stated Iris.
4. "How long is the small intestine?" questioned Rosie.
5. "My temperature is 99°. Am I sick?" asked Penny.
6. "Most people have more than 100,000 hairs on their heads," said Mr. Adams.
7. Gino asked, "Is a sneeze faster than a fastball?"
8. "How many times does my heart beat each day?" asked Vera.

#3305 Daily Skills Practice–Grades 3–4 163 ©Teacher Created Materials, Inc.

Page 164

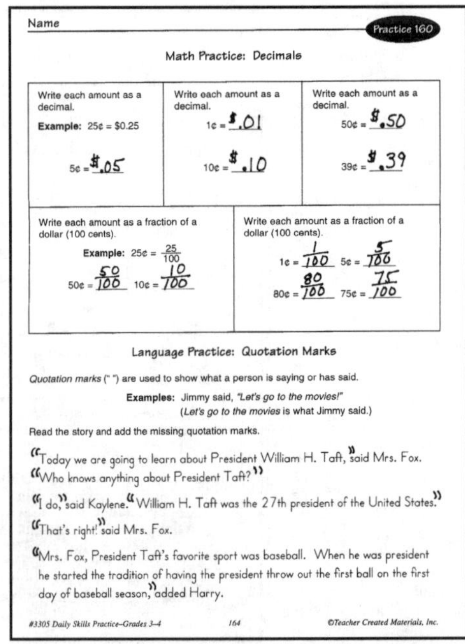

Name

Practice 160

Math Practice: Decimals

Write each amount as a decimal.	Write each amount as a decimal.	Write each amount as a decimal.
Example: 25¢ = $0.25 5¢ = $.05	1¢ = $.01 10¢ = $.10	50¢ = $.50 39¢ = $.39

Write each amount as a fraction of a dollar (100 cents).	Write each amount as a fraction of a dollar (100 cents).
Example: 25¢ = $\frac{25}{100}$ 50¢ = $\frac{50}{100}$ 10¢ = $\frac{10}{100}$	1¢ = $\frac{1}{100}$ 5¢ = $\frac{5}{100}$ 80¢ = $\frac{80}{100}$ 75¢ = $\frac{75}{100}$

Language Practice: Quotation Marks

Quotation marks (" ") are used to show what a person is saying or has said.

Examples: Jimmy said, *"Let's go to the movies!"*
(*Let's go to the movies* is what Jimmy said.)

Read the story and add the missing quotation marks.

"Today we are going to learn about President William H. Taft," said Mrs. Fox. "Who knows anything about President Taft?"

"I do," said Kaylene. "William H. Taft was the 27th president of the United States."

"That's right," said Mrs. Fox.

"Mrs. Fox, President Taft's favorite sport was baseball. When he was president he started the tradition of having the president throw out the first ball on the first day of baseball season," added Harry.

#3305 Daily Skills Practice–Grades 3–4 164 ©Teacher Created Materials, Inc.

Page 165

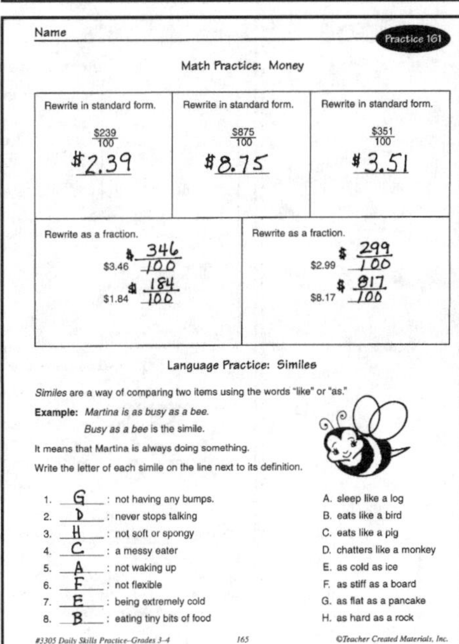

Name

Practice 161

Math Practice: Money

Rewrite in standard form.	Rewrite in standard form.	Rewrite in standard form.
$\frac{\$239}{100}$ = $2.39	$\frac{\$875}{100}$ = $8.75	$\frac{\$351}{100}$ = $3.51

Rewrite as a fraction.	Rewrite as a fraction.
$3.46 = $\$\frac{346}{100}$ $1.84 = $\$\frac{184}{100}$	$2.99 = $\$\frac{299}{100}$ $8.17 = $\$\frac{817}{100}$

Language Practice: Similes

Similes are a way of comparing two items using the words "like" or "as."

Example: *Martina is as busy as a bee.*
Busy as a bee is the simile.

It means that Martina is always doing something.

Write the letter of each simile on the line next to its definition.

1. G : not having any bumps. — A. sleep like a log
2. D : never stops talking — B. eats like a bird
3. H : not soft or spongy — C. eats like a pig
4. C : a messy eater — D. chatters like a monkey
5. A : not waking up — E. as cold as ice
6. F : not flexible — F. as stiff as a board
7. E : being extremely cold — G. as flat as a pancake
8. B : eating tiny bits of food — H. as hard as a rock

#3305 Daily Skills Practice–Grades 3–4 165 ©Teacher Created Materials, Inc.

Page 166

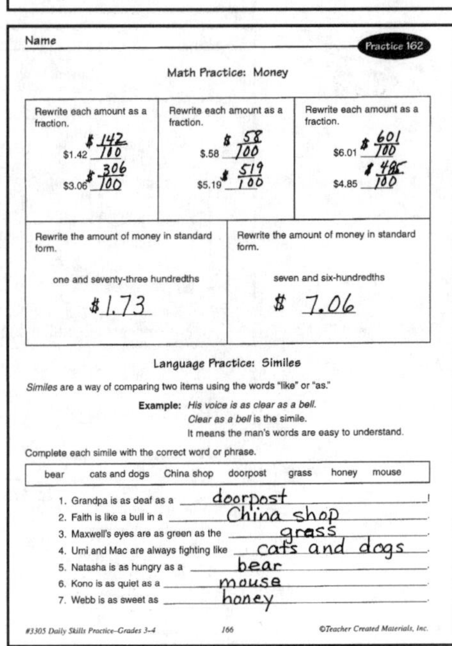

Name

Practice 162

Math Practice: Money

Rewrite each amount as a fraction.	Rewrite each amount as a fraction.	Rewrite each amount as a fraction.
$1.42 = $\$\frac{142}{100}$ $3.06 = $\$\frac{306}{100}$	$.58 = $\$\frac{58}{100}$ $5.19 = $\$\frac{519}{100}$	$6.01 = $\$\frac{601}{100}$ $4.85 = $\$\frac{485}{100}$

Rewrite the amount of money in standard form.	Rewrite the amount of money in standard form.
one and seventy-three hundredths $1.73	seven and six-hundredths $ 7.06

Language Practice: Similes

Similes are a way of comparing two items using the words "like" or "as."

Example: *His voice is as clear as a bell.*
Clear as a bell is the simile.
It means the man's words are easy to understand.

Complete each simile with the correct word or phrase.

bear	cats and dogs	China shop	doorpost	grass	honey	mouse

1. Grandpa is as deaf as a doorpost.
2. Faith is like a bull in a China shop.
3. Maxwell's eyes are as green as the grass.
4. Umi and Mac are always fighting like cats and dogs.
5. Natasha is as hungry as a bear.
6. Kono is as quiet as a mouse.
7. Webb is as sweet as honey.

#3305 Daily Skills Practice–Grades 3–4 166 ©Teacher Created Materials, Inc.

Page 167

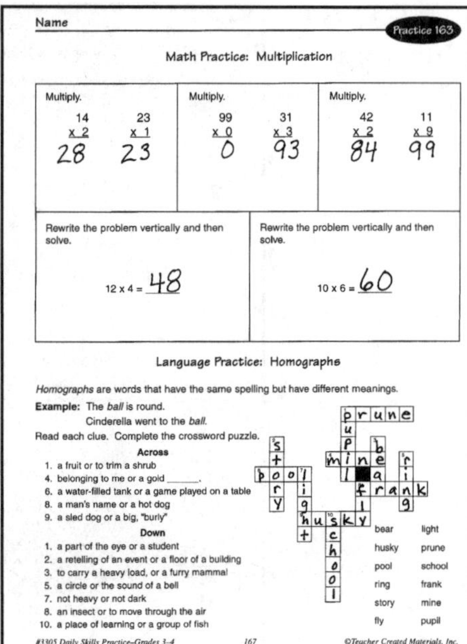

Name ______ Practice 163

Math Practice: Multiplication

Multiply.	Multiply.	Multiply.
14 x 2 = 28 23 x 1 = 23	99 x 0 = 0 31 x 3 = 93	42 x 2 = 84 11 x 9 = 99

Rewrite the problem vertically and then solve.	Rewrite the problem vertically and then solve.
12 x 4 = 48	10 x 6 = 60

Language Practice: Homographs

Homographs are words that have the same spelling but have different meanings.

Example: The *ball* is round.
Cinderella went to the *ball*.

Read each clue. Complete the crossword puzzle.

Across

1. a fruit or to trim a shrub
4. belonging to me or a gold ______.
6. a water-filled tank or a game played on a table
8. a man's name or a hot dog
9. a sled dog or a big, "burly"

Down

1. a part of the eye or a student
2. a retelling of an event or a floor of a building
3. to carry a heavy load, or a furry mammal
5. a circle or the sound of a bell
7. not heavy or not dark
8. an insect or to move through the air
10. a place of learning or a group of fish

bear	light
husky	prune
pool	school
ring	frank
story	mine
fly	pupil

#3305 Daily Skills Practice–Grades 3–4 167 ©Teacher Created Materials, Inc.

Page 168

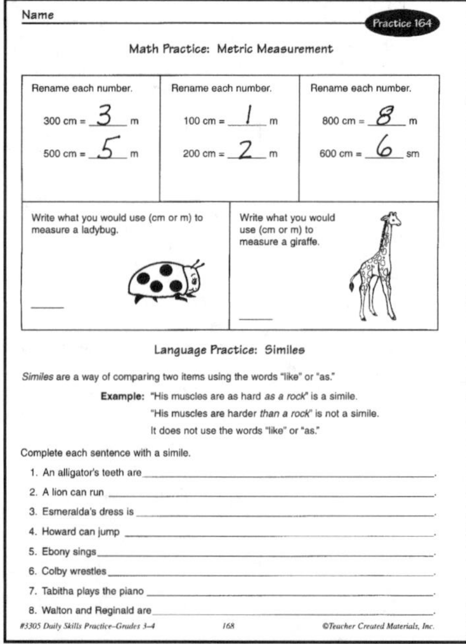

Name ______ Practice 164

Math Practice: Metric Measurement

Rename each number.	Rename each number.	Rename each number.
300 cm = 3 m 500 cm = 5 m	100 cm = 1 m 200 cm = 2 m	800 cm = 8 m 600 cm = 6 sm

Write what you would use (cm or m) to measure a ladybug.	Write what you would use (cm or m) to measure a giraffe.
____	____

Language Practice: Similes

Similes are a way of comparing two items using the words "like" or "as."

Example: "His muscles are as hard *as a rock*" is a simile.
"His muscles are harder *than a rock*" is not a simile.
It does not use the words "like" or "as."

Complete each sentence with a simile.

1. An alligator's teeth are ______.
2. A lion can run ______.
3. Esmeralda's dress is ______.
4. Howard can jump ______.
5. Ebony sings ______.
6. Colby wrestles ______.
7. Tabitha plays the piano ______.
8. Walton and Reginald are ______.

#3305 Daily Skills Practice–Grades 3–4 168 ©Teacher Created Materials, Inc.

Page 169

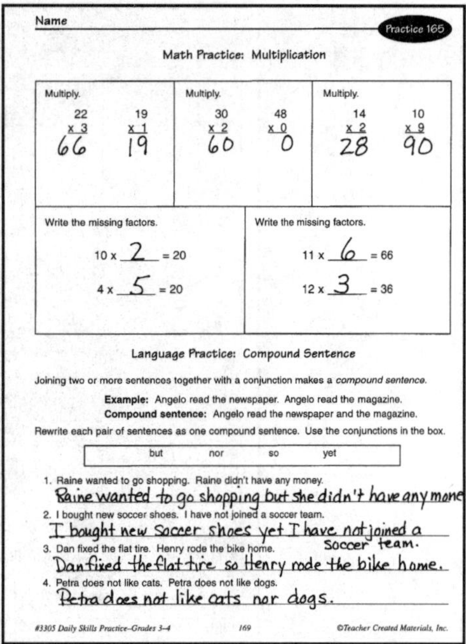

Name ______ Practice 165

Math Practice: Multiplication

Multiply.	Multiply.	Multiply.
22 x 3 = 66 19 x 1 = 19	30 x 2 = 60 48 x 0 = 0	14 x 2 = 28 10 x 9 = 90

Write the missing factors.	Write the missing factors.
10 x 2 = 20 4 x 5 = 20	11 x 6 = 66 12 x 3 = 36

Language Practice: Compound Sentence

Joining two or more sentences together with a conjunction makes a *compound sentence*.

Example: Angelo read the newspaper. Angelo read the magazine.
Compound sentence: Angelo read the newspaper and the magazine.

Rewrite each pair of sentences as one compound sentence. Use the conjunctions in the box.

but	nor	so	yet

1. Raine wanted to go shopping. Raine didn't have any money.
Raine wanted to go shopping but she didn't have any money
2. I bought new soccer shoes. I have not joined a soccer team.
I bought new Soccer shoes yet I have not joined a Soccer team.
3. Dan fixed the flat tire. Henry rode the bike home.
Dan fixed the flat tire so Henry rode the bike home.
4. Petra does not like cats. Petra does not like dogs.
Petra does not like cats nor dogs.

#3305 Daily Skills Practice–Grades 3–4 169 ©Teacher Created Materials, Inc.

Page 170

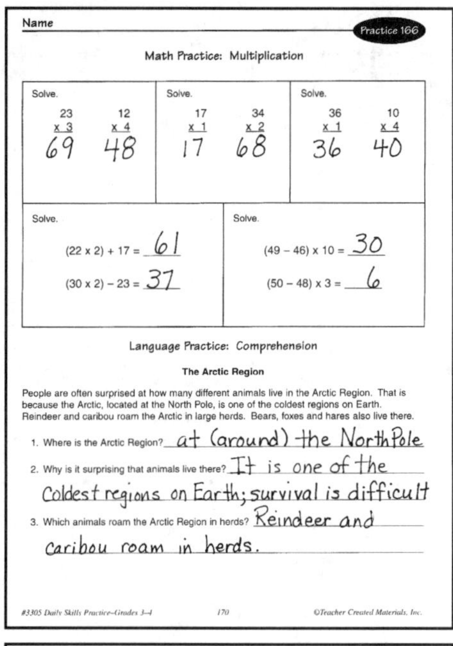

Name ______ Practice 166

Math Practice: Multiplication

Solve.	Solve.	Solve.
23 x 3 = 69 12 x 4 = 48	17 x 1 = 17 34 x 2 = 68	36 x 1 = 36 10 x 4 = 40

Solve.	Solve.
(22 x 2) + 17 = 61 (30 x 2) – 23 = 37	(49 – 46) x 10 = 30 (50 – 48) x 3 = 6

Language Practice: Comprehension

The Arctic Region

People are often surprised at how many different animals live in the Arctic Region. That is because the Arctic, located at the North Pole, is one of the coldest regions on Earth. Reindeer and caribou roam the Arctic in large herds. Bears, foxes and hares also live there.

1. Where is the Arctic Region? at (around) the North Pole
2. Why is it surprising that animals live there? It is one of the Coldest regions on Earth; survival is difficult
3. Which animals roam the Arctic Region in herds? Reindeer and caribou roam in herds.

#3305 Daily Skills Practice–Grades 3–4 170 ©Teacher Created Materials, Inc.

Page 171

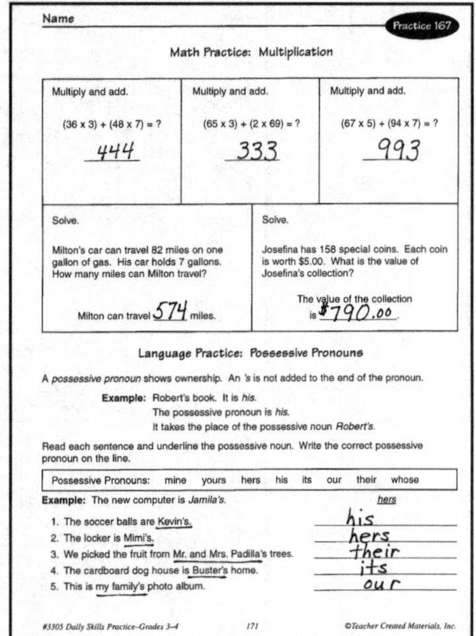

Name ______ Practice 167

Math Practice: Multiplication

Multiply and add.	Multiply and add.	Multiply and add.
(36 x 3) + (48 x 7) = ? 444	(65 x 3) + (2 x 69) = ? 333	(67 x 5) + (94 x 7) = ? 993

Solve.	Solve.
Milton's car can travel 82 miles on one gallon of gas. His car holds 7 gallons. How many miles can Milton travel? Milton can travel 574 miles.	Josefina has 158 special coins. Each coin is worth $5.00. What is the value of Josefina's collection? The value of the collection is $790.00

Language Practice: Possessive Pronouns

A *possessive pronoun* shows ownership. An *'s* is not added to the end of the pronoun.

Example: Robert's book. It is *his*.
The possessive pronoun is *his*.
It takes the place of the possessive noun *Robert's*.

Read each sentence and underline the possessive noun. Write the correct possessive pronoun on the line.

Possessive Pronouns: mine yours hers his its our their whose

Example: The new computer is *Jamila's*. hers

1. The soccer balls are Kevin's. his
2. The locker is Mimi's. hers
3. We picked the fruit from Mr. and Mrs. Padilla's trees. their
4. The cardboard dog house is Buster's home. its
5. This is my family's photo album. our

#3305 Daily Skills Practice–Grades 3–4 171 ©Teacher Created Materials, Inc.

Page 172

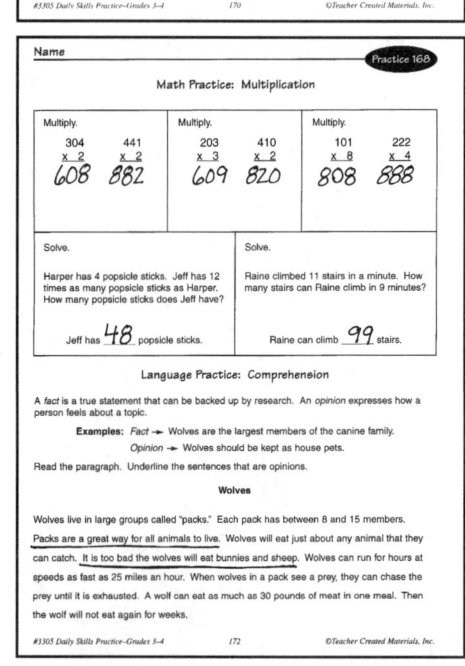

Name ______ Practice 168

Math Practice: Multiplication

Multiply.	Multiply.	Multiply.
304 x 2 = 608 441 x 2 = 882	203 x 3 = 609 410 x 2 = 820	101 x 8 = 808 222 x 4 = 888

Solve.	Solve.
Harper has 4 popsicle sticks. Jeff has 12 times as many popsicle sticks as Harper. How many popsicle sticks does Jeff have? Jeff has 48 popsicle sticks.	Raine climbed 11 stairs in a minute. How many stairs can Raine climb in 9 minutes? Raine can climb 99 stairs.

Language Practice: Comprehension

A *fact* is a true statement that can be backed up by research. An *opinion* expresses how a person feels about a topic.

Examples: *Fact* → Wolves are the largest members of the canine family.
Opinion → Wolves should be kept as house pets.

Read the paragraph. Underline the sentences that are opinions.

Wolves

Wolves live in large groups called "packs." Each pack has between 8 and 15 members. Packs are a great way for all animals to live. Wolves will eat just about any animal that they can catch. It is too bad the wolves will eat bunnies and sheep. Wolves can run for hours at speeds as fast as 25 miles an hour. When wolves in a pack see a prey, they can chase the prey until it is exhausted. A wolf can eat as much as 30 pounds of meat in one meal. Then the wolf will not eat again for weeks.

#3305 Daily Skills Practice–Grades 3–4 172 ©Teacher Created Materials, Inc.

Page 173

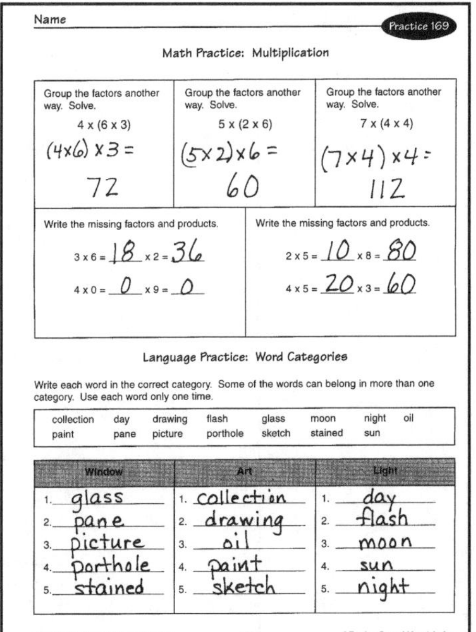

Name ______ Practice 169

Math Practice: Multiplication

Group the factors another way. Solve. 4 x (6 x 3)	Group the factors another way. Solve. 5 x (2 x 6)	Group the factors another way. Solve. 7 x (4 x 4)
(4x6) x3 = 72	(5x2)x6 = 60	(7x4)x4 = 112

Write the missing factors and products.	Write the missing factors and products.
3 x 6 = 18 x 2 = 36	2 x 5 = 10 x 8 = 80
4 x 0 = 0 x 9 = 0	4 x 5 = 20 x 3 = 60

Language Practice: Word Categories

Write each word in the correct category. Some of the words can belong in more than one category. Use each word only one time.

collection day drawing flash glass moon night oil paint pane picture porthole sketch stained sun

Window	Art	Light
1. glass	1. collection	1. day
2. pane	2. drawing	2. flash
3. picture	3. oil	3. moon
4. porthole	4. paint	4. sun
5. stained	5. sketch	5. night

#3305 Daily Skills Practice–Grades 3–4 173 ©Teacher Created Materials, Inc.

Page 174

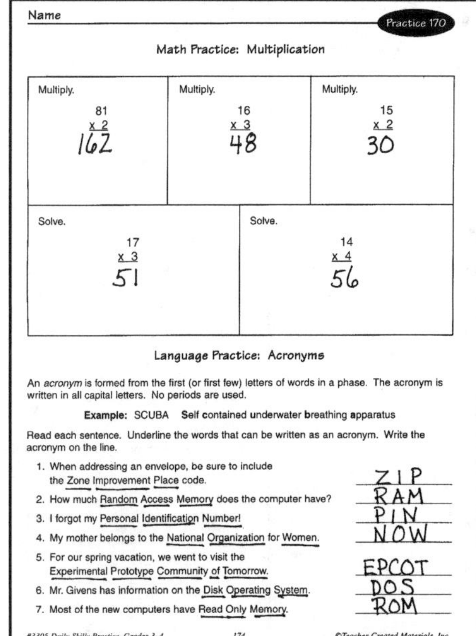

Name ______ Practice 170

Math Practice: Multiplication

Multiply. 81 x 2	Multiply. 16 x 3	Multiply. 15 x 2
162	48	30

Solve. 17 x 3	Solve. 14 x 4
51	56

Language Practice: Acronyms

An *acronym* is formed from the first (or first few) letters of words in a phase. The acronym is written in all capital letters. No periods are used.

Example: SCUBA **Self contained underwater breathing apparatus**

Read each sentence. Underline the words that can be written as an acronym. Write the acronym on the line.

1. When addressing an envelope, be sure to include the Zone Improvement Place code. ZIP
2. How much Random Access Memory does the computer have? RAM
3. I forgot my Personal Identification Number! PIN
4. My mother belongs to the National Organization for Women. NOW
5. For our spring vacation, we went to visit the Experimental Prototype Community of Tomorrow. EPCOT
6. Mr. Givens has information on the Disk Operating System. DOS
7. Most of the new computers have Read Only Memory. ROM

#3305 Daily Skills Practice–Grades 3–4 174 ©Teacher Created Materials, Inc.

Page 175

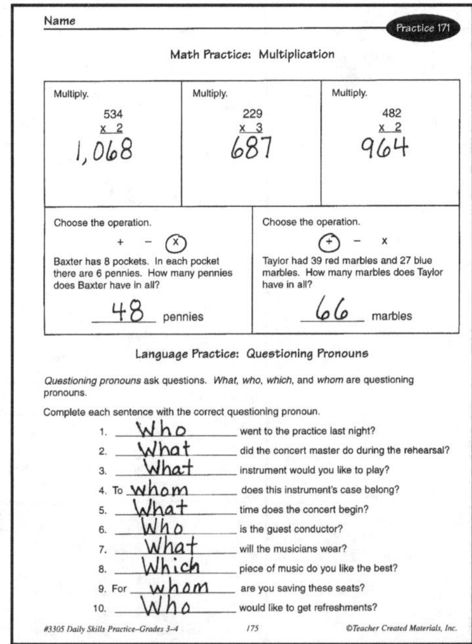

Name ______ Practice 171

Math Practice: Multiplication

Multiply. 534 x 2	Multiply. 229 x 3	Multiply. 482 x 2
1,068	687	964

Choose the operation. + − (x)	Choose the operation. (+) − x
Baxter has 8 pockets. In each pocket there are 6 pennies. How many pennies does Baxter have in all? 48 pennies	Taylor had 39 red marbles and 27 blue marbles. How many marbles does Taylor have in all? 66 marbles

Language Practice: Questioning Pronouns

Questioning pronouns ask questions. *What, who, which,* and *whom* are questioning pronouns.

Complete each sentence with the correct questioning pronoun.

1. Who went to the practice last night?
2. What did the concert master do during the rehearsal?
3. What instrument would you like to play?
4. To whom does this instrument's case belong?
5. What time does the concert begin?
6. Who is the guest conductor?
7. What will the musicians wear?
8. Which piece of music do you like the best?
9. For whom are you saving these seats?
10. Who would like to get refreshments?

#3305 Daily Skills Practice–Grades 3–4 175 ©Teacher Created Materials, Inc.

Page 176

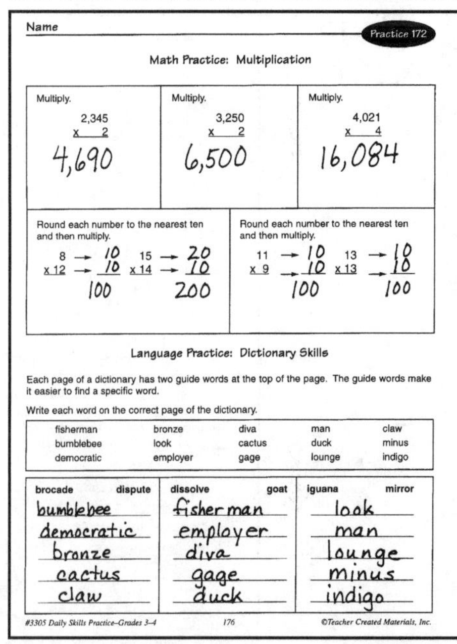

Name ______ Practice 172

Math Practice: Multiplication

Multiply. 2,345 x 2	Multiply. 3,250 x 2	Multiply. 4,021 x 4
4,690	6,500	16,084

Round each number to the nearest ten and then multiply.	Round each number to the nearest ten and then multiply.
8 → 10, x 12 → 10 = 100; 15 → 20, x 14 → 10 = 200	11 → 10, x 9 → 10 = 100; 13 → 10, x 13 → 10 = 100

Language Practice: Dictionary Skills

Each page of a dictionary has two guide words at the top of the page. The guide words make it easier to find a specific word.

Write each word on the correct page of the dictionary.

fisherman bronze diva man claw bumblebee look cactus duck minus democratic employer gage lounge indigo

brocade — dispute	dissolve — goat	iguana — mirror
bumblebee	fisherman	look
democratic	employer	man
bronze	diva	lounge
cactus	gage	minus
claw	duck	indigo

#3305 Daily Skills Practice–Grades 3–4 176 ©Teacher Created Materials, Inc.

Page 177

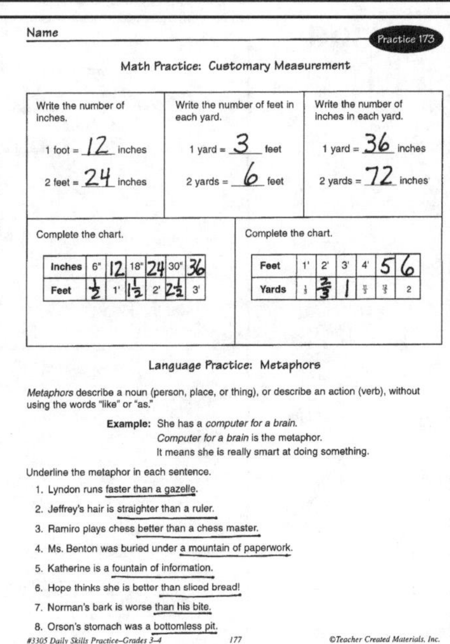

Name ______ Practice 173

Math Practice: Customary Measurement

Write the number of inches.	Write the number of feet in each yard.	Write the number of inches in each yard.
1 foot = 12 inches	1 yard = 3 feet	1 yard = 36 inches
2 feet = 24 inches	2 yards = 6 feet	2 yards = 72 inches

Complete the chart.

Inches	6"	12	18"	24	30"	36
Feet	1/2	1'	1 1/2	2'	2 1/2	3'

Complete the chart.

Feet	1'	2'	3'	4'	5	6
Yards	1/3	2/3	1	4/3	5/3	2

Language Practice: Metaphors

Metaphors describe a noun (person, place, or thing), or describe an action (verb), without using the words "like" or "as."

Example: She has a *computer for a brain.*
Computer for a brain is the metaphor.
It means she is really smart at doing something.

Underline the metaphor in each sentence.

1. Lyndon runs faster than a gazelle.
2. Jeffrey's hair is straighter than a ruler.
3. Ramiro plays chess better than a chess master.
4. Ms. Benton was buried under a mountain of paperwork.
5. Katherine is a fountain of information.
6. Hope thinks she is better than sliced bread!
7. Norman's bark is worse than his bite.
8. Orson's stomach was a bottomless pit.

#3305 Daily Skills Practice–Grades 3–4 177 ©Teacher Created Materials, Inc.

Page 178

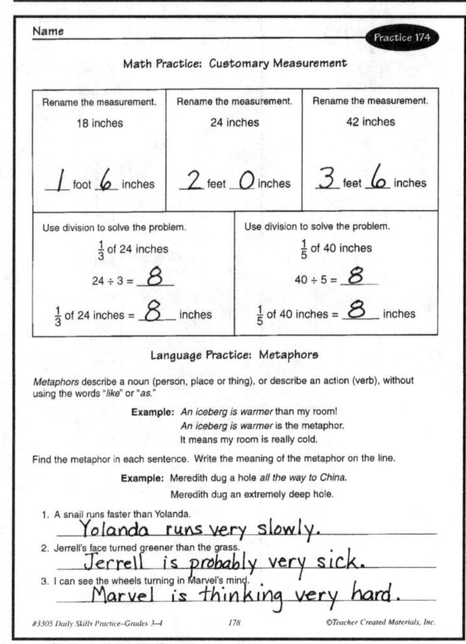

Name ______ Practice 174

Math Practice: Customary Measurement

Rename the measurement. 18 inches	Rename the measurement. 24 inches	Rename the measurement. 42 inches
1 foot 6 inches	2 feet 0 inches	3 feet 6 inches

Use division to solve the problem.	Use division to solve the problem.
1/3 of 24 inches	1/5 of 40 inches
24 ÷ 3 = 8	40 ÷ 5 = 8
1/3 of 24 inches = 8 inches	1/5 of 40 inches = 8 inches

Language Practice: Metaphors

Metaphors describe a noun (person, place or thing), or describe an action (verb), without using the words "*like*" or "*as*."

Example: *An iceberg is warmer* than my room!
An iceberg is warmer is the metaphor.
It means my room is really cold.

Find the metaphor in each sentence. Write the meaning of the metaphor on the line.

Example: Meredith dug a hole *all the way to China.*
Meredith dug an extremely deep hole.

1. A snail runs faster than Yolanda.
Yolanda runs very slowly.
2. Jerrell's face turned greener than the grass.
Jerrell is probably very sick.
3. I can see the wheels turning in Marvel's mind.
Marvel is thinking very hard.

#3305 Daily Skills Practice–Grades 3–4 178 ©Teacher Created Materials, Inc.

Page 179

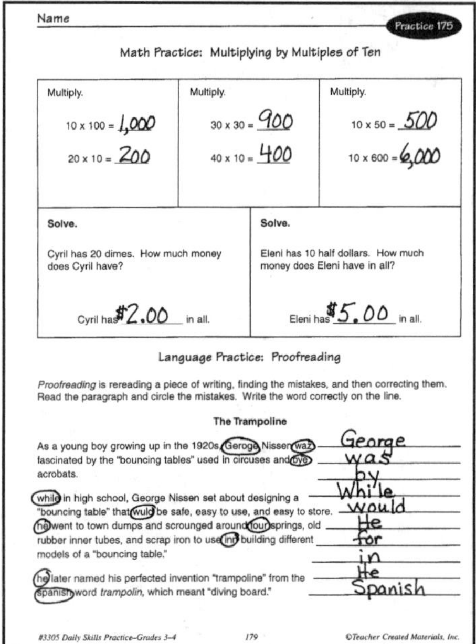

Name ______ Practice 175

Math Practice: Multiplying by Multiples of Ten

Multiply.	Multiply.	Multiply.
10 x 100 = 1,000	30 x 30 = 900	10 x 50 = 500
20 x 10 = 200	40 x 10 = 400	10 x 600 = 6,000

Solve.	Solve.
Cyril has 20 dimes. How much money does Cyril have?	Eleni has 10 half dollars. How much money does Eleni have in all?
Cyril has $2.00 in all.	Eleni has $5.00 in all.

Language Practice: Proofreading

Proofreading is rereading a piece of writing, finding the mistakes, and then correcting them. Read the paragraph and circle the mistakes. Write the word correctly on the line.

The Trampoline

As a young boy growing up in the 1920s, George Nissen waz fascinated by the "bouncing tables" used in circuses and bye acrobats. — George, was, by

while in high school, George Nissen set about designing a "bouncing table" that wuld be safe, easy to use, and easy to store. he went to town dumps and scrounged around four springs, old rubber inner tubes, and scrap iron to use ine building different models of a "bouncing table." — While, would, He, for, in

he later named his perfected invention "trampoline" from the spanish word *trampolin*, which meant "diving board." — He, Spanish

#3305 Daily Skills Practice–Grades 3–4 179 ©Teacher Created Materials, Inc.

Page 180

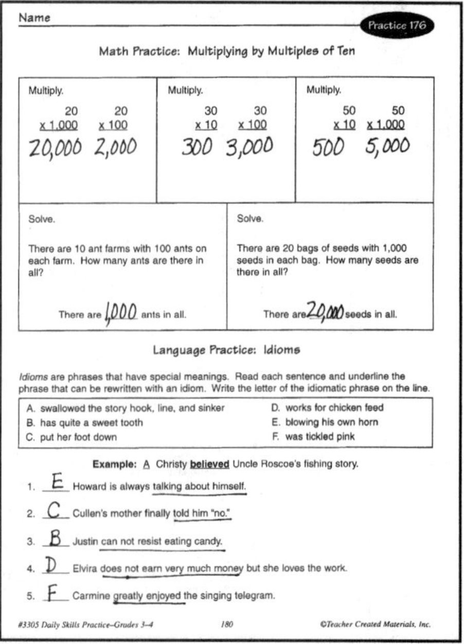

Name ______ Practice 176

Math Practice: Multiplying by Multiples of Ten

Multiply.	Multiply.	Multiply.
20 x 1,000 = 20,000; 20 x 100 = 2,000	30 x 10 = 300; 30 x 100 = 3,000	50 x 10 = 500; 50 x 1,000 = 5,000

Solve.	Solve.
There are 10 ant farms with 100 ants on each farm. How many ants are there in all?	There are 20 bags of seeds with 1,000 seeds in each bag. How many seeds are there in all?
There are 1,000 ants in all.	There are 20,000 seeds in all.

Language Practice: Idioms

Idioms are phrases that have special meanings. Read each sentence and underline the phrase that can be rewritten with an idiom. Write the letter of the idiomatic phrase on the line.

A. swallowed the story hook, line, and sinker	D. works for chicken feed
B. has quite a sweet tooth	E. blowing his own horn
C. put her foot down	F. was tickled pink

Example: A Christy **believed** Uncle Roscoe's fishing story.

1. E Howard is always talking about himself.
2. C Cullen's mother finally told him "no."
3. B Justin can not resist eating candy.
4. D Elvira does not earn very much money but she loves the work.
5. F Carmine greatly enjoyed the singing telegram.

#3305 Daily Skills Practice–Grades 3–4 180 ©Teacher Created Materials, Inc.

Page 181

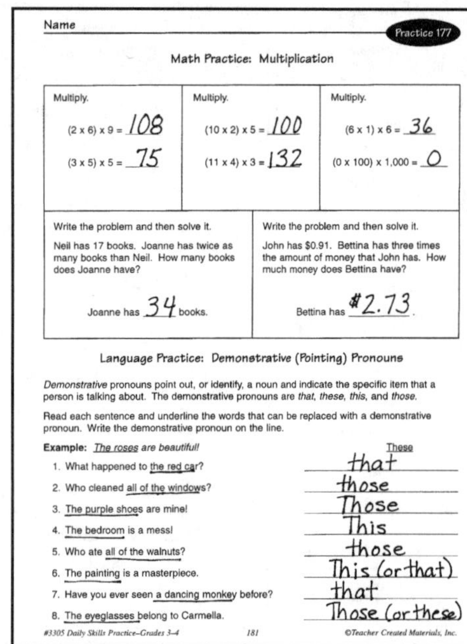

Name ______ Practice 177

Math Practice: Multiplication

Multiply.	Multiply.	Multiply.
(2 x 6) x 9 = 108	(10 x 2) x 5 = 100	(6 x 1) x 6 = 36
(3 x 5) x 5 = 75	(11 x 4) x 3 = 132	(0 x 100) x 1,000 = 0

Write the problem and then solve it.	Write the problem and then solve it.
Neil has 17 books. Joanne has twice as many books than Neil. How many books does Joanne have?	John has $0.91. Bettina has three times the amount of money that John has. How much money does Bettina have?
Joanne has 34 books.	Bettina has $2.73.

Language Practice: Demonstrative (Pointing) Pronouns

Demonstrative pronouns point out, or identify, a noun and indicate the specific item that a person is talking about. The demonstrative pronouns are *that, these, this,* and *those.*

Read each sentence and underline the words that can be replaced with a demonstrative pronoun. Write the demonstrative pronoun on the line.

Example: *The roses are beautiful!* These

1. What happened to the red car? that
2. Who cleaned all of the windows? those
3. The purple shoes are mine! Those
4. The bedroom is a mess! This
5. Who ate all of the walnuts? those
6. The painting is a masterpiece. This (or that)
7. Have you ever seen a dancing monkey before? that
8. The eyeglasses belong to Carmella. Those (or these)

#3305 Daily Skills Practice–Grades 3–4 181 ©Teacher Created Materials, Inc.

Page 182

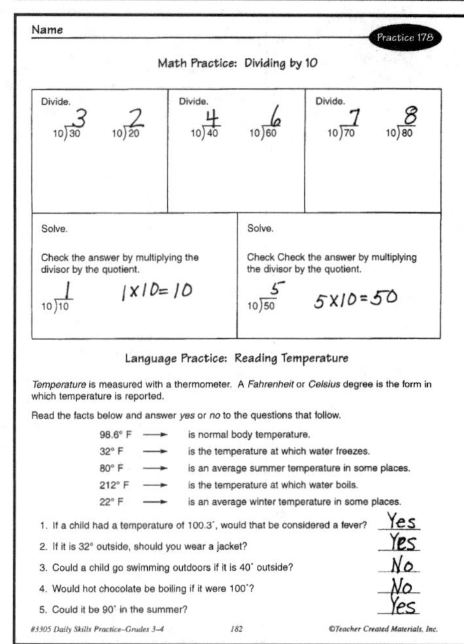

Name ______ Practice 178

Math Practice: Dividing by 10

Divide.	Divide.	Divide.
30 ÷ 10 = 3; 20 ÷ 10 = 2	40 ÷ 10 = 4; 60 ÷ 10 = 6	70 ÷ 10 = 7; 80 ÷ 10 = 8

Solve.	Solve.
Check the answer by multiplying the divisor by the quotient.	Check Check the answer by multiplying the divisor by the quotient.
10 ÷ 10 = 1; 1 x 10 = 10	50 ÷ 10 = 5; 5 x 10 = 50

Language Practice: Reading Temperature

Temperature is measured with a thermometer. A *Fahrenheit* or *Celsius* degree is the form in which temperature is reported.

Read the facts below and answer *yes* or *no* to the questions that follow.

- 98.6° F → is normal body temperature.
- 32° F → is the temperature at which water freezes.
- 80° F → is an average summer temperature in some places.
- 212° F → is the temperature at which water boils.
- 22° F → is an average winter temperature in some places.

1. If a child had a temperature of 100.3°, would that be considered a fever? Yes
2. If it is 32° outside, should you wear a jacket? Yes
3. Could a child go swimming outdoors if it is 40° outside? No
4. Would hot chocolate be boiling if it were 100°? No
5. Could it be 90° in the summer? Yes

#3305 Daily Skills Practice–Grades 3–4 182 ©Teacher Created Materials, Inc.

Page 183

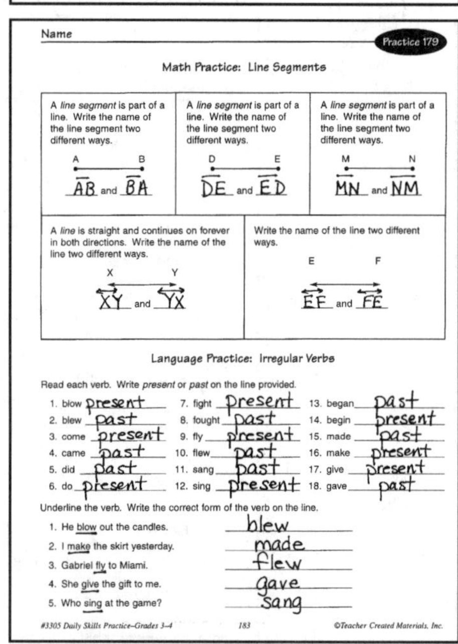

Name ______ Practice 179

Math Practice: Line Segments

A *line segment* is part of a line. Write the name of the line segment two different ways.	A *line segment* is part of a line. Write the name of the line segment two different ways.	A *line segment* is part of a line. Write the name of the line segment two different ways.
$\overline{AB}$ and $\overline{BA}$	$\overline{DE}$ and $\overline{ED}$	$\overline{MN}$ and $\overline{NM}$

A *line* is straight and continues on forever in both directions. Write the name of the line two different ways.	Write the name of the line two different ways.
$\overleftrightarrow{XY}$ and $\overleftrightarrow{YX}$	$\overleftrightarrow{EF}$ and $\overleftrightarrow{FE}$

Language Practice: Irregular Verbs

Read each verb. Write *present* or *past* on the line provided.

1. blow present	7. fight present	13. began past
2. blew past	8. fought past	14. begin present
3. come present	9. fly present	15. made past
4. came past	10. flew past	16. make present
5. did past	11. sang past	17. give present
6. do present	12. sing present	18. gave past

Underline the verb. Write the correct form of the verb on the line.

1. He blow out the candles. blew
2. I make the skirt yesterday. made
3. Gabriel fly to Miami. flew
4. She give the gift to me. gave
5. Who sing at the game? sang

#3305 Daily Skills Practice–Grades 3–4 183 ©Teacher Created Materials, Inc.

Page 184

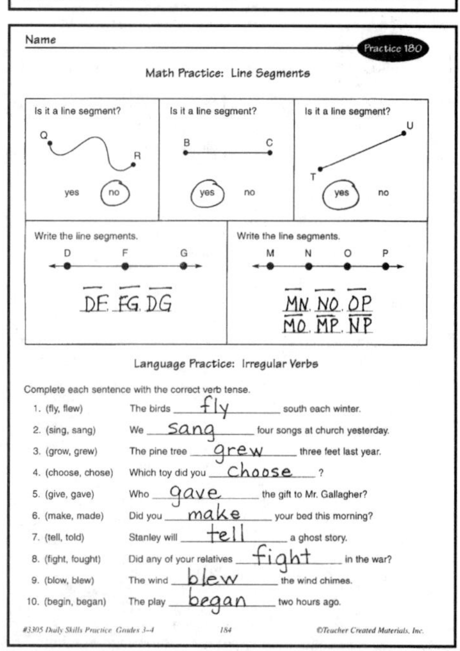

Name ______ Practice 180

Math Practice: Line Segments

Is it a line segment?	Is it a line segment?	Is it a line segment?
yes (no)	(yes) no	(yes) no

Write the line segments.	Write the line segments.
$\overline{DF}$ $\overline{FG}$ $\overline{DG}$	$\overline{MN}$ $\overline{NO}$ $\overline{OP}$ $\overline{MO}$ $\overline{MP}$ $\overline{NP}$

Language Practice: Irregular Verbs

Complete each sentence with the correct verb tense.

1. (fly, flew) The birds fly south each winter.
2. (sing, sang) We sang four songs at church yesterday.
3. (grow, grew) The pine tree grew three feet last year.
4. (choose, chose) Which toy did you choose?
5. (give, gave) Who gave the gift to Mr. Gallagher?
6. (make, made) Did you make your bed this morning?
7. (tell, told) Stanley will tell a ghost story.
8. (fight, fought) Did any of your relatives fight in the war?
9. (blow, blew) The wind blew the wind chimes.
10. (begin, began) The play began two hours ago.

#3305 Daily Skills Practice–Grades 3–4 184 ©Teacher Created Materials, Inc.

Page 185

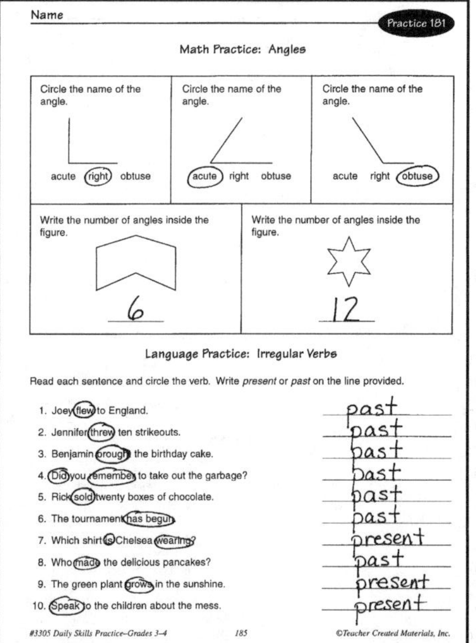

Name | Practice 181

Math Practice: Angles

Circle the name of the angle.	Circle the name of the angle.	Circle the name of the angle.
acute (right) obtuse	(acute) right obtuse	acute right (obtuse)

Write the number of angles inside the figure.	Write the number of angles inside the figure.
6	12

Language Practice: Irregular Verbs

Read each sentence and circle the verb. Write *present* or *past* on the line provided.

1. Joey (flew) to England. past
2. Jennifer (threw) ten strikeouts. past
3. Benjamin (brought) the birthday cake. past
4. (Did) you (remember) to take out the garbage? past
5. Rick (sold) twenty boxes of chocolate. past
6. The tournament (has begun). past
7. Which shirt (is) Chelsea (wearing)? present
8. Who (made) the delicious pancakes? past
9. The green plant (grows) in the sunshine. present
10. (Speak) to the children about the mess. present

#3305 Daily Skills Practice–Grades 3–4 185 ©Teacher Created Materials, Inc.

Page 186

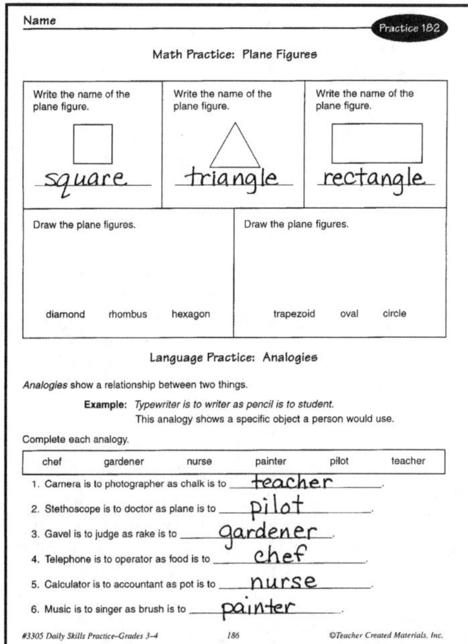

Name | Practice 182

Math Practice: Plane Figures

Write the name of the plane figure.	Write the name of the plane figure.	Write the name of the plane figure.
square	triangle	rectangle

Draw the plane figures.	Draw the plane figures.
diamond rhombus hexagon	trapezoid oval circle

Language Practice: Analogies

Analogies show a relationship between two things.

Example: *Typewriter is to writer as pencil is to student.* This analogy shows a specific object a person would use.

Complete each analogy.

chef	gardener	nurse	painter	pilot	teacher

1. Camera is to photographer as chalk is to teacher.
2. Stethoscope is to doctor as plane is to pilot.
3. Gavel is to judge as rake is to gardener.
4. Telephone is to operator as food is to chef.
5. Calculator is to accountant as pot is to nurse.
6. Music is to singer as brush is to painter.

#3305 Daily Skills Practice–Grades 3–4 186 ©Teacher Created Materials, Inc.

Page 187

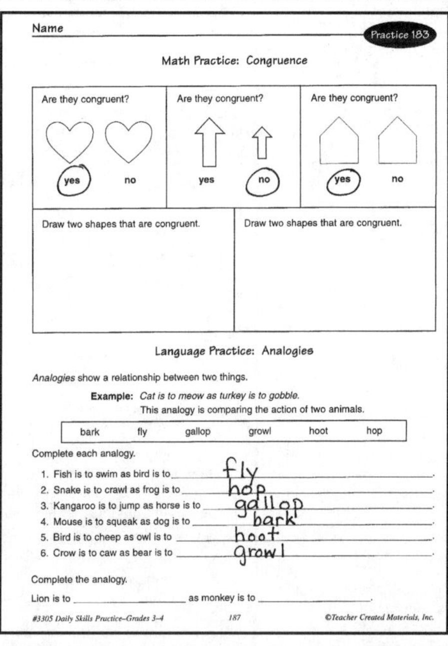

Name | Practice 183

Math Practice: Congruence

Are they congruent?	Are they congruent?	Are they congruent?
(yes) no	yes (no)	(yes) no

Draw two shapes that are congruent.	Draw two shapes that are congruent.

Language Practice: Analogies

Analogies show a relationship between two things.

Example: *Cat is to meow as turkey is to gobble.* This analogy is comparing the action of two animals.

bark	fly	gallop	growl	hoot	hop

Complete each analogy.

1. Fish is to swim as bird is to fly.
2. Snake is to crawl as frog is to hop.
3. Kangaroo is to jump as horse is to gallop.
4. Mouse is to squeak as dog is to bark.
5. Bird is to cheep as owl is to hoot.
6. Crow is to caw as bear is to growl.

Complete the analogy.

Lion is to ________ as monkey is to ________.

#3305 Daily Skills Practice–Grades 3–4 187 ©Teacher Created Materials, Inc.

Page 188

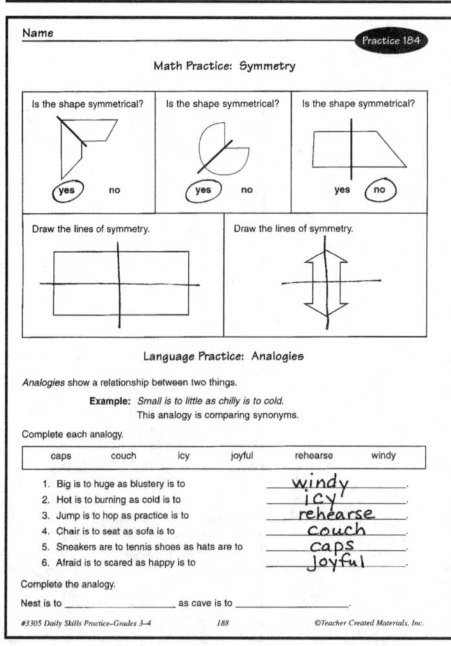

Name | Practice 184

Math Practice: Symmetry

Is the shape symmetrical?	Is the shape symmetrical?	Is the shape symmetrical?
(yes) no	(yes) no	yes (no)

Draw the lines of symmetry.	Draw the lines of symmetry.

Language Practice: Analogies

Analogies show a relationship between two things.

Example: *Small is to little as chilly is to cold.* This analogy is comparing synonyms.

Complete each analogy.

caps	couch	icy	joyful	rehearse	windy

1. Big is to huge as blustery is to windy.
2. Hot is to burning as cold is to icy.
3. Jump is to hop as practice is to rehearse.
4. Chair is to seat as sofa is to couch.
5. Sneakers are to tennis shoes as hats are to caps.
6. Afraid is to scared as happy is to joyful.

Complete the analogy.

Nest is to ________ as cave is to ________.

#3305 Daily Skills Practice–Grades 3–4 188 ©Teacher Created Materials, Inc.

Page 189

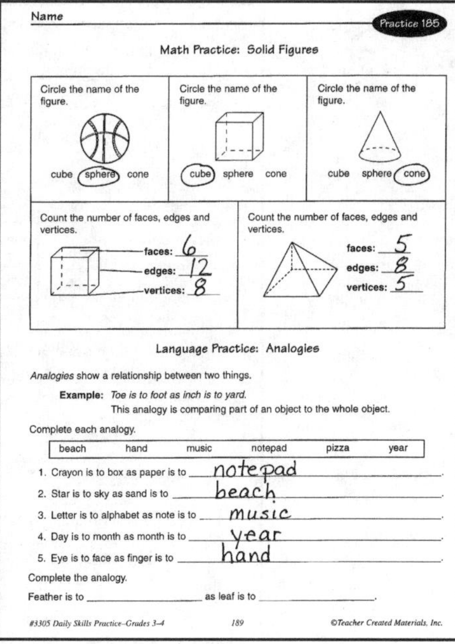

Name | Practice 185

Math Practice: Solid Figures

Circle the name of the figure.	Circle the name of the figure.	Circle the name of the figure.
cube (sphere) cone	(cube) sphere cone	cube sphere (cone)

Count the number of faces, edges and vertices.	Count the number of faces, edges and vertices.
faces: 6 edges: 12 vertices: 8	faces: 5 edges: 8 vertices: 5

Language Practice: Analogies

Analogies show a relationship between two things.

Example: *Toe is to foot as inch is to yard.* This analogy is comparing part of an object to the whole object.

Complete each analogy.

beach	hand	music	notepad	pizza	year

1. Crayon is to box as paper is to notepad.
2. Star is to sky as sand is to beach.
3. Letter is to alphabet as note is to music.
4. Day is to month as month is to year.
5. Eye is to face as finger is to hand.

Complete the analogy.

Feather is to ________ as leaf is to ________.

#3305 Daily Skills Practice–Grades 3–4 189 ©Teacher Created Materials, Inc.

Page 190

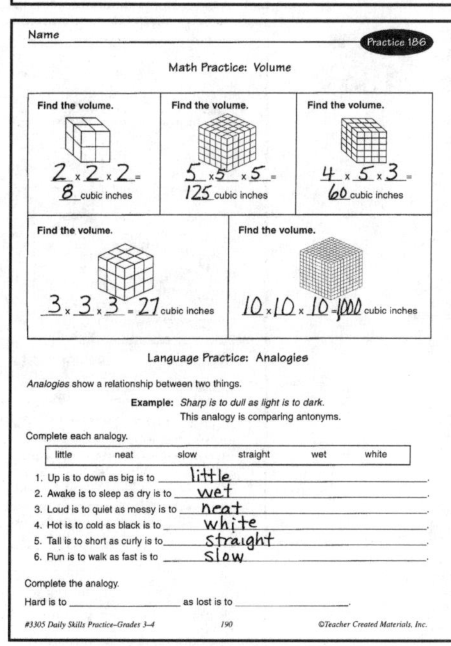

Name | Practice 186

Math Practice: Volume

Find the volume.	Find the volume.	Find the volume.
2 x 2 x 2 = 8 cubic inches	5 x 5 x 5 = 125 cubic inches	4 x 5 x 3 = 60 cubic inches

Find the volume.	Find the volume.
3 x 3 x 3 = 27 cubic inches	10 x 10 x 10 = 1000 cubic inches

Language Practice: Analogies

Analogies show a relationship between two things.

Example: *Sharp is to dull as light is to dark.* This analogy is comparing antonyms.

Complete each analogy.

little	neat	slow	straight	wet	white

1. Up is to down as big is to little.
2. Awake is to sleep as dry is to wet.
3. Loud is to quiet as messy is to neat.
4. Hot is to cold as black is to white.
5. Tall is to short as curly is to straight.
6. Run is to walk as fast is to slow.

Complete the analogy.

Hard is to ________ as lost is to ________.

#3305 Daily Skills Practice–Grades 3–4 190 ©Teacher Created Materials, Inc.

Page 191

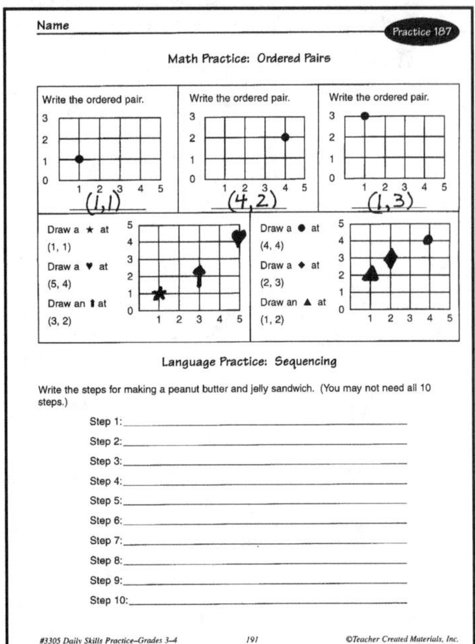

Name ______________________ Practice 187

Math Practice: Ordered Pairs

Write the ordered pair.	Write the ordered pair.	Write the ordered pair.
(1,1)	(4,2)	(1,3)

Draw a ★ at (1, 1)
Draw a ♥ at (5, 4)
Draw an ⬆ at (3, 2)

Draw a ● at (4, 4)
Draw a ◆ at (2, 3)
Draw an ▲ at (1, 2)

Language Practice: Sequencing

Write the steps for making a peanut butter and jelly sandwich. (You may not need all 10 steps.)

Step 1: ____________________
Step 2: ____________________
Step 3: ____________________
Step 4: ____________________
Step 5: ____________________
Step 6: ____________________
Step 7: ____________________
Step 8: ____________________
Step 9: ____________________
Step 10: ____________________

#3305 Daily Skills Practice–Grades 3–4 191 ©Teacher Created Materials, Inc.

Page 192

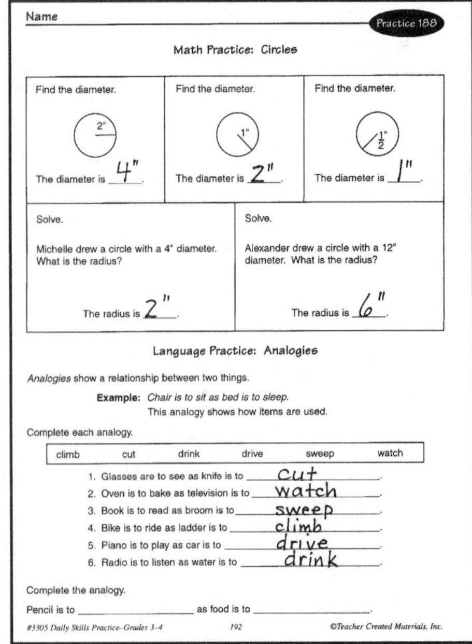

Name ______________________ Practice 188

Math Practice: Circles

Find the diameter.	Find the diameter.	Find the diameter.
2" — The diameter is 4".	1" — The diameter is 2".	½" — The diameter is 1".

Solve.

Michelle drew a circle with a 4" diameter. What is the radius?

The radius is 2".

Solve.

Alexander drew a circle with a 12" diameter. What is the radius?

The radius is 6".

Language Practice: Analogies

Analogies show a relationship between two things.

Example: *Chair is to sit as bed is to sleep.*
This analogy shows how items are used.

Complete each analogy.

climb	cut	drink	drive	sweep	watch

1. Glasses are to see as knife is to cut.
2. Oven is to bake as television is to watch.
3. Book is to read as broom is to sweep.
4. Bike is to ride as ladder is to climb.
5. Piano is to play as car is to drive.
6. Radio is to listen as water is to drink.

Complete the analogy.

Pencil is to ______________ as food is to ______________.

#3305 Daily Skills Practice–Grades 3–4 192 ©Teacher Created Materials, Inc.

Page 193

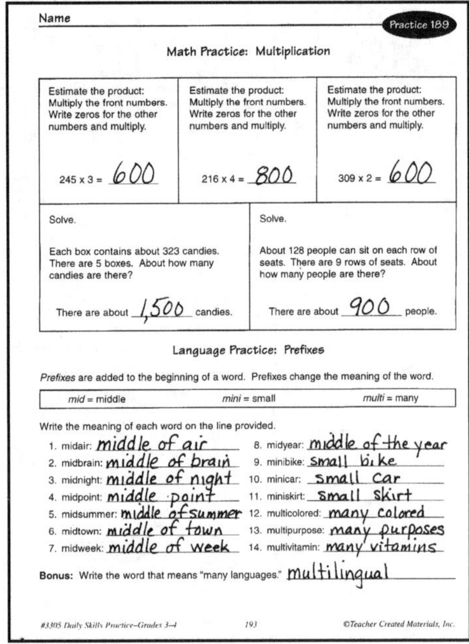

Name ______________________ Practice 189

Math Practice: Multiplication

Estimate the product: Multiply the front numbers. Write zeros for the other numbers and multiply.	Estimate the product: Multiply the front numbers. Write zeros for the other numbers and multiply.	Estimate the product: Multiply the front numbers. Write zeros for the other numbers and multiply.
245 x 3 = 600	216 x 4 = 800	309 x 2 = 600

Solve.

Each box contains about 323 candies. There are 5 boxes. About how many candies are there?

There are about 1,500 candies.

Solve.

About 128 people can sit on each row of seats. There are 9 rows of seats. About how many people are there?

There are about 900 people.

Language Practice: Prefixes

Prefixes are added to the beginning of a word. Prefixes change the meaning of the word.

mid = middle	*mini* = small	*multi* = many

Write the meaning of each word on the line provided.

1. midair: middle of air
2. midbrain: middle of brain
3. midnight: middle of night
4. midpoint: middle point
5. midsummer: middle of summer
6. midtown: middle of town
7. midweek: middle of week
8. midyear: middle of the year
9. minibike: small bike
10. minicar: small car
11. miniskirt: small skirt
12. multicolored: many colored
13. multipurpose: many purposes
14. multivitamin: many vitamins

Bonus: Write the word that means "many languages." multilingual

#3305 Daily Skills Practice–Grades 3–4 193 ©Teacher Created Materials, Inc.

Page 194

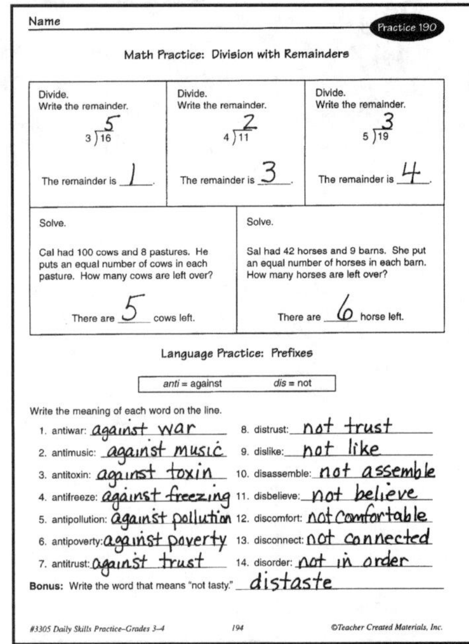

Name ______________________ Practice 190

Math Practice: Division with Remainders

Divide. Write the remainder.	Divide. Write the remainder.	Divide. Write the remainder.
3)16 = 5	4)11 = 2	5)19 = 3
The remainder is 1.	The remainder is 3.	The remainder is 4.

Solve.

Cal had 100 cows and 8 pastures. He puts an equal number of cows in each pasture. How many cows are left over?

There are 5 cows left.

Solve.

Sal had 42 horses and 9 barns. She put an equal number of horses in each barn. How many horses are left over?

There are 6 horse left.

Language Practice: Prefixes

anti = against	*dis* = not

Write the meaning of each word on the line.

1. antiwar: against war
2. antimusic: against music
3. antitoxin: against toxin
4. antifreeze: against freezing
5. antipollution: against pollution
6. antipoverty: against poverty
7. antitrust: against trust
8. distrust: not trust
9. dislike: not like
10. disassemble: not assemble
11. disbelieve: not believe
12. discomfort: not comfortable
13. disconnect: not connected
14. disorder: not in order

Bonus: Write the word that means "not tasty." distaste

#3305 Daily Skills Practice–Grades 3–4 194 ©Teacher Created Materials, Inc.

Page 195

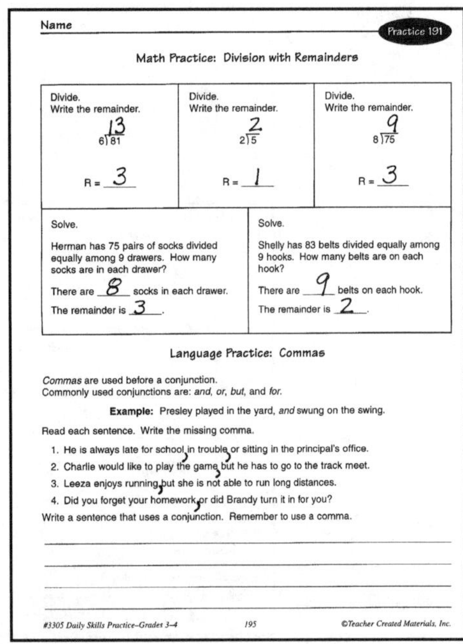

Name ______________________ Practice 191

Math Practice: Division with Remainders

Divide. Write the remainder.	Divide. Write the remainder.	Divide. Write the remainder.
6)81 = 13	2)5 = 2	8)75 = 9
R = 3	R = 1	R = 3

Solve.

Herman has 75 pairs of socks divided equally among 9 drawers. How many socks are in each drawer?

There are 8 socks in each drawer.
The remainder is 3.

Solve.

Shelly has 83 belts divided equally among 9 hooks. How many belts are on each hook?

There are 9 belts on each hook.
The remainder is 2.

Language Practice: Commas

Commas are used before a conjunction.
Commonly used conjunctions are: *and, or, but,* and *for.*

Example: Presley played in the yard, *and* swung on the swing.

Read each sentence. Write the missing comma.

1. He is always late for school, in trouble, or sitting in the principal's office.
2. Charlie would like to play the game, but he has to go to the track meet.
3. Leeza enjoys running, but she is not able to run long distances.
4. Did you forget your homework, or did Brandy turn it in for you?

Write a sentence that uses a conjunction. Remember to use a comma.

____
____
____
____

#3305 Daily Skills Practice–Grades 3–4 195 ©Teacher Created Materials, Inc.

Page 196

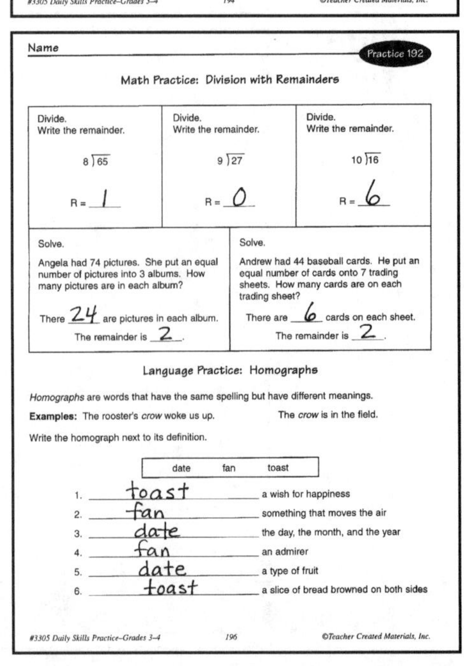

Name ______________________ Practice 192

Math Practice: Division with Remainders

Divide. Write the remainder.	Divide. Write the remainder.	Divide. Write the remainder.
8)65	9)27	10)16
R = 1	R = 0	R = 6

Solve.

Angela had 74 pictures. She put an equal number of pictures into 3 albums. How many pictures are in each album?

There 24 are pictures in each album.
The remainder is 2.

Solve.

Andrew had 44 baseball cards. He put an equal number of cards onto 7 trading sheets. How many cards are on each trading sheet?

There are 6 cards on each sheet.
The remainder is 2.

Language Practice: Homographs

Homographs are words that have the same spelling but have different meanings.

Examples: The rooster's *crow* woke us up. The *crow* is in the field.

Write the homograph next to its definition.

date	fan	toast

1. toast — a wish for happiness
2. fan — something that moves the air
3. date — the day, the month, and the year
4. fan — an admirer
5. date — a type of fruit
6. toast — a slice of bread browned on both sides

#3305 Daily Skills Practice–Grades 3–4 196 ©Teacher Created Materials, Inc.

Page 197

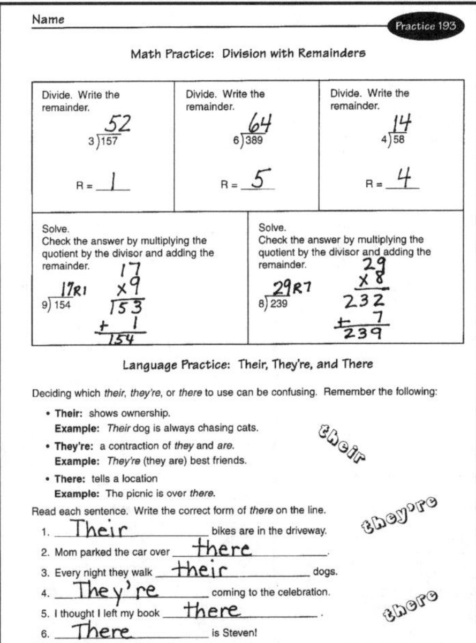

Name

Practice 193

Math Practice: Division with Remainders

Divide. Write the remainder. 3)157 = 52, R = 1	Divide. Write the remainder. 6)389 = 64, R = 5	Divide. Write the remainder. 4)58 = 14, R = 4

Solve. Check the answer by multiplying the quotient by the divisor and adding the remainder. 9)154 = 17R1; 17 × 9 = 153; + 1 = 154

Solve. Check the answer by multiplying the quotient by the divisor and adding the remainder. 8)239 = 29R7; 29 × 8 = 232; + 7 = 239

Language Practice: Their, They're, and There

Deciding which *their, they're,* or *there* to use can be confusing. Remember the following:

- **Their:** shows ownership.
  Example: *Their* dog is always chasing cats.
- **They're:** a contraction of *they* and *are.*
  Example: *They're* (they are) best friends.
- **There:** tells a location
  Example: The picnic is over *there.*

Read each sentence. Write the correct form of *there* on the line.

1. Their bikes are in the driveway.
2. Mom parked the car over there.
3. Every night they walk their dogs.
4. They're coming to the celebration.
5. I thought I left my book there.
6. There is Steven!

#3305 Daily Skills Practice–Grades 3–4 197 ©Teacher Created Materials, Inc.

Page 198

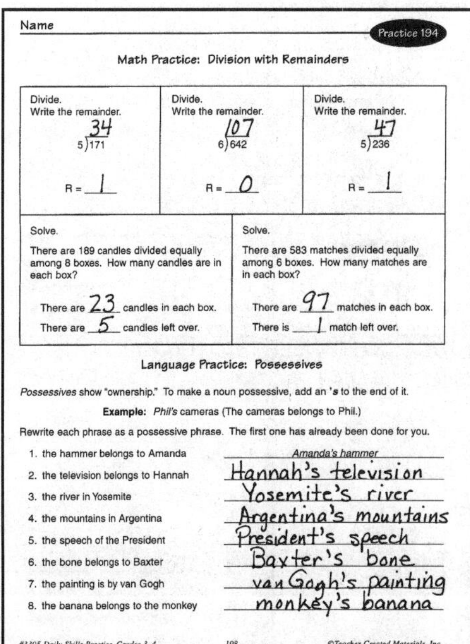

Name

Practice 194

Math Practice: Division with Remainders

Divide. Write the remainder. 5)171 = 34, R = 1	Divide. Write the remainder. 6)642 = 107, R = 0	Divide. Write the remainder. 5)236 = 47, R = 1

Solve. There are 189 candles divided equally among 8 boxes. How many candles are in each box? There are 23 candles in each box. There are 5 candles left over.

Solve. There are 583 matches divided equally among 6 boxes. How many matches are in each box? There are 97 matches in each box. There is 1 match left over.

Language Practice: Possessives

Possessives show "ownership." To make a noun possessive, add an *'s* to the end of it.

Example: *Phil's* cameras (The cameras belongs to Phil.)

Rewrite each phrase as a possessive phrase. The first one has already been done for you.

1. the hammer belongs to Amanda — *Amanda's hammer*
2. the television belongs to Hannah — Hannah's television
3. the river in Yosemite — Yosemite's river
4. the mountains in Argentina — Argentina's mountains
5. the speech of the President — President's speech
6. the bone belongs to Baxter — Baxter's bone
7. the painting is by van Gogh — van Gogh's painting
8. the banana belongs to the monkey — monkey's banana

#3305 Daily Skills Practice–Grades 3–4 198 ©Teacher Created Materials, Inc.

Page 199

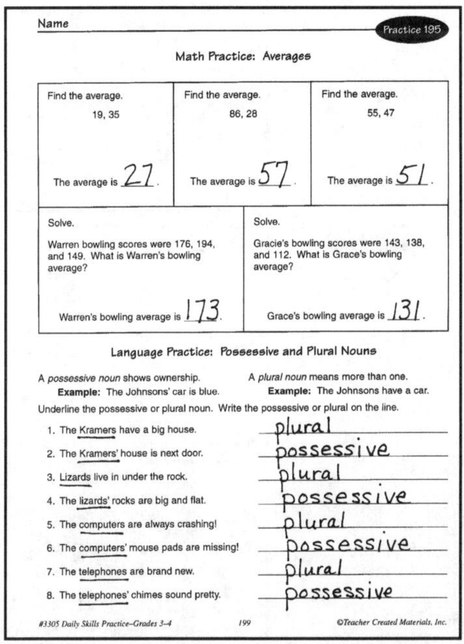

Name

Practice 195

Math Practice: Averages

Find the average. 19, 35 The average is 27.	Find the average. 86, 28 The average is 57.	Find the average. 55, 47 The average is 51.

Solve. Warren bowling scores were 176, 194, and 149. What is Warren's bowling average? Warren's bowling average is 173.

Solve. Gracie's bowling scores were 143, 138, and 112. What is Grace's bowling average? Grace's bowling average is 131.

Language Practice: Possessive and Plural Nouns

A *possessive noun* shows ownership. **Example:** The Johnsons' car is blue.

A *plural noun* means more than one. **Example:** The Johnsons have a car.

Underline the possessive or plural noun. Write the possessive or plural on the line.

1. The Kramers have a big house. — plural
2. The Kramers' house is next door. — possessive
3. Lizards live in under the rock. — plural
4. The lizards' rocks are big and flat. — possessive
5. The computers are always crashing! — plural
6. The computers' mouse pads are missing! — possessive
7. The telephones are brand new. — plural
8. The telephones' chimes sound pretty. — possessive

#3305 Daily Skills Practice–Grades 3–4 199 ©Teacher Created Materials, Inc.

Page 200

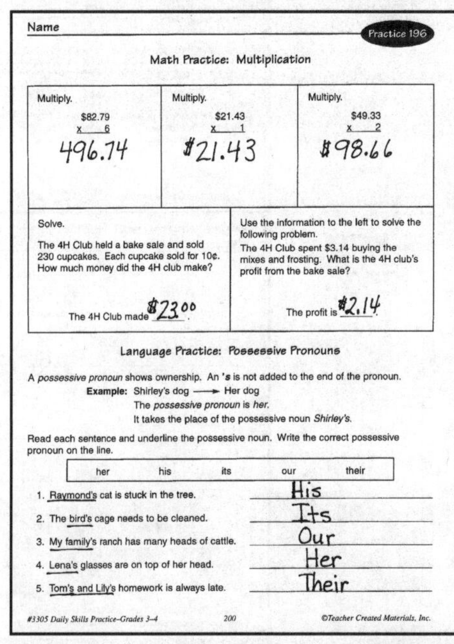

Name

Practice 196

Math Practice: Multiplication

Multiply. \$82.79 × 6 = 496.74	Multiply. \$21.43 × 1 = \$21.43	Multiply. \$49.33 × 2 = \$98.66

Solve. The 4H Club held a bake sale and sold 230 cupcakes. Each cupcake sold for 10¢. How much money did the 4H club make? The 4H Club made \$23.00.

Use the information to the left to solve the following problem. The 4H Club spent \$3.14 buying the mixes and frosting. What is the 4H club's profit from the bake sale? The profit is \$2.14.

Language Practice: Possessive Pronouns

A *possessive pronoun* shows ownership. An *'s* is not added to the end of the pronoun.

Example: Shirley's dog → Her dog
The *possessive pronoun* is *her.*
It takes the place of the possessive noun *Shirley's.*

Read each sentence and underline the possessive noun. Write the correct possessive pronoun on the line.

her	his	its	our	their

1. Raymond's cat is stuck in the tree. — His
2. The bird's cage needs to be cleaned. — Its
3. My family's ranch has many heads of cattle. — Our
4. Lena's glasses are on top of her head. — Her
5. Tom's and Lily's homework is always late. — Their

#3305 Daily Skills Practice–Grades 3–4 200 ©Teacher Created Materials, Inc.

Page 201

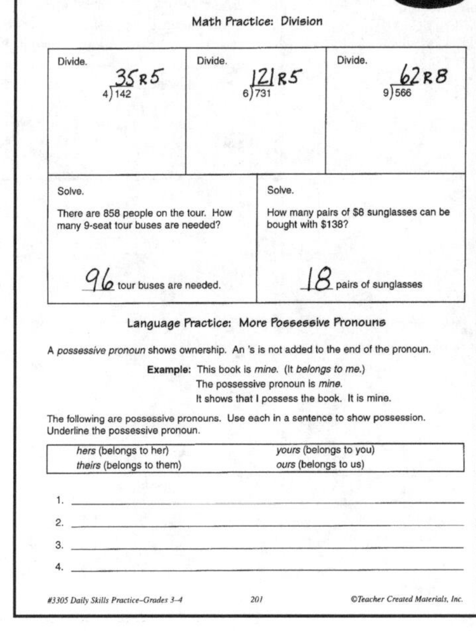

Name

Practice 197

Math Practice: Division

Divide. 4)142 = 35R5	Divide. 6)731 = 121R5	Divide. 9)566 = 62R8

Solve. There are 858 people on the tour. How many 9-seat tour buses are needed? 96 tour buses are needed.

Solve. How many pairs of \$8 sunglasses can be bought with \$138? 18 pairs of sunglasses

Language Practice: More Possessive Pronouns

A *possessive pronoun* shows ownership. An 's is not added to the end of the pronoun.

Example: This book is *mine.* (It *belongs to me.*)
The possessive pronoun is *mine.*
It shows that I possess the book. It is mine.

The following are possessive pronouns. Use each in a sentence to show possession. Underline the possessive pronoun.

hers (belongs to her)	*yours* (belongs to you)
theirs (belongs to them)	*ours* (belongs to us)

1. ______
2. ______
3. ______
4. ______

#3305 Daily Skills Practice–Grades 3–4 201 ©Teacher Created Materials, Inc.

Page 202

Name

Practice 198

Math Practice: Division

Divide. 7)225 = 32 R1	Divide. 1)491 = 491	Divide. 8)573 = 71R5

Solve. The concert tickets cost \$8 each. The choir has \$825. How many tickets can they buy? The choir club can buy 103 tickets.

Solve. Each night a different number of people (653, 375, 491, 702) attend the concert. What is the average number of attendance? The average number is 555.

Language Practice: Research Report

When writing a research report, it is important to use your own words.

Money

Example: Feathers, beads, stones, and shells were once used as money.
Instead of money, people used feathers, beads, stones, and shells.

Rewrite each sentence using your own words.

1. In Burma, their coins were called "flower silver" because of the flower design on each piece of silver.
2. In Mexico, cacao (chocolate) beans were used for money.
3. At one time, Ethiopians used bars of rock salt for money.
4. Coins were first made during the 17th century.

#3305 Daily Skills Practice–Grades 3–4 202 ©Teacher Created Materials, Inc.

Page 203

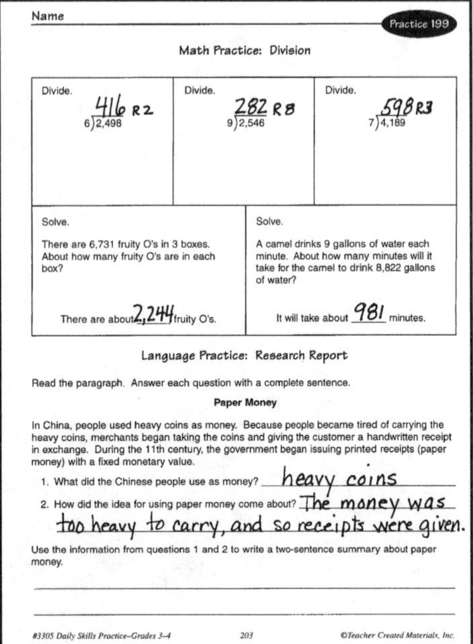

Name ______ Practice 199

Math Practice: Division

Divide.	Divide.	Divide.
$6\overline{)2{,}498}$ = 416 R2	$9\overline{)2{,}546}$ = 282 R8	$7\overline{)4{,}189}$ = 598 R3

Solve.	Solve.
There are 6,731 fruity O's in 3 boxes. About how many fruity O's are in each box? There are about 2,244 fruity O's.	A camel drinks 9 gallons of water each minute. About how many minutes will it take for the camel to drink 8,822 gallons of water? It will take about 981 minutes.

Language Practice: Research Report

Read the paragraph. Answer each question with a complete sentence.

Paper Money

In China, people used heavy coins as money. Because people became tired of carrying the heavy coins, merchants began taking the coins and giving the customer a handwritten receipt in exchange. During the 11th century, the government began issuing printed receipts (paper money) with a fixed monetary value.

1. What did the Chinese people use as money? heavy coins
2. How did the idea for using paper money come about? The money was too heavy to carry, and so receipts were given.

Use the information from questions 1 and 2 to write a two-sentence summary about paper money.

#3305 Daily Skills Practice–Grades 3–4 203 ©Teacher Created Materials, Inc.

Page 204

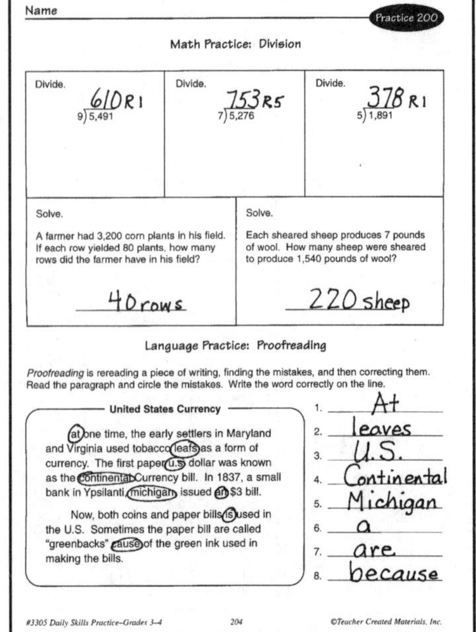

Name ______ Practice 200

Math Practice: Division

Divide.	Divide.	Divide.
$9\overline{)5{,}491}$ = 610 R1	$7\overline{)5{,}276}$ = 753 R5	$5\overline{)1{,}891}$ = 378 R1

Solve.	Solve.
A farmer had 3,200 corn plants in his field. If each row yielded 80 plants, how many rows did the farmer have in his field? 40 rows	Each sheared sheep produces 7 pounds of wool. How many sheep were sheared to produce 1,540 pounds of wool? 220 sheep

Language Practice: Proofreading

Proofreading is rereading a piece of writing, finding the mistakes, and then correcting them. Read the paragraph and circle the mistakes. Write the word correctly on the line.

United States Currency

at one time, the early settlers in Maryland and Virginia used tobacco leafs as a form of currency. The first paper u.s. dollar was known as the continental Currency bill. In 1837, a small bank in Ypsilanti, michigan, issued an $3 bill.

Now, both coins and paper bills is used in the U.S. Sometimes the paper bill are called "greenbacks" cause of the green ink used in making the bills.

1. At
2. leaves
3. U.S.
4. Continental
5. Michigan
6. a
7. are
8. because

#3305 Daily Skills Practice–Grades 3–4 204 ©Teacher Created Materials, Inc.

Page 205

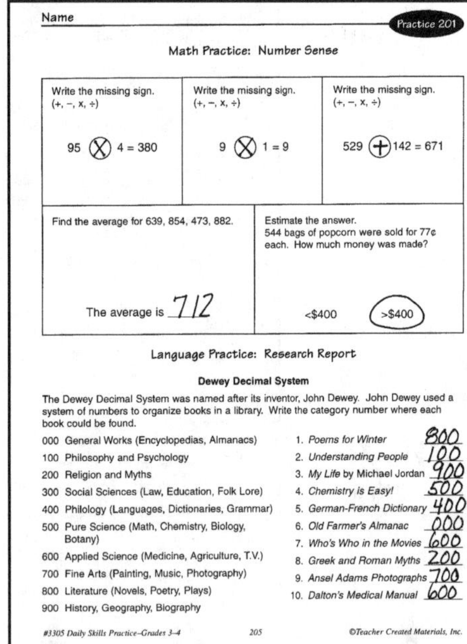

Name ______ Practice 201

Math Practice: Number Sense

Write the missing sign. (+, –, x, ÷)	Write the missing sign. (+, –, x, ÷)	Write the missing sign. (+, –, x, ÷)
95 (x) 4 = 380	9 (x) 1 = 9	529 (+) 142 = 671

Find the average for 639, 854, 473, 882.	Estimate the answer. 544 bags of popcorn were sold for 77¢ each. How much money was made?
The average is 712	<$400 (>$400)

Language Practice: Research Report

Dewey Decimal System

The Dewey Decimal System was named after its inventor, John Dewey. John Dewey used a system of numbers to organize books in a library. Write the category number where each book could be found.

000 General Works (Encyclopedias, Almanacs)
100 Philosophy and Psychology
200 Religion and Myths
300 Social Sciences (Law, Education, Folk Lore)
400 Philology (Languages, Dictionaries, Grammar)
500 Pure Science (Math, Chemistry, Biology, Botany)
600 Applied Science (Medicine, Agriculture, T.V.)
700 Fine Arts (Painting, Music, Photography)
800 Literature (Novels, Poetry, Plays)
900 History, Geography, Biography

1. *Poems for Winter* 800
2. *Understanding People* 100
3. *My Life* by Michael Jordan 900
4. *Chemistry is Easy!* 500
5. *German-French Dictionary* 400
6. *Old Farmer's Almanac* 000
7. *Who's Who in the Movies* 600
8. *Greek and Roman Myths* 200
9. *Ansel Adams Photographs* 700
10. *Dalton's Medical Manual* 600

#3305 Daily Skills Practice–Grades 3–4 205 ©Teacher Created Materials, Inc.

Page 206

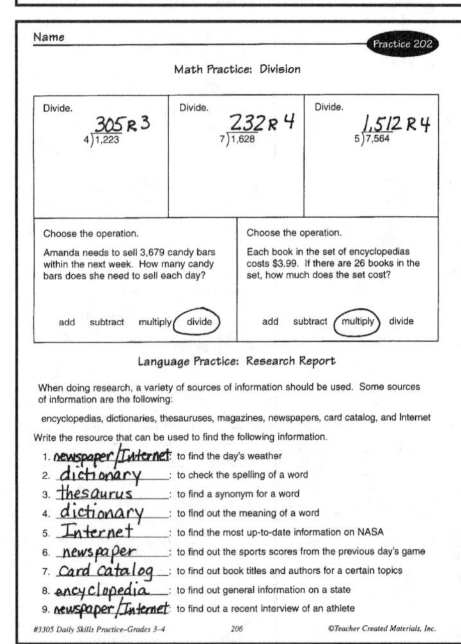

Name ______ Practice 202

Math Practice: Division

Divide.	Divide.	Divide.
$4\overline{)1{,}223}$ = 305 R3	$7\overline{)1{,}628}$ = 232 R4	$5\overline{)7{,}564}$ = 1,512 R4

Choose the operation.	Choose the operation.
Amanda needs to sell 3,679 candy bars within the next week. How many candy bars does she need to sell each day? add subtract multiply (divide)	Each book in the set of encyclopedias costs $3.99. If there are 26 books in the set, how much does the set cost? add subtract (multiply) divide

Language Practice: Research Report

When doing research, a variety of sources of information should be used. Some sources of information are the following:

encyclopedias, dictionaries, thesauruses, magazines, newspapers, card catalog, and Internet

Write the resource that can be used to find the following information.

1. newspaper/Internet: to find the day's weather
2. dictionary: to check the spelling of a word
3. thesaurus: to find a synonym for a word
4. dictionary: to find out the meaning of a word
5. Internet: to find the most up-to-date information on NASA
6. newspaper: to find out the sports scores from the previous day's game
7. card catalog: to find out book titles and authors for a certain topics
8. encyclopedia: to find out general information on a state
9. newspaper/Internet: to find out a recent interview of an athlete

#3305 Daily Skills Practice–Grades 3–4 206 ©Teacher Created Materials, Inc.